MAN-MACHINE COMMUNICATION

Information Sciences Series

Editors

ROBERT M. HAYES
Vice President
Becker-Hayes, Inc.

JOSEPH BECKER
President
Becker-Hayes, Inc.

Consultants

CHARLES P. BOURNE
Director, Advanced Information Systems Division
Programming Services, Inc.

HAROLD BORKO
UCLA

Joseph Becker and Robert M. Hayes:
INFORMATION STORAGE AND RETRIEVAL

Charles P. Bourne:
METHODS OF INFORMATION HANDLING

Harold Borko:
AUTOMATED LANGUAGE PROCESSING

Russell D. Archibald and Richard L. Villoria:
NETWORK-BASED MANAGEMENT SYSTEMS (PERT/CPM)

Charles T. Meadow:
THE ANALYSIS OF INFORMATION SYSTEMS, A PROGRAMMER'S
INTRODUCTION TO INFORMATION RETRIEVAL

Launor F. Carter:
NATIONAL DOCUMENT-HANDLING SYSTEMS FOR SCIENCE AND
TECHNOLOGY

George W. Brown, James G. Miller and Thomas A. Keenan:
EDUNET: REPORT OF THE SUMMER STUDY ON INFORMATION
NETWORKS CONDUCTED BY THE INTERUNIVERSITY COMMUNI-
CATIONS COUNCIL (EDUCOM)

Perry E. Rosove:
DEVELOPING COMPUTER-BASED INFORMATION SYSTEMS

F. W. Lancaster:
INFORMATION RETRIEVAL SYSTEMS

Ralph L. Bisco:
DATA BASES, COMPUTERS, AND THE SOCIAL SCIENCES

Charles T. Meadow:
MAN-MACHINE COMMUNICATION

Man-Machine Communication

CHARLES T. MEADOW

Center for Computer Sciences and Technology
National Bureau of Standards

Wiley-Interscience

A DIVISION OF JOHN WILEY & SONS

NEW YORK · LONDON · SYDNEY · TORONTO

TO HARRIET

How often has my spirit turned to thee!

Information Sciences Series

Information is the essential ingredient in decision making. The need for improved information systems in recent years has been made critical by the steady growth in size and complexity of organizations and data.

This series is designed to include books that are concerned with various aspects of communicating, utilizing, and storing digital and graphic information. It will embrace a broad spectrum of topics, such as information system theory and design, man-machine relationships, language data processing, artificial intelligence, mechanization of library processes, non-numerical applications of digital computers, storage and retrieval, automatic publishing, command and control, information display, and so on.

Information science may someday be a profession in its own right. The aim of this series is to bring together the interdisciplinary core of knowledge that is apt to form its foundation. Through this consolidation, it is expected that the series will grow to become the focal point for professional education in this field.

Preface

I became interested in communication between man and computers as a result of my work in information retrieval, which convinced me that the most important and interesting problems in that field were those of how the user of an informational retrieval system made known his wants to the computer, used a computer as an instrument for browsing, and finally obtained his results. It quickly became apparent that here were a fascinating interplay of computer programming, engineering design, library science, education, and psychology and also, most critical of all, an insight into human behavior.

I use the term *man-machine communication* in the context of interactive, or conversational, communication between a man and a computer. Excluded by this definition are the more elemental forms of communication between men and machines, such as the entry of a program into a machine and the recovery of results at a later time. These elemental forms are common to all uses of a computer and imply a form of master-slave relationship between the programmer and the computer. In the world of conversational systems, we are involved with give and take, or mutual exchange of information, between two systems each of which enjoys some independence of action.

Although the field of interactive systems is in its infancy, it has caught the fancy of many people, both within and outside the profession of computer science. The essence of the problem is to achieve effective communication between two quite different organisms, or systems. One of these is capable of creative thinking, high-speed correlation, and decision-making under uncertainty, but is slow at calculation, reading, and writing and is error-prone. The other has limited intellectual powers but does high-speed calculation, reading, and writing and rarely makes errors. The analogy between man-computer interaction, given these characteristics, and the biological concept of symbiosis, in which dissimilar organisms are mutually dependent for life support, was first proposed by J. C. R. Licklider; we shall have more to say about this concept in Chapter 1.

Interactive systems are now being applied to information retrieval, instruction, engineering design, text-editing, artistic design, and a host of other tasks. Some notable successes have been achieved, but not as many as I feel there should have been by this time. Some of the reasons for this lag in progress are discussed in Chapter 13. The worlds of journalism and popular science seem to assume that all the problems will be overcome and that we shall find highly intelligent, conversational computers being used in, and indeed dominating, all phases of our lives. I do not find the idea of becoming dominated by a computer a particularly pleasing prospect. I do not think such domination will come about, mainly because I believe man will retain his control over his computers. I hope this book will play some small part in dispelling the fears of those who may share my displeasure at the thought of computer domination, but may not now share my optimism. Behind all the apparent magic of a computer is a program, which, if it doesn't quite have feet of clay, at least has statements written in FORTRAN by a human programmer.

This book is an introduction to the elements, methods, and problems of interactive systems and is tutorial in tone. It is intended for both users and designers of conversational systems: those who actually operate them as well as those who design the overall systems in which they are used. I would expect, primarily, to draw my readers from among the designers of information systems and such prospective users as teachers, writers, librarians, lawyers, design engineers, and professional managers. The book is a survey and is not intended as an exhaustive text. The reader wishing to pursue any topic in detail will have to seek further, but I have provided references to help him do so.

The general plan of the book is to show what kinds of things have been done and, roughly, how they work. It is oriented to the point of view of the user and the software designer, both roles I myself have often played. I have tried to describe the nature of conversation between man and machine—how it looks to the user and how the designer made it look that way. Since the logic is, to a large extent, independent of hardware, hardware is considered sparingly, but program logic is sometimes described in detail.

The book is divided into three parts. Part I covers the basic elements of interactive systems: the hardware, or mechanical devices used in man-machine communication; computer programming; computer time-sharing; and natural language processing. Part II covers basic systems that are fully interactive programming systems, of significance in themselves but often found as components of larger systems. Finally, in Part III, we consider a representative set of advanced applications and conclude with a summary of the major problems of man-machine communications systems and a preview of what is to come. Applications to be described were selected principally to show a variety of techniques. Some existing applications are not covered here, and there surely will be more to come.

Most of this text was written while I was employed by the International Business Machines Corporation, and readers will note a tendency on my part to refer to IBM products and projects rather frequently. Obviously, these are the products and projects with which I was then most familiar, and their developers have been my friends and colleagues for many years. The use of IBM systems for illustrative purposes in no way limits the generality of the principles described, nor does it imply endorsement on my part or the absence of similar, competitive products in the marketplace.

Because this is a survey, not a presentation of original research, little of the work reported is my own, and I have tried to be meticulous in acknowledging the sources of all material covered. In addition to these citations I have included at the end of most chapters a list of recommended readings. These are usually readily available as hard-cover books or periodicals. But this is a changing field. Although the principles do not change much, the technology does. As a practical matter, it was necessary to stop adding new references more than a year before the publication date. To help close this gap, abstracting journals and printed indexes to the periodical literature are, of course, available to the reader. For a single, comprehensive source, I recommend the series *Annual Review of Information Science and Technology,* edited by Carlos A. Cuadra and published by John Wiley & Sons (Volumes 1 and 2 in 1966 and 1967) and Encyclopaedia Britannica, Inc. (Volumes 3, 4, and 5 in 1968, 1969, and 1970). Each volume of this series surveys and reviews hundreds of publications in the field that appeared in print the year before the *Annual Review* was published.

I am greatly in the debt of many people who helped make this book possible. Principal among them are three who generously gave me their time to read the manuscript and, having done so, their advice:

James Martin of IBM, Dr. Michael J. Seven of Harvey Mudd College, and Thomas N. Pyke, Jr., of the National Bureau of Standards. Mrs. Eva Lambert was, as usual, both competent and patient in typing the manuscript. My thanks go also to many friends who helped with pictures and reference materials, notably Charles L. Baker (International Computing Company), Paul Bradshaw (IBM), Evan Evans (IBM), Janice Lourie (IBM), William M. Newman (University of Utah), and I. J. Seligsohn (IBM). Special appreciation is due to Harry M. McConnell of Wiley for his help at a difficult time.

CHARLES T. MEADOW

Washington, D. C.
December, 1969

Contents

MAN-MACHINE COMMUNICATION

Part I

Elements Of
Interactive Systems

Chapter One

Introduction

1.1 THE NATURE OF MAN-MACHINE COMMUNICATION

Man communicates with machines in many ways. One of the simplest of these is by pressing a button that starts, stops, or in some way changes the action of a machine. On a higher plane, computer programmers communicate with their machines by writing sequences of commands that the computer is then asked to execute. As traditionally carried out, this form of communication is a monolog—the programmer writes his commands and then the machine executes them without further interaction with its mentor. These monologs can be long. If there is such a thing as an average program, it consists of probably 1000 commands, but some programs contain 100,000 commands.

Our intent in this book is confined to treatment of a relatively new development, *interactive communication*, or dialog, between men and computers. Interactive communication is two-way communication, each party providing feedback to the other, usually each indicating whether the last utterance of the other was understood and supplying results, or progress indications, for any action that was requested. Speed of response is an important element in interaction. Without trying to reduce this to a specific number, we generally expect responses in seconds—soon enough that, for the man, everything related to the dialog remains fresh in his

3

mind. When the response time is, say, a full day, a great deal of forgetting and relearning is involved. Other interactions require responses in fractions of seconds, a general characteristic of graphic communication. Brodey and Lindgren give us this picture of the essence of interactive communication, compared with communication by exchange of written messages.

" . . . As a dialogue [the] exchange of [printed] information and concept is very seriously limited by the medium even if you respond with letters and questions. It is a long-distance exchange, with terrific time delays between sender and receiver. Although it has certain advantages, it is a rather tenuous one-dimensional dialogue.

"Let us then take the example of two people talking together. One is trying to explain something to the other. He starts by throwing out an explanation, constantly assessing by the other's expression whether or not anything is getting across. The listener may be obviously puzzled or may show a glimmer of understanding. *He* is listening for something in the explanation that sounds like something he already knows, so that he can link it up conceptually with a structured inner map that he already has organized. By his expressions, by his gestures, by his questions, he reveals to his interlocuter or teacher what he does not understand. By his 'errors,' by his lack of comprehension, by his verbal responses, the teacher judges how 'far off' he is, and he takes new tacks, thinks of new analogies, and so on. Everyone of us has had this experience of learning a new concept, a new idea, stretching out and changing a point of view we already held; and everyone of us has had the experience of trying to explain something to someone else. Intuitively, we know what this process is like, but we have no formal language to describe and to predict how it occurs. It is still an art." [1]

We define man-machine communication as two-way conversation that is goal-oriented—aimed toward the accomplishment of a specific objective—and in which both parties contribute a necessary function. Each performs a role of which the other is not capable. Usually the man provides creativity and originality, makes decisions, or analyzes complex patterns or arrays of data. The computer's main contribution tends to be fast and accurate storage and retrieval of large quantities of information and extremely rapid calculation. We have, then, two dissimilar systems or organisms, working toward a common goal and dependent, each upon the other, in its attainment. The term *symbiosis* describes a similar phenomenon as it occurs in nature, except that biological organisms in symbiosis need not share a common goal. J. C. R. Licklider, writing what is perhaps the pioneering paper in this field, tells why man-machine symbiosis is needed, on the basis of some of his own experiences, and describes what it is. The narrative quoted here recounts an analysis he made of some of his own professional working habits.

"About 85 per cent of my 'thinking' time was spent getting into a position to think, to make a decision, to learn something I needed to know. Much more time went into finding or obtaining information than into digesting it. Hours went into the plotting of graphs, and other hours into instructing an assistant how to plot. When the graphs were finished, the relations were obvious at once, but the plotting had to be done in order to make them so. At one point, it was necessary to compare six experimental determinations of a function relating speech-intelligibility to speech-to-noise ratio. No two experimenters had used the same definition or measure of speech-to-noise ratio. Several hours of calculating were required to get the data into comparable form. When they were in comparable form, it took only a few seconds to determine what I needed to know.

"Throughout the period I examined, in short, my 'thinking' time was devoted mainly to activities that were essentially clerical or mechanical: searching, calculating, plotting, transforming, determining the logical or dynamic consequences of a set of assumptions or hypotheses, preparing the way for a decision or an insight. Moreover, my choices of what to attempt and what not to attempt were determined to an embarrassingly great extent by considerations of clerical feasibility, not intellectual capability."

.   .   .   .

"As has been said in various ways, men are noisy, narrow-band devices, but their nervous systems have very many parallel and simultaneously active channels. Relative to men, computing machines are very fast and very accurate, but they are constrained to perform only one or a few elementary operations at a time. Men are flexible, capable of 'programming themselves contingently' on the basis of newly received information. Computing machines are single-minded, constrained by their 'preprogramming.' Men naturally speak redundant languages organized around unitary objects and coherent actions and employing 20 to 60 elementary symbols. Computers 'naturally' speak nonredundant languages, usually with only two elementary symbols and no inherent appreciation either of unitary objects or of coherent actions.

"Present-day computers are designed primarily to solve preformulated problems or to process data according to predetermined procedures. The course of the computation may be conditional upon results obtained during the computation, but all the alternatives must be foreseen in advance. (If an unforeseen alternative arises, the whole process comes to a halt and awaits the necessary extension of the program.) The requirement for preformulation or predetermination is sometimes no great disadvantage. It is often said that programming for a computing machine forces one to think clearly, that it disciplines the thought process. If the user can think his problem through in advance, symbiotic association with a computing machine is not necessary.

"However, many problems that can be thought through in advance are very difficult to think through in advance. They would be easier to solve, and they could be solved faster, through an intuitively guided trial-and-error processing in which the computer cooperated, turning up flaws in the reasoning or revealing unexpected turns in the solution. Other problems simply cannot be formulated without computing-machine aid. Poincare anticipated the frustration of an important group of would-be computer users when he said, 'The question is not, "What is the answer?" The question is, "What is the question?" ' One of the main aims of man-computer symbiosis is to bring the computing machine effectively into the formulative parts of technical problems." [9]

Recently the idea of man-machine communication and its applications have received much attention in computer literature and even in the popular press. For example, schoolroom use of computers to assist the teacher has begun with some fanfare. The idea of an intellectual partnership of man and a machine tends to be associated only with computers and is often regarded with dread, as a forerunner of the domination of man by his machines. But this form of partnership is not new, nor does it, of itself, portend any grave consequences for mankind. Here is an excerpt from Jan de Hartog which, while relatively recent, surely portrays a feeling that has been with man since he first set out to sea.*

". . . I had no idea that I had finally entered into that most ancient, mystical relationship between man and matter: the comradeship between a sailor and his ship. I was at last, in my turn, imbuing a piece of man-made machinery with a personality of its own, linked to it by a bond of loyalty and devotion, an umbilical cord of love. . . . I knew, with the high-plumed presumption of the inexperienced young male, that she would never disobey me again, but would repay my devotion with idolatry. From now on she would be consumed with only one desire: to comply with the slightest of my wishes—slave, comrade, concubine; alter

* From *The Captain* by Jan de Hartog. Copyright © 1966 by Littra, A. G. Reprinted by permission of Atheneum Publishers.

ego of Narcissus, spectral partner in the imaginary dialogue of the Masters after God." [4]

1.2 THE HISTORY OF MAN-MACHINE COMMUNICATION

Teaching machines represent probably the earliest use of man-machine interaction on the level we wish to consider. First reported in 1926 by Pressey [12] and later by Skinner, [14] these are basically devices for testing or teaching. The machine, in some form, "asks" a question, the student answers it, and then some checking is done of his answer. Used in this way, the machine is, at the least, an efficient testing device. If it is also used to present some tutorial material to the student, it can teach him as well as test him. Early teaching machines required the student either to answer by pressing a button of some sort or to write a reply and then compare it with a previously hidden, correct answer. In the former case the machine could tell whether or not the answer was right; in the latter case the student's own judgment was needed, although his answers could be recorded for later viewing and checking by the teacher. This technique gives the student an important benefit —immediate response by the machine to an action by him. As soon as the student gives his reply to a question, the reply is checked (or a correct answer is displayed to him so that he can check) and he knows almost immediately whether he is right or wrong. This immediate *reinforcement* has been proved a strong factor in the rate of learning. If the same student had to turn in a paper to be graded by the teacher and wait a day or two for the results, he would learn less both from his correct answers and from his mistakes.

Teaching machines have evolved into *computer-assisted instruction,* the use of a general-purpose computer as a teaching machine. The greater capability of the computer for logical analysis and data processing, as compared to early teaching machines, makes it truly an interactive device. Not only can we get immediate feedback but also the machine's reaction can be tailored more specifically to student actions, detecting and responding to the exact nature of an error, not just to the fact of right or wrong. The computer also offers the author of a teaching course greater flexibility in changing sequences of presentation on the basis of student performance, a capability for the machine to answer the student's questions (as in providing a dictionary look-up service), and a calculating capability for the student.

Another major landmark, not exactly a system but a classical definition of the problem of man-machine interaction, came from Vannevar Bush, [2] in a paper published in 1945. As part of a general description of the problems and potential of scientists in the aftermath of World War II he hypothesized a device called *memex* which would be a mechanized, personal library, a desk-size device storing large quantities of microfilm. The collection on film could be indexed and retrieved on demand and new notes and documents could easily be added to it. Except for variations in the actual hardware that has evolved, which has tended to take a different turn, Bush set a goal for an interactive information storage and retrieval system that is still not realized.

An important development for man-machine communication is the use of graphic information for both computer input and output. The computer can display graphic images—pictures—on a cathode ray tube for convenient viewing by a man. It takes only a fraction of a second to "draw" a highly complex image. The man, by methods we shall describe later, can also draw these pictures and transmit them to the computer, and can identify points and regions on them to the computer. In this way man and machine can communicate in terms of spatial relationships and can do so rapidly. The alternatives, converting the relationships into tedious strings of numbers or using slower, computer-driven plotting machines, both vastly increase the time involved and remove the element of high-speed interaction.

The use of computer-controlled graphic output as an interactive technique seems, like so many computer innovations, to have originated at MIT. A well-known early project involved calculating the trajectory of a ball dropped from a given height and given some forward momentum. The path of the ball was computed, and a picture of the ball following this path in *real time* (i.e., the pictured ball moved at the same speed as an actual ball would) was displayed on a cathode ray tube. The interactive value was derived in the following way. A student was asked to set up the equations of motion and then write a program to solve them.[3] His program was then executed by the computer and, if correct, would show the ball following a prescribed trajectory. If the equations were wrong, the ball would miss its path. As a result, the student got an immediate indication of whether his program was correct and some indication of what, if anything, went wrong. The alternative would have been to have the computer print out a series of coordinates that the ball was passing through and to compare these with a set of coordinates computed by hand. The graphic method is not only more vivid but also more fun.

Later, MIT was also the scene of one of the greatest advances in man-machine communication with the development of a prototype for a semiautomatic air defense system for the United States, one in which a computer received information directly from radar, processed it, remembered it, displayed it, and helped to make decisions based on it.[13] The computer went on to do all the calculations needed to plan an intercept, if necessary, but always worked under the overall control of a man who made the key decisions. To make these decisions, displays were needed showing the geography of the region, the tracks of aircraft passing by, flight plans indicating what aircraft were expected, and the details of each track, present or expected, including identification of the aircraft, its altitude, exact course, and speed. No single display could show all the needed information with all possibly essential detail. An air defense officer viewing a display was able to ask the computer to vary the information displayed, to bring out more detail, to enlarge or contract an image, to remove information from a screen, or to retrieve data stored in memory. If some critical item developed while the officer was otherwise occupied, the computer was able to call his attention to the item by making the display blink or by sounding an audible alarm. However the officer came to begin working on a problem, he was able to take several different views of a situation and to ask for more information before rendering a decision. When the system was finally put into operation, it was known as SAGE [5] (for Semi-Automatic Ground Environment) and consisted of a network of control centers. Each center had two large computers and banks of cathode ray display tubes, each with dozens of switches and keys for the entry of data, and a light pen for selecting points in a display about which more information was wanted or on which some special function was to be performed.

More recently we have seen a broadening of the applications of man-machine communication. Use of a computer for engineering design (see Figure 1.1) is now reported as a reality at a number of installations, including General Motors Research Laboratories,[7] where work has been in progress since the 1950s. The most widely known system for preparing drawings by computer, called *Sketchpad*,[15] was created by Ivan Sutherland at MIT's Lincoln Laboratory. Beside these systems for entering graphic information into a computer, we now have interactive information retrieval systems and interactive systems for information acquisition, editing, and instruction, all of which will be covered in detail in later chapters.

Many of the modern interactive systems depend upon *time-sharing*, a method that allows a computer to serve more than one user at a time. Time-sharing does not, of itself, make interaction possible (the SAGE work did not have this benefit, for example), but it makes interaction economical, and we may expect that bringing interactive systems into practical day-to-day use will depend largely upon the flexibility and

Figure 1.1 An engineering designer working at a CRT console. *Photo courtesy IBM Corp.*

economics of future time-sharing systems. Fano and Corbato * look upon this development as one of crucial importance in the development of the industry.

"The history of the modern computer has been characterized by a series of quantum leaps in our view of the machine's possibilities. To mention only two of the crucial advances, the application of electronics, vastly increasing the computer's speed of operation, and later the invention of special languages, facilitating communication with the machine, each in its turn opened new vistas on the computer's potentialities. Within the past few years the technique called time-sharing has again stimulated the imagination. It has created an unexpected new order of uses for the computer." [6]

---

* From Fano and Corbato, "Time-Sharing on Computers," copyright © 1966 by Scientific American, Inc. All rights reserved.

1.3 HOW INTERACTIVE SYSTEMS ARE USED

We cannot yet claim that the day of the interactive system as a commonplace is at hand. But we do find an increasing number of applications and increasing interest in extending the idea into more and more new fields. Chapters 6 through 12 of this book survey some of the major applications, discussing each in some detail. Here we shall briefly sketch them to provide a general frame of reference.

We have divided the applications into *(a)* a basic set primarily concerned with exchanging information and *(b)* a set of advanced applications that tend to make use of the basic set. We have identified the following four as the important basic applications.

Information Acquisition. This involves the entry of data into a computer through an interactive process wherein the data are checked on entry, errors are fed back immediately, and the power of the computer can be used to elicit only needed information. In this way the need for redundant transcription and transmission of data is reduced.

Information Retrieval. This application concerns the recovery of information that has been stored in a computer, again using conversational techniques to assure that information needed has been fully identified and that the user can browse to find what he really wants. Retrieval is often a prerequisite for the entry of data because originators of information may find it necessary to ask questions before making a decision about what is to be entered into files. For example, a committee headed by Dr. G. W. King made a study of the Library of Congress [8] and discovered, along with other findings, that catalogers spend as much as 60 per cent of their time searching in the existing catalog for information needed to complete catalog entries for new acquisitions. The King committee recommended the extensive use of interactive systems for cataloging as well as retrieval operations.

Editing. We are finding the computer of great value in storing text material and assisting in its preparation for publication. The principal part of this activity consists of accepting raw text input and allowing the author to make changes—adding or deleting material and moving portions of it around. If we can do these things, we can also accept and edit nontextual, or highly structured, material that also needs editing, such as formatted library catalog records or computer programs.

Instruction. We have already briefly described the role of the computer as a teaching machine. From the point of view of the computer program, the instructional process might be considered that of asking a student questions, the answers to which are already known, and comparing his responses with the known information. In information acquisition the computer asks for information it does not already have, and in information retrieval it works with the user to ascertain what is wanted. Only in instructional systems (and not always there) do we have a situation in which the computer asks its user essentially to confirm existing information and then acts differently according to whether he can or cannot confirm it.

The more advanced group of applications are concerned with producing a useful output through joint action of man and machine. These are much closer to man-computer symbiosis than are any of the basic applications just described. The outputs may be a directly usable product —a computer program or an electronic circuit diagram—or a decision affecting a business or military enterprise. Three such applications have been selected for review.

Interactive Programming. In a reversal of the tale that the shoemaker's children often go barefoot, computer programmers have turned attention to their own art, and one of the most effective applications of man-machine communication is that of producing computer programs. *Interactive programming* is a term often used interchangeably with *time-sharing,* but the two are different. Although the former is usually an application of the latter, either can exist without the other, and we shall take pains to keep these concepts separate.

Design. Viewed abstractly, the process of design is the creation of an information structure, or model, often highly complex and frequently expressing relationships that cannot be easily verbalized, such as shape or color. The *design* must be differentiated from the *product.* The former is information descriptive of the latter. We can use a computer to provide valuable assistance in evolving the design—the information set—and then use the design separately to develop the product. Sometimes the computer can also be used in product development. From this viewpoint the design for a textile fabric (Figure 1.2) is not different from the design for a building or an electronic circuit. In the textile application a designer first uses the computer to assist in the design of a fabric and then can harness the machine directly to the job of controlling a loom to produce the fabric previously designed.[10]

Decision-Making. A decision made by a military commander or a business or government executive is rarely an abstract choice between *yes* and *no*—it is as much the design of a plan or a strategy as it is a

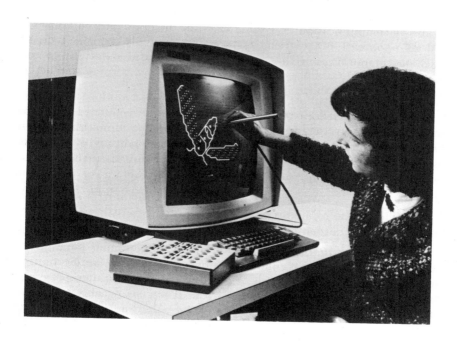

Figure 1.2 A textile designer working through the CRT. *Photo courtesy J. Lourie.*

selection from among clearly defined and differentiated alternatives. By their very nature, interactive systems do not decide for a man; rather, they assist him to make a decision by supplying needed information and occasionally reminding him of what he has to do to make, and fully specify, a decision. Here the computer has not lived up to our expectations (or perhaps, fears), in that computer decision-making is largely limited to cases in which the variables are relatively few and are well defined. Unfortunately, management in general has the opposite situation—many ill-defined variables to work with. Computer programs lack inference-drawing capability; they cannot suggest original ideas, or, at least, they are not very good at it. Hence command and management systems today largely employ combinations of information retrieval and simulation. The machine recovers information on demand and makes requested tests, but does not decide or suggest.

1.4 THE ELEMENTS OF MAN-MACHINE COMMUNICATION

Communication between man and machine requires that there be means of communication and some capacity on both sides to interpret and act upon each other's remarks. Some of the basic elements of man-machine communication that occur frequently in working systems are the following.

Hardware   We must be concerned with actual transducers or means of conveying and transforming signals in either direction between the versatile but imprecise and error-prone man and the unimaginative but stalwart computer. In Chapter 2 we will review many of the types of communication terminals and "interface" equipment in current use.

Programming.   The computer must be programmed to carry out its end of a conversation. Moreover, since programming consists of a man providing the computer with a list of instructions that it will then execute, the real burden of man-machine communication falls on man.

Natural Language Communication.   It is becoming common for designers of man-machine communications systems to strive for natural language as the medium of conversation. What this term means exactly tends to vary somewhat in different circumstances, since what is natural for one man may not be for another. The trend, however, is toward simplifying the act of communication and requiring less and less formal training for an operator or user of an interactive system. Hence a large and growing discipline is devoted to computer interpretation of natural language; and, although there is much overlap with man-machine communication, the two are not coincident.

At present, in the overwhelming majority of interactive systems, natural language can be avoided, and it is avoided because of the difficulty of using it. Our Chapter 5 serves mainly to introduce the reader to the subject and familiarize him with the formidable nature of the problem.

1.5 THE FUTURE OF INTERACTIVE SYSTEMS

It appears to us that man-machine interaction is going to become *the* way of problem-solving. People today who are problem-solvers—whether physicists, physicians, programmers, or ship's navigators—expect to be provided with certain basic tools. Depending on the profession, these may include stethoscopes, slide rules, telephones, drawing instruments, and other equipment. In the future, much of the work of these professionals will change from direct use of their instruments—that is, from personally making measurements or performing calculations—to telling a computer what measurements to make and what calculations to perform. Problem-solvers will ask the computer for information and will give the computer their results. Men will not longer be able to compete in these professional areas without the computer, just as today a physician cannot meet professional standards of practice without the use of the most modern instruments. And, just as we now accept as perfectly natural and desirable the use of machinery to extend man's physical limitations (a telephone to amplify his voice, or a microscope to amplify his vision), we will come to accept as perfectly natural his use of a computer to amplify his intellect. William Orr suggests, "There is really only one 'application' of Conversational Computers, and that is *whatever you do during the course of a normal work day.*"[11]

But we shall find the computer not to be restricted to the list of applications we have given. Because the computer is a versatile and programmable medium for communication with other machines, we will find it in use to control laboratory experiments, to produce works of art, and to provide active assistance in composing other forms of programs. It may well become as ubiquitous and necessary a medium for the communication and amplification of man's thoughts as the telephone and the typewriter are today.

REFERENCES

1. Brodey, Warren M., and Nilo Lindgren, "Human Enhancement through Evolutionary Technology," *IEEE Spectrum*, 4, 9 (September 1967), 87–97.
2. Bush, Vannevar, "As We May Think," *Atlantic Monthly*, **176**, 1 (July 1945), 101–108.
3. Davis, Ruth M., "A History of Automated Displays," *Datamation*, 11, 1 (January 1965), 24–28.
4. De Hartog, Jan, *The Captain*, Atheneum, New York, 1966, p. 171.
5. Everett, R. R., C. A. Zraket, and H. D. Bennington, "SAGE—A Data-Processing System for Air Defense," *Proceedings of the Eastern Computer Conference, 1957*, The Institute of Radio Engineers, New York, December 1957, pp. 148–155.
6. Fano, R. M., and F. J. Corbato, "Time-Sharing on Computers," *Scientific American*, **215**, 3 (September 1966), (also in *Information*, W. H. Freeman, San Francisco, 1966, pp. 76–95).
7. Jacks, Edwin L., "A Laboratory for the Study of Graphical Man-Machine Communication," *Proceedings of the Fall Joint Computer Conference, 1964*, San Francisco, pp. 343–350.
8. King, Gilbert W., et al., *Automation and The Library of Congress*, Library of Congress, Washington, D.C., 1963, p. 80.
9. Licklider, J. C. R., "Man-Computer Symbiosis," *IRE Transactions on Human Factors in Electronics*, **HFE–1** 1 (March 1960), 4–11.

10. Lourie, Janice R., and Abie M. Bonin, "Computer-Controlled Textile Designing and Weaving," *Proceedings of the IFIPS Conference, 1968,* Edinburgh.
11. Orr, William D., ed., *Conversational Computers,* John Wiley, New York, 1968, p. vii.
12. Pressey, S. L., et al., "Pressey's Self-Instructional Test-Scoring Devices," *Teaching Machines and Programmed Learning,* A. A. Lumsdaine and Robert Glaser, eds., National Education Association, Washington, D.C., 1960, Part II, pp. 32–93.
13. Sackman, Harold, *Computers, System Science and Evolving Society,* John Wiley, New York, 1967, pp. 91–167.
14. "Skinner's Teaching Machines and Programming Concepts," in Lumsdaine and Glaser, *op. cit.* (Reference 12) , pp. 94–256.
15. Sutherland, Ivan E., "Sketchpad, A Man-Machine Graphical Communication System," *Proceedings of the Spring Joint Computer Conference, 1963,* Spartan Books, New York, pp. 329–346.

Chapter Two

Interactive Communication Devices

2.1 INTRODUCTION

Meaningful communication between a man and a machine requires that each be able to present information to the other in a meaningful way and, of course, be able to sense the information provided by the other. Speeds or reading and writing and general perceptive ability vary widely. We are not dealing with communication between similar organisms here, and the differences between man and machine in the perception, interpretation, processing, and transmission of information are vitally important in the design of information systems. Computers are far faster at most of the communications tasks—reading, writing, and drawing diagrams. Man is faster and far more versatile at interpreting complex patterns in data. To bring these complementary capabilities together in a team is the major purpose of interactive computing systems.

The data-processing industry is developing an ever greater variety of interface equipment and is making it more reliable and easier to use. The increased use of telephone or other common-carrier communications networks makes computers more readily available to a greater number of people. Hardware availability, however, is not the main problem. Each use of a computer for man-machine communication requires a careful analysis of what information is to be transmitted in each direction, how it is to be transmitted or displayed, and when or under what conditions it is to be transmitted or displayed. In some communications systems the number and the composition of possible messages are severely limited, as is the case when we dial telephone numbers. Only limited message types can be transmitted, and only certain number combinations are admissible. Within these limitations the system operates easily and efficiently. If one were to insist on dialing the name of a friend, rather than his telephone number, however, the result would have to be an error message or a wrong number. The system may allow for more elaborate conversational elements than simply telephone numbers and recorded responses to incorrectly dialed numbers, but it must then be carefully programmed to generate and interpret them.

In this chapter we survey a number of representative interface devices, that is, the devices used to pass information between man and machine. The field has become far too large to attempt an exhaustive survey. Indeed, this would serve no purpose, for the equipment offered on the market changes rapidly, while the principles remain basically the same. We will generally refrain from any discussion of the advantages of the individual devices, leaving advocacy for later chapters on the various applications of man-machine communication.

Our approach in this chapter will be to start with the more traditional and better-known keyboard devices and the linkages between the communications terminals and the existing communications networks, and then to introduce the more modern and esoteric devices involving graphic and audio and visual information presentation. All the equipment described herein is, or has been, in use somewhere.

A note on terminology will be helpful—a typewriter, cathode ray tube, or other interface device is at one end of a communications network that links it to a computer. It is then, a *terminal* device, and we often speak of a typewriter, etc., as a terminal in this sense. Also, with our modern penchant for packaging, we often find one or more devices built into a desk or table, called a *console*. The word *console* is often used interchangeably with *terminal* to indicate the device used to receive information from, or transmit it into, the network connected to the computer. The network may be part of the nation's telephone system, or it may be a single cable directly attached to the computer.

2.2 KEYBOARD TERMINALS

Probably the most commonly available communication device is essentially an electric typewriter. Even in the very early computers a typewriter was available for printing output, for modifying a program that had malfunctioned, or for use by the operator to control the computer. Today, most computers still have such a terminal for use as a control device, but it is now almost exclusively used by the machine operator, as there are more efficient ways of getting output or of modifying a program. Keyboard terminals are in frequent use, however, as remote input-output devices, located far from the computer and connected through telephone lines. Although the keyboards used vary somewhat, there is now a tendency toward standardization so that all generate a compatible transmission code.

Typewriter-type terminals have the following characteristics. Transmission speed is about 15 characters per second. The reliability is high; they are very easy to use. Their deficiencies are primarily their lack of speed (which becomes increasingly important as the computer's ability to generate large volumes of data rapidly increases) and their lack of graphic capability, or the ability to transmit two-dimensional structures. They *can* be used to generate graphic material, such as bar graphs and outline maps, but at a slow rate of speed. Some common examples of these terminals are the Model 37 Teletype, the IBM 1052 keyboard printer, and the IBM 2740 communication terminal. The last of these is very similar to a conventional, office electric typewriter; it is shown in Figure 2.1.

Many applications of man-machine communications systems involve primarily the transmission of coded messages using very restricted vocabularies. Requests for the quotation of a stock price, an inventory level, or the status of a bank account fall into this category. When the vocabulary is so restricted, it is more convenient for users to press a single button, key, or switch that represents one of the stereotyped messages than to have to type the full message each time on a typewriter. We would, of course, have the user remember that A stands for "Give me the price of _____" and B stands for "Stock symbol follows," but an easier approach is to devise a special keyboard each of whose keys has a particular meaning. Keys are arranged in rows, and the device is often called a *matrix keyboard* because of this regular arrangement. A common example is found in some cafeterias that employ such a device for their cashiers. Each button is labelled with the name of a food item offered that day. The cashier has only to strike the keys corresponding to the items purchased. She does not have to remember the price of each item. The cash register, on the other hand, associates each key with a price, rather than the name of the item, and a correct bill is quickly produced. A matrix keyboard is illustrated in Figure 2.2.

Sometimes we may have too many possible coded messages to fit on a

Figure 2.1 The IBM 2740 terminal. *Photo courtesy IBM Corp.*

Figure 2.2 The IBM 1094 matrix keyboard. *Photo courtesy IBM Corp.*

single keyboard matrix, yet we do not desire either to have multiple keyboards or to revert to a typewriter and lose the advantage of single-key input. What can be done then is to change the meaning of keys. This can be achieved by using a cardboard or plastic overlay to a matrix keyboard, which has printed on it different sets of meanings for keys. Since the computer knows only what key was struck, not what message was intended, it needs some means of telling which of several possible meanings was intended. The overlay is made with a keylike appendage, which transmits to the computer a coded message identifying the overlay and hence telling the computer how to interpret the single key that the user has struck. In effect, use of this device sends two characters to the computer, one identifying the overlay and one the key. An overlay is shown in Figure 2.3.

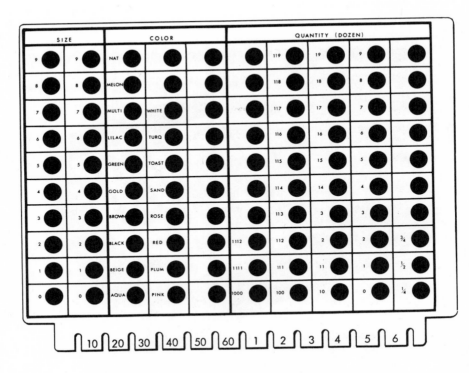

Figure 2.3 An overlay for the matrix keyboard. The numbered tabs at the bottom may be removed in different patterns to enable different overlays to have different codes. *Photo courtesy IBM Corp.*

Matrix keyboards have the advantage of greater ease and speed of entry of information and therefore require less training for an operator. But they have a more limited vocabulary than typewriters. Keying speed may be about the same as for a typewriter, but each key conveys more than a single character's meaning. An example is the IBM 1092 Programmed Keyboard, which has a 10 $\times$ 15 matrix of keys and as many as 48 different overlays, or "Keymats."

Another interesting form of keyboard, which we find in increasing use, is the Touch-Tone® or Touch-Calling telephone. As used in the home or office, the Touch-Tone® is an ordinary-appearing telephone with the rotary dial replaced by an array of twelve pushbuttons. The two additional buttons, beyond those needed for the ten numeric digits, have arbitrary meanings. Each different user may assign different meanings to them. They can be used to denote the end of a field, the end of a message, the presence of an error is the last transmission, the use of an alternate code for the ten numeric buttons, or any other meaning agreed upon by both the sender and the computer program at the receiving end.

One technique for using the extra keys allows alphabetic information to be transmitted. The assumption must be made that most characters sent will be numeric, for extra effort is required for the alphabetic characters. The "dial" is arranged as shown in Figure 2.4, letters being associated with numbers as they are in conventional telephone dials. The letters Q and Z, which usually do not appear on the dial, are assumed to be associated with the number 1. The 11th button (*) preceding a number button means to take the first (leftmost) alphabetic character associated with the number. Thus *2 means A. The 12th button (#) means to take the rightmost associated letter, so #2 means C. The combination *# denotes the middle alphabetic character, and

Figure 2.4*a* The Touch-Tone® telephone. *Photo courtesy AT & T Co.*

hence B is *#2. Still more codes can be made by using sequences of three or more combinations of * and #.

The telephone is used mostly in information retrieval applications where specific information is requested by entering a number or series of codes. When this form of alpha-numeric input is combined with audio output (see Section 2.7), an interactive system results. Because the input by the human user is slow, these conversations must be restricted in nature. But we cannot overestimate the advantage of a "communica-

Figure 2.4*b* An enlargement of the Touch-Tone® "dial." *Photo courtesy AT & T Co.*

tions terminal" that is so readily and universally available, that serves as a useful office machine when not needed for data transmission, that is familiar to most users and that, of course, is already connected into a giant communications network. An early weakness, the lack of an associated printer to give both a written record of what was transmitted and a printed form of response from the computer, is now being overcome. Such written records are desirable in many of the commercial applications for which this means of communication is otherwise so admirably suited. Having now introduced the question of tying the terminal into the communications network, let us examine this problem further before proceeding with a discussion of other terminal devices.

2.3 COMMUNICATIONS INTERFACES

We can connect a communications terminal to a computer by directly wiring the terminal to the computer or to a control unit specifically designed to connect the central computer with terminals, storage, and input and output units. In this way we build a small network within the computer system. The terminals are then semipermanently attached; that is, they are connected by cables, and, although they retain some freedom of movement, they cannot be moved from room to room or building to building. This is called *hard wiring*. The alternative approach is to connect the terminals to a common carrier network and also connect the computer, or its input-output controller, to the same network. The advantages, when this approach is permitted by terminal design, are that wire and cables are not paid for when not actually in use, that terminals may be freely moved about, and that users may be remotely located. (Terminal-to-computer conversations have been held through trans-Atlantic cable and Telstar. Typical directly connected cable lengths, on the other hand, are of the order of tens of feet, although up to 2000 feet is often permissible.)

A typewriter terminal costs on the order of $50 to $100 per month, and the charge for a telephone network interface (such as the Bell System 103A Data Set) is around $30 per month. This, in addition to the cost of actual line usage, is all the investment required for a new user of an existing on-line computing system. When the terminal is the telephone itself, or is an existing teletype that is part of a company's existing teletype network, the cost to attach a computer is quite low, a fact that enhances the attractiveness of this approach. The cost of using the computer itself is not included in these estimates.

As an alternative to the Bell Data Set as a means of coupling a terminal to a telephone line, there is now coming into use an *acoustic coupler*[5] which is wired to the terminal. By placing the handset of any telephone into the coupler, the terminal is connected into the network (Figure 2.5). The acoustic coupler is small and easily portable. When it is used together with a small, portable typewriter terminal, a completely portable terminal results. This can be highly useful to salesmen, who can place an order with their home offices immediately after making a sale, or to news reporters, who can type their stories in the telephone booth nearest the scene of the event being covered and communicate directly with an automatic typesetting system.

Whatever network is involved, at the computer the channel control or input-output control unit must be able to service a number of lines leading to terminals and combine their traffic streams into a single high-speed data stream going into the central computer. Since it takes about $\frac{1}{15}$ second to transmit a character through a keyboard and only a few millionths of a second to store it in the computer, we need these control, or multiplexing, devices to compact the data and to free the

Figure 2.5 An acoustic coupler. *Photo courtesy Anderson Jacobson, Inc.*

main computer from having to wait for each input character. This process may be roughly compared to the use of small feeder airlines bringing passengers from many points into a major airport, where they board larger, faster planes for a long-distance trip. It would not be economical to travel directly between each small airport and the larger, more distant air terminal.

2.4 REMOTE SENSING DEVICES

In some applications it is desirable to transcribe information into machine-readable form before it is presented for use in a data-processing system. For example, some libraries use a prepunched book card together with a punched-card user identification to process a circulation transaction, or charge-out. The librarian at the charge desk need only insert the book card and the punched identification card in a mechanical reader to make a record of the charge. This reduces the work of the librarian and permits the computer to handle the sending of notifications for overdue books and the keeping of up-to-date records of book inventory and location. There is a variety of these devices. We shall describe the IBM 1030 family of such machines.

A single device, the IBM 1031 Input Station,[10] can be configured in a number of ways to provide different combinations of reading capabilities (see Figure 2.6). It can read standard 80-column punched cards and plastic badges equivalent to 22-column-wide punched cards (the type now frequently used for identification cards and implied in our example of a library check-out procedure). This device is also able to read from a cartridge, a device about the size of a punched card but a half-inch thick. As many as 12 columns of information can be "dialed" into the cartridge by sliding levers to the appropriate number positions in the columns. The cartridge is then read as if it were a punched card. This permits the operator at an input station to vary the data he transmits to the computer. It is also possible to make manual entry of information (numeric or blank only) directly into the system by manipulating slides in what amounts to a semipermanently fixed cartridge. Thus, for very changeable information, direct entry can be used. For more slowly changing but repetitive information, a cartridge is preferred. When the data can be pretranscribed well before use, a punched card or punched badge is feasible. A number of combinations are possible, permitting for example, a full-size card, a badge, and manual entry all as input forms from a single station.

Input stations such as these, in addition to their application in

Figure 2.6 Components of the IBM 1030 data collection system. *Photo courtesy IBM Corp.*

library activities as we have mentioned, can be used in factories, particularly job shops, where work passes from one station to another and the exact operation to be performed may vary from item to item. It becomes important, then, to record what was done and how long it took. These stations can also be used in warehousing operations to record receipts and shipments, or in a variety of other inventory control operations.

Clearly, the limit on this form of input is that it cannot transmit complicated messages unless they have been prepunched. The advantage lies in the ease with which it can transmit an uncomplicated message. The 1030 system can be made interactive by combining the input possibilities mentioned with a remote printer or card punch. A 1033 Printer can be attached, through which the computer can transmit to the man at the remote station, confirming his input, giving him special instructions, or requesting retransmission if an error has been found. A remotely punched card can be attached to newly received merchandise, for example, and used thereafter as an inventory control card, to be read by the 1031 when the material is withdrawn from storage.

The 1030 system components can be cable-attached to a computer or connected to common-carrier networks. As many as eight satellite 1030's can be connected to a control 1030, which then communicates with the computer. The satellite stations cost about half what the control stations cost, and these, in turn, cost about the same as a type-writer-style terminal.

2.5 CATHODE RAY TUBES

The cathode ray tube (CRT) has been used as an output device almost continuously since the modern era of computers began. Its speed of operation and ability to present graphic material are essential in many applications. The basic principle of operation[6] is quite simple. A beam of electrons enters the tube from the rear (see Figure 2.7), and its point of impact on the back of the tube face is controlled by electromagnetic fields set up across the path of the beam. By varying the strength of the fields the beam is moved vertically and horizontally. As no mechanical motion is involved, this is an extremely fast operation. When the beam hits the back of the tube face, it strikes a phosphor-coated surface and causes light to be emitted. By varying the composition of the coating, different degrees of persistence of this light can be achieved. A CRT used for computer output usually has relatively low persistence. This leads to the requirement that a display be regenerated often if it is to

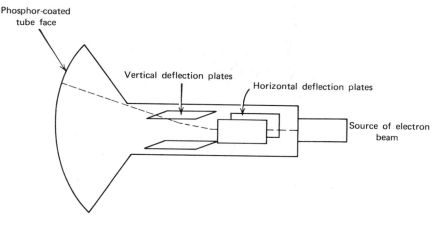

Figure 2.7 Schematic of a CRT. The deflection plates are one of several possible means of setting up the magnetic fields that control the positioning of the electron beam.

appear stable. Images must be regenerated about 30 times a second in order to have the appearance of being continuous and to avoid an irksome flicker.

Cathode ray tubes may be generally grouped into either of two classes, as far as the computer output devices are concerned. There are small, relatively inexpensive terminals that can display only a limited repertoire of characters, and these in fixed positions on the screen, just as a typewriter is restricted in the choice and positioning of its characters. A display device of this type is illustrated in Figure 2.8. A larger, more expensive class of terminals can generate any character and position it anywhere.

Character formation can be under program control, that is, the characters can be formed by displaying a pattern of dots or line segments. If this is done, there is no restriction on the size or style of characters.

Figure 2.8 The IBM 2260 display terminal. *Photo courtesy IBM Corp.*

Some terminals have a built-in character generator. When this is the case, electronic circuits generate the dot pattern. This arrangement, while faster, gives less flexibility in the choice of characters. Another form of character generator is a template into which an array of shapes has been cut. The electron beam is guided by one magnetic field through the appropriate image pattern on the template, and then a second field positions the beam on the tube face.

The larger terminals have a vector- or line-drawing capability. When the terminal is provided with the origin and the end point of a line, a segment connecting these points is automatically generated. Sets of these segments may be used to generate characters, maps, graphs, or other images. The large amount of information that must be supplied to a terminal to generate such a complex display is too much for the typical low transmission speed communications systems we have previously described. Generally, then, the larger CRT's are connected directly to computers through cables.

Figures 1.1 and 1.2 (pp. 10 and 13) show displays generated on a large, vector-drawing display terminal.

2.6 GRAPHIC INPUT DEVICES

The cathode ray tubes we have described are not, in themselves, inter-active devices, but in use they are combined with some form of input system to make them so. There is usually a keyboard, which is sufficient for many applications. Sometimes there are both a typewriter and a matrix keyboard, the latter for entering frequently used commands to the computer on what to display and how to do it. A tool that permits graphic communication through a CRT is called a *light pen*[8] (Figure 2.9). Its name derives from its shape, which resembles an ordinary pen, and the fact that it communicates by sensing light and, in some uses, by leaving a path of light on the face of the CRT.

The light pen contains a sensing apparatus that is triggered whenever it is held close to the tube face (in some cases, it is switched on by pressing against the face of the tube) and senses the spot of displayed light under itself when the spot is intensified in a regeneration cycle. When the spot is sensed, the pen sends a signal to the computer. This signal contains, in effect, the coordinates of the point where light was sensed, that is, the pen says, "I have sensed light at location x, y." The computer program must be able to interpret this message. It must know what it had displayed at point x, y and what meaning to ascribe to the selection of this point by the light pen. As we shall see in Chapter 11, if the

Figure 2.9 A light pen. *Photo courtesy National Bureau of Standards.*

computer is properly programmed, the pen may be moved across the face of the tube, a light pattern will appear to follow it, and the track made by this combination can be displayed as a sequence of dots. In this way, the user can draw any figure he wishes and the computer, by recording the locations of the dots, can keep a record of the line or curve.

The light pen is an excellent means for making quick selections among displayed alternatives. If the computer displays a list of possibilities, the user can select the one he wants by pointing to it with his light pen (Figure 2.10). The computer can be programmed to acknowledge the choice and to confirm it by blinking, underlining the selected item, erasing all others, and so on. The pen is even more valuable when a user wants to communicate in terms of position or shape. For example, the pen can easily inform the computer that its user wants to move some (indicated by pen) element of a display from its current position to another (indicated) position on the screen. This capability is useful in

Figure 2.10. Using the light pen to select an item on a list. *Photo courtesy J. Lourie.*

editing text, for example, where the editor may want to move a word to a different position in a sentence or to add a new word to a sentence. In perhaps its most interesting application, the user traces a track across the face of a CRT and indicates to the computer that this is to be the new shape of some structure, such as an automobile body, he is designing.

One difficulty with light pens is that they "illuminate" an area larger than a single spot, that is, they sense, not just a single dot on the tube face, but rather a small area, and they cannot discriminate among spots within this area. To the human user, they seem to point to, or *illuminate*, the area rather than a point. The programs in use must be able to interpret for themselves what is mean by a light pen message anywhere in the neighborhood of a given point. This also means that light pens are not very accurate for drawing. Another inconvenience has to do with the way in which CRT consoles are usually assembled. The CRT itself tends to be mounted so that the tube face is vertical, or nearly so, and directly facing the user (see Figure 2.10). Drawing with an imprecise instrument in this way can be cumbersome.

The RAND Tablet[1] is a means of conveying graphic images to a computer in an easier, more comfortable manner than by use of the light pen. It consists of an array of 1024×1024 grid elements embedded in a flat surface. Its user "writes" by means of a device much like a light pen, but one that is pressure sensitive to give the feel of an ordinary pen or pencil. As the pen moves across the surface of the tablet, the grid intersections that it passes over make known their positions to the computer and, again, a trace of the pen's path results. In this case, the path is then displayed on the face of a CRT, used in conjunction with the tablet. In this way, the user gets a visual image of what he has drawn, but the image appears at a different place—on the CRT, not on the tablet. Critics argue that it is unnatural to see the result of a drawing appear elsewhere than the surface on which is was traced. Proponents reply that the greater naturalness of the manner of writing compensates for this and, furthermore, that the view of the drawing is entirely uncluttered by the user's hand and arm. We might add that any keyboard transcriber operates in this way—the visual image that results from depressing a key appears, not *on* the key, but elsewhere, on a printed page or on a CRT, and people have no particular trouble adapting to this feature.

2.7 AUDIO OUTPUT DEVICES

Two kinds of audio output devices permit a computer to be programmed to play recorded messages to a system user. The unit of recording varies from a single word to a full message of paragraph or page length. A program decides which unit or combination of units to play to the user.

The simpler of the audio systems is the one first introduced as part of an instructional system. Messages are recorded on an ordinary, home-type audio tape recorder. The messages can vary in length. Each is preceded and followed on the tape by a high-pitched tone that can be sensed by the computer. To locate message n the computer has only to start at the top of the tape and count n tones to know that it has positioned the tape in the correct place. This approach can be used in combination with other modes of presentation to provide an oral explanation of a picture or diagram displayed through other means, or simply to vary the manner of presentation to keep up the student's interest. A disadvantage is that the time required to traverse the tape can be quite long; and, unless the messages are recorded in approximately the sequence in which they will be played, a delay in the conversational process is introduced. Since the whole object of computer-assisted instruction is to be able to skip around in a course on the basis of how the student responds to earlier questions, exact presequencing cannot always be done.

Another approach is represented by IBM's Audio Response Units.[4] The earlier model of the device made use of analog recordings of individual words, or portions of words, in short, fixed-length, analog memory units. In the newer of several models that have been produced, message units are stored as digital representations of the analog signal, and these are converted back into analog form when selected and retrieved for presentation. In other words, what is stored is a set of numbers representing the signal to be transmitted. These numbers are converted back into sound only when ready for use. This technique requires special apparatus to convert sound signals into numeric form for storage and then numbers back into sound signals. However, the approach permits use of the regular computer memory for storage of messages, rather than requiring special analog recordings that employ a different form of memory from the one utilized by the computer for other purposes. This approach also has the advantage of permitting expansion of the message store without purchase of new equipment. Usually, a long list of commonly used words is prerecorded, perhaps augmented by a list of words peculiar to the specific application, and a program assembles messages as needed.

The main application of these devices is to respond to telephone inquiries, say for a current stock price, the inventory level of a given item, or the credit status of a department store customer. In these applications a stream of data enters the computer to update a file, perhaps recording changes in stock prices. In this case, the telephone inquirer designates the symbol of the stock about which information is wanted by "dialing" on a Touch-Tone® telephone. A program searches a file to recover the current value of the stock price and then uses this information to search another file to recover the message units needed to assemble a message that will announce the price, perhaps the words "Four eight and one half" to denote a price of $48.50. This kind of response needs only a very limited vocabulary.

These audio response units can operate in a conversational mode in the sense that the caller can ask a new question as soon as he receives a response to the previous one. There is an automatic cut-off if, after a response, the caller takes no action for a specified period of time, which may vary between about 5 and 10 seconds. If this period of grace is exceeded, the caller must dial again if he has another question to ask. As long as he asks something, though, he can keep the line open and can carry on a continuous conversation for as long as is meaningful to him. Since the only terminal needed for operation with an audio response unit is a telephone, a system can be set up relatively inexpensively and can serve a large number of users.

It must be realized, however, that, to carry on a truly general conversation, a large vocabulary is needed, as is a great deal of programming logic to assemble the outgoing messages. To obtain valid conversational outputs, many forms of the basic words would have to be stored—plurals, possessives, different tenses, and so on. The programming required to assemble well-structured sentences would probably be excessive. Hence we must expect these machines to remain limited to fairly simple question-and-answer applications for yet a few years, with more elaborate messages prerecorded in their entirety. In the long term, however, we may anticipate highly versatile computer-created speech.

2.8 VIDEO OUTPUT DEVICES

In addition to graphic images that may be generated with line segments and dot patterns on cathode ray tubes, it is possible to have other forms of computer-generated video displays. Combining computer output, traditionally in the form of numbers or simple graphs, with high-quality graphic imagery has long been a goal of computer engineers.[3] A common example of such usage is the superposition of computer-generated aircraft tracks and intelligence data onto colored maps for use in military command posts. This provides a combination of good geographic detail, not available with outline maps drawn by a CRT, and up-to-the-minute information, posted by a computer as soon as received and then correlated with previous data.

One such device is the Iconarama,[7] which generates slides for projection in a choice of colors. The slides are made by starting with a glass plate covered with an opaque material. A computer-controlled stylus etches away the coating to make the curves or figures desired. A projector system using colored filters permits display of the results on a large screen on which may also be projected maps or other prepared material. The map backgrounds can be provided by conventional color-film projectors. The result is easy to read and can be used in a lighted room. The weakness is the time required to etch a slide and the fact that slides cannot be erased; to change information a new slide must be generated. An Iconarama display is shown in Figure 2.11.

When the information to be displayed does not change, or changes only every few days, not every few minutes, conventional photographic projection techniques can be used under computer control. Again, we

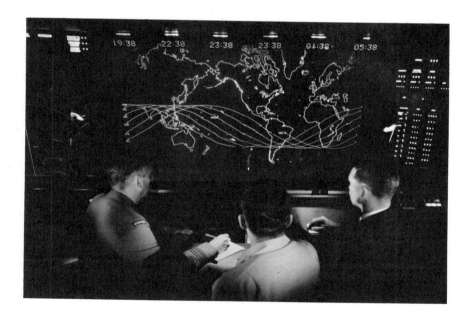

Figure 2.11 Using the Iconorama display to track the Gemini V spacecraft. *NASA photo.*

find these techniques used with instructional systems. The IBM 1401–1440 Computer Assisted Instruction system included a standard 35-millimeter slide projector so wired as to provide for random access by the computer, that is, the computer could request that any given slide be projected next. Most ordinary projectors proceed only in sequence from slide n to $n + 1$. Once selected, the slide is projected, from the rear, onto a glass screen that is part of the student's console. The main advantage of the slides is to indicate color or spatial concepts difficult to verbalize or to show through the CRT. The slides can also be used for the presentation of text, however, and in this application offer the author of a course the advantages of color, a greater variety of type styles, and a change from the use of typewriter or CRT. In a newer instructional system, a similar concept is used, but the images are stored on strips of 16-millimeter film. This provides a greater storage capacity with about the same projection quality. Both systems suffer somewhat from delays when nonsequential access is desired.

Digital television[2] is a new form of display in which digital information is fed from a computer into a television system and displayed on an ordinary TV screen. This is one way of achieving the mixing of rapidly changing digital data with high-quality graphic background material, for two pictures can be combined in the television, with the result that the digital information appears overlaid on the graphic display. There are some other advantages, even when mixing is not required. The projected image is steadier and hence easier to view over a long period without undue eye strain. Also, a CRT is limited, in the number of line segments or points it can display, by the size of its buffer memory and by the the regeneration time. An overcrowded display may not be able to be completely regenerated in one cycle. If this happens the viewer will see a badly flickering picture.

We can now use video, or television, tape recordings together with a computer.[9] These work in somewhat the same way as the audio tape-playing device mentioned above. Video recordings can be quite valuable in information retrieval applications. When documents are recorded on microfilm, for example, they can be retrieved but the images cannot be transmitted to distant consoles, except by use of relatively slow facsimile equipment. The video recordings, on the other hand, can be transmitted electronically without removing the original from the file. Also, records can easily be copied, a feature that enables system users to file like records near each other.

On the basis of this development, we should be able to look forward to long-distance retrieval of color motion pictures for immediate viewing at consoles. This may prove valuable for instruction in many fields—for example, surgery, where films of new procedures can be made immediately available to doctors and medical students anywhere in the world; art, where the holdings of one museum can be immediately viewed in any other museum; or vocational training, where it may not be feasible to provide copies of film for small numbers of people, but it may be possible to provide remote video through a computer-assisted instruction system.

Regardless of the progress made in improving communications equipment, we must remember that use of these devices is controlled by a computer and that the computer is controlled by a program written by a man. Ultimately, then, a man must anticipate all conversational situations that may arise and must prepare for the appropriate response on the part of the machinery. His skill in doing so, rather than anything innate in the hardware, determines the success of the interactive system.

REFERENCES

1. Davis, M. R., and T. O. Ellis, "The RAND Tablet, A Man-Machine Graphical Communications Device," *Proceedings of the Fall Joint Computer Conference, 1964,* San Francisco, pp. 325–331.
2. Hendrickson, Herbert C., "A High-Precision Display System for Command and Control," *Information Display,* July-August 1967, pp. 32–36.
3. Hobbs, L. C., "Display Applications and Technology," *Proceedings of the IEEE,* **54,** 12 (December 1966) , 1870–1884.
4. *IBM 7772 Audio Response Unit,* Form A27–2711, IBM Corp., White Plains, N.Y., 1966.
5. Lewin, M. H., "Portable Electronic Keyboard for Computer Input by Telephone," *IEEE Transactions,* **EC–16,** 3 (June 1967), 332–334.
6. Marsh, M. D., "Display and Storage Tubes," *Electronic Industries,* **25,** 4 (April 1966) , 54–61.
7. Schmidt, George W. N., "The Iconorama System," *Datamation,* **11,** 1 (January 1965) , 31–34.
8. Sutherland, Ivan E., "Sketchpad, a Man-Machine Graphical Communication System," *Proceedings of the Spring Joint Computer Conference, 1963,* Spartan Books, New York, pp. 329–346.
9. *VIDEOFILE Document Storage and Retrieval System,* Form F–100, Ampex Corporation, Redwood City, Calif., 1967.
10. *1030 Data Collection System,* Form A24–3018, IBM Corp., White Plains, N.Y. (undated) .

RECOMMENDED ADDITIONAL READING

1. Davis, Ruth M., "A History of Automated Displays," *Datamation,* **11,** 1 (January 1965) , 24–28.
2. *IBM Tele-processing Systems Summary,* Form A24–3090, IBM Corp., White Plains, N.Y., 1964.

3. Luxenberg, H. R., "Survey and History of the State-of-the-Art," *Computer Graphics,* Thompson, Washington, D.C., 1967, pp. 23–38.

4 Van Dam, Andries, *A Survey of Pictorial Data Processing—Techniques and Elements,* Moore School Report 66–19, The University of Pennsylvania, Philadelphia, 1965. (Also available from Clearinghouse for Federal Scientific and Technical Information, National Bureau of Standards, Washington, D.C., as AD 626 155.)

5. Van Dam, Andries, "Computer Driven Displays and Their Use in Man/Machine Interaction," *Advances in Computers,* Vol. 7, F. L. Alt and M. Rubinoff, eds., Academic, New York, 1966, pp. 239–290.

Chapter Three

Programming

3.1 INTRODUCTION TO PROGRAMMING

This chapter is a brief, nonrigorous introduction to computer programming. It assumes a minimal familiarity with computers, but none with programming. There are several exercises that should be done to give readers without previous experience a feel for what a professional computer programmer must do. The reader already familiar with programming may safely skip the chapter.

We have chosen the programming language FORTRAN[1] for illustration because it is probably the most common one in use. To achieve a degree of understanding sufficient for actual programming, the reader must spend the time to read a more detailed textbook and to become familiar with actual operations at some computer center. Several standard works on FORTRAN are listed in the bibliography to this chapter.

3.1.1 What Is a Computer?

A computer is a machine that performs arithmetic and other data-processing operations as directed by a human programmer. Our discussion is limited to *digital* computers, which comprise the great majority of commercial computers in use today.

A digital computer is one that represents numbers by recording the digits that make up the number—13 requires the recording of a 1 and a 3. This is contrasted with an *analog* computer, which represents numbers by analogy. The number 13 might be represented by 13 volts of electrical potential, for example, or by a distance of 13 millimeters on a slide rule, without any explicit representation of the 1 or the 3.

3.1.2 Data Processing

The basic arithmetic operations that a computer can perform need no definition here. *Data processing* refers to such operations as searching files, rearranging information, printing, editing, or other functions usually characterized as being highly repetitive and applied to large masses of information.

Think, for a moment, what it takes for a teacher to post a set of test grades to a class list and then to compute each student's semester grade and enter it on a grade-reporting form. This is certainly not difficult or intellectually challenging. But the teacher must look up the name of each student for whom he has a test score, copy the grade into the column reserved for this test on the class register, and then go through the class list and compute a semester grade—presumably the average of several tests—for each student. Once computed, the semester grade is entered on the register and transcribed onto a grade-reporting form. Involved are searching the class list, copying the test score, a small amount of computation to find the grade, copying again when the overall grade is computed, and copying for a third time to make up the grade-reporting form. This is a typical set of data-processing functions.

3.1.3 Programming

A computer differs fundamentally from other machines in one important sense: It performs only functions it is explicitly programmed to perform. It has no inherent problem-solving capability; that is, the machinery itself performs no useful work unless it is instructed what to do. Preparing a set of instructions is sometimes called *coding,* and a program sometimes called *code.* The program, or set of instructions on what to do, is written in advance of the execution of the function and then stored in the computer. This is the derivation of the term *stored program,* which applies to most digital computers. Some computers have programs built in, or they must read in externally stored commands one at a time for execution.

We cannot operate automobiles, cranes, or simple machines like hammers in this way. The must be controlled by a human intelligence at the moment they perform a stated function. Sometimes, though, machine tools can be driven by a computer, which is, in turn, controlled by a program.

A computer has only a small set of commands that it can carry out. If any given function is to be performed, a programmer must describe it to the computer in terms of this limited instruction repertoire.

Think about the special care you take when instructing a small child how to do something he has never done before. He understands only a limited number of words. He cannot foresee or imagine what will happen when he tries the task. You must explain everything to him and foresee for him the contingencies that he cannot visualize.

This is why a programmer's job is difficult. He must not only interpret the function in terms of the computer-comprehensible commands, but also foresee all contingencies and make provision for them. When a programmer does not do this correctly, you get someone else's bill from your favorite department store.

The programmer, then, describes a job in terms of computer instructions, foresees all contingencies for erroneous data or other errors, writes these plans in computer instruction terms, and stores the result in the computer. Then the computer can execute the commands. A formal procedure for performing a calculation is called an *algorithm*. We are all familiar with an algorithm, or procedure, for performing long division.

Most of the time, the programmer will make some small errors and the program does not work well, or perhaps not at all. Then the programmer must test the program and change it until it does perform satisfactorily. This so-called "debugging" is expensive and time consuming, but it is absolutely essential. Writing a large program without error is too rare an event to depend on.

3.2 ORGANIZATION OF A COMPUTER

In general, the functions a computer can perform are to read and write data, process these data, store them, and move them between the components of the computer. The computer can read a punched card, add up the numbers punched on it, store this information within the computer, and then type out the sum on a typewriter. To understand how it does these things, let us first look at the components of the computer.

3.2.1 Components

Many computer components (See Figure 3.1) can be explained by analogy with human counterparts. For example, a computer has sensory and signal-producing components. It can do some reading of printed matter, and it can sense holes in punched cards or the existence of magnetized spots on magnetic tape. Today, computers actually can speak by playing selected, prerecorded messages from a tape recorder. They can produce other forms of signals, the most common being the printed page, punched cards, magnetic tape, and images on a CRT. Thus a computer has many means of communication and is highly versatile, both in sensing (input) and in producing signals (output).

Like a man, a computer has a memory. Whenever it reads, it reads data into its memory. When it wants to write or to send a signal, it takes information from its memory. For a computer to process data, the data have to be in its memory first.

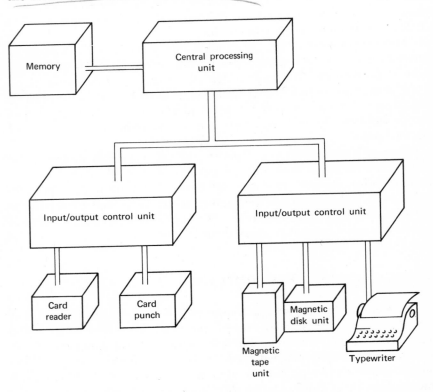

Figure 3.1 Schematic representation of the major components of a computer.

The main work of a computer is performed in the *central process-ing unit* (CPU), where arithmetic is done, data are processed, and deci-sions are made concerning what to do next. The CPU interprets the machine's repertoire of instructions. It may carry them out itself or order another component, such as a card reader, to comply with a com-mand.

Let us take a closer look at the three major groups of components: input/output components, the memory, and the CPU.

3.2.2 Input/Output Components

The best-known medium for communicating with a computer is the punched card. Holes are punched or not punched in precisely determined locations, and the patterns of holes represent numbers, letters, and punctuation. Figure 3.2 shows some examples. The com-puter has a card reader which takes one card at a time from a stack, interprets the holes, and then sends the resulting information into the CPU for transmission to memory.

Similarly, the computer can order a pattern of holes to be punched into a card by the card punch. Of course, the information comprising the pattern must first have been stored in the computer's memory.

Magnetic tape works the same way as punched cards, except that instead of holes there are tiny magnets (Figure 3.3) made or sensed by electric currents. These magnets are created on magnetic material coated onto a plastic tape base. Magnetic tape is a more compact storage medium, and characters can be both written and sensed on the tape with far greater speed than they can on punched cards.

To type a message on a typewriter, the computer "tells" the type-writer what key to use. Essentially, instead of providing the typewriter with a pattern of holes or magnets, the computer gives it the number of a key. Thus the letters QWERT YUIOP might be printed by striking keys 1 through 10 in succession.

3.2.3 The Memory

Most modern computers have at least two kinds of memory and may have more. They differ in size and in speed of storage or recall. The main memory consists of thousands of tiny magnetic cores—dough-nut-shaped elements about $\frac{1}{8}$ inch or less in diameter. Each core or magnet represents a single "bit" of information, either a zero or a one, and up to eight cores may be used to represent a complete character. The decimal numeral 1 might be represented by 00000001, and the letter A

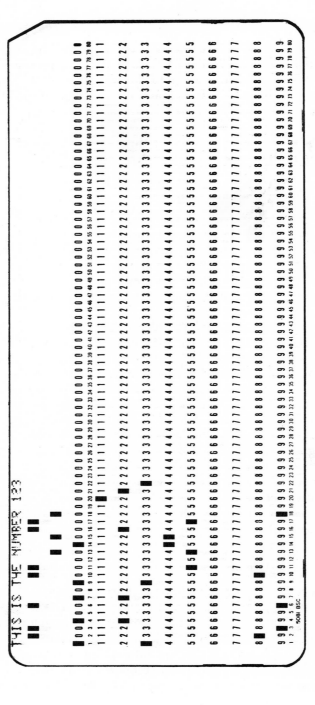

Figure 3.2 Character representation in a punched card.

46

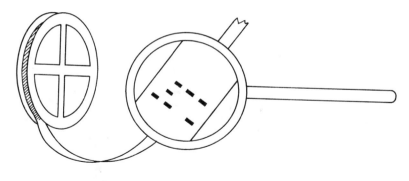

Figure 3.3 Magnetic tape character representation. Magnetized areas on the tape are not visible, but they would have this appearance if they were.

might be 00100001, with the first one-bit in this character being used to differentiate A from 1.

Each character, or sometimes a group of characters called a *word* (what else is a word but a group of characters?), has an *address*. The address is simply the location in memory of the character or word. The first character is at location 1, the one-hundredth character is at location 100, and so on.

Magnetic core memory is "fast." Information can be stored in it and retrieved from it very rapidly. Typical storage or retrieval times are around one millionth of a second.

Most computers also have an auxiliary memory. It works on the same general principles but typically is larger, slower, and less expensive. One of the most common forms of auxiliary memory is the magnetic disk. This looks and works much like a phonograph record, except that recording is done by magnetizing spots on the disk and sensing them later. The minimum unit of storage is usually larger, being at least a word and sometimes a full *track*, which is a ring of recorded data all around the disk. Figure 3.4 shows a schematic of magnetic disk recording.

A typical elapsed time for reading or recording on disks is ten millionths of a second for a character. Since reading or writing must be done in larger units, however, it may take a thousand times as long to read a full track or to write one.

Magnetic tape can also be used as an auxiliary memory. We can read from and write on tape as rapidly as on disks, but we cannot always reach quickly the spot on the tape we want. If we have just started to

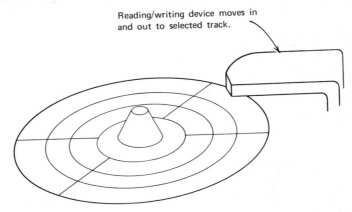

Reading/writing device moves in
and out to selected track.

Figure 3.4 Magnetic disk storage. The division of the disk into tracks (rings), and the tracks into sectors, is shown. Character recording within a sector is similar to the recording on a magnetic tape.

read a tape at its beginning and we find that the information we want is at the end, it may take several minutes of reading to get there. Meanwhile, the computer has to wait for its information. On a magnetic disk, however, we can move the reading and writing mechanism, on an armlike member, directly across the disk to any track we want, much as we can manually move the arm of a phonograph to any band on a phonograph record.

Any location in magnetic core memory can be reached as fas as any other position. There is no time delay in moving from one part to any other. This characteristic is called *random accessibility,* meaning that any point selected at random can be reached from any other point in equal time. However, it takes more time on a magnetic disk to reach a point two tracks away than to reach a point one track away from the present arm position. And obviously, with magnetic tape, it takes much longer to reach a point far away. Thus, although magnetic disks are frequently termed random access devices, this is a misnomer.

Reading and writing activities in all the memories are initiated and controlled by the central processing unit.

3.2.4   The Central Processing Unit

We have seen a computer so far as a system of input and output machines and several forms of memory for storing information. This is analogous to a large warehouse with loading docks, mail rooms, telephones, and storage spaces. But so far we have not considered how material is controlled in its flow through this assembly of components.

The CPU's main job is to interpret instructions. To do this it has to know where to find an instruction and what the instruction says. Then it can carry out the command.

The instructions, by the way, are stored in the same memory as the data. Since instructions to the machine are numeric codes, they even look like data. The number string 10001 might mean a price of $100.01, or it might be that 100 means *read* and 01 means *the card reader*, so that 10001 could mean *read a card*. If the computer is asked to interpret a number as a command, it will attempt to do so. If, by mistake, we give it today's date and ask it to "execute" that command, the computer will try. Sometimes, by coincidence, a randomly selected number will have meaning as a command, and then the computer acts quite strangely.

To get the computer to add two numbers together, we must provide the CPU with the following information: (1) where the command to add the numbers is stored, that is, in which memory location it is written that the computer is to perform this addition; (2) what two numbers are to be added—again, the numbers are given in terms of the address locations where they are stored; (3) where the sum is to be placed—in what memory location.

The machine obtains its information in these simple steps, illustrated in Figure 3.5.

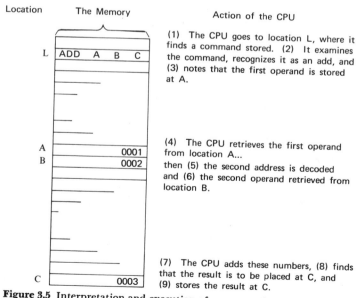

Figure 3.5 Interpretation and execution of a command.

1. It gets an instruction from memory location L.
2. The instruction is interpreted as an add command.
3. The address of the first number to be added is found.
4. The number at that address is retrieved.
5. The address of the second number is recovered from the command.
6. The second number is retrieved from memory.
7. The two numbers are added.
8. The address where the sum is to be placed is recovered from the add command.
9. The sum is stored at that address.

The programmer is not required to lay out each of these steps in detail, but he must provide the information required.

3.3 PROGRAMMING COMMANDS AND LANGUAGES

As we have said, there are different kinds of computer instructions. Some are concerned with arithmetic, some with reading or writing, some with still other functions. There are also different ways in which we can tell a computer what we want to do, that is, different programming languages, some easier for people to use, some easier for a computer to interpret.

3.3.1 Arithmetic Commands

The arithmetic commands that a computer can carry out are the four basic operations with which we are all familiar: add, subtract, multiply, and divide. In each case, the computer must know where to find the numbers and where to put the result of an operation. In discussing these and the other commands to follow, we will use a simplified form of the programming language FORTRAN. A programming language is a means of conveying instructions to the computer. FORTRAN is one of several languages that enable the programmer to use notation familiar to him, particularly if he is doing mathematical work.

To perform an arithmetic operation in a computer we must recognize that what we are doing is getting some numbers from their storage locations, doing something to them, and putting the result in some memory location. In FORTRAN terminology, we are *assigning* a value, the result, to that memory location.

To make it easy for the programmer, FORTRAN lets us call locations by names rather than numbers. Therefore we could call the *location* of the first number x and the location of the second number y, and we could have a command that says, "Assign to location RESULT the value of X added to Y." To write this symbolically, we would say, RESULT = X + Y.

The equal sign in FORTRAN means *is assigned the value* or *set equal to*. It denotes an operation, not a condition. As simple a statement as A = B means, "Assign to A the value found at B," or "Go to location B, find the number there and put that number in location A."

All of the following are proper FORTRAN assignment statements:

$$A = B$$
$$A = B + C$$
$$A = B - C$$
$$A = B * C$$
$$A = B / C$$

The sign * means to multiply. The result of each of these commands would be to set a new value in location A, and the new values would be, respectively, B, the sum of B and C, the difference between B and C, the product of B and C, and the quotient of B divided by C.

FORTRAN makes it possible to perform far more complex operations than these by combinations of the basic steps, but we will not go into them here.

3.3.2 Instruction Sequence

Implicit in a FORTRAN command, such as those in the preceding section, is an instruction to the computer to pick up the next command from the next sequential location in memory. That is, if two successive commands are

$$A = B + C$$
$$D = 2 * A$$

the first command implicitly tells the computer to execute the second command next. A portion of the CPU called the *instruction counter* keeps track of what command is to be executed next and informs the CPU so that it can find the appropriate command in memory.

3.3.3 Types of Programming Languages

The computer, as a piece of machinery, does not understand the FORTRAN language. Hence the symbolic statements, such as A = B + C, must be translated into commands that the machine does understand, called *machine language commands*. These are much more detailed and much harder for people to learn. It may take several machine language commands to carry out the operation specified by one FORTRAN language command.

A computer program called a *compiler* translates the FORTRAN program into a machine language program. In fact, FORTRAN stands for FORmula TRANslator. In its translated form, the program no longer uses symbolic addresses. Every address is the actual number of the memory element within the computer. Therefore, when we write A = B + C, the compiler must first assign actual addresses to A, B, and C and must thereafter use these actual, or *absolute,* addresses in its translated coding. We will find this point of some significance when time-sharing is described in Chapter 4.

Other examples of programming languages that differ from the machine language into which they are translated are COBOL, ALGOL, and PL/I. There is yet another class of languages, called *assembly languages,* which are very much like machine languages but are a little easier to use. An assembly language is more rigidly structured and is usually easier for the machine to interpret than a machine language, although it is harder for people to learn. For example, to add two numbers in an assembly language, we might write some commands such as these:

1.   BR 100
2.   AD 200
3.   ST 100

where command 1 *br*ings a number from address 100 to a special location, 2 *ad*ds the number at 200 to the number previously brought in, and 3 *st*ores the sum back in location 100.

The relatively minor translation process from an assembly language to machine language is called an *assembly,* and the program that performs the translation is termed an *assembler.*

3.3.4   Input/Output Commands

Now that we have learned how to compute numbers, we have to learn how to bring data into a computer and write results out. We will continue to use simplified but proper FORTRAN statements.

Reading numbers or words into the computer requires that the computer know several items of information. Where is the information now? Where is it to be put, once read? What does it look like; in particular, how many characters does it have? The last question is important because the answer determines how many characters or words of memory must be set aside to receive the data.

If there were only one input device on a computer, and if all data elements were, say, five-character numbers, an input command could have the form

READ A

where A stands for (is a symbolic address representing) the location into which the number is to be put. But few computer systems are so simple, and hence more information is needed.

A real FORTRAN read statement looks like this:

READ (D, F) A

where D specifies what input *device* to use, F tells where another FORTRAN statement can be found that gives the *format* of the incoming data, and A is to be the *address* of the data. So this statement tells the computer to read some information, whose form is described in statement F, from input device D, and put the data at location A.

The format statement might look like this, if the information were a five-character integer:

FORMAT (I5)

The format statement is not a command. It is a description of data.

Now, if the card reader were device number 1, a command to read a five-character number and put it at location A looks like

99   FORMAT (I5)
100   READ (1,99) A

The numbers to the left are FORTRAN statement numbers that may be assigned by the programmer, need not be consecutive, and are needed at all only when a statement is referred to by another statement. The 99 is the READ statement refers to statement number 99, which describes the format.

To read two numbers from the same card, one five digits long and one three digits long, we could write

103   FORMAT (I5, I3)
104   READ (1,103) A, B

Writing is done very much the same, but the direction is reversed. To punch the number that is at location A onto a card (if the card punch is device 2), we write

108   WRITE (2,99) A

Remember that statement 99 is a previously written format statement specifying a five-digit integer.

3.3.5 An Example

Let us see what an actual program might do with a combination of input-output and arithmetic commands. Suppose we have a card with three numbers punched on it, each five characters long. We want to read this card, compute the average of the numbers, and punch another card with the result on it. Here is what we can do.

1   FORMAT (I5, I5, I5)
     READ (1,1) A, B, C

So far we have defined what our input looks like, and have read it from the card reader into locations A, B, and C. Now, we do the arithmetic.

$$D = A + B$$
$$D = D + C$$

The first of these statements sets D equal to the sum of the numbers at A and B. The second command adds what is already at D to what is stored at C. We now have the sum of the contents of A, B, and C stored in D. The mean, or average, is found by dividing by 3; hence

$$M = D / 3$$

Now we have the number we want, in M, but have yet to punch it out. For this we need another format statement:

$$6 \quad \text{FORMAT} \quad (I5)$$

and a punch command:

$$\text{WRITE} \quad (2, 6) \quad M$$

And we are done. Note that the statement numbers need not have been in order or consecutive. Also, we need to number only statements that are going to be referred to by other statements. That is why the arithmetic and input-output statements have no numbers.

If we had wanted to print the result, instead of punching it, we would have selected another output device. This would require only a change of device number in the write statement.

The astute reader, at this point, will feel that computer programming is a tedious activity and that it seems to take an inordinate amount of trouble to find the average of three numbers. Also, he may wonder what would happen if there were 300 cards and he had to find a mean for each. Would he have to write this program over again 300 times?

To a certain extent computer programming is tedious, and we have made no attempt to disguise this. We want to insure that the reader appreciates how each detail must be accounted for. In actual practice, however, the same person does not have to account for everything, and one way to lessen the tedium is for programmers to use the work of others to reduce their own efforts.

Our sample program could be simplified, for example, by using the full capability of FORTRAN notation. The entire calculation could have been done in a single statement, this way:

$$M = (A + B + C) / 3$$

The computer would interpret this just the way you do—add the three numbers, A, B, and C, together and then divide the sum by 3. We have avoided using such complex statements because of all the syntactical rules of the FORTRAN language that go along with them.

Now let us consider what to do about the possibility that we might have 300 cards to work with.

3.3.6   Branching Commands

We said earlier that an implicit part of each command is that the computer is to get the next statement from the immediately following memory location. This has been true in each of our examples except for format statements, which, it will be recalled, are not commands; they are advisory in nature and hence are not executed.

If we had 300 cards and had to find the mean of the numbers on each, it should be clear that the same arithmetic statements should do for each card. If we could find a way to *use* them over and over again, we would not have to *write* them over and over again. Since this situation is a very common one, commands are available that enable us to do just this.

Commands that change the sequence of execution of program statements are called *branching commands,* meaning that the computer is to branch from its position in a sequence of commands to another point in the program. The simplest of these is the GO TO.

The GO TO tells the computer to get its next command or statement at the location named. GO TO 3 tells the computer to change its normal sequence, find statement 3, execute it, and continue in sequence from there.

The statements

```
1    N = 0
2    N = N + 1
3    GO TO 2
```

will add 1 to N continuously (see Figure 3.6). If statements 2 and 3 are executed 500 times, the value of the number in N will be 500.

Below is the program we wrote earlier to read three numbers from one card and find the mean. We have changed it only by affixing a number to the first read statement and regrouping the statements.

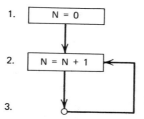

Figure 3.6 A simple branching sequence.

```
1   FORMAT (I5, I5, I5)
6   FORMAT (I5)
2   READ (1,1) A, B, C
    D = A + B
    D = D + C
    M = D / 3
    WRITE (2,6) M
```

If, to the end of this program, we affix GO TO 2, the program will read a card, compute the mean of the three numbers found there, punch a card with the mean, and go back for another card. This continues as long as there are cards ready to be read. The program is illustrated by a *flow chart* in Figure 3.7.

So, we have found an easy way to get 300 averages without having to write the same program over again 300 times.

3.3.7 Conditional Commands

Suppose, now, we want to find whether there are any computed averages higher than 25 and, if so, to make a separate list of them. Making a list is no problem, but if we are to separate averages over 25 from those under, a new kind of command is required.

This is our introduction to one of the most powerful and useful groups of commands—conditional or decision-making commands. What we would like is a command that can look at a number and then do one

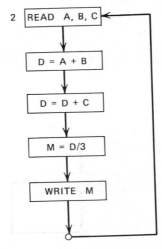

Figure 3.7 Repetitive use of program commands.

thing if the number has a particular property and something else if it does not.

The simplest test is whether or not the number has the value zero. FORTRAN gives us such a statement, called IF. It sends the computer along one branch of the program if a number is zero, along another branch if the number is less than zero, and along still a third branch if the number is greater than zero.

We could write an IF statement this way:

$$\text{DIFF} = \text{M} - 25$$
$$\text{IF (DIFF) 2, 2, 10}$$
$$10 \quad \text{WRITE (2,6) M}$$
$$\text{GO TO 2}$$

This program (see Figure 3.8) computes the difference between the mean, M, and the threshold value, 25. If DIFF is greater than zero, then M is greater than 25. In this case, the program branches to statement 10, writes out the mean, and branches back into the main program (at Statement 2 of the program illustrated on p. 56) to read another input card. If DIFF is less than or equal to zero, then M is less than 25 or equal to 25 and we have no wish to record the mean. In either case, the program branches back to statement 2 for a new input card.

Another kind of decision-making situation is encountered when we want to do something a fixed number of times. Suppose, for example,

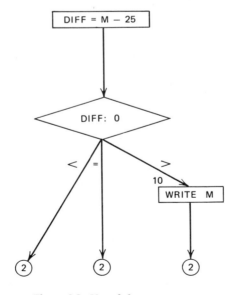

Figure 3.8. Use of the IF statement.

we had to add a column of 100 numbers. Even to write all of the 100 steps in one long FORTRAN statement would be tiresome. Because this kind of problem also arises often in programming, a special command has been developed specifically to control repetition of statements.

To add a column of 100 numbers, we could do this: set SUM initially to zero and then add the hundred numbers to SUM, one at a time. If each number is punched on a separate card, the program might look like this

```
1       FORMAT (I5)
        SUM = 0
        READ (1, 1) X
        SUM = SUM + X
```

After the fourth statement, the value of SUM is the value of the first number read into location X. We now want to repeat the third and fourth statements 99 more times. Therefore we introduce the command DO, which means to execute a specified set of statements. The command must tell which statements are to be executed and how many times they must be carried out.

Here is what the full program would be:

```
1       FORMAT (I5)
        SUM = 0
        DO 2 K = 1, 100, 1
        READ (1, 1) X
2       SUM = SUM + X
```

This program causes the statements (indicated by shading) beginning with the first one after the DO and continuing through the statement number indicated, in this case 2, to be executed 100 times. The DO statement also tells the computer to execute these commands under control of a counter, K, which is initially set to 1, has 1 added to it each time, and has a limit of 100. When K gets to the value 100, execution stops.

What, in effect, is happening is this:

```
        K = 1
        SUM = 0
3       READ (1, 1) X
        SUM = SUM + X
        J = K - 100
        IF (J) 4, 5, 5
4       K = K + 1
        GO TO 3
5       Continue the program
```

This program, which is shown schematically in Figure 3.9, adds 1 to a counter each time a card is read and a new number is added to SUM.

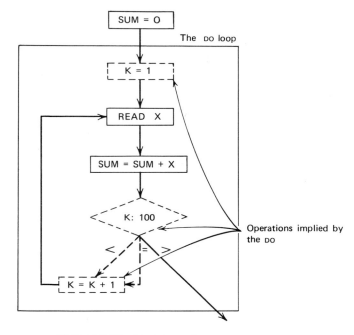

Figure 3.9 The DO statement.

The difference, J, between this count and 100 is computed; and if J is less than zero (K less than 100) we add 1 to K, at statement 4, and go back for another input card at statement 3. If J is greater than, or equal to, zero (K greater than or equal to 100), we go on with the program.

This is quite a bit of programming to accomplish a basically simple control function—the execution of a set of commands repetitively. That is why the DO command was created.

To summarize its usage, the DO has four information elements. In general, it can be written DO s INDEX $= N_1, N_2, N_3$. Here s indicates a statement number. All statements after the DO, down to and including statement number s are to be executed under control of the DO. This set of statements is said to comprise a DO *loop*. INDEX is the address of a number to be used as a counter, or *index* as it is more commonly designated in programming jargon. The first time the DO statement is encountered, the INDEX number is set to value N_1. Thereafter, each time the DO loop is repeated, the number at N_3 is added to INDEX until the value of N_2 is reached. When INDEX reaches the value of N_2, execution of the loop ceases and the next statement executed is that following s. N_1 is called the *initial value,* N_2 the *limit,* and N_3, the *increment* of the index variable, or number.

A rule to remember is that the last command in the group of statements covered by a DO must be executed each time the loop is repeated. This is necessary because the test to see whether or not the loop is to be repeated again is made after completion of the loop. We mention this point because it is possible to include DO loops within DO loops, or *nest* them, or to branch around within a loop. The programmer must remember that he must always end a loop by executing the last statement, the statement named in the DO statement itself. Thus, although branching is permitted, we cannot branch from the middle of the loop back to the DO statement and expect all the looping controls to perform correctly. To initiate another iteration from a point within the loop, branching must be done to the end of the loop, not the beginning. Figure 3.10 illustrates this rule graphically.

Requiring that all branches converge at or before the end of the loop is an artificial constraint to which the programmer must adhere. In order to have a command that can always be executed regardless of how many different branches there may be within a DO, a null command, CONTINUE, has been created. The CONTINUE statement causes no action to be taken, but allows for a statement that can be branched to from anywhere in the program and is convenient for use at the end of a DO loop.

With the three commands, GO TO, IF, and DO, that affect the sequence of operations of a program highly complex decisions can be made. The programmer's job is to state the problem and the decision criteria in terms of these simple commands. This is not always easy.

3.4 AN EXAMPLE

Suppose that we have punched grades on each of four tests for a class of 50 students onto cards and we want to find who is the best student in the class. The programmer must immediately ask what the criterion is for selecting the best student.

For the time being, we will ignore the possibility of a tie; that is, we will assume no two students can have the same average. Will it be necessary to compute each student's average to find the best performer? Or will his *total* do as well for the purpose at hand?

Try to work out the program yourself. Remember that there are four test grades, which are two-digit integers, on each of 50 record cards. If we assume the cards are in alphabetic order, then knowing the card

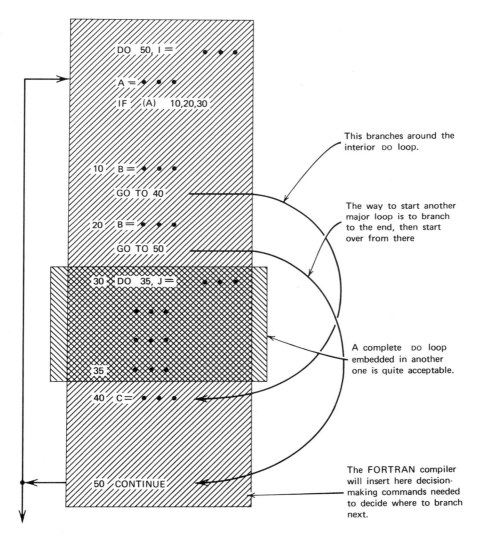

Figure 3.10 Branching within a DO loop.

sequence number identifies the student for us, since we can easily find out who student number 3 is. His name need not be punched in the card.

There is usually more than one correct way to write any program; hence we cannot have you check your program line for line with our solution. Work out your own solution, then read ours, and see whether you have taken care of all the elements. The program text is shown below, and a flow chart is given in Figure 3.11.

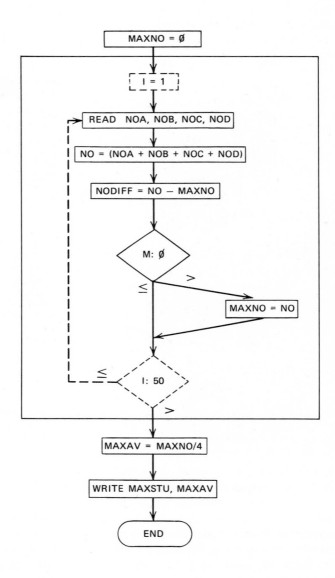

Figure 3.11 Highest-grade program.

Program Example

Program Statement	*Comment*
1 FORMAT (I2, I2)	
2 FORMAT (I2, I2, I2, I2)	
MAXNO = 0	Will be used to store highest sum.
DO 7 I = 1, 50, 1	
4 READ (1, 2) NOA, NOB, NOC, NOD	Read in four grades, NOA, NOB,
NO = NOA + NOB	. . . , for one student. Compute
NO = NO + NOC	student's total score, using simple
NO = NO + NOD	arithmetic statements allowing only one operation per statement.
NODIFF = NO − MAXNO	Compute difference between this student's total and previously recorded high.
IF (M) 6,6,5	Branch to: 6 if less than previous high; 6 if equal to previous high (we assumed this could not happen); 5 if a new high.
5 MAXNO = NO	Set MAXNO to the new high.
MAXSTU = I	This records the sequence number of the current high student.
6 CONTINUE	Dummy command having the effect of branch back to statement 4 for another card or, if the DO loop has been executed 50 times, continue with the next sequential statement.
8 MAXAV = MAXNO/4	Now change the high *total* to an *average*.
WRITE (2,2) MAXSTU, NOSTU, MAXNO	Write out the sequence number of the winning student and the high average.
END	

When checking your program against this one, the important thing is whether you can explain why the programs differ. There are a few peculiarities of our solution that should be explained but that become important only if the reader is going to take up programming seriously. In that case, a more detailed FORTRAN manual is required.

Note that each of our data names begins with the letter I, N, or M. In FORTRAN, variables beginning with these letters are automatically considered to be integers. Otherwise, they may be numbers stored in other forms, such as fractions, which we shall not go into here. This usage follows mathematical convention, where the letters i, j, k, l, m, and n are often used to denote integers.

Since we have an IF statement within the set of commands controlled by a DO, it is important that, regardless of which path we take from the IF, we end at the "bottom" of the DO. Thus we have made use of the CONTINUE statement.

Every program must conclude with an END statement.

3.5 DATA REPRESENTATION

So far, all our examples have been stated in terms of individual numbers stored at known locations. That is, when we had 50 student records, they were all kept on cards and read in, one record at a time, each succeeding record going into the same memory locations used by the last record. In practice, this procedure is too cumbersome. We often want to keep lists completely within the computer, and we need a handy way to address elements of a list.

We also want, in actual practice, to be able to deal with information other than integers. With student records, for example, we would certainly like to have the student's name and be able to use this, rather than his sequence number in a class, to refer to him.

Even with numbers, we may find that having to set the exact length of a number in advance of computing it can lead to trouble. In many problems, we cannot predict what the resulting numbers will look like and hence do not know how many spaces to reserve for them. Furthermore, in scientific applications, we are often interested in no more than four or five significant digits and may not want to reserve ten spaces or characters to handle more information than is needed.

FORTRAN can accommodate all these requirements. There are actually several kinds of data representation, and we shall look at three: (1) fixed-point numbers, which are the kind we have been working with; (2) alphabetic information; and (3) so-called floating-point numbers, which enable the computer to use the far easier scientific notation for handling numbers of widely varying size.

3.5.1 Alphabetic Information

Suppose, in our student record illustration, we had put the student's name on the card, as well as his test scores. FORTRAN allows us to read in, and later write, this name so long as we properly identify it to the program as alphabetic, not numeric, data. This notification is done through the format statement. Where we have previously called every-thing an integer and have used the notation I*n* to denote an integer of *n* characters, we now introduce the notation A*n*.

If we have reserved the first 15 characters on a card for the student's name, we can read the name into the computer with this combination of commands:

20 FORMAT (A15)

READ (1,20) STUDENT

Memory location STUDENT now contains a 15-character student name. That name can be written in a similar way:

WRITE (2,20) STUDENT

To read a card containing both alphabetic and numeric information, the format statement must completely describe all the data. In our example, we would have to use this format statement:

FORMAT (A15, I2, I2, I2, I2)

Now you should be able to revise the program you wrote to find the best student. This time, instead of writing the student's sequence number, give his name and grade.

3.5.2 Floating-Point Numbers

The number 135 can be written as 13.5×10. Similarly, the number .135 can be written as 13.5×10^{-2}, when 10^{-2} is one one-hundreth, or 1 divided by 100. This is a convenient way to write numbers, especially those that will vary widely in magnitude. It has the advantage of requiring essentially the same number of characters, or space on a page, regardless of the magnitude of the number. Thus 135000000000000 is 13.5×10^{13}, and .000000000000135 is 13.5×10^{-14}. It should be obvious that this is a great convenience to the programmer who has to be concerned with how much of his memory is used to store numbers.

Computers use a very similar notation. For example, 135 might be written .135 (2), which means that .135 is to be multiplied by 10^2. It is not necessary to write the multiplication sign or the 10. Actually, the parentheses are not written either, but they are convenient for use in printed material. The computer might see this number as 1352. Of course, it would have to be programmed to understand that the first three digits represent the basic number *(mantissa)* and the last digit represents the *exponent*. In practice, both these numbers are longer than in this example.

With FORTRAN, the computer does all the work of converting numbers into this format. If a card has the number 135 punched into it, the programmer may tell the computer to read in the number, but assume it has a decimal point after the first digit (1.35) and then convert it to the floating-point notation. The number as stored might be 1351, meaning multiply .135 by 10 to revert to 1.35.

The format statement to handle floating-point input tells how many total digits there are and where the decimal point is to be assumed. FORMAT F3.2 means there are three digits to be read and the decimal point is to be assumed to be two places from the right end.

3.5.3 Arrays

Suppose we wanted to compute a class average for our list of students and then write out the names of all those whose grades were above average. We could not use the approach employed so far, of reading in and working on a single student record at a time, unless we read in all student records twice, once to compute the average and again to see which students exceeded it.

To solve this problem and many others, we would like to store all our data in the memory first and then do our computations and decision-making with all information at hand. Although we can do this with the commands presented so far, a new memory location name would be required for each new card we read in. If this is true, we cannot use the same program statements over again for each new student whose grade we want to compute.

To get around this problem, FORTRAN enables us to define lists, or arrays, of information and to use position in the list as a means of addressing information. In other words, FORTRAN enables us to store all the student names in memory and to address the first name as STUDENT(1), the second as STUDENT(2), and so on.

Moreover, FORTRAN allows us to refer to the location of an element of an array symbolically. We can use an address such as STUDENT(N) to refer to the nth name in the array. N, in this case, is just another variable, or number. It, too, is the name of a memory location at which an integer is stored. That integer tells which array element is being addressed. For example, the commands

$$N = 13$$
$$\text{WRITE } (2,20) \text{ STUDENT(N)}$$

cause the 13th name in the array of student names to be written out.

Let us review this briefly. FORTRAN permits naming arrays of memory locations, as well as individual locations. The nth element is addressed by using the array name *subscripted* with (N). The subscript may be a number, referring to an exact location, as STUDENT(5), or it may be a symbolic reference, as STUDENT(N).

If the symbolic reference is used, the program goes to the memory location indicated by the subscript, in this case N, and finds the number stored there. That number is used as a numeric subscript. Thus

$$N = 5$$
$$\text{WRITE } (2,20) \text{ STUDENT}(N)$$

has the same meaning as

$$\text{WRITE } (2,20) \text{ STUDENT}(5)$$

Now let us restate the student grade problem. There are 50 punched cards containing student information. On each card, the first 15 columns are devoted to the student's name. Thereafter, there are four test results, each taking two columns.

Perform the following computations. Find each student's average grade. Then compute the class average. Write out the names of all students with grades higher than the class average. Write a program to do these things, and compare your results with ours by referring to the text below and the flow chart in Figure 3.12.

Program Example

Program Statement	*Comment*
1 FORMAT (A15, I2, I2, I2, I2)	
FORMAT (A15, I2)	
KLASS = 0	Will be used to compute the class
MAXNO = 0	average.
DO 4 K = 1,50,1	
READ (1,1) STUDENT (K) , NOA (K) ,	Read in the student's name and
NOB (K) , NOC (K) , NOD (K)	four test scores.
NO (K) = NOA (K) + NOB (K)	Compute student's average as be-
NO (K) = NO (K) + NOC (K)	fore.
NO (K) = NO (K) + NOD (K)	
NO (K) = NO (K) /4	
4 KLASS = KLASS + NO (K)	Add student average to class total. End of DO loop.
KLASS = KLASS/50	Compute class average.
DO 6 J = 1,50,1	
M = NO (J) − KLASS	Compute difference between a student's average and the class average.
IF (M) 6,6,5	Branch to 5 if student is above average, to 6 otherwise.
5 WRITE (2,2) STUDENT (J) , NO (J)	Write student name and average.
6 CONTINUE	

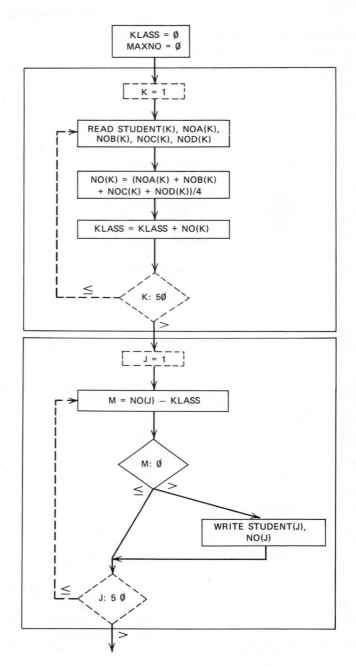

Figure 3.12 Grades-above-average program.

3.6 SUBROUTINES

Sometimes we will want to perform the same calculation at several different points in a program. Other times we want to perform a calculation so common that we feel sure some other programmer has already written a program to do the work. A form of program that helps to solve these problems is called a *subroutine*. A subroutine is a program that is intended to be used as a part of another program. The special feature of a subroutine is that, when it is finished or has been executed, control returns to the point in the larger program from which the subroutine was entered.

When a programmer wants to use a subroutine, he uses the command CALL, followed by the name of the subroutine. Hence, CALL SIN(x) might be used to call into play a subroutine that will compute the trigonometric sine of the number x. When the calculation is finished, control returns to the command immediately following the CALL. We might, then, have the sequence

> READ (1,1) x
>
> CALL SIN (x)
>
> GO TO 37

This program will read a number, x, compute its sine, and then branch to instruction 37 in the program.

When writing a subroutine, we use the command RETURN instead of GO TO to branch back to the calling program. In this way the subroutine need contain no addresses of the calling program and hence can be used in any calling program. This makes it easy for programmers to exchange subroutines with each other, thereby saving the cost and time of duplicate programming.

Sometimes subroutines are so commonly used that they become part of the programming language. Actually, SIN is one of these. To simplify its use, a programmer may assume that FORTRAN will compute the sine for him. He may, then, write Y = SIN(x) instead of CALL SIN(x), Y = x.

3.7 CONVERSATIONAL PROGRAMMING

Since this book is about man-machine communication, we should consider how to write programs that can converse with people.

First, we must remember that a communications terminal is just another input or output device. In FORTRAN notation, it might be addressed by another number in the read or write statement, just as we have used 1 for a card reader, 2 for a card punch, and so on. We might adopt, for discussion's sake, the convention that 9 is a typewriter terminal that can be read from or written on.

Second, we must consider what we mean by a conversation. What steps do we expect the computer to perform in order to have conversation?

3.7.1 Conversational Elements

Regardless of the purpose of the conversation, we will find the following elements almost invariably involved.

First, a message is sent from computer to man, by way of a communications terminal. This message may be in textual, pictorial, or graphic form, or it may be so simple as the unlocking of a keyboard to enable the human being to send his message.

Second, the man responds to the machine-generated message. Again, the choice of medium is wide. He may type in a text message or use a light pen.

Third, the computer analyzes the man's response. Here is where the cleverness of the programmer comes into play, for the sophistication (perhaps the entire success of the conversation) depends, in the next step, on the computer's ability to "speak" meaningfully to the man, that is, at a nontrivial level of discourse. Restriction to *yes/no* or other multiple choice replies necessarily limits the effectiveness of a conversation. Being able to recognize subtle differences between actual and anticipated responses enables the computer to appear more intelligent in its responses.

The fourth step encompasses the processing of responses, in which we include making the decision on what to do next. Processing may also include storing, performing some elaborate mathematical calculation, or editing a reply. The branching decision is that of deciding which conversational step to operate next. In order to make this decision, a great deal of processing may be required. For example, in instructional applications, we find that authors of such programs may want to branch a student to different material, depending on his total performance in the course, up to the point where the decision is being made. Hence the branching decision is made, not just on the basis of the last student response, but on the basis of an analysis of all his answers to all previous questions.

But the same basic problem of the machine and its program working out a reaction to the student's message arises whatever the application. An architect designing a building may signify that he desires to add a new line, that he wishes the existing drawing of the building to be rotated on the viewing screen, that he wants a photograph made of it, or that he would like to change a previous line. The conversational program must make it easy for him to specify his intent and then be able to recognize and carry out the decision. Once the machine completes its processing and makes its decision, a new message-response-process cycle begins.

3.7.2 Transmitting the Message

The programmer using FORTRAN or another high-order language is little concerned with the actual transmission of the message to the terminal. He need only place his message in memory and execute a write command, just as he does to punch out a message on a card.

The programmer's main concern is to write and store all the messages he is going to use. Remember that the computer does not create messages; it merely transmits them. The programmer must anticipate every message he may need and see to it that all of them are stored in memory, accessible to his conversational program.

The programmer can use message fragments and transmit more than one when he is ready to send a message. For example, if he has stored the messages THANK YOU and VERY MUCH, he can transmit the text THANK YOU VERY MUCH by using two successive write statements or by transmitting two variables with one write statement. The same fragments can also be used in other messages, as THANK YOU, SIR.

Although there is no specific limitation on the number of messages that may be stored, memory is expensive and each message must be composed by a programmer and stored in advance of use. We can see, then, the degree of ingenuity required of the programmer who must handle a great variety of conversational situations with a limited repertoire of messages.

3.7.3 Receiving the Message

The FORTRAN programmer has little difficulty writing a message-receiving program, although some other person, another programmer, has to have written a program that continually scans all input lines into the computer, reads in whatever messages are coming, and stores them for use by the conversational program. Messages coming in too rapidly to be processed by the FORTRAN program may have to be queued, or stored, until the program is ready for them. All this action is assumed by the FORTRAN programmer when he issues his read command.

Reading in a response imposes few requirements on the conversational programmer, except that he has to be sure to reserve enough memory space for the response. If necessary, he may have to tell the responder how long a message is permitted and, of course, a decision must be made on what to do if the limitation is exceeded.

3.7.4 Analyzing the Response

Once again, here is the crucial step for the programmer and the user of a conversational program. The programmer has now caused the computer to ask a question, it has received an answer, and now it must check to see what the answer was and prepare to take action as a result.

Suppose, for example, we want to ask a mechanical designer for the diameter of a hole he has specified in a part. The computer asks, WHAT DIAMETER? He replies, 2.1. What can the program do? It would be a favor to the designer to check whether this answer is reasonable, to ascertain the units of the dimension, and to record it in a file for later use, possibly in documentation.

Within the limits of the part or machine the designer is working on, it may be obvious that holes must be between 0.001 inch and 6.0 inches in diameter. If the answer falls outside the stated limits, the reason may be that it is an incorrect number or that the reply is not a number at all. Certainly, there will be a difference in what the computer should reply if the designer gives an out-of-tolerance number and if he gives no number at all. We will see in future chapters how use of *nonresponsive* answers can make for more meaningful interaction. A nonresponsive answer is one intended, not to answer the last question asked, but instead to shift the subject of conversation.

For example, a nonresponsive answer might ask for the retrieval of some fact from the computer's files. The machine designer might, in response to the question asking for the diameter of a hole, answer, WHAT ARE THE LIMITS? His answer is not responsive to the question, but he never intended that it be. The programmer must anticipate that such responses could be made, test for them, and, if they occur, take action accordingly.

If he allows these options, the programmer is faced with some extra complications. He does not know whether the characters he is to test are letters or numbers. Hence he does not know what form of read, write, and processing commands he can use. He may have to treat all responses as alphabetic, detect the presence of numbers by character-by-character analysis, and then, if the answer is numeric, convert the resulting character string into a number.

For example, if the responder means to answer 13, the program may have to look at each character, test it against each possible digit, and construct the proper number. To do this, we shall have to introduce another programming technique that is allowed in FORTRAN. Previously, the IF statement was followed by a branch to any of three addresses, depending on whether a particular number was less than, equal to, or greater than zero. Another way to use the IF statement is to base branching on whether a given expression is true or false. We shall show only one of several possible ways to use this form of IF, which is called the *logical* IF.

The expression to be evaluated is a statement of equality or inequality between two variables, designated by their symbolic addresses. If we have numbers stored at locations A and B, we can write an expression IF A = B and we can do one thing next if A equals B and another thing if A is not equal to B. Instead of the = sign in a logical IF statement, FORTRAN requires us to use the symbol, .EQ.. After the IF A.EQ.B we write a GO TO. (FORTRAN permits a wider range of expressions here, but, like our restriction of only one arithmetic operation per command, this simplification is made in the interest of avoiding syntactic detail.) If the expression is true, that is, if A is equal to B, we execute the GO TO statement. If the expression is false, we do not execute it but instead go on to the statement next after the IF. The full statement, then, is

IF (A.EQ.B) GO TO n

with the program branching to statement n if A equals B.

Here is how we might code the response analysis when we allow a responder to give us either a number or, say, the reply ASK, which might be used to permit him to ask a question of the computer. Assume we have asked for what would normally be a three-character number in reply. These characters are stored for us at location REPLY. We shall treat REPLY as an array of three one-character elements. We will have to have stored an array called DIGIT, consisting of the digits 0, 1, 2, ... We will also have to store the letters A, S, and K in array ASK. The program to follow is diagrammed in Figure 3.13.

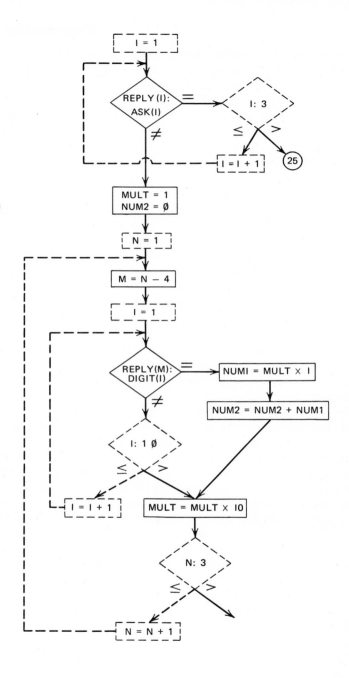

Figure 3.13 A conversational program segment.

Program Example

Program Statement	*Comment*
DO 1 I = 1,3,1	If the first character of the response
IF (REPLY (I) .EQ.ASK (I)) GO TO 1	is A, go to statement 1 and proceed
GO TO 2	to compare the reply with the let-
1 CONTINUE	ters A,S,K. The first failure to match
GO TO 25	confirms that REPLY ≠ ASK, and we
	can go on with the program.
2 MULT = 1	These numbers will be used below.
NUM2 = 0	
3 DO 5 N = 1,3,1	Prepare to look at three characters.
4 M = 4−N	When N is 1, M is 3, so we look at
	the rightmost digit first.
6 DO 10 I = 1,10,1	Prepare to test a character of REPLY
	against each of the ten digits.
7 IF (REPLY (M) .EQ.DIGIT (I)) GO TO 9	Go to 9, when the digit in the reply
	matches the digit in the array DIGIT.
	At this time, I will have the numeric
	value we want.
8 GO TO 10	
9 NUM1 = MULT*I	MULT is 1 for the ones position, ten
NUM2 = NUM2 + NUM1	when we check the ten position, etc.
GO TO 5	As soon as we have a match, we stop
10 CONTINUE	looking for more.
5 MULT = MULT*10	When all done with the ones digit
	of REPLY, we change the value of
	MULT for the tens digit. The DO
	statement (3) causes us to branch
	back to statement 4 at this point.

It would be a worthwhile exercise to assume a response of any three digits and to follow the execution of this program completely, seeing how the digits are transformed into a number. Note that the DO loop beginning at statement 3 will always be executed three times but the one beginning at 6 will be executed from one to ten times for each of the three major loops. If the low-order, or units, digit of REPLY is 2, we would execute the following string of statements (after checking for an alphabetic reply): 2, 3, 4, 6, 7, 8, 10, 6, 7, 8, 10, 6, 7, 9, 5, . . . , which assumes that array DIGIT begins with 0, 1, 2, 3, ... A good way to follow the program is to set up a number of columns on a piece of paper, one for the statement number and one for each variable, that is, MULT, NUM2, etc. Record a statement number and the value of the number stored at the named location; then go on to the next statement, as the program would, until you have completely converted your three-digit number.

This program has at least one intentional flaw. Can you find it?

The program makes no provision for replies that do not contain exactly three digits. The reply 32 would not be properly converted, because the third digit is missing and would not match any of the numbers in DIGIT. Can you revise the program to handle this?

3.7.5   Processing Responses

Response processing, once an analysis has been made to determine what form of reply has been received, is just like any other form of programming. A careful analysis in advance will assure that the processing steps are appropriate to the type of answer received. For example, if a test has been made to assure that a diameter is within tolerance, the answer may safely be converted, say from inches to centimeters; but if it had not been ascertained first that the reply was numeric, this calculation would produce a nonsense value.

3.7.6   The Branching Decision

Our conversational program has now asked a question, received an answer, analyzed this answer, and taken some action. It is now ready to proceed to the next question. Where to go will probably depend upon what reply was received. The greatest single value of using a computer in a conversational mode is that a careful analysis can be made of responses, a great many variations in them discerned, and different actions taken. If branching were always to the next question, the conversation would have little claim to sophistication.

In fact, then, the programmer will probably write many more questions and response analyses than he will use in any one conversation.

3.8 SUMMARY

Programming consists of telling a computer every step it must take to solve a problem or perform any useful task. This is done by providing it with a list of specific instructions that it is to carry out. Although programmers may make use of programs written by others, it is their obligation to insure that every facet of the job has been described and every contingency foreseen. In conversational systems, in particular, it is important to realize that incoming messages can contain errors and that often the effectiveness of an interactive system will hinge upon the way in which it handles errors.

REFERENCES

1. McCracken, Daniel D., *A Guide to ALGOL Programming*, John Wiley, New York, 1962.
2. McCracken, Daniel D., *A Guide to COBOL Programming*, John Wiley, New York, 1963.
3. Organick, Elliot I., *A FORTRAN Primer*, Addison-Wesley, Reading, Mass., 1963.
4. Weinberg, Gerald M., *PL/I Programming Primer*, McGraw-Hill, New York, 1966.

RECOMMENDED ADDITIONAL READING

1. Brooks, Frederick P., Jr., and Kenneth E. Iverson, *Automatic Data Processing*, System/360 Edition, John Wiley, New York, 1968.
2. Flores, Ivan, *Computer Software*, Prentice-Hall, Englewood Cliffs, N.J., 1965.
3. Galler, Bernard A., *The Language of Computers*, McGraw-Hill, New York, 1962.
4. Knuth, Donald E., *The Art of Computer Programming*, Vol. 1, *Fundamental Algorithms*, Addison-Wesley, Reading, Mass., 1968.
5. Leeds, H. and G. Weinberg, *Computer Programming Fundamentals*, McGraw-Hill, New York, 1966.
6. McCracken, Daniel D., *A Guide to FORTRAN Programming*, John Wiley, New York, 1962.
7. Nicol, Keith, *Elementary Programming and ALGOL*, McGraw-Hill, New York, 1965.
8. Pollack, Seymour V., *A Guide to FORTRAN IV*, Columbia University Press, New York, 1965.
9. Rosen, Saul, *Programming Systems and Languages*, McGraw-Hill, New York, 1967.
10. Wegner, Peter, *Programming Languages, Information Structures, and Machine Organization*, McGraw-Hill, New York, 1968.

Chapter Four

Time-Sharing

4.1 INTRODUCTION

Time-sharing is a method of sharing a computer or allocating its resources, among several users. A general-purpose digital computer is actually a collection of subsystems with widely varying characteristics. Typically, the greater part of the total system is idle while only one or two components are performing some operation. Most time-sharing systems have as their main purpose the servicing of man-machine communication consoles that operate at far lower speeds than does the central computer. Man-machine processing would be prohibitively expensive if the computer were forced to stand idle while the man composed a message and transmitted it at 10 to 15 characters per second. Indeed, many authors define time-sharing solely in terms of servicing people at consoles. However, we prefer a more general definition, namely, that time-sharing is a method of operating a computer which allows more than one program to be in operation at one time, optimizes the allocation of computer systems resources to meet the demands of all these programs, and guarantees each user that his program will be serviced within some stated time period. The demands of users' programs may vary, and that is why we prefer to avoid the assumption that human beings at consoles are the only users. For example, it is quite reasonable to consider, as the basis for the design of a time-sharing system, overall efficiency of use of computer time, or response to nonhuman communications demands, as well as to consider the rate of response to human beings who are in a conversational mode.

No computer with a single processor actually operates more than one program in its CPU at one time. That is, the computer interprets and executes only one command at one time, although there may be overlap between command execution in the main processor and input or output operations. But what can be done is to switch rapidly back and forth, from operating a small portion of one program to a portion of another, and to do this so fast that human users do not realize that they are not receiving the full attention of the computer. In this way, more than one program can use the CPU while the slower input/output operations are in progress. Getting the computer to do this switching is a complex operation, one which is, itself, performed under the control of a complex computer program usually called a *time-sharing monitor*. The programs that share the computer under the monitor's control are called *user programs,* since they are supplied by the users of the time-sharing system.

Let us look more closely at the computer and program characteristics that make time-sharing possible. First, the components of a computer act at vastly different speeds. The electric typewriter terminals operate, usually, at a maximum of 15 characters per second. To transmit the string *John Smith* requires 15 characters and a full second. The characters are four case shifts (two up-shifts and two down-shifts), a space, an end-of-message symbol, and, of course, the letters *johnsmith.* During this second, some computers could have executed five million internal operations if left free to do so while the console operator was typing. Once the character string is in the computer, it might take only a few microseconds to compare the message with another character string, as might be done in an instructional system. Storing the message on a disk memory, though, might require something on the order of tens of milliseconds. And there are input and output operations of still longer duration—searching a magnetic tape, for example, may tie up several minutes of computer time.

Once an input or output operation is initiated, most modern computers allow it to proceed while the central processor returns to operation of a program. If the program must await the completion of the input or output operation before proceeding (for example, it might order the retrieval of some data from a tape and be unable to continue until these data are available), the entire computer is bound up in awaiting the results of a painfully slow operation. With overlapping operations, on the other hand, we are allowed to initiate a tape search, then return to

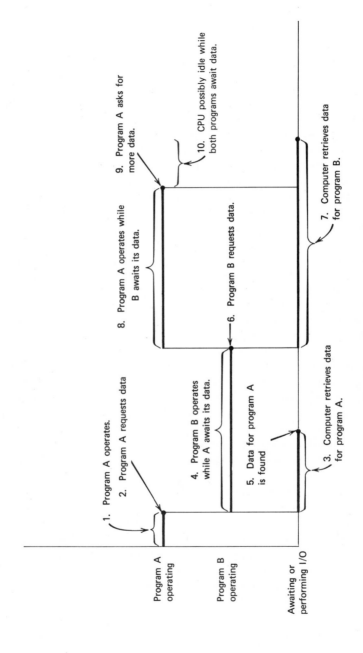

Figure 4.1 Multiprogram operation.

some other program, and operate it until a signal is received that our tape search is completed and the needed data are available. The computer may then return to the first program and complete it, or at least operate it until the next I/O operation is called for, as shown in Figure 4.1.

What will this switching cost? To operate two small programs in this way, very little. Beside the two user programs, there is a requirement for a small amount of additional program execution time for the monitor to handle the interrupting of one program and the initiation of the other one. But, from the point of view of the user whose program otherwise would not have been run at all, this is a small price to pay.

A second characteristic of computers that makes time-sharing possible is that different programs will use different mixes of the available resources. One program may be a heavy user of input and output components, performing relatively little computation but much data movement. Another may be a mathematical program, using few data but performing a great many functions on the data. Whereas time-sharing among a group of programs with similar resource requirements might not be profitable, because most programs would often be queued up waiting for the use of the same components, a diversity of demand helps to make sharing profitable, for the programs are not so often competing for the same devices and are quite ready to permit use by other programs of components that they themselves do not require.

Finally, there is the set of computer programs that involve man-machine communication. In these applications of computers, programs are called into use, or invoked, by people at consoles. Here a relatively small amount of computer processing is needed to respond to any stimulus provided by the man, but high-speed reaction by the computer is desired. In other words, the may may take several minutes to compose a message and a few additional seconds to type it, but he then wants the machine to reply instantaneously. This characteristic requires high performance on the part of the computer, but only for a very limited period. Most of the time there is nothing to do; hence the climate for time-sharing is present.

One of the major applications of time-sharing is for on-line programming systems. In these systems, programmers enter their programs directly into the computer through a console and the program is able to be executed immediately, or at worst in a short amount of time. Turn-around time—the elapsed time between the submission of a program to a computer center and the receipt of results of its operation by the programmer—can be reduced from hours or days to seconds. We discuss some of the techniques and benefits of this mode of operation in Chapter 10. Other applications of time-sharing are for computer-assisted instruction, data editing, and graphic design (Chapters 8, 9, and 11, respectively). Most of these applications have the characteristic that many users are involved and the amount of computing any one of them wants at any particular time is limited.

Time-sharing, then, allows the simultaneous utilization of many computer resources to the net economic advantage of each user. It does not affect what is physically possible on any given computer. Hence time-sharing is not what makes man-machine communication possible, but it is what makes it *economical*. How many or what percentage of the computer's components are in use simultaneously depends on the particular time-sharing monitor and hardware in use and on the specific problem mix in operation at any one time. The trick is to make the system sufficiently economical to enable users to employ a computer that they would not otherwise have been able to afford.

4.2 BASIC ELEMENTS OF A TIME-SHARING SYSTEM

The usual approach to time-sharing is to load several programs into a computer's memory and operate them one at a time. As one program is interrupted, another begins operating. An interruption can be caused by the initiation of an input or output operation, a time-consuming task that can be executed in parallel with computation if some computation can be found to do while awaiting the I/O result. Interrupts can also be triggered by a timing mechanism, to insure, say, that a long-running mathematical program does not monopolize the system.

Operating in this mode requires a monitor program or operating system, to keep track of what program is operating, what I/O operations are in progress, and where data are to be placed upon arrival. The monitor's duties also include making the decision on what program to execute next and performing the I/O operations on behalf of the individual programs. In other words, in order to perform an input operation, a time-sharing user program requests that the monitor perform the operation. In this way, by having all programs deal with a central source, all such operations are coordinated and executed in the most efficient manner possible. Figure 4.2 illustrates the relationships among the monitor and the user programs and their respective data.

Usually a time-sharing system allows more than one user program, or portions of user programs, to be in core memory at one time, although it is possible to have time-sharing in which the complete portion of memory devoted to user programs is replaced each time a program is

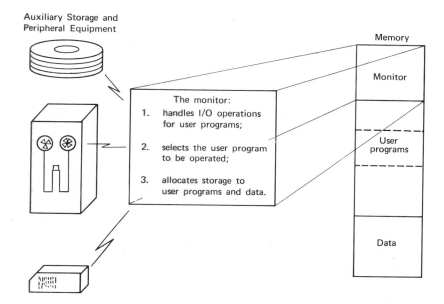

Figure 4.2 Role of the monitor program.

interrupted. To understand time-sharing, then, we must first see how memory is allocated among the competing programs and how conflicts regarding their demands for data from files are resolved.

4.2.1 Relocation of Programs

A machine language program, when ready to be executed, contains internal references to addresses in the computer's memory. Consider a program segment that occupies, say, 100 computer words and has within it a statement calling for a branch to location 50. This is normal and meaningful, but suppose the program were stored, not in locations 1 through 100 or 0 through 99, but in 500 through 599. Certainly, if we are going to store fragments of more than one program at one time, we cannot locate all of them starting with location 0. Only one program can have location 50 within its allocated storage space.

Usually, memory is set aside in units called *pages*. These have possibly 1000 characters each. Any given program may require more than one page, but when we are ready to load a new program into memory we never really know in advance which page areas are free. Therefore we must be prepared to load a segment of any program into any available page, and this means we must be prepared to adjust all addresses in a program segment to the location of the free page. This is called *relocation*. Programs are initially assembled relative to a base location of 0, and adjustments are made to relocate the program relative to whatever location is available when the program is ready to be run.

Relocation requires that each program statement containing an address reference be tagged as such. When the program is loaded into core memory, each such statement is modified by adding the address of the page to the address of the command. Thus a reference to location 50, in a program to be relocated to a page beginning at location 7000, would become address 7050. This can be accomplished in either of two general ways: (1) the time-sharing monitor program can scan the user program being loaded and make any address adjustments indicated by the tags (see Figure 4.3), or (2) the computer may be constructed to be able to add a number stored in a particular location to any program address, automatically. In the second case, when the monitor loads the user program the location of the page is stored at some designated location, and when the user program is executed the base address is automatically added to the address given in the program, as shown in Figure 4.4.

It can be seen that either approach requires some work on the part of the monitor, adding further to the overhead cost of operating a time-sharing system. If the automatic address modification feature is used, the costs of the *computer hardware* must go up. In the case of program

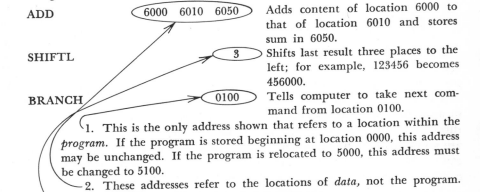

Program Stored in Memory	*Comment*
ADD ⟨6000 6010 6050⟩	Adds content of location 6000 to that of location 6010 and stores sum in 6050.
SHIFTL ⟨3⟩	Shifts last result three places to the left; for example, 123456 becomes 456000.
BRANCH ⟨0100⟩	Tells computer to take next command from location 0100.

1. This is the only address shown that refers to a location within the *program*. If the program is stored beginning at location 0000, this address may be unchanged. If the program is relocated to 5000, this address must be changed to 5100.

2. These addresses refer to the locations of *data*, not the program. They are unaffected by relocation of the program.

3. This is not an address and is not affected by relocation of either the program or the data.

Figure 4.3. Address modification for relocation.

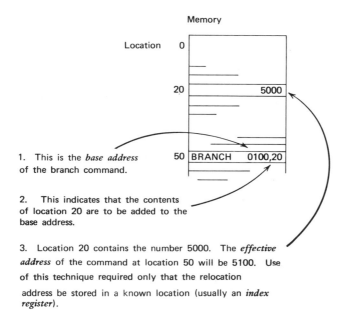

1. This is the *base address* of the branch command.

2. This indicates that the contents of location 20 are to be added to the base address.

3. Location 20 contains the number 5000. The *effective address* of the command at location 50 will be 5100. Use of this technique required only that the relocation address be stored in a known location (usually an *index register*).

Figure 4.4 Automatic address modification.

relocation, the cost of *using* a computer goes up. Either way, there is a price to be paid for relocation, and the system designer or purchaser must determine whether the return on this added investment justifies the cost.

4.2.2 Allocation of Memory to User Programs

It may well be that any given user program cannot fit into the amount of core memory available. Certainly, with the need to store the time-sharing monitor and the need to keep several programs ready for operation, lack of space is a highly unlikely contingency. This is why paging was developed, so that only portions of a program need be in memory at one time. The number of pages required for a complete user program is not a critical factor, since no attempt is made to load all of them at once.

Assume that a single page of a user program has been loaded, is being executed, and contains a branch to a location outside its own page.

The monitor must then find where the page containing the target address is stored. At minimum, the monitor must look in core memory to find where the page is and then hand control over to it, but it may not find the page in core memory. In this case, an input operation is necessary to retrieve the program page from wherever it is stored (probably on a disk or drum), resulting in an interrupt of the same type as that caused by a data retrieval operation. Clearly, the more pages of a program that are stored in core memory, the lower is the probability of an interrupt to get more program pages.

We can see that deciding how many pages of any program to store in core memory at one time is another function of the monitor. It is physically possible to store as little as one page for each program, but that means a high probability of costly interrupts to find new pages. Instead, the entire memory available to user programs may be devoted to a single program, which minimizes interruptions of this program but causes a larger disruption when control of the machine is turned over to another program.

The monitor is also faced with deciding what to do when a user programs calls for some data. Data also occupy space in memory. The total picture becomes one of an ever-changing assignment of memory pages to programs and their data, with the monitor being responsible for keeping track of what is stored where and for deciding what to do in the event of competition for space by programs or data.

4.2.3 Access to Data

We have already pointed out that the time-sharing monitor handles all actual input and output transactions on behalf of the users' programs. Because more than one of these programs may want to use the same data storage or transmission component at the same time, another burden is placed on the monitor to schedule these operations and to keep certain difficulties from arising.

Let us consider some of the major tasks and decisions with which the monitor must cope on behalf of a user program in handling data. If retrieving data is involved, the monitor must first find where the information is. A key factor is whether or not the information is already in core memory, either put there earlier by the program being processed or by another user program. If the data are in core, a time-consuming auxiliary memory search is avoided. If they are not in core, the auxiliary search must be initiated, but first the monitor must find out whether the memory device is available at the moment. For example, if six magnetic tapes are attached to a single tape control unit, this unit, as well as the individual tape, must be free. If either is not free, a notation must be made in a waiting list (queue), showing what data are wanted from what device, and the requirement will be fulfilled when the equipment is free.

For this, we can see the implication of a need for a *queue management program* within the monitor—one that periodically examines the waiting lists and the available resources, and decides what actions to take. It should be obvious that the efficiency of queue management plays a great role in determining the overall efficiency of the monitor.

When a data record requested by a user program is finally located, the monitor must find some room in core memory to store it. Now we face the same problem as we did in finding room to store program elements that are brought in from auxiliary storage. The utilization of core may change considerably between the time a request for a data record is made and the time it is delivered. Hence the amount of pre-planning that can be done for data storage is limited, and the core allocation decision must be made as the data arrive. If no core space is available, the monitor must decide either to remove some existing material (write over it), to hold the new data in a buffer, if available, until some core area becomes free, or even to abandon the data and retrieve the record again later when space is available. The last option, although logically acceptable, would be an expensive strategy to follow.

Finally, one of the most important monitor tasks in regard to data is to protect information "belonging" to one program from encroachment, intentional or not, by another program. In addition to protecting data records, a time-sharing system must be able to protect *programs* from being misused by other programs. It is particularly important, of course, to insure that the monitor cannot be modified by a user program. Suppose two user programs are allowed to use the same file, perhaps a personnel file. One might be a file maintenance program and the other a processing program. If a change is being posted to the file by the maintenance program, there may be a short interval during which the file has been only incompletely modified and currently reflects neither the old nor the new version, but a combination that is meaningless. An example is shown in Figure 4.5. Here a record of the file occupies portions of two tracks on a disk, and the maintenance program is in the process of changing them. It is possible for the processing program to retrieve the new version of the first part of a record and the old version of the second part. The change of an employee's record illustrated could result in the misinterpretation of the information in the manner shown.

The monitor can overcome this problem by "locking" the file in process of being changed until the alteration is complete. In this way, any other program needing to use the file may have to wait but is always

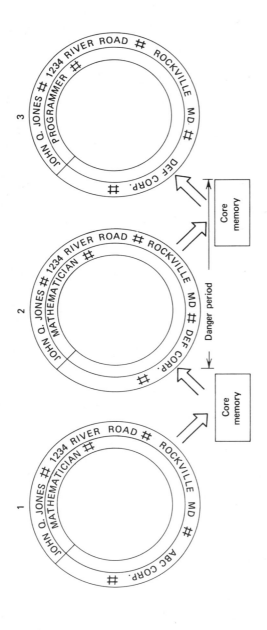

1. This is the original status of a record on a disk. The record for John Q. Jones occupies parts of two tracks. This record is to be changed to show a new employer, DEF Corp., and a new job title, Programmer. To do this, the first track is read into core memory, modified, and rewritten in corrected form (2).

2. Now the second track related to Jones is read into core memory and modified. It is then rewritten onto the disk (3).

3. After the first track has been corrected, but before the second one has been rewritten, the disk contains erroneous information (2) because it shows the new employer but the old job title. This false information would be fed to any program accessing the file during the danger period indicated.

Figure 4.5 The need for file protection.

sure of eventually getting a complete record. Locking may be as simple an action as setting an indicator to show that a change is in progress and seeing to it that the monitor always checks all such indicators before retrieving information from any file. The monitor would refuse to retrieve data from a locked file.

The added time for these operations is small. The delay imposed on overall execution is not fixed but depends on the degree of mutual dependency of the user programs. If there is a high degree of dependency, which would mean a high probability of interference in each other's file operations, it might be desirable to perform the locking operations on a record level, instead of a file level. This would decrease interference significantly but would raise, equally significantly, the amount of storage required for the indicators and the time to check the tables.

The problem of interference can exist when dealing with core-stored files as well as with auxiliary files, and a similar lockout procedure can be used. Some computers have more than one processor; these have a built-in mechanism to prevent interference when two programs try to access the same location in a jointly used magnetic core memory at exactly, or nearly, the same time. Some kind of priority system chooses between programs vying at the same time, and a fixed but small delay is imposed on the loser. Normally, this delay is insignificant; but if the two programs were doing extensive search or processing operations in the same core-located file, one program could be significantly inhibited.

Occasionally, one program wishes to permanently lock all others out of its files. A program that handles students' examination grades, for example, may want to be sure that no other program in the time-sharing system is able to gain access to the files, for either search or maintenance. In other situations, a program may wish to lock others out only for maintenance, while freely allowing retrieval. This may be the case in regard to a dictionary used in information retrieval. It may be desirable to control carefully the *changing* of the dictionary, but not to restrict *references* to it. This form of control can be handled by extending the concept of the lockout indicator, from a single bit showing that the file is open or closed, to a list, for each file, of the programs or users to be permitted to retrieve data from a file and those permitted to modify this file.

Finally, another solution to the problems of handling data by a time-shared program is to prohibit storing files in auxiliary memory, requiring all data to be stored in core and to be accessible to only one program. The data become, effectively, part of the program. Because many data-handling problems are thereby overcome or simplified, the overall system operates at high speed and efficiency. However, the programs, in these cases, cannot make use of auxiliary memory for storage; hence the size of the files with which they can deal is severely restricted. Furthermore, it is difficult for one program to retrieve data from files maintained by another. Therefore this approach is totally unacceptable for general-purpose work, since it excludes many types of programs. But it does permit the operation of largely mathematical programs, which, because of the absence of data-handling delays, operate at very high speed.

4.2.4. The Monitor Program

We have successively added new responsibilities to the monitor program each time we added a new facility that we would like in our time-sharing system. Allocation of core, queue management for I/O operations, and file protection—all these can be complex program operations. The more efficiently the allocations are done the more efficiently the overall system will operate, but greater efficiency is probably bought at the cost of greater running time for the monitor. Moreover, running time for the monitor is nonproductive time. It must be charged to overhead, and its costs distributed over the cost of operating all the user programs. It is not at all difficult for a monitor to require so much running time as to nullify all the advantage of its own existence. This is part of what caused the lag between the demonstration of the technical feasibility of time-sharing and its economic success in the marketplace. (Hardware considerations were also involved.)

4.3 TIME-SHARING SYSTEMS

In Section 4.2 we described some of the requirements for a time-sharing monitor and some of the options open to the systems designer. In this section we shall consider some examples of systems that demonstrate different approaches to the major questions.

4.3.1. Types of Systems

There are two main bases for classifying time-sharing systems: the goals they try to accomplish and the design of the monitor. We shall use monitor design as the basis for our review in Section 4.3.2. As to goals, we can recognize systems that are:

1. *Limited application systems,* severely restricting the nature of the user program that can be run on them.
2. *Limited repertoire systems,* in which no restriction is directly placed on the application of users' programs, but restriction is placed on the logical functions they can perform.

3. *Unlimited or nearly unlimited systems,* which aim to allow the using programmer complete freedom to run any program he wants, or any program he could run if he were in complete control of the computer.

Examples of limited application systems are computer-assisted instruction (CAI) and on-line data-editing systems. A CAI system,[8] for example, allows the programmer (in this case the author of a course) to enter only a limited form of program (his teaching program). The CAI time-sharing system is intended mainly for administration of the course to the student. Mostly, then, the time-sharing system is executing programs with a number of users simultaneously, but these users are students, not programmers. Far less processing is required on the student's input than of a computer programmer's input in an on-line programming system. Although an instructional program can do arithmetic and can produce printed output, one would not expect to write a payroll program in this form. Instructional programs are also severely restricted in the complexity of the mathematical programs they can run.

A data-editing system [18] is somewhat the same. It allows users to give it a limited number of commands, all concerned only with text entry and editing, and makes no provision whatever for general-purpose programming. These systems can be efficient so long as they are used for the applications intended. A computer system that handles only a single application is said to be *dedicated* to that application. It is possible to perform teaching and editing functions under a more general system, but a dedicated system usually is able to perform a particular application either faster or less expensively, or both.

A limited repertoire system, as suggested previously, allows its users to work on any application but does not give them a full range of programming commands. For example, the JOSS,[1, 3] APL,[13] QUIKTRAN,[14] and the original BASIC [9] time-sharing systems, which are primarily for mathematical users, do not allow the using programmer to search or otherwise manipulate files stored in auxiliary memory. Data can be read from consoles but cannot be placed on magnetic tape or disk, under user control, and later searched or retrieved. These systems also place a limit on the size of a program. The user willing to cope with these limitations gains, in return, a fast-response system that is economical to use and easy to learn.

We introduce here another classification of a time-sharing system—according to whether or not it interprets user commands as they are executed or before they are executed. An *interpretive* system leaves the user's program in symbolic form until a statement is ready to be executed.

Only then is the symbolic text examined and the necessary computer language commands determined. In a *compiled* system, a user's entire symbolic program is translated into machine language before any part of it is executed.

An interpretive system is slower in operation, obviously, because the interpretation time must be added to the execution time of each symbolic command. On the other hand, there are distinct advantages to an interpretive system. Commands can be entered and executed one at a time, a desirable feature if the user is doing some calculations for which he wants immediate response or if he wishes to edit data he has just entered. Also, commands can easily be changed, and as soon as the change is made the program is again ready for execution. There is no delay for compilation.

An interpretive system requires less core storage for user programs that are being executed. Thus it imposes a far less difficult memory allocation problem. Essentially, only one program, the interpreter, is operating and the users' programs are treated as *data* for this program. We may also say that the computer is dedicated to the operation of the interpreter. There is no need for relocation, since all commands are symbolic anyway. When a program statement not in core is referred to, the operation of the user program is interrupted and a read is initiated to bring in the needed statements. In the meantime, another user program is begun or resumed. Although it would be highly inefficient to do this, as little as a single statement of each user program could be put in core at one time, leaving almost the entire memory for the storage of data and for the monitor. For practical use, more commands should be stored, with an attempt made to minimize the number of interrupts for new program statements.

A compromise between interpretive and compiler systems involves the use of an *incremental compiler,* which can compile independent commands or a group of commands and execute them on demand, and can allow symbolic changes to be made to a program. Changes are made without the requirement for a complete recompilation of the original program. That is, the incremental compiler can allow the using programmer to change some statements in his symbolic program, compile only the changes, and modify the previously compiled, machine language version of the program.

4.3.2. A Survey of Techniques

We shall give a brief comparison of four of the principal kinds of time-sharing systems, varying according to monitor design. Some of the monitor techniques can be used with limited or unlimited repertoire systems and in interpretive or compile mode.

Commutation. A commutating system rotates control among a set of programs, with each program taking its turn according to its assigned position in sequence. The program whose turn it is operates or declines to operate and then turns over control to its successor, either directly or thorugh a small monitor. This technique is illustrated in Figure 4.6. Such a technique was used with SAGE,[6] one of the first real-time computer systems. A commutating, or single-thread,[12] system places minimum demand on the monitor, which need only arrange for the requisite data to be available for the user programs and then call a user program when its turn arises. Little time is lost in decision-making about what program to run or in evaluating priorities. Some programs may find that there is nothing for them to do in a given cycle. When it is possible that a program will not have a task to perform in some cycles, the author of the program should arrange to test for this condition first.

Cycles may be of fixed length or variable. If the length is fixed and there has been little input activity in any one cycle, the entire system may have to idle because many of the programs have no task. This might be the case if the cycle time were tied to the sweep time of a radar

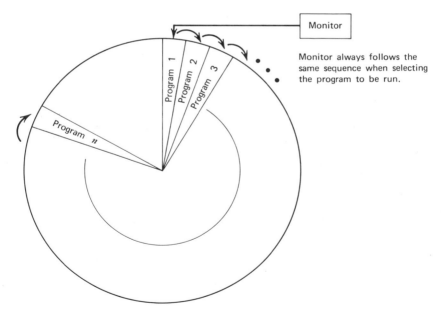

Figure 4.6 Commutating monitor.

antenna (as was the case in SAGE) and no inputs were forthcoming in any given sweep. When its cycle time is thus governed, the computer must sample the communication line to the radar at fixed intervals, and all programs must be designed to permit this to happen under the maximum incoming-data load. Nothing can be done with the spare time when no data arrive during a specific cycle.

A commutating, or cycling, system benefits from a less complex monitor and devotes less computer time to overhead. However, it does not handle asynchronous inputs well, or widely varying processing loads on the individual program. In short, it is not particularly well adapted to general-purpose computing, but works well in a controlled environment where the data rate and processing required are predictable.

If communication with the terminal devices can be delegated to a separate, communicating computer, or multiplexor,[10] the commutating method can be used with interpretive systems. A fixed amount of time is devoted to each user program, and all I/O operations are handled by the multiplexor, which provides data on demand to the main computer and carries the latter's messages to the terminals of individual users.

Multiprogramming. Multiprogramming does not necessarily imply time-sharing, but it deserves mention because many such systems are coming into use. There is one main difference between multiprogramming and time-sharing; the lack, in multiprogramming, of a guaranteed limit on the time devoted to running any one program. Without this limit, there can be no guarantee of minimum response time to any given user. Typically, a multiprogramming monitor [5, 4] will operate several programs simultaneously, but switch control only when an I/O call is issued, not on the lapse of a time interval. (See Figure 4.7.) A small (in memory space and amount of data) mathematical program that uses long periods of time without external references may monopolize a multiprogramming system until it is completed.

If the multiprogramming monitor can handle interrupts, as most modern systems can, the system can be made more responsive to users, still without elapsed time limitations. Thus program A initiates an input operation and, on doing so, turns over control to program B, which is prepared to run for a long time without the need of input or output operations. When the data for A arrive, however, the computer is interrupted and the monitor then resumes operation of program A or at least has the data ready for A when B is done.

By assigning priorities to programs, greater or lesser emphasis can be placed on programs that make heavy use of I/O. If program A in our previous example were given precedence, whenever some I/O operation

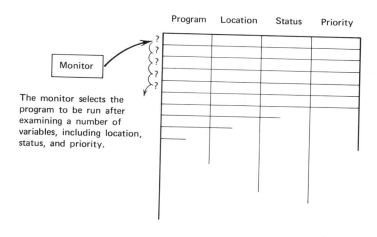

Figure 4.7 Multiprogramming monitor.

that it initiated was completed, program B would be halted and A allowed to resume until it had to stop for more data.

By dividing the core memory available to users into several *partitions*,[16] each large enough to contain a full user program, the costs and delays of continually moving and relocating programs are saved. The programs need be relocated only when initially loaded; thereafter, each will operate from the same partition until it completes operation.

A multiprogramming system such as this is a compromise between full time-sharing and single-program operation. Although it cannot handle a large number of user programs and it cannot guarantee rapid response to the needs of each one, it places a relatively low demand on the monitor and hence saves overhead costs. If care is taken in the selection of the programs to be loaded simultaneously, it is possible to achieve a high degree of responsiveness to users with a multiprogramming system, particularly if a large number of programs are loaded that are primarily message handlers for low-speed communications terminals. This is the case with computer-assisted instruction, for example; the amount of processing of a student message tends to be low and the number of terminal communications operations is likely to be high.

Multiprogramming with Time-Slicing. In a full time-sharing system [8, 15] time-slicing, or elapsed-time interrupting, is added to other multiprogramming features. In addition, steps are taken to allow the using programmer to assume that he has the entire computer, not just a partition, at his disposal. The time-sharing monitor takes care of the addressing difficulties caused by the allocation of only a small fraction of core memory to any one program, and (let us repeat) the monitor handles all input and output operations for the using programmer. As long as the monitor is able to handle relocation and reallocation of core, and as long as a user program can address only one core location at a time, the apparent effect of a full memory can be achieved by rapid shuffling of data and programs within core memory and between core and auxiliary memory. Queuing of requests for the use of input and output facilities is handled by the monitor. Hence the using programmer is free to write his programs as if he were the sole client of the computer system.

Each user program is assured of its chance to operate at least once in every nt seconds, where t is the maximum time interval for a program and n is the number of user programs in the system. The actual time between "shots" can be much less because user programs are interrupted *either* by the lapse of t seconds *or* the initiation of I/O operations, whichever comes first. On the other hand, a priority system can be imposed that may allow for the designation of some programs as more important than others or may give precedence to programs making small demands for memory space.

Virtual Systems.   In a typical time-sharing system the using programmer assumes he has the full core memory available to him although he actually uses only a small part of it at any one time. As to other system components, he must conform with the actual configuration of the resources in the system. The assumption of full memory has led to the use of the term *virtual memory* in the sense that the programmer essentially visualizes this amount of memory but does not physically have the use of it.

An extension of this concept leads to the complete virtual system [17] (see Figure 4.8), wherein a programmer may see or visualize whatever system he wants (within some limits) and leaves it to the monitor program to adjust addresses and reallocate resources to achieve the desired effect. One immediate advantage of the virtual system concept is that the programmer can assume a very large core memory, perhaps millions of characters, adequate to hold all the data needed for his particular problem. He, then, does not need to worry about programming input and output operations. He assumes all the data are always available to him in core. The monitor may have to work at a furious rate to perform

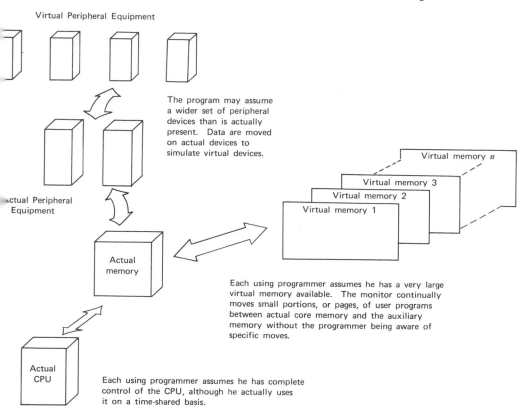

Figure 4.8 Virtual systems.

actual I/O operations and thus have required data actually available when needed. This becomes a way of having the computer, through the virtual system monitor, do a great deal of the work that the using programmer would otherwise have to perform himself.

Even with his large, virtual core, the using programmer may want to exercise control of some I/O facilities. He may want to display information or to transmit it to or accept it from remote terminals. He may have so many data that use of auxiliary memory is required. The virtual system allows him to assume whatever virtual components he wishes, so long as the monitor has been equipped to simulate them. He may want to write a program that will eventually operate on a large computer with two data channels, whereas the physical computer on which the virtual system is operated perhaps has only one. The using programmer may ignore this discrepancy. He writes as if there were channels 1 and 2 and leaves it to the monitor to simulate them for him. The monitor, then, may actually get information from, and put it on, only a single auxiliary device, while logically simulating the action of two channels. It takes no more time to do all this in terms of the use of actual core memory by the *user program*. Of course, where the programmer expected two operations to be either simultaneous or immediately sequential in time, the virtual system may impose a long delay while it carries out the simulation of two data channels, so that the elapsed time of a program may vary considerably from what it would be in single-program operation.

Because all resources are controlled by the monitor, rather than by individual programmers not working in concert, the net efficiency of computer use may be very high. Although conclusive figures are not available, preliminary work indicates that application of this concept can, potentially, lead to highly efficient use of a computer system, even though the monitor clearly induces some overhead costs.

Sharing of Physical Components.   Another technique that can be used to increase the efficiency of operation of a computer, or to improve reaction time, is the physical sharing of facilities. Most commonly, this technique is employed in *multiprocessing* systems,[11] in which more than one processor or central computer is used to handle the computing load (Figure 4.9). Entirely separate programs can be running in each of the processors, with each processor having access to all of the core and

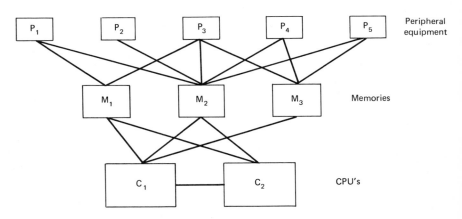

Figure 4.9 Multiprocessing system. Two or more CPU's share one or more memory units and peripheral devices. The processors may work jointly on one program or may run independent programs. Failure of any single unit in such a system may leave the system still able to perform.

auxiliary memory devices and I/O devices. In this way, one program need not wait for all the programs in front of it to complete a turn. It is optional whether or not time-sharing or some other facility-sharing technique is used within each of the processors.

This technique is particularly desirable in applications where high computer reliability is mandatory, as in an air traffic control system.[2] If one processor malfunctions, its work load can be divided among the others. More processors (and other components) than are needed for normal operation may be put into the system to achieve high reliability without the cost of full duplication of resources.

4.4 AN EXAMPLE

A complete description of a time-sharing system would require far more detail than is consistent with the level of this book. Therefore we shall present a highly simplified, fictional example.

4.4.1. Program Selection

Assume a computer with a fairly large memory, the exact size not being important to this discussion. We can arbitrarily decide to partition the memory into three major patrs, one devoted to storage of the time-sharing monitor program, one for user programs, and one for storage of data for the user programs. The unit of storage, or the minimum amount of memory to be allocated, will be a page of such size as to permit perhaps 50 pages of program to be in core at once. The data portion need not be the same size but may be assumed so for convenience. The actual page sizes and amount of core available for programs and data should be determined experimentally for any system, possibly being a variable subject to change as user patterns alter.

We shall make the general rule that user programs are to be interrupted when any of the following conditions is met:

1. A program initiates a data input or output operation.

2. A program calls, or branches, to a point in the program that is not resident in core memory; hence an input operation is required for a page of the program.

3. A program runs for t milliseconds without finishing or initiating an I/O operation.

Assume that we have loaded several programs into memory, loading, say, the first page of each program into successive page areas of memory, taking advantage of the relocation capabilities of the monitor. Control is passed to the first of these programs, which then runs until one of the conditions listed above is met. Suppose the interrupt is caused by an input operation. This command immediately invokes the monitor, which initiates the read operation. The monitor now must decide what program to run next; since the system has just begun operation, there is little information to consider. The monitor might just as well select the next program in line and initiate the program numbered two. Let us assume that program 2 runs for a while and then comes to a point where it calls for a subroutine that is not stored in the same page as the calling program segment. Once again, we must stop the program, initiate an input operation, and consider what program to run next.

This time, however, our decision is more difficult to make. Now we want to consider whether to go on to program 3 or to check on the input operation for program 1 and, if completed, to return to the first program. We can begin to see how rapidly the situation becomes foggy and impossible to prescribe like a simple, cookbook procedure. Let us see, then, what records the monitor program would have had to keep and what some of the alternatives are for a decision-making procedure.

For the monitor to decide what program to operate next, it must certainly know what programs are waiting for turns. Hence a list of such programs is a requirement. A program entirely resident on a disk or drum cannot be operated directly. It has to be retrieved first, relocated, and loaded. Therefore the monitor needs to know where each page of each program is permanently stored. A table containing this information, together with other tables to be described later, is shown in Figure 4.10.

In the example we have used, we found that when program 2 ended its turn we were uncertain whether to go on to program 3 or to return to program 1. Regardless of which decision we would make in this situation, a requirement is that we know (a) why program 1 was stopped, and (b) whether the input operation that caused the stop is completed or not. Here, then, are two more items of information to be maintained by the monitor. We record the status of each program, showing why it stopped and what event it is waiting for. We also need a table of all incomplete input and output operations, showing the status of each and the program for which the operation is to be, or was, performed. We can also look ahead and realize the need for a table of locations of data pages. This will enable any using program to find the location in core of data it has requested. Such a table will also permit another program to find and use the same data without having to repeat input operations—a very significant time saving if it can be achieved. (Continue to

List of Ready Programs

1
2
3
4
5
. .
i

List of Ready Programs Interrupted by Clock

1
2
3
4
. .
k

Status of Programs in Queue

Program No.	Page No.	Location	Status	Priority	Reason Stopped	Time Stopped	Identity of Data Record Being Awaited

Data Page Locations

Data Page	Location

Pending I/O Operations

Unit Addressed	Record Identity	Requesting Program No.	Status

Figure 4.10 Tables used by a time-sharing monitor.

bear in mind that we are setting up a hypothetical system and are not able to include all of the many details that a real system might need or use to achieve greater efficiency.)

These tables of program status and data location will be used in two major monitor functions—deciding what program to execute next and deciding where to store data and program pages as they are read into the computer, that is, the problem of memory allocation.

In Figure 4.11, we have diagrammed an algorithm for selecting the next program. It is based only on the information contained in the tables shown in Figure 4.10. To start with (*A* in the flow chart) we look at each program in the current list to find those in a ready state. A program is in the ready state when it is ready to operate, with all needed data or other program pages in core. Any program waiting for the completion of an I/O command is not ready. Neither is a program page that has run to completion and turned over control to another page of the same program; nor, of course, a program that is completely finished. At *B*, a list is made of all programs currently in the ready state, from this list, the monitor will select the program to be executed next.

A program that communicates with on-line terminals needing rapid servicing will require high priority in our time-sharing system. Whenever one of these programs is ready, we give it precedence (*C* in Figure 4.11) over all other programs that are also ready. When any program is selected by the monitor, its entry in the program status list must be modified (*D*) to show that it is now in operation; then the monitor turns over control (*E*) to this program.

If no high-priority programs are ready, or none existent, we look (*F*) for a program that was interrupted, the last time it ran, by the interval timer. If we give precedence to such programs, we can promise a high degree of utilization of core and the central processor, and gain time for the completion of the I/O operations now in progress. Thus more programs can compete the next time the monitor goes through this decision process. Some time-sharing systems operate these programs in a fashion that gives them ever longer time periods for operation, spaced by ever longer time-out periods. For example, we might allow a program to operate for 200 milliseconds. If the program is interrupted by time, not an I/O command, we make it skip its next turn, then on the third try give it 400 milliseconds, skip it again, and next give it, perhaps, 800 milliseconds. What we will be doing, it should be recalled, is setting up a greater number of I/O operations between heavy-duty compute intervals, so that, even with a large number of I/O calls, the computer is nearly always busy.

The flow chart of Figure 4.11 shows a test (*G*) for the amount of

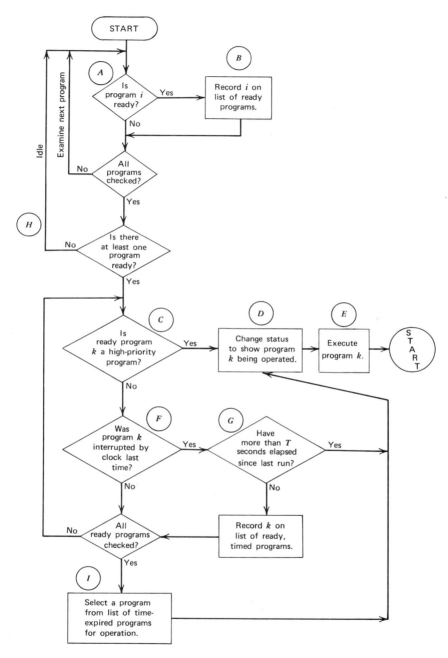

Figure 4.11 A program selection algorithm.

time elapsed since our time-interrupted program last ran. If it has run too recently, we skip it for now, using this simple decision rule as a substitute for the more elaborate one just described. If a program was in the ready state but bypassed because it had run too recently, we must record this in case we end up with no other program qualified to run; then we will ignore the minimum-time-since-last-run criterion.

If there were no programs in the ready state, we would return to the top of the decision program (*H*), in effect idling until some program changed its status by having an I/O command completed. Or we could go to another part of the monitor, which would await the arrival of messages from the I/O channels, and return to this scheduling algorithm only when a change of state occurred. Note, at the bottom of Figure 4.11 (*I*), that the fact that we reach the end of the list can mean only one thing: there is at least one program which is in the time-interrupted status but has not waited long enough since its last run. In order for us to have reached point *C* in the flow chart at least one program must have been ready; and if this program has been a high-priority one, we would have selected it immediately and never hit the end of the list.

4.4.2 Memory Allocation

Our memory allocation program is illustrated in Figure 4.12. We use a very simple one. There is a table (see Figure 4.10) of core memory locations showing what is stored there, and from the program status table the status of what is stored there can be found. A similar table tells the status of data transactions. When new information arrives in the computer, it goes to a buffer, or staging area, to await reassignment. If this is a new program page, we look in the program area (remember that we have arbitrarily decided to store programs in one part of memory and data in another) for free space. We would label a page area as free if the program previously there had indicated that it was completed and did not need to be run again. If there is any such space, we put the new program page there and go to the scheduling algorithm.

If there is no completely free space, we must look for the space that will cause us the least disruption and cost. In this case we have decided that this will be space containing a program page that has completed its run but that may be used again by its parent program. Even though the page may be used again, it is not the one now standing in line to be run and we cannot predict how soon it will be needed. We will use the first such page we can find for the new program segment.

If there are no pages that have completed operation, as an arbitrary decision for illustrative purposes we will look for a page awaiting com-

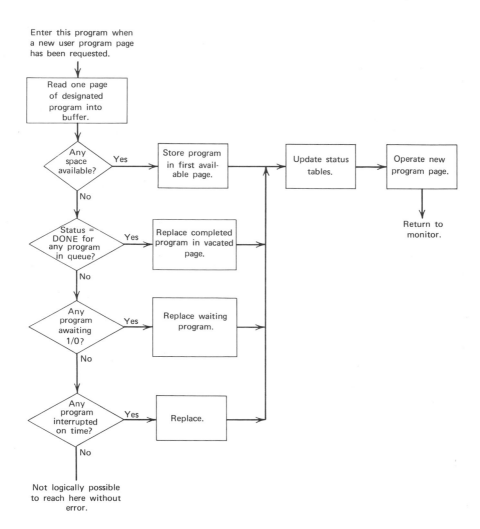

Figure 4.12 A memory allocation algorithm.

pletion of an I/O operation, since it is possible that the new page can be executed and set free before the data for the other page arrives. If this does not happen, we will have caused ourselves some extra work by writing over a page awaiting an input operation, then having to read this page back in again, and possibly being faced with exactly the same space shortage as that now facing us. But, if the system is in a full-load status, we must take some risks or have no place to put information just read in.

In this example, we want to give the greatest protection to program segments interrupted by time, for we know we will want to execute these exact pages when their turns arrive. If they are overwritten, we are certain they will have to be read in again.

By the status definitions we have used, there must be a program page in one of the states we have checked. Hence there is no possibility of having no place to put new incoming programs, even though we do take a risk of putting one in a somewhat undesirable location.

Incoming data can be treated in the same way. If there is no free space, we have to consider writing over some data awaiting use, and we give priority to data for programs that are now awaiting other data or other program pages; that is, we will overwrite these last. If none of these can be found, we will have to erase data for a program stopped on a time limit and then, of course, read these data back in again later, when the program comes up again.

4.3.3. Input/Output Queue Management

Also required is an input/output queue management program that maintains a list of all commands awaiting operation, the status of each, and the status of the I/O channels and devices. Whenever an operation is completed or a facility becomes free, a new operation can be executed and the status of the completed one changed. A simplified flow chart of such a program is shown in two parts in Figure 4.13. Part *a* shows how an input request is initiated, and part *b* illustrates management of the queue. This program makes no use of priorities; it always starts at the top of the waiting list and performs, in order, whatever operations it can.

Finally, Figure 4.14 illustrates the interrelationship of all the individual programs we have developed. This shows a portion of the monitor, the part that would be executed immediately upon the completion of a user program. First, the status of the program just completed is changed, and, if necessary, a message is sent to the queue management program ordering it to take cognizance of the need for a new I/O operation. Then the I/O queue is scanned to see whether any operations, upon which some program is depending, have been completed since the last time this part of the monitor operated. If so, the appropriate status changes are posted; and, if it was an input operation, the memory allocation program is invoked, while in the case of an output operation the core areas that held the data are freed. Finally, the program-selection program is called.

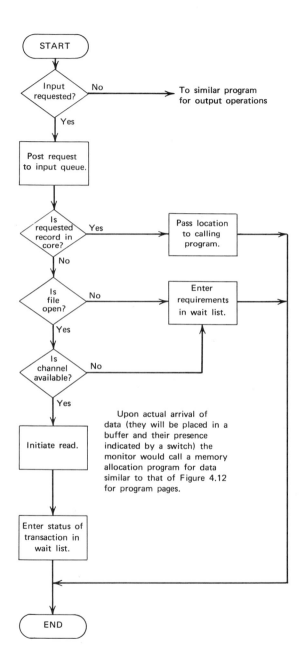

Figure 4.13*a* Initiate-input request.

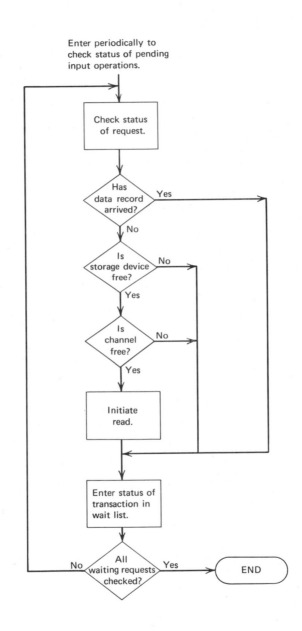

Figure 4.13*b* Input queue management.

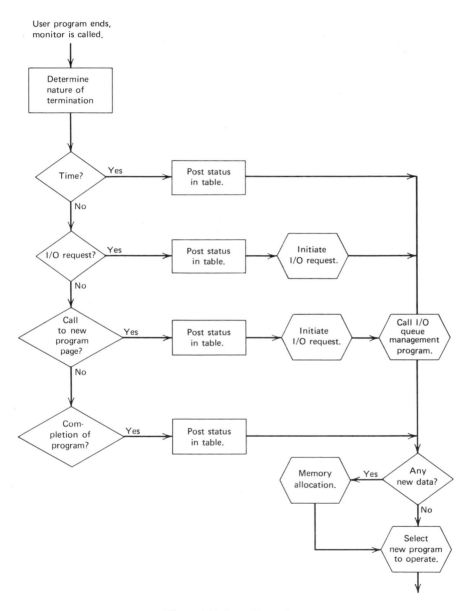

Figure 4.14 Overall monitor.

If no user program is ready or waiting to operate, the monitor can idle in this loop, repeatedly checking the queues to find status changes that would enable the operation of a new program.

We will not again go this deeply into the mechanics of time-sharing, although a similar time-sharing system is assumed in many of the applications we shall discuss in Chapters 6 through 12.

REFERENCES

1. Baker, C. L., *JOSS: Introduction to a Helpful Assistant*, Memorandum RM–5058–PR, The RAND Corp., Santa Monica, Calif., July 1966.
2. Blakney, G. R., L. F. Cudney, and C. R. Eickhorn, "An Application-Oriented Multiplocessing System, II, Design Characteristics of the 9020 System," *IBM Systems Journal*, **6**, 2 (1967), 80–94.
3. Bryan, G. E., and E. W. Paxson, *The JOSS Notebook*, Memorandum RM–5367–PR, The RAND Corp., Santa Monica, Calif., 1967.
4. Codd, E. F., "Multiprogramming," *Advances in Computers*, Vol. 3, F. L. Alt and M. Rubinoff, eds., Academic, New York, 1963, pp. 78–153.
5. Critchlow, A. J., "Generalized Multiprocessing and Multiprogramming Systems," *Proceedings of the AFIPS 1963 Fall Joint Computer Conference*, Spartan Books, New York, 1963, pp. 107–126.
6. Everett, R. R., C. A. Zraket, and H. D. Bennington, "SAGE—A Data Processing System for Air Defense," *Proceedings of the Eastern Computer Conference, 1957*, The Institute of Radio Engineers, New York, December 1957, pp. 148–155.
7. Fano, R., "The MAC System: The Computer Utility Approach," *IEEE Spectrum*, **2**, 1 (January 1965), 56–64.
8. *IBM 1500 Operating System, Computer-Assisted Instruction, Coursewriter II*, Form CAI–4036–1, IBM Corp., White Plains, N.Y. (undated).
9. Kemeny, John G., and Thomas E. Kurtz, *Basic Programming*, John Wiley, New York, 1967.
10. Martin, James, *Programming Real-Time Computer Systems*, Prentice-Hall, Englewood Cliffs, N. J., 1965, p. 158.
11. *Ibid.*, pp. 40, 255.
12. *Ibid.*, p. 158.
13. Pakin, Sandra, *APL/360 Reference Manual*, Science Research Associates, Chicago, 1968.
14. *QUIKTRAN User's Guide*, Form E20–0240, IBM Corp., White Plains, N.Y.
15. Schwartz, J. I., C. Coffman, and C. Weissman, "A General-Purpose Time-Sharing System," *AFIPS Conference Proceedings*, **26** (1964), 455–464.
16. Wegner, Peter, *Programming Languages, Information Structures and Machine Organization*, McGraw-Hill, New York, 1968, pp. 72–73.
17. *Ibid.*, pp. 80–90.
18. *1440/1460 Administrative Terminal System (ATS) Description*, Form H20–0129, IBM Corp., White Plains, N.Y. (undated).

RECOMMENDED ADDITIONAL READING

1. Corbato, F. J., et al., *The Compatible Time-Sharing System: A Programmer's Guide,* The MIT Press, Cambridge, Mass., 1963.

2. Fano, R. M., and F. J. Corbato, "Time-Sharing on Computers," *Information,* W. H. Freeman, San Francisco, 1966. pp. 76–95.

3. McCarthy, John, "Time-Sharing Computer Systems," *Management and the Computer of the Future,* M. Greenberger, ed., The MIT Press and John Wiley, Cambridge, Mass., and New York, 1962, pp. 220–248.

4. Pyke, Thomas N., Jr., "Time-Sharing Computer Systems," *Advances in Computers,* Vol. 8, Academic, New York, 1967, pp. 1–45.

5. Scherr, Allan L., *An Analysis of Time-Shared Computer Systems,* The MIT Press, Cambridge, Mass., 1967.

6. Ziegler, James R., *Time-Sharing Data Processing Systems,* Prentice-Hall, Englewood Cliffs, N.J., 1967.

Chapter Five

Natural Language
Communication

5.1 INTRODUCTION

The ability to "talk" to a computer in natural language has long been a dream both of computer people and of science fiction writers. A major step in this direction was taken around 1951, when serious work on automatic language translation was begun. In machine translation a computer is given a text in one language and is expected to produce an equivalent text in another language.

Another source of interest in natural language communication is the field of information retrieval. Here we find that a major weakness of many systems, particularly the earlier ones, was the cumbersome, artificial language that users were required to learn. Since often the users were not mathematically inclined, a language that demanded of them a logical equation, couched in terms not familiar to them (in fact, rather like a computer program), was a psychological barrier. When, in addition, they were asked to take the unfamiliar step of completely describing the object of their search beforehand, results were disappointing.

Similar difficulties arose in indexing documents for storage in these retrieval systems. Once again, unfamiliar artificial languages were devised, and indexers or catalogers had to become fluent in them. As a result both the cataloger and the retriever were working with unfamiliar languages. Although the development of better artificial languages is clearly one of the possible solutions to this problem, interest has developed in dealing entirely in natural language. There are now a number of retrieval systems that can be queried in natural language or in a language that approximates a natural one.

We are also finding interest in natural language communication in other fields. In computer-assisted instruction it is sometimes desirable to have students answer questions in their own terms, that is, write essays, and to have the computer able to analyze the answers and then reply in kind. In various design automation activities, such as computer programming, a nonspecialist can be enabled to design a program without having to work in a detailed programming language. Whether the end result is a program or perhaps eventually a circuit design or architectural design, the designer would work in a language familiar to him, with all the burden put on the computer for translating his requirements into the detail needed by the program.

In spite of this widespread interest, natural language communication has been something of a will-o'-the-wisp since mechanical translation activities began, with any number of projects being undertaken but few convincing natural language communications resulting. There has been a certain degree of progress, of course, and some systems appear quite practical if one permits certain restrictions either in the content of messages or in the syntax that can be used. Our object in this chapter is to convey to the reader some indication of the nature of the problems and the degree of difficulty of their solution.

At this point we should introduce a word of caution. As mentioned above, the day of man-machine natural language conversation among intellectual equals is not at hand. We have no formulas by which the exact meaning of a natural language statement can be made known unambiguously to a computer. For that matter, we have no way of *assuring* unambiguous communication among highly intelligent human beings, particularly those with different cultural backgrounds that establish different frames of reference and perhaps different meanings for the same set of words. If a computer is to carry out a truly intelligent conversation in natural language, it must be enabled to recognize all the many syntactic and semantic variations of such language. This has never been done. The approaches to natural language conversation that have produced the most useful results have tended to be based either on simplification of the language used or on mere statistical interpretation of a text, with no attempt to resolve fine points of meaning. In either case, the present state of the art is such that we must consider whether the advantages that we intuitively feel would accrue from the use of natural language would remain after the language or its interpreter has been severely restricted. In other words, perhaps an artificial language would have worked as well, with less interpretation cost, in the long run.

5.2 SOME APPROACHES TO NATURAL LANGUAGE ANALYSIS

In this section we review a representative set of language-processing techniques. Not all are conversational, but the possible use of each technique as part of a larger conversational system should be apparent. The techniques span the following: extraction of key words from a text and use of the array of extracted words as the basis for further communication; restricted language, in which both vocabulary and syntax are heavily constrained, yet the language appears natural; a system that permits unrestricted syntax by the human being but requires that he remain within a given context; and, finally, nonconversational translation of languages.

5.2.1 Key Word Extraction

To some extent, the gist of a natural language, narrative text can be represented by a list of the most frequent information-bearing words used in the text. What constitutes an information-bearing word is very much open to question and may well vary from document to document or person to person, but it is generally agreed that *the, and, or,* and so on convey no substantive information about document content. Similarly, most people would agree that, in this paragraph, the following words do bear substantive information: *natural, language, narrative, text, information, words, document.*

A number of programs exist that compile lists of *key words* from a text. One way to do this is to build a thesaurus and declare that any word in this thesaurus is "key" if it appears in a document.[1] This technique is useful when dealing with a highly specialized field in which key terms may be relatively unambiguous. An opposite approach is to make a dictionary of "common" words, delete them from the text, and then declare that any remaining word occurring with a frequency greater than n is "key." This concept was first introduced by H. P. Luhn[8] and, when put into practice, yields a compromise between precision of indexing and cost of indexing. Both these approaches would benefit from a thesaurus which groups together synonyms and near synonyms, even if just by eliminating variations in form of the same basic word. It is also possible to eliminate high-frequency words on the basis of their high usage rate alone, since usually the most frequent words are common words.

Here is a simplified key word extraction procedure, distilled from several systems. We will show how it would apply to a few short documents. The procedure has two basic steps:

1. Truncate all words to six characters. This both simplifies the handling of data in fixed-word-length computers and eliminates many ending variations on the same root word by amputation of the problem.

2. Look up each truncated word in a common word dictionary. If the word is found, discard it. Otherwise, enter the word on the list of selected words.

Figures 5.1 through 5.3 show three short "documents," each accom-

---

Computer programming consist of writing a list of instructions to be executed by a computer. To do so, a task that the computer is to perform must be stated in terms of the limited number of commands the machine is able to recognize and carry out. Here is where the skill of the programmer manifests itself. Programming, say, a payroll system means to describe it in terms of the precise set of arithmetic instructions, input-output and decision-making commands that will cause a computer to convert a set of weekly time cards into a correct set of paychecks for thousands of employees.

a	7	employees	1	means	1	so	1
able	1	executed	1	must	1	stated	1
and	2					system	1
arithmetic	1	for	1	number	1		
				of	10	tasks	1
be	2	here	1	out	1	terms	2
by	1			output	1	that	2
		in	2	input	1	the	6
cards	1	instructions	2	paychecks	1	thousands	1
carry	1	into	1	payroll	1	time	1
cause	1	is	3	perform	1	to	6
commands	2	it	1	precise	1		
computer	4	itself	1	programmer	1	weekly	1
consists	1			programming	2	where	1
convert	1	limited	1			will	1
correct	1	list	1	recognize	1	writing	1
decision	1	machine	1	say	1		
describe	1	making	1	set	3		
do	1	manifests	1	skill	1		

Figure 5.1 Text sample and word frequency distribution, I.

When we consider a computer as a teaching machine, we find ourselves with a highly versatile device which is capable both of extending a teachers' capabilities and of being limited by them. Teaching through a computer requires a high degree of computer programming skill and a great deal of skill in understanding how students will react to the machine. The teacher must anticipate—by writing a program that will do it for him—all the possible answers his students might give to his questions and then he must be able to program the computer to respond to each student in such a way as to make him learn from his mistakes, if any.

a	9	each	1	machine	2	teacher	1
able	1	extending	1	make	1	teacher's	1
all	1			might	1	teaching	2
and	3	find	1	mistakes	1	that	1
answers	1	for	1	must	2	the	4
anticipate	1	from	1			them	1
any	1			of	4	then	1
as	2	give	1	ourselves	1	through	1
		great	1			to	6
be	1			possible	1		
being	1	he	1	program	2	understanding	1
both	1	high	1	programming	1		
by	2	highly	1			versatile	1
		him	2	questions	1		
capable	1	his	3			way	1
capabilities	1	how	1	react	1	we	2
computer	4			requires	1	when	1
consider	1	if	1	respond	1	which	1
		in	2			will	2
deal	1	is	1	skill	2	with	1
degree	1	it	1	student	1	writing	1
device	1			students	2		
do	1	learn	1	such	1		
		limited	1				

Figure 5.2 Text sample and word frequency distribution, II.

panied by an alphabetized list of words contained in it and their frequencies of occurrence. Figure 5.4 shows the effect of (1) truncating words at six characters to reduce ending variations and (2) applying a low-frequency cut-off of one occurrence and a high-frequency cut-off of five occurrences. The words that remain after this purely statistical process, but that might reasonably be expected to be removed by referral to a common word list, are marked with an asterisk (*). Unfortunately, each of the lists loses some intuitively significant words, designated by a dagger (†), through these procedures. The existence of such words indicates the need for a more sophisticated technique for practical use.

This two-step procedure establishes a list of words that, together

A computer is able to carry out a limited repertoire of instructions or commands. A list of such instructions provided to a computer for a specific purpose is called a program. The art of programming lies in selecting the right sequence of commands to provide the best solution to a problem—one which recognizes all possible variations in input, takes a minimum amount of time for the computer to execute, and which is written in such a way that it can be modified if the problem conditions change. Another factor in the programming art is the amount of time it takes the programmer to write the program and insure that it is error-free.

a	9	error	1	minimum	1	selecting	1
able	1	execute	1	modified	1	sequence	1
all	1					solution	1
amount	2	factor	1	of	6	specific	1
and	2	for	2	one	1	such	2
another	1	free	1	or	1		
art	2			out	1	takes	2
		if	1			that	2
be	1	in	4			the	9
best	1	input	1	possible	1	time	2
		instructions	2	problem	2	to	6
called	1	insure	1	program	2		
can	1	is	5	programmer	1		
carry	1	it	3	programming	2	variations	1
change	1			provide	1		
commands	2	lies	1	provided	1	way	1
computer	3	limited	1	purpose	1	which	2
conditions	1	list	1			write	1
				recognizes	1	written	1
				repertoire	1		
				right	1		

Figure 5.3 Text sample and word frequency distribution, III.

with bibliographic data, can now serve as the index of a document, the approximate equivalent of the information on a library catalog card. Such a file could be queried in the same way as if the key words had been selected by the indexer or if traditional subject headings were used.

Key word extraction can also be used for composing the query to a file. Suppose that instead of a "formatted" query of the type illustrated in Figure 5.5, which is written in an artificial language, a library user could write a short essay describing the material he wants or is interested in. This essay could then be key-word indexed, just as the documents are, and searching accomplished by having the computer compare the two lists of key words. Many different match criteria are possible. We could declare the query and the document indexes to be matched if one-fourth of the query key words appear in the document index; of course, we could vary this threshold in either direction. An example of

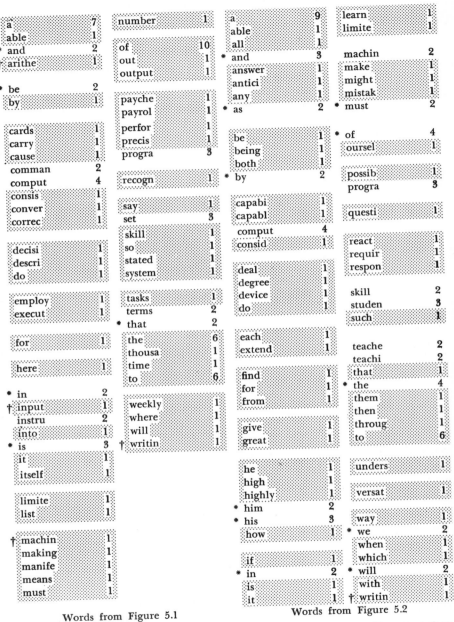

a	7	number	1
able	1	of	10
* and	2	out	1
† arithe	1	output	1
* be	2	payche	1
by	1	payrol	1
cards	1	perfor	1
carry	1	precis	1
cause	1	progra	3
comman	2	recogn	1
comput	4	say	1
consis	1	set	3
conver	1	skill	1
correc	1	so	1
decisi	1	stated	1
descri	1	system	1
do	1	tasks	1
employ	1	terms	2
execut	1	* that	2
for	1	the	6
here	1	thousa	1
* in	2	time	1
† input	1	to	6
instru	2	weekly	1
into	1	where	1
* is	3	will	1
it	1	† writin	1
itself	1		
limite	1		
list	1		
† machin	1		
making	1		
manife	1		
means	1		
must	1		

Words from Figure 5.1

a	9	learn	1
able	1	limite	1
all	1	machin	2
* and	3	make	1
answer	1	might	1
antici	1	mistak	1
any	1	* must	2
* as	2	* of	4
be	1	oursel	1
being	1	possib	1
both	1	progra	3
* by	2	questi	1
capabi	1	react	1
capabl	1	requir	1
comput	4	respon	1
consid	1	skill	2
deal	1	studen	3
degree	1	such	1
device	1	teache	2
do	1	teachi	2
each	1	that	1
extend	1	* the	4
find	1	them	1
for	1	then	1
from	1	throug	1
give	1	to	6
great	1	unders	1
he	1	versat	1
high	1	way	1
highly	1	* we	2
* him	2	when	1
* his	3	which	1
how	1	* will	2
if	1	with	1
* in	2	† writin	1
is	1		
it	1		

Words from Figure 5.2

Figure 5.4 Key word selection. Words from Figures 5.1 and 5.2 are (1) truncated at six characters and (2) rejected (shown by shading) if they occur only once or five or more times. Words marked * would normally be deleted by a common word dictionary.

118

REQUESTOR'S NAME	=	I. ASKEM
FILE NAME	=	CATALOG
SUBJECT	=	COMPUTER $\times$ (PROGRAMMING $+$ USE $+$ APPLICATION) $\times$ PROBLEM
DATE	$\geq$	1965
RETRIEVE		FULL DOCUMENT

Figure 5.5 Example of an artificial query language.

this type of query and the matching key words are shown in Figure 5.6.

The advantage of this approach is its ease of use by the searcher. He need learn no special language. He provides only what amounts to a tutorial description of his area of interest. But there are also disadvantages, primary among them the fact that, if the searcher does not receive from the system what he considers an adequate response, he may not be able to figure out why, or what to do next. Since he does not know the precise logic the computer is using in translating his request into a retrieval search, it is not clear what caused the trouble: whether some word in his request causes the elimination of too may candidates,

Query: Find documents on the subject of computer programming or on how the computer is used in the solution of problems, with emphasis on programming the problem solution.

Key Words in Query		Statistically Selected Key Words
computer	2	computer
documents	1	of
emphasis	1	on
find	1	programming
how	1	solution
in	1	
is	1	
of	2	
on	3	
or	1	
problem	1	
problems	1	
programming	2	
solution	2	
subject	1	
the	4	
used	1	
with	1	

Figure 5.6 A natural language query.

whether he is too general in his description, or too specific. Although there are solutions to these problems, too, they tend to return to the realm of special languages and knowledge of the mechanics of the system's operation.

An additional problem is that the searcher who is able to describe his material in a very detailed and specific way will lose the benefit of this detail because the interpreting program will see only a list of key words, not a syntactic statement. For each new problem, however, there is a solution. To counter the loss of syntactic information, we can make use of a concordance and allow the searcher to specify the relative positions of words that he wants in his documents. He could, then, require the occurrence of the words *information* and *retrieval* in that order, in the same sentence and with fewer than three words intervening. This would allow for selection of such phrases as *information storage and retrieval, information retrieval,* or *information or data retrieval.* He may also specify that a given set of words co-occur in the same sentence or paragraph. Although this does not have quite the specificity of syntax, it is far more precise than selection on the basis of a list of key words remaining after common word deletion. Techniques such as those described in this paragraph were employed successfully in Project LITE,[4] a system designed to retrieve legal information.

5.2.2 Restricted Language

An entirely different approach to natural language communication can be taken by restricting the syntax of the language and the frame of reference of the vocabulary terms. In this technique any statement in the restricted language is a valid natural language statement, but not conversely. On the other hand, any syntactic construction that can once be specified to the language interpretation program can be reused thereafter—the system can be open-ended in its syntactic analysis capability.

The DEACON project,[3] conducted by General Electric, is an example of this kind of system. Frederick Thompson, originator of DEACON, gives this example of an ambiguous sentence, the kind that makes us turn to the use of a restricted language for practical, man-machine discourse:[10] "John believes Mary lies."

Here is an example of a question that DEACON can interpret and answer: WHO IS COMMANDER OF THE 638TH BATTALION? Working from the end of the sentence, DEACON will recognize that the question mark denotes that this is a question. Although this may seem obvious, it is the mark, not the syntax, that so classifies the sentence for DEACON. A declarative sentence ends with an exclamation point. The word

BATTALION is looked up in a thesaurus wherein certain attributes of a battalion in general are specified, with one attribute being its very presence in the thesaurus, for only in that way can a vocabulary element have formal existence. Thus it can be quickly ascertained that the name or designation of a battalion may be 638TH. We are now able to look up 638TH BATTALION in the thesaurus and henceforth to deal with this two-word phrase as denoting a single entity.

The word THE is essentially a modifier of the phrase 638TH BATTALION, and upon its recognition as an article and as a modifier of a legitimate substantive phrase, it can be ignored. Hence THE 638TH BATTALION is equivalent to 638TH BATTALION.

The word OF points out that what precedes it is an attribute of what follows. Since what follows has been found to be a proper substantive, it remains only to check that a valid substantive precedes OF in order for the longer phrase to be valid. We must have the program remember, then, that it should next be encountering an attribute of the 638th Battalion.

COMMANDER is a valid attribute of THE 638TH BATTALION. Hence we now know that the phrase COMMANDER OF THE 638TH BATTALION indicates a single entity that, in a sense, is an attribute of the battalion.

WHO IS is a functional phrase that, coupled with the question mark encountered at the end of the sentence, tells the program that the information sought is what follows IS. DEACON, then, has translated the original sentence, WHO IS THE COMMANDER OF THE 638TH BATTALION, into RETRIEVE THE NAME OF THE COMMANDER OF THE 638TH WHICH IS A BATTALION. We might have written this query in the form

RETRIEVE NAME FOR

UNIT TYPE = BATTALION

UNIT NAME = 638TH

POSITION = COMMANDER

The natural language expression WHO IS ... has been found to be unambiguous and could be translated into this form in a straightforward manner.

In natural language we might have worded our question, "Who has the 638th?" This is perfectly valid usage in the military context, "who has" being understood to mean "who commands"; and the expression *638th*, with nothing for it to modify, will be understood to mean the most obvious 638th, in case there is more than one. Which is the most obvious one is clearly a function of who is asking the question. Although DEACON could be trained to cope with this usage, we cannot envisage explicitly identifying every possible syntactic usage (correct as well as incorrect) of natural language. A system user who is told only that he is dealing with a natural language system might easily employ a syntax not recognizable by the system and be unable to communicate. To use the system effectively, he must be taught what the limitations of the language are, how the machine responds to illegal usages, and how he can recover from communications failures.

5.2.3   Unrestricted Language

Joseph Weizenbaum[11,12] has produced a program called *Eliza*, which, like the Shaw character, can be taught to converse increasingly well. It is a most interesting program to consider because of the smoothness and apparent sophistication of the conversations, which impose virtually no syntactic restrictions on its human conversational partners. The program assumes the human conversant is remaining within an overall context, but it does very little in the way of carrying information over from one portion of the conversation to another. It will not remember what its human partner said an hour ago. An advanced version of *Eliza*, however, seems to be progressing toward a longer memory span.

Figure 5.7 shows a brief sample of early *Eliza* in a conversation written to resemble a psychiatric interview. It should be noted that the requirement for the human conversant to remain in an overall context is restricted to his continued willingness to act (compose messages) as if he were the patient in the interview.

Man: 1.   men are all alike

Machine: 1.   IN WHAT WAY

            2.   they're always bugging us about something or other

            2.   CAN YOU THINK OF A SPECIFIC EXAMPLE

            3.   well, my boyfriend made me come here

            3.   YOUR BOYFRIEND MADE YOU COME HERE

            4.   he says i'm depressed much of the time

            4.   I AM SORRY TO HEAR YOU ARE DEPRESSED

Figure   5.7   Brief *Eliza*-like conversation.[12] *J. Weizenbaum,* Communications of the ACM, *Volume 10, No. 8, August* 1967; *copyright* © 1967, *Association for Computing Machinery, Inc.*

Some longer examples are shown in Figure 5.8. Let us see what kind of sentence analysis logic is needed for this much conversation. The basic concept is to set up certain standard sentence or phrase patterns that may be input to the machine and then to formulate an output sentence based on the input. The rule for recognizing an input pattern is called a *decomposition rule,* and one for reformulation is termed a *reassembly rule.* For example, if the input is HELLO 0 (0 implies any string of characters occurring in this relative position. Hence HELLO followed by anything is a recognizable pattern), the machine reply might be simply HOW DO YOU DO.

A more sophisticated set of rules will use input terms in the output sentence. For example, a decomposition rule could be 0 I AM 0, and a reassembly rule might be WHY ARE YOU 3, the 3 specifying a direct copy of segment 3 of the input sentence, the segments being the phrase represented by the first 0, I AM, and the phrase represented by the second 0. Thus, if the input were OH, I AM TIRED, the output would be WHY ARE YOU TIRED.

Another technique is to change the person of pronouns. If the input sentence reads I DISLIKE DOGS, *Eliza* can change the form and add new words to give WHY DO YOU DISLIKE DOGS? Bear in mind that *Eliza* makes no attempt to understand the words *tired* and *dogs* in these examples.

When the input sentence does not conform to one of the anticipated patterns, a "content-free" message is sent by *Eliza,* which essentially masks the machine's lack of comprehension and keeps the conversation going. In the short conversation shown in Figure 5.7, the first machine response is of this character. It would appear to have meaning following virtually any declarative sentence.

The second machine response, although not actually using any of the words of the preceding input, is obviously context-dependent. This machine response can be triggered by the discovery of ALWAYS in the input sentence, signalling a generalization on the part of the man. A reasonable-sounding response to a generalization is to ask for a specific case.

Exchange 3 shows the use of input words in the output message, with a change of person. The WELL can be discarded. The remainder is of the form

1st person pronoun/noun/verb/1st person pronoun/verb/adverb

The machine reply is generated by converting ME to YOU and MY to YOUR and then repeating the basic sentence. To the responder, this has the appearance of asking for more information. For the programmer, it merely represents a way to make an intelligent-appearing output response related to the input.

Exchange 4 requires the program to recognize *depressed* as an unde-sirable state and then to apply logic similar to that used in line 3. This form of recognition would have to be accomplished by the programmer's anticipating the words that he feels would indicate a state of depression or using a thesaurus to relate words to a concept. This procedure can be tedious, but that is a price that must be paid for communication at this level. Remember, though, that the program we have been illustrating was intended to simulate a psychiatric interview, so that extra effort to recognize a state of depression is not far fetched. It would be quite another thing to expect this program to reply in context if the inter-viewee had stated I'M SLICING MY DRIVES. This admission also indicates something of a state of depression, but the program would probably react with a content-free reply.

The *Eliza* programs seem to work quite well—almost too well, in fact, for they can be deceiving even to programmers. Any given *Eliza* program requires the human conversant to remain in context, and the machine's responses are then programmed to appear to remain in context. The conversation we have shown is not the same as an interrogation program written by a psychiatrist with the intention of diagnosing or treating a patient. There is no implication by Weizenbaum that this program has therapeutic value, but one could easily be fooled into thinking so. An application of *Eliza* that has some value to its user is illustrated in Figure 5.8, which shows a segment of an instructional use.[9] Without detailed analysis we can see the role of inferred context here, for the student actually passes little information to the program. Nevertheless the conversation intuitively seems able to teach and to do so in an interesting way that maximizes self-discovery and the exploration of new ideas by the student.

5.2.4 Translating Natural Language

A natural language translation project that achieved a fair degree of success in a field not distinguished by many triumphs was developed by IBM for the U. S. Air Force.[2] This project considered machine trans-lation to consist of three major steps: *lexical recognition* (basically, a dictionary problem—one of recognizing what word we are dealing with) , *syntax* (recognizing the structural patterns in a text so that words may be classified as to part of speech or role in the structure) , and *semantics* (the resolution of multiple meanings not resolved in earlier steps) .

Because translation requires so many table-search operations, a special-purpose computer was developed, based on a high-speed, high-capacity disk memory. It is not a stored-program computer; the program to do the translation is not explicitly stored as a sequence of commands. Rather, each dictionary entry contains codes that tell the computer what to do in the event a string of input characters matches a dictionary item. Information is written on the disk by a photographic process, rather than by the more popular magnetic means, and the disk has a capacity of 30 million bits with an average access time of 35 milliseconds, both admirable figures for 1961, when the work was completed.

The machine works basically by taking a string of input (or *source language* text) and looking it up in the dictionary. The machine is so designed that the longest possible match will be discovered first. For example, if the input string is HERRINGBONE, it will be translated (if matched by a dictionary word) as a single term. If this string is not matched by a dictionary argument, it would probably find separate matches on the substrings HERRING and BONE and the idiomatic nature of the word would be lost in a literal translation. Idioms longer than a single word, even full sentences, can be stored as well.

A typical entry in the dictionary has the form shown below, but first we should agree on some terminology. An *entry* is the complete package of a word, its definition, and any accompanying instructions to the computer. An *argument* is the input word, the word being looked up, or the word about which a definition is given. An entry, then, is of the form[5]

$$\alpha A_1 A_2 \ldots C \tau T_1 T_2 \ldots \alpha$$

where α is a boundary marker, denoting the beginning of one entry and the ending of the previous one.

$A_1 A_2 \ldots$ represent the characters of the *argument*, written, of course, in the source language.

C represents one or more control characters whose functions are defined below. These control characters largely replace the function of a stored program in other computers.

τ denotes the start of the output string, or *target*, the characters that are the translation of the argument.

$T_1 T_2 \ldots$ are the characters of the *target*.

A string of input characters is loaded into an area of memory, called a *buffer,* and a search is begun. The search, as we have said, is programmed to find the longest possible match between characters of the input string and dictionary arguments. This is done by starting at the beginning, in normal alphabetical order, and searching from A toward Z until the first argument is found that is beyond the input string in the

PLEASE CONSIDER HOW WE MIGHT SYNCHRONIZE TWO CLOCKS TO READ THE 'SAME TIME'. ONE OF THESE CLOCKS IS IN SAN FRANCISCO, THE OTHER IS IN NEW YORK. AS YOU THINK ABOUT THE PROBLEM, ASK ME ANY QUESTIONS THAT OCCUR TO YOU. WHEN YOU ARE READY TO PROPOSE A SYNCHRONIZATION METHOD, TYPE 'READY'. THEN I WILL QUIZ YOU ABOUT YOUR PROPOSED METHOD.

what do you mean by synchronize

FOR THE PRESENT MAKE USE OF THE EVERYDAY MEANINGS OF SUCH PHRASES AS 'SAME TIME' AND 'SYNCHRONIZE'. LATER WE WILL DISCUSS THE MEANING OF THESE TERMS MORE CAREFULLY

may i use telegraph signals

CERTAINLY, FEEL FREE TO USE TELEGRAPH

ready

NOW I WILL QUIZ YOU ON YOUR SYNCHRONIZATION METHOD DOES YOUR METHOD OF SYNCHRONIZATION INVOLVE THE PROPAGATION OF SOME SIGNAL—OR MATERIAL OBJECT—FROM ONE PLACE TO ANOTHER

yes

WHAT KIND OF PROPAGATING SIGNAL OR TRAVELING OBJECT DO YOU PROPOSE TO USE

a watch

WILL YOUR WATCH MOVE AT A SPEED VERY MUCH SMALLER THAN THE SPEED OF LIGHT

of course

GOOD. TRAVELLING CLOCKS CAN BE USED TO SYNCHRONIZE DISTANT CLOCKS TO ARBITRARILY HIGH ACCURACY IF THEY TRAVEL SLOWLY ENOUGH. YOU MAY LEAVE THE PROBLEM BY PUSHING THE 'QUIT' BUTTON TWICE. IF YOU WOULD LIKE TO EXPLORE FURTHER THE MATTERS OF PRINCIPLE ASSOCIATED WITH OTHER METHODS, CHOOSE ANOTHER WAY TO COMMUNICATE BETWEEN THE DISTANT CLOCKS WHAT KIND OF PROPAGATING SIGNAL OR TRAVELING OBJECT DO YOU PROPOSE TO USE

light

Figure 5.8 Use of *Eliza* for instruction.[9] *J. Weizenbaum,* Communications of the ACM, *Volume 10, No. 8, August 1967; copyright © 1967, Association for Computing Machinery, Inc.*

alphabet. Then the search moves backward. If the input string is DICTIONARIES, for example, and the dictionary has it

D

•

•

•

DICTION

DICTIONAR

DICTIONARY

DICTUM

the search will proceed from A to DICTIONARY and then reverse until some

WELL, OF COURSE THE LIGHT SIGNAL WILL NOT FOLLOW THE CUR-
VATURE OF THE EARTH. SO LET US ASSUME THAT SOME SYSTEM
OF RELAY TOWERS IS USED. NOW LET ME ASK, WILL THE LIGHT SIG-
NAL TRAVEL DIRECTLY BETWEEN NEW YORK AND SAN FRANCISCO
OR WILL THE LIGHT SIGNAL TRAVEL TO OR FROM SOME INTER-
MEDIATE POINT

it will travel from st louis in both directions

IS YOUR INTERMEDIATE POINT EQUIDISTANT FROM NEW YORK
AND SAN FRANCISCO

let's say it is, yes

MY UNDERSTANDING IS THAT YOU EXPECT TO USE TWO SIGNALS
AND THAT THESE SIGNALS WILL EITHER CONVERGE ON OR BE
SENT OUT FROM A POINT EQUIDISTANT FROM NEW YORK AND SAN
FRANCISCO. IS MY UNDERSTANDING ON THIS POINT CORRECT

yes

WILL THIS PAIR OF SIGNALS CONVERGE ON THE INTERMEDIATE
POINT OR BE SENT OUT FROM THIS POINT
they will be sent from the point
WILL THE TWO SIGNALS LEAVE THE INTERMEDIATE POINT AT THE
SAME TIME

certainly

AHA, I'VE GOT YOU. YOU ARE TRYING TO SYNCHRONIZE THE NEW
YORK AND SAN FRANCISCO CLOCKS TO READ THE 'SAME TIME'
HOW CAN IT BE VALID TO ASSUME A 'SAME TIME' FOR THE DEPAR-
TURE OF A PAIR OF SIGNALS FROM THE MIDPOINT

because the pair of signals leave from the same point

RIGHT
THE PHRASE 'SAME TIME' HAS AN UNAMBIGUOUS MEANING WHEN
APPLIED TO EVENTS THAT OCCUR NEAR THE SAME POINT IN SPACE.
NOW YOU ARE GOING TO CONTINUE YOUR ARGUMENT BY SAYING
THAT THE TWO SIGNALS THAT START FROM THE MIDPOINT AT THE
SAME TIME WILL PRESUMABLY REACH NEW YORK AND SAN FRAN-
CISCO AT THE SAME TIME. THESE SIGNALS CAN THUS BE USED TO
SYNCHRONIZE THE NEW YORK AND SAN FRANCISCO CLOCKS. IS
THIS THE WAY YOUR ARGUMENT WILL CONTINUE

yes

ONE FINAL QUESTION. WHAT ASSUMPTION ARE YOU MAKING
ABOUT THE SPEEDS OF THE TWO SIGNALS THAT TRAVEL IN OPPO-
SITE DIRECTIONS
that these speeds are equal
VERY GOOD. YOU HAVE DEVISED A VALID METHOD FOR SYNCHRO-
NIZING TWO CLOCKS, ONE IN NEW YORK AND ONE IN SAN FRAN-
CISCO. I AM NOW RETURNING YOU TO THE CTSS SYSTEM

Figure 5.8 Continued

match is achieved. In this case the longest match is with DICTIONAR which
would have some control characters with it indicating that a suffix is expected and where to search for the suffix in the dictionary. A minimum
match is guaranteed by including individual letters in the dictionary, so
that, at worst, there would be a transliteration from source into target
language (or alphabet). Normally, when a match occurs, the target
string is typed as output. Then the characters of the input string that

matched the argument are shifted out of the input buffer, and an equal or smaller number of new characters are shifted in. In our example here, we might shift out DICTIONAR, bringing in IESb (b = blank) as the four leading characters of the input string. This sequence of operations can be varied by use of the control characters.

If the control character μ appears in an entry, followed by another character designated by ρ, the input string matching this entry causes emission of the target as usual, but also causes ρ to be *prefixed* to the remaining characters in the input string. Suppose the input is $I_1I_2I_3 \ldots I_{10}$ and a match has been found for $I_1I_2I_3$ with an entry of the form

$$\alpha I_1 I_2 I_3 \; \mu\rho \; \tau \; \text{TRANSLATION} \; \alpha$$

Then the word TRANSLATION is printed, and the character ρ is moved to the leftmost position of the remaining input string, which becomes $\rho \; I_4 I_5 \ldots$. The ρ need not represent a printable character in either the source or the target alphabets. It may be simply a code used to pass a message to the computer instructing it to translate the following characters with the understanding that state or condition ρ exists, perhaps that a masculine gender has been established, or a past tense. The ρ characters may be used to denote subject context as well as grammatical conditions.

The character ν used in the argument allows any character in the corresponding position of the input string to match. Thus CAT, as input, matches CAν as an argument. So do CAB, CAD, CAM, and so on. Figure 5.9 shows a schematic diagram of the search logic.

However conscientious the lexicographers, situations will arise in which there is more than one possible meaning of an input word and no obvious way to choose among the alternatives. The translator handles such a case by typing out all remaining candidates and leaving it to a human editor to make the final decision. This brings to mind the fact that the objective of a good mechanical translation system need not be to provide publication-quality translations directly. If it can be assumed that all computer output will be reviewed by an editor, the translation program can be relieved of a very heavy burden and need concentrate only on conveying the sense of the input into the target language.

5.3 AN EXAMPLE

For our example, let us take the role of the author of a computer-assisted instruction course that allows students to give text answers. The author has the task of composing a program that will analyze a

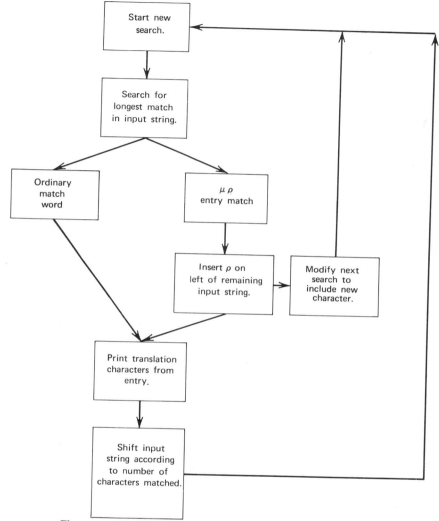

Figure 5.9 Search logic for language translator.[5] *Courtesy IEEE.*

student reply and then compare it, or a processed version of it, with a correct reply supplied by the author. The program must decide whether, or to what extent, the two replies match and what should be done in each recognizable case.

Authors of CAI courses are more interested in teaching than in programming, and they must compromise between a thorough analysis requiring a complex program and a more superficial analysis that can be programmed easily. Computer running time is also a consideration, one that will probably correlate with the complexity of the program. Hence the author will not necessarily want to use the full bag of tricks available in language translation programs.

As in the *Eliza* instructional example, the author *may* find that fluidity of conversation is less important than the ability to discern what the student is trying to say in a single paragraph. Hence he may choose to impose restrictions upon the student (e.g., use a series of short, numbered paragraphs, discussing subject 1 in paragraph 1, . . .) , and he may be unashamed to have his program ask the student the meaning of any word that it does not recognize. In short, he has the opposite situation of the first *Eliza* program illustrated. He has a clearly defined, practical goal to reach. The nature of the conversation that takes place along the way may be of secondary importance to him.

We assume the following repertoire of commands for the course author. Since these are clearly not sufficient for intelligent, two-way discourse, it will be required of the author that he phrase his questions so as to channel the student into desired paths and that he make provision for responses that his program cannot recognize. The commands are as follows:

1. *Common word deletion.* A dictionary is used to remove "non-information-bearing" words from a response.

2. *Punctuation deletion.*

3. *Concordance creation.* Words in a response are ordered alphabetically, with the relative position in the original order stored with the word.

4. *Word frequency count.* The occurrences of each word in the response are counted.

5. *Thesaurus creation and word analyzer.* This can be used to convert different synonyms and forms of a word into a common form to simplify subject analysis.

Note that there is no syntactic analysis here. Any analysis of *groups of words* is left to the author to program for himself. Also, each of these functions would be called as a subroutine in the teaching program, in any order desired by the author. For example, he can call for the concordance-building subroutine before or after removing common words. He should normally delete punctuation before building a concordance in order to remove, for example, the difference between a capitalized word and the same word written in lower case. However, if punctuation is deleted first, an artificial end-of-sentence and end-of-paragraph indicator will have to be put into the text so that the concordance builder can keep track of locations. Before seeing how these facilities might actually be used, let us look more closely at how they work individually.

5.3.1   Common Word Deletion

An alphabetically ordered list of common words will be used for this purpose. Approximately 70 different words in conventional English usage will account for about half the total text.[6] Simple elimination of articles, prepositions, and forms of the verb *to be* will reduce the number of remaining words quite significantly.

As an interesting exercise, you might try composing a list of 50 common words and then eliminating these words from a randomly selected paragraph of this text or from a newspaper article. After this has been done, list the remaining words and see how well you think the list describes the subject matter of the original article or paragraph. Almost always there will be some meaningless words on the list, but we must balance the cost of the effort to remove them with the cost of inefficiencies that result from retaining them.

5.3.2   Punctuation Removal

On a standard keyboard the punctuation marks to be removed are . , ; : ' " ? / () and whatever special symbols are present—the character $ ¢ & and so on. On a communications terminal the up-shift, or case shift, necessary to print most of these characters may be a transmitted character, although it does not print. Thus the numeral 4 is transmitted as 4, but the character $ may be transmitted as ↑ 4 ↓ (↑ for up-shift, ↓ for down-shift). On older teletype terminals, all numerals are uppercase characters and require shift characters as well as key, or printing, characters. To make the decision whether or not to delete a character, in this case 4, it is necessary to consider its context—is it to be printed as indicated (4) or as an alternate character ($)?

Punctuation removal also entails standardization of spacing. As far as word boundaries are concerned, any number of consecutive spaces is equivalent to one space. Extra spaces may be used, by convention, to indicate the end of a sentence or of a paragraph. Commonly, the sequence . b b ↑ (b represents a space or blank which is a transmitted character) signals a new sentence. The period ends the previous sentence, two spaces are skipped, and the initial character of the next sentence is capitalized. This does not work, however, for some teletype terminals, which may have only one case for letters. A convention such as this for denoting the start of a new sentence reduces the chances of the computer making two sentences of MR. SMITH GOES TO TOWN. A new paragraph can be indicated by two carriage returns, followed by a tabulate character or by some fixed number of spaces for indentation.

As we have pointed out, we would probably want to retain a few special symbols to indicate sentence and paragraph boundaries for use by the concordance-building program.

5.3.3 Concordance Creation

A concordance program would probably be written to use a space as a word boundary and the special symbols whose need was pointed out above as sentence and paragraph boundaries. Each word from the text would be entered into the concordance, which would be maintained in alphabetic order, with a notation of location of occurrence, probably position within sentence, sentence number, and paragraph number. Recall that we are dealing with short essays here and have no need for higher organizational entities than the paragraph. As new words are added, they are listed in order. When a word that is already in the concordance is encountered again, only the new location, or address, need be given.

5.3.4 Word Frequency Counting

Much of the logic of word frequency counting is the same as that of concordance building. A list must be made of all words in a text (before or after the elimination of common words, but definitely after the elimination of punctuation). However, instead of recording the locations that would be needed for a concordance, a simple count of the number of occurrences is sufficient. The set of words and accompanying counts is called the *word frequency distribution* of the text. This distribution can be used as an aid in determining whether a student's response to a question approximates the answer written by the author. If the distributions are nearly the same, the texts may be assumed to be closely matched. We must remember, though, that we are measuring a correlation here, and this is not a causal relationship. We cannot prove that, if two word frequency distributions are nearly the same, the original texts are also nearly the same. But the converse is probably true, and the original proposition may hold often enough to justify using this technique for instructional purposes (but perhaps not for final examinations).

The definition of a match can vary. One measure of closeness of fit is

$$m = \sum_i \frac{|a_i - s_i|}{a_i}$$

where a_i is the frequency of occurrence of word i in the author's text, s_i is the frequency of the same word in the student text, $|a_i - s_i|$ means the *absolute value* of $a_i - s_i$ (or the sign ignored), and the symbol $\sum_i$ means to add this entire expression as evaluated for all words in the author's list. If the two distributions are identical, the value of m is zero. If all the s_i are zero (none of the student's words are in the author's distribution), the value of m is the number of words in the author's list. If the two distributions are similar, but not identical, the value of m will be small, but higher than zero.

Look back at Figures 5.1 through 5.3. The first and the last of these are quite similar. The paragraph in Figure 5.2 expresses a different thought, although still related to computer programming, obviously the main subject of the other paragraphs. Figure 5.10 gives the word frequency distributions for these paragraphs, in raw form, and Figure 5.11 shows a condensed list with high- and low-frequency words omitted. To compile this second group of words, we used the frequency cut-offs within each document and then listed any word that remained in any document with its frequency in each. Finally, a value of m is computed for each document pair, using the second word list.

5.3.5 Thesaurus and Word Analyzer

With a large enough thesaurus we would have no need for word analysis. The basic idea is to equate words that convey the same concept, particularly to eliminate minor differences of spelling or inflection—for example, to equate WRITE, WRITES, and WRITING.

To avoid an excessively large thesaurus we would like to be able to identify prefixes and detach them from the root word. The language translation scheme described in Section 5.2.4 could perform this function. Another approach is simply to truncate all words at, say, six characters, thus eliminating a large number of variations but introducing ambiguities not previously present. This technique neatly equates ADVANCe, ADVANCes, and ADVANCing but confounds us by equating COMMUNicate, COMMUNity, and COMMUNist. Nonetheless, as a "quick and dirty" approximation, it has some merit, for we would be really bothered only when a student writes about communists when we thought he should be discussing communities. Even if this happens, there should be enough other words, not so easily confused, that could serve for distribution matching.

If we did have to use a word analyzer, we might store certain pre-

Truncated Word	¶1	¶2	¶3	Truncated Word	¶1	¶2	¶3	Truncated Word	¶1	¶2	¶3	Truncated Word	¶1	¶2	¶3
a	7	9	9	device	–	1	–	make	–	1	–	set	3	–	–
able	1	1	1	do	1	1	–	making	1	–	–	skill	1	2	–
all	–	1	1	each	–	1	–	manife	1	–	–	so	1	–	–
amount	–	–	2	employ	1	–	–	means	1	–	–	soluti	–	–	1
and	2	3	2	error	–	–	1	might	–	1	–	specif	–	–	1
anothe	–	–	1	execut	1	–	1	minimu	–	1	–	stated	1	–	–
answer	–	1	–	extend	–	1	–	mistak	–	1	–	studen	–	3	–
antici	–	1	–	factor	–	–	1	modifi	–	1	–	such	–	1	2
any	–	1	–	find	–	1	–	must	1	2	–	system	1	–	–
arithe	1	–	–	for	1	1	2	number	1	–	–	takes	–	–	2
art	–	2	–	free	–	–	1	of	10	4	6	tasks	1	–	–
as	–	2	–	from	–	1	–	one	–	1	–	teache	–	2	–
be	2	1	1	give	–	1	–	or	–	1	–	teachi	–	2	–
being	–	1	–	great	–	1	–	oursel	–	1	–	terms	2	–	–
best	–	–	1	he	–	1	–	out	1	–	1	that	2	1	2
both	–	1	–	here	1	–	–	output	1	–	–	the	6	4	9
by	1	2	–	high	–	1	–	payche	1	–	–	them	–	1	–
called	–	–	1	highly	–	1	–	payrol	1	–	–	then	–	1	–
can	–	–	1	him	–	2	–	perfor	1	–	–	thousa	1	–	–
capabi	–	1	–	his	–	3	–	possib	–	1	1	throug	–	1	–

cause	1	—	—
change	—	—	1
comman	2	—	2
comput	4	4	3
condit	—	—	1
consid	—	1	—
consis	1	—	—
conver	1	—	—
correc	1	—	—
deal	—	1	—
decisi	1	—	—
degree	—	1	—
descri	1	—	—

	2	2	4
in	2	2	4
input	1	—	1
instru	2	—	2
insure	—	—	1
into	1	—	—
is	3	1	5
it	1	1	3
itself	1	—	—
learn	—	1	—
lies	—	—	1
limite	1	1	1
list	1	—	1
machin	1	2	—

	3	3	5
progra	3	3	5
provid	—	—	1
purpos	—	—	1
questi	—	1	—
react	—	1	—
recogn	1	—	1
repert	—	—	1
requir	—	1	—
respon	—	1	—
right	—	—	1
say	1	—	—
select	—	—	1
sequen	—	—	1

	6	6	6
to			
unders	—	1	—
variat	—	—	1
versat	—	1	—
way	—	1	1
we	—	2	—
weekly	1	—	—
when	—	1	—
where	1	—	—
which	—	1	2
will	1	2	—
with	—	1	—
write	—	—	1
writin	1	1	—
writte	—	—	1

Figure 5.10 Raw word frequency distributions.

Truncated Word	Frequency			
amount	– – 2			
and	2 3 2			
art	– – 2			
as	– 2 –			
be	2 1 1			
by	1 2 –			
comman	2 – 2			
comput	4 4 3	$m_{1,2} = 11.7$	(number words $= 19$)	
for	1 1 2			
him	– 2 –			
his	– 3 –	$m_{2,3} = 24.3$	(number words $= 23$)	
in	2 2 4			
instru	2 – 2			
is	3 1 5			
it	1 1 3	$m_{1,3} = 11.3$	(number words $= 19$)	
machin	1 2 –			
must	1 2 –			
proble	– – 2			
progra	3 3 5			
provid	– – 2			
set	3 – –			
skill	1 2 –			
studen	– 3 –			
such	– 1 2			
takes	– – 2			
teache	– 2 –			
teachi	– 2 –			
terms	2 – –			
that	2 1 2			
time	1 – 2			
we	– 2 –			
which	– 1 2			
will	1 2 –			

Figure 5.11 Condensed word frequency distributions.

fixes and suffixes, such as a-, con-, sub-, anti- or -ing, -ed, -ation, and delete these whenever they are found. This will leave only the root word, which is then not necessarily either a properly spelled English word or the actual root (SITTING minus -ING = SITT). However, there is no need for good looks in our system, and we can fill out thesaurus with these roots as well as with properly spelled words. Again, we remind the reader that we are discussing quick approximations that may be useful and economical in on-line instructional systems, not techniques for use on conventional language translation programs.

5.3.6   Using the Commands

Suppose we have asked a student to describe computer programming. He might have given the answer shown in Figure 5.1, and the instructor might have supplied the paragraph of Figure 5.3 as his standard against which student replies are to be judged. The instructor's program for evaluating student replies must include processing of his own model response as well as the student reply. We show, below, the steps the instructor might have taken to perform this analysis and, in Figures 5.12 through 5.16, the results of applying these operations to the two replies.

1. Remove punctuation (Figure 5.12).
2. Delete common words (Figure 5.13).
3. Convert words to thesaurus classes (Figure 5.14).
4. Build concordance (Figure 5.15).
5. Compute word frequency distribution (Figure 5.16).
6. Compute m.
7. If $m \geqslant 25$, consider distributions to have matched, give grade of A.
8. If $m \geqslant 20$, consider distributions partially matched, give grade of C.
9. If $m < 20$, assume failure to match, tell student his response was inadequate, ask for another answer.

---

computer programming consists of writing a list of instructions to be executed by a computer. to do so a task that the computer is to perform must be stated in terms of the limited number of commands the machine is able to recognize and carry out. here is where the skill of the programmer manifests itself. programming say a payroll system means to describe it in terms of the precise set of arithemetic instructions input output and decision making commands that will cause a computer to convert a set of weekly time cards into a correct set of paychecks for thousands of employees.

(*a*) Student response

Figure 5.12 Removal of punctuation.

a computer is able to carry out a limited repertoire of instructions or commands. a list of such instructions provided to a computer for a specific purpose is called a program. the art of programming lies in selecting the right sequence of commands to provide the best solution to a problem one which recognizes all possible variations in input takes a minimum amount of time for the computer to execute and which is written in such a way that it can be modified if the problem conditions change. another factor in the programming art is the amount of time it takes the programmer to write the program and insure that it is error free.

(*b*) Instructor's model response

Figure 5.12 Removal of punctuation (*Continued*).

---

computer programming consists writing list instructions executed computer. task computer perform stated terms limited number commands machine able recognize carry. skill programmer manifests. programming payroll system means describe terms precise set arithmetic instructions input output decision making commands cause computer convert set weekly time cards correct set paychecks thousands employees.

(*a*) Student response with common words deleted

computer able carry limited repertoire instructions commands. list instructions provided computer specific purpose called program. art programming lies selecting right sequence commands provide best solution problem recognizes possible variations input minimum amount time computer execute written way modified problem conditions change. factor programming art amount time programmer write program insure error free.

(*b*) Instructor's model with common words deleted

Figure 5.13 Removal of common words.

---

computer program consist write list instruction execute computer. task computer perform state term limit number command machine able recognize carry. skill program manifest. program payroll system mean described term precise set arithmetic instruction input output decision make command cause computer convert set week time card correct paycheck thousand employee.

(*a*) Student reply

computer able carry limit repertoire instruction command. list instruction provide computer specific purpose call program. art program lie select right sequence command provide best solution problem recognize possible variation input minimum amount time computer execute write way modify problem condition change. factor program art amount time program write program insure error free.

(*b*) Instructor's model

Figure 5.14 Reduction to thesaurus classes.

able	2–1	input	4–11	program	1–2
arithmetic	4–9	instruction	1–6		3–2
			4–10		4–1
card	4–22	limit	2–6		
carry	2–12	list	1–5	recognize	2–11
cause	4–16				
command	2–8	machine	2–9	set	4–8
	4–15	make	4–14		4–19
computer	1–1	manifest	3–3	skill	3–1
	1–8	mean	4–4	state	2–4
	2–2			system	4–3
	4–17	number	2–7		
consist	1–3			task	2–1
convert	4–18	output	4–12	term	2–5
correct	4–23				4–6
		paycheck	4–24	time	4–21
decision	4–13	payroll	4–2		
describe	4–5	perform	2–3	week	4–20
			4–1	write	1–4
employee	4–26	precise	4–7		
execute	1–7				

(a) Concordance of student response

able	1–2	factor	4–1	provide	2–3
amount	3–17	free	4–10		3–8
	4–4			purpose	2–6
art	3–1	input	3–15		
	4–3	instruction	1–6	recognize	3–12
			2–2	repertoire	1–5
best	3–9	insure	4–9	right	3–5
call	2–7	lie	3–3	select	3–4
carry	1–3	limit	1–4	sequence	3–6
change	3–26	list	2–1	solution	3–10
command	1–7			specific	2–5
	3–7	minimum	3–16		
computer	1–1	modify	3–23	time	3–18
	2–4				4–5
	3–19	possible	3–13		
condition	3–25	problem	3–11	variation	3–14
			3–24		
error	4–10	program	2–8	way	3–22
execute	3–20		3–2	write	3–21
			4–2		4–7
			4–6		
			4–8		

(b) Concordance of instructor's model

Figure 5.15 Concordances.

able	1	limit	1	set	2
arithmetic	1	list	1	skill	1
				state	1
card	1	machine	1	system	1
carry	1	make	1		
cause	1	manifest	1	task	1
command	2	mean	1	term	2
computer	4			thousand	1
consist	1	number	1	time	1
convert	1				
correct	1	output	1	week	1
				write	1
decision	1	paycheck	1		
describe	1	payroll	1		
		perform	2		
employee	1	precise	1		
execute	1	program	3		
input	1	recognize	1		
instruction	2				

(a) Student distribution

able	1	input	1	recognize	1
amount	2	instruction	2	repertoire	1
art	2	insure	1	right	1
best	1	lie	1	select	1
		limit	1	sequence	1
call	1	list	1	solution	1
carry	1			specific	1
change	1	minimum	1		
command	2	modify	1	time	2
computer	3				
condition	1	possible	1	variation	1
		problem	2		
error	1	program	5	way	1
execute	1	provide	2	write	2
factor	1	purpose	1		
free	1				

(b) Instructor's model distribution

Figure 5.16 Word frequency distributions.

5.4 CONCLUSION

There is some difference of opinion among research and development workers in the field as to whether the effort to achieve man-machine natural language communication is worth the effort. It has also been questioned whether what we call *natural language* is necessarily the most natural language to use for problem solving.[7] The point made is that an activity such as telling a computer how to perform an intricate function in detail may best be done by using a precisely defined vocabulary and a syntax suitable to the function. Nonetheless, the lure of natural language communication is with us, and we may expect to see a continuing trend toward its use, or its approximation, in all forms of man-machine communication.

REFERENCES

1. Artandi, Susan, and Stanley Baxendale, *Project Medico, First Progress Report,* Graduate School of Library Science, Rutgers, The State University, New Brunswick, N. J., January 1968

2. Craft, J. L., E. H. Goldman, and W. B. Strohm, "A Table Look-up Machine for Processing of Natural Languages," *IBM Journal of Research and Development,* **5,** 3 (July 1961), 192–203.

3. Craig, James A., Susan C. Berezner, Homer C. Carney, and Christopher R. Longyear, "DEACON: Direct English Access and Control," *Proceedings of the AFIPS 1966 Fall Joint Computer Conference,* Spartan Books, New York, 1966, pp. 365–380.

4. Dietmann, Donald C., "Using LITE for Research Purposes," *U. S. Air Force JAG LAW Review,* VIII, 6 (November-December 1966), 11–19.

5. Galli, E. J., "The Stenowriter—A System for the Lexical Processing of Stenotypy," *IRE Transactions on Electronic Computers,* April 1962, pp. 187–199.

6. Herdan, G., *Language as Choice and Chance,* P. Noordhoff N. V., Groningen, 1956, p. 15.

7. Ingerman, P. Z., in a review of "Foundations of the Case for Natural-Language Programming," by Mark Halpern, in *Computing Reviews,* **8,** 2 (March-April 1967), 128.

8. Luhn, H. P., "The Automatic Creation of Literature Abstracts," *IBM Journal of Research and Development,* **2,** 2 (April 1958), 159–65.

9. Taylor, Edwin, quoted in Weizenbaum, "Contextual Understanding by Computers" (see Reference 11).

10. Thompson, Frederick B., "English for the Computer," *Proceedings of the 1966 AFIPS Fall Joint Computer Conference,* Spartan Books, New York, 1966, pp 349–364.

11. Weizenbaum, Joseph, "Contextual Understanding by Computers," *Communications of the ACM,* **10,** 8 (August 1967), 474–480.

12. Weizenbaum, Joseph, "ELIZA—A Computer Program for the Study of Natural Language Communication Between Man and Machine," *Communications of the ACM,* **9,** 1 (January 1966), 36–45.

RECOMMENDED ADDITIONAL READING

1. Bar-Hillel, Yehoshua, *Language and Information*, Addison-Wesley, Reading, Mass., 1964.
2. Borko, Harold, *Automated Language Processing*, John Wiley, New York, 1967.
3. Cherry, Colin, *On Human Communication*, 2d Ed., The MIT Press, Cambridge, Mass., 1966.
4. Edmundson, H. P., *Natural Language and the Computer*, McGraw-Hill, New York, 1963.
5. Locke, W. N., and A. D. Booth eds., *Machine Translation of Languages*, Technology Press of the Massachusetts Institute of Technology and John Wiley, Cambridge, Mass., and New York, 1955.
6. Oettinger, Anthony G., *Automatic Language Translation*, Harvard University Press, Cambridge, Mass., 1960.

Part II Basic Interactive Systems

Chapter Six

Information Retrieval

6.1 INTRODUCTION

Information retrieval is the selective recovery of information from storage. It uses criteria supplied by a requestor to discriminate between wanted and unwanted information. The information retrieved may be directly useful data, such as telephone numbers, or references to other information, such as catalog or index cards. Instead, it may be text, pictures, or records in other media which will have to be further read or scanned for the information actually desired. Some authors distinguish between systems that retrieve directly useful data and those that retrieve only records to be further scanned, the former being called *data* or *fact retrieval systems* and the latter *document retrieval systems*. We prefer not to make this distinction in a definition but to consider an information retrieval system to be one that retrieves symbols from a store, regardless of the form of the symbols or the purpose they are to serve. Indeed, the difference between facts and unevaluated documents may vary from user to user.

A working retrieval system needs to be concerned not only with putting information into files, but also with taking it out and changing the content of files. The last aspect of information retrieval is not always recognized for the important role it plays, but unless files contain correct information we cannot get what we want from them. Keeping files current can easily take as much effort and ingenuity as searching them. A retrieval system, then, acquires information, stores it, maintains it, and retrieves it. In most systems a substantial amount of work in these areas is performed by human beings, even if machine supported. For example,

145

in most libraries or document collections, the items are indexed manually and the index is stored in the computer for use in the retrieval process. But it is likely that more manpower is devoted to preparing these input records than to preparing retrieval requests or, in an all-manual system, to performing retrieval searches. Some systems—IBM's ITIRC,[8] for example—do not catalog documents in the traditional sense but prepare an abstract that is then entered into the computer in its entirety. ITIRC, however, requires careful coding of the search requests. This is done manually, and then the search is carried out automatically. It seems, therefore, that some amount of human effort is needed in the catalog-store-retrieve cycle, but different systems make different selections of the phases to be mechanized.

Information retrieval, in the broad context we shall consider, has two major facets: (1) *file processing,* or the mechanics of designing, organizing, searching, and modifying files of information; and (2) *language*—the design of languages for document description in index records or queries, the interpretation of these languages by search and file maintenance programs, the strategy of query formulation, and the evaluation of the results of a query.

The file-handling aspects of retrieval pervade almost all areas of data processing, even the purely scientific computing field. In space exploration, for example, vast quantities of raw information are taken from telemetry signals, recorded, and then later used, as needed, for particular computations. In order to do this, individually useful data sets must be extracted from the totality of information collected. Information retrieval also plays a large part in time-sharing computer operations, where rapid and efficient retrieval of data as well as of program segments is required.

It is the language aspect of information retrieval that has traditionally received the most attention. The major difference between a system that retrieves portions of programs for a time-sharing system and one that retrieves documents from a library is the certainty with which the time-sharing system designer knows what his search criteria will be. Contrast this degree of certainty with the problem encountered by a librarian, who cannot anticipate what users will want to search for, except within quite general bounds. Much of the effort that goes into retrieval systems, then, is devoted, not so much to the mechanics of retrieval, as to the design of languages. Indexing languages are needed that are general enough to describe documents well but also specific enough to be interpreted by a computer program. Query languages must also be well balanced between expressiveness, efficiency, and effectiveness. We must recognize that, in cataloging or indexing a book, we are replacing its contents with a few simple descriptors expressed in what is usually a primitive language, and that this index will serve as the basis for making decisions on what documents we want to retrieve, even if the retrieval criteria we wish to use are quite complex or subtle. The selection of the indexing language and the skill with which it is used play a far greater role in determining retrieval system effectiveness than any other single factor.

The earliest on-line information retrieval systems tended to be concerned mostly with file processing and involved relatively few language difficulties. They were systems concerned with airline reservations, inventory status, stock price quotations, and the like. Systems with significant language-processing functions were reported in the literature but never achieved general acceptance or popularity.[3] The opportunity for rapid interaction with a computer, however, is appealing to those faced with language problems. Hence systems with this capability have been postulated for many years,[1, 4] for they give the user the chance to browse rapidly and to utilize the speed of the machine to enable him to make numerous trials in his efforts to overcome the many ambiguities of indexing languages. In this way, man can put himself "in the loop" in the semantic decision-making process and not be forced to have all decisions made vicariously, on the basis of a deterministic program that is instructed what to do in every definable case but cannot cope with the inevitable unrecognizable situation.

In this chapter, we shall review the principal elements of an information retrieval system, then consider the role of interactive, or on-line, systems, and finally describe a hypothetical system in operation.

6.2 ELEMENTS OF AN INFORMATION RETRIEVAL SYSTEM

We shall consider an information retrieval system as consisting of six elements, although some may not be explicit in any given system. Briefly, these are:

1. Files of information.
2. A language for expressing this information.
3. A language for querying the files, certainly related to the language of the files but not necessarily identical to it.
4. A search program that scans files on the basis of the query and recovers the specified information.
5. Search strategy, a concept used by the searcher in deciding how to formulate a query, to evaluate its results, and to iterate the process.

6. A maintenance program for making additions, changes, or deletions in the files.

6.2.1. Files

We can look at the basic unit of information to be stored in a retrieval system as a *record,* a set of data elements about a single entity or subject. A typical record is a library catalog card or a bank statement. Both are physically distinct from other records of their respective files and entirely concerned with a single subject (book or depositor), although they may make reference to other records or files (as a catalog card may suggest "see ———"). Records consist of information *fields, sets,* or *arrays.* Records, in turn, are members of files. A *file* is then an array of records.

A *field* is a set, or grouping, of characters or bits. It may be a number, name, line of natural language text, or code. Fields, in turn, may also be grouped into sets. Thus the imprint of a book is the collection of fields concerning its publication—the publisher, place, and date. An *array* is a set of identically structured elements, either of fields or of sets. We might have an array of temperature readings, one per hour, or an array of papers published by an author, each element of the array containing title, date, and publisher.

The terminology of information retrieval is not settled, and the reader may find the terms just defined used in somewhat different senses in the literature. Some new terminology is now coming into play, to a large extent to differentiate more clearly between the information structures stored in a system and the physical memory configuration in which these structures are stored. Records, for example, are not always physically distinct from each other, for it may be wasteful of space to make them so. For example, how can we store 81-character records on 80-column punched cards? Logically, it is perfectly permissible to start the next record in the column following the end of the last one, so that record 2 would start in column 2 of card 2, record 3 would start in column 3 of card 3, etc. This, of course, can make processing of the file something of a challenge; however, the storage is compact, and where there is enough information and storage is expensive, cost may be the dominating consideration.

In the terminology coming into prominence, we have characters, as before, but these are sometimes called *bytes,* since they are not always used to represent a printed character, but are the smallest unit of data transference between major computer components. Characters comprise *words* or *fields,* the term *word* being ambiguous and referring either to a field of arbitrary length or to a fixed number of characters that comprise a unit of addressing and data transference by the computer. These are grouped into *arrays,* defined as before, or *structures,* which are sets of fields, not necessarily all the same. Array elements can be structures as well as repeating fields. What was termed a *record* now may be called a *major structure,* and a *file* a *data set.* Using these terms frees us to employ *file* to mean a physical unit of storage and *record* to designate a physical subdivision of a memory unit. Thus a card reader can be a file and a card a record, or a disk unit can be a file and a track a record. Figure 6.1 shows these structural relationships graphically.

File organization [6] is concerned with how smaller- or lower-order structural elements are combined to make larger ones, and how they are sequenced within the larger structures. Elements of an array (for example, records of a file) are usually put in order according to the value of some field within the array element. A file of records about bank accounts will probably be in order, or sorted, on the field *customer name* or *customer account number.* This field is called the *sort key.* Implicitly a part of each record is a statement of where the next record is to be

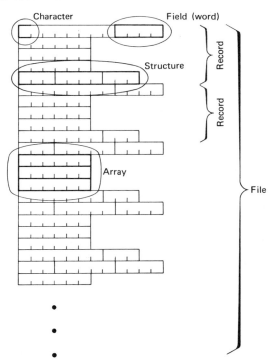

Figure 6.1 Structural elements of a file.

found—the next record in alphabetic order will be the next physical record in the file. This indicator is often termed a *pointer*. By making the pointer to the next logical record or array element explicit, a number of interesting file organization techniques are possible. This means we want to store, in each record, the location of the next logical record and not leave this to be understood.

Let us pause first to consider the burden imposed by the requirement that the next logical record always be the next physical record. This may seem the "natural" way to organize a file, and it is certainly the most common. But what happens when we want to insert a new record into a file? We must push apart the existing ones in order to make the insertion. This is simple enough when the records are cards standing upright in an incompletely filled file drawer. Complications begin to arise, however, when the drawer becomes full, and it is necessary to move some cards from the back of one drawer or tray to the front of the next, a process that may have to be repeated more than once until a drawer with free space is finally encountered. In a computer the records, on magnetic disk or a magnetic tape, cannot be so conveniently pushed along to make room for new ones. If records are to be moved from their positions on these memory media, they must be recopied from the old to the new positions. This is expensive and can consume far more time than was required to find the position into which the insertion was to be made. Thus, as we have previously noted, file maintenance time can far exceed search time in a retrieval system.

Now let us consider the file organizations that make use of an explicit pointer, or linkage, from one element to the next.[5] A *chain* consists of a set of records or array elements that contain explicit pointers instead of the implicit assumption that the next logical record follows in the next physical position. The structure within the record may remain the traditional one, in which the next logical field is the adjacent physical field. A chain is illustrated in Figure 6.2. Use of this structure would permit a librarian changing a catalog file to make a notation on an existing card that the next logical card is to be found in the last drawer in the file, where all the excess space is collected. The new last card would then point to the card following the position where the insert was logically made. This requires a bit of bookkeeping on the part of the librarian, but no wholesale relocation of cards. In a computer, these changes can be made within the existing disk records, with no requirement for any records to be recopied in order to insert a new record in a file. This is not a particularly simple system for people to use and is not recommended as such. Whereas index cards are relatively easy for people to move, the recording of pointers is comparatively

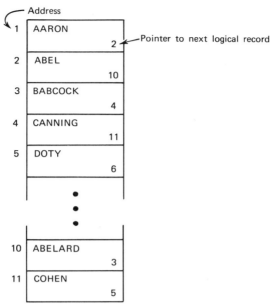

Figure 6.2 A chained file. Each record contains a pointer to the next logical record, which need not be the next physical record.

difficult. For computers, dealing with records on disk memories, the conditions are reversed.

A *list* is a chain of individual data elements. In the usual definition, a list may be referred to, from a point outside itself, only at its top, or first, logical element. A list consists of *cells* that contain, in pure form, a *datum* and a *pointer*, although either of these may have to serve a dual role. For example, a special symbol must be placed in either field of the cell to indicate the end of the list, that is, the fact that no information follows. A list structure is illustrated in Figure 6.3. It is possible to use more than one datum or more than one pointer in any cell.

A list may have another list as an element. This can easily be accomplished by replacing a datum with a pointer to the beginning of another list, with the pointer originally in this cell used to point to the next logical element of the original list. The datum must then be capable of indicating whether it is being used as an item of data or as a pointer to a subordinate list. Any single datum in a list can be expanded into a sublist by changing the datum part of the cell into a pointer to the sublist. For example, suppose we have a cell of an existing list that is used to store a single number representing *location*. We wish, now, to be more explicit and to change this into a list of numbers showing *lati-*

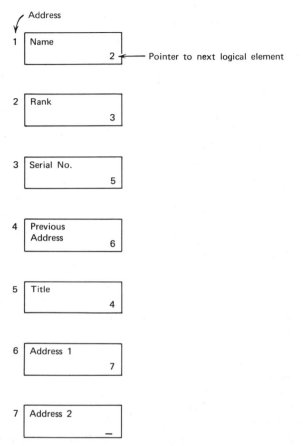

Figure 6.3 A list. Each cell points to the next logical cell comprising an information structure. Any cell (here *previous address*) may, in turn, point to a sublist rather than contain a datum.

tude, longitude, and *altitude.* To do this we can convert the original location datum to a pointer to *latitude,* make the pointer in the latitude cell point to *longitude,* and make *longitude* point to *altitude.* The pointer in the altitude cell can point back to the old location cell (now the *top* of a new sublist), or it can simply indicate *end of list.* This is shown in Figure 6.4.

Lists are useful to programmers when the structure, as well as the content, of files is subject to frequent change. Although the searching of a list may be less efficient than the searching of a contiguous file, changing the structure of an existing record is no more difficult than changing the content of a conventionally organized file.

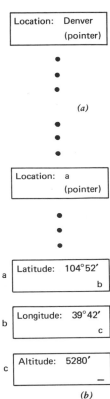

Figure 6.4 Creating a sublist. (*a*) *Location* is initially a single datum within a list, here shown as a city name. We now wish to expand the method of representing location and to use three fields: *latitude, longitude,* and *altitude*. (*b*) The datum in the *location* cell is replaced with a pointer to a newly created sublist of three elements concerned with location data.

A *ring* is similar to a list, but each field points to the location of the next logical one. The last field points back to the first. The search program (for such a technique is almost certainly restricted to computer systems) can start searching at any point in the ring and is always assured it will find the pointer to the next field. In this way structures can be expanded in size whenever convenient, added, or deleted in their entirety. Rings are of great significance in graphic processing, where, with a single stroke of a light pen, a designer can create, delete, or change a complex information structure. Moreover, each element in a ring may be a member of another ring. In the illustration in Figure 6.5 the group of fields *name—rank—serial number—address—title* constitutes a ring. A *ring structure* is created if we link all names in a ring, perhaps pointing in alphabetical order; all ranks, perhaps in seniority; and so on.

It is always desirable to sequence a file on the basis of the field to be used as a search term. If personnel records are always to be searched on the basis of Social Security number, this field becomes the basis for sequencing, or the sort key. When we cannot predict the search fields, or when we know there will be more than one (as is generally the case), we may have to do a search with no ordering of records to guide us and to speed the process. In other words, when we search on the basis of a sort key, we can tell when we are getting "near," we may be able to compute an approximate starting point (there is no use looking in the first of twenty file drawers for the W's), and we can easily tell when we have passed all possible records that could satisfy the query. On the other hand, to search a library catalog on, say, *publisher,* means looking

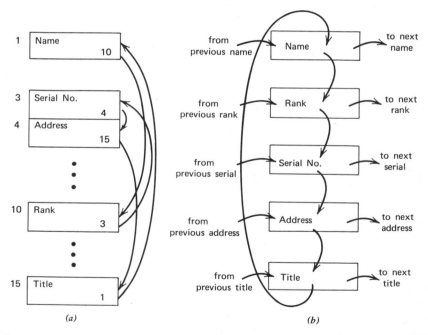

(a)   (b)

Figure 6.5 A ring structure. (*a*) A *ring* is a list in which the last element points to the first, and entry can be at any element. (*b*) A *ring structure* is an interconnected set of rings. Here, a ring descriptive of an individual person contains elements linked to a ring of names, a ring of all majors, a ring of all residents of Alexandria, etc.

at each card, for the order of the file provides us no help. To overcome this problem, we can create indexes of files, or tables that tell what record contains a given value of a given field. We could create an index for each field of a record, but this is rarely necessary.

Figure 6.6 illustrates a file, sorted on *name* with indexes for two additional fields, which provide a ready reference from these fields to record numbers. Thus searches on the sort key, *name,* or on the two fields for which there are indexes, can be carried out quickly and efficiently. A search on any other field, say *location,* however, would require a tedious search of every record. Because the indexes represent a rearranging of the information they contain, they are often called *inverted indexes* or *cross indexes.* The use of some equivalent of these indexes is virtually required in on-line systems, if machine interaction with a man is to be carried out at a useful rate.

List, ring, or chain structures, although alleviating some structural problems, do not remove our concern for file sequence. Even though the fields comprising a record are physically scattered, they are connected by pointers to the next field of a record and to the beginning of the next

Main File - sorted on name

AARON	CAPT.	PILOT
WASHINGTON		
ABEL	LT.	NAVIGATOR
LOS ANGELES		
ABELARD	MAJ.	PERSONNEL OFFICER
CHICAGO		
BABCOCK	MAJ.	PILOT
WASHINGTON		
CANNING	CAPT.	PHYSICIAN
HONOLULU		
COHEN	LT.	PILOT
WASHINGTON		

Inverted File - rank

CAPT.	AARON
	CANNING
LT.	ABEL
	COHEN
MAJ.	ABELARD
	BABCOCK

Inverted File - occupational specialty

NAVIGATOR	ABEL
PERSONNEL OFFICER	ABELARD
PHYSICIAN	CANNING
PILOT	AARON
	BABCOCK
	COHEN

Figure 6.6 Inverted index files.

logical record. When we search a file for a given logical record, we use this chain of pointers to find the desired record. But there are not necessarily pointers from every field to the next record containing the same or the "next" value of the field. In other words, we must still devote energy to assist a search program to find the "next" record and to decide how many different interpretations of "next" we will allow. The decisions will effect storage space (for pointers) and search time (more pointers reduce search time).

6.2.2. Languages for File Data

Much of information retrieval has to do with the interpretation and translation of languages. A document or other information to be retrieved is represented by an information record written in some language, which may be natural English but more probably is an artificial language designed just for the purposes of simplifying the storage and retrieval of information. A book coming into a typical library is classified by subject and then has catalog cards made out for it, describing its title, author, subject, publisher, etc. Although some of this description is in natural language, some is in a condensed, highly structured language used to describe subjects. Most libraries actually use two kinds of classification— a single hierarchical term under which the book is to be physically filed, and possibly several subject headings for which catalog card entries are made. If the user of a library is adept at expressing his needs in these terms, he can accomplish effective retrieval. If he is not so skilled or does not use the library staff to help him, he may easily miss the material he wants.

Other artificial languages may be devised to represent other forms of information. Thus, to store and process data on inventory status, a corporation might devise a language to describe each of its products by a product-type code, specific item code, color code, and shipping weight. For example, a single code might contain numbers representing the following: kitchen appliances (product type), portable dishwasher (specific product), white (color), and 200 pounds (shipping weight); and these might be combined into a compact numeric field such as 12 1234 1 2, where the individual numbers stand for the four items described.

The use of artificial languages and codes did not originate with the advent of data processing. They serve the same purpose in nonmechanized systems, that of compacting information records and simplifying filing operations, particularly in the sense of having a uniform system for all persons who use the file. What is peculiar to data processing is that the computer must to some extent interpret these codes and languages, and any slight errors, inconsistencies, or mismatches cannot be resolved by a quick mental decision by the searcher. If, for example, a clerk searching an inventory file for white dishwashers assumes the color code is w, he will quickly see that all the codes are numeric and will realize that white has to be represented by some code other than w. If he asks the computer to make such a search, however, it may well blindly continue to search for w and never discover that this code is nonexistent in the language. Of course, the computer can be programmed to look for errors in coding, and one of the major design decisions of a retrieval system is the extent to which such error checks are to be made automatically, and the procedure to be followed when a mistake is detected.

We call the language used to express information stored, maintained, and searched by a retrieval system an *index language*. The requirements for a language that represents information in a retrieval system are (1) that it express the concepts needed to an adequate degree, (2) that it be sufficiently unambiguous, (3) that it be compact in its use of storage space, and (4) that it be inexpensive to use. The importance of each of these factors will, of course, vary considerably from user to user and application to application. A language that is adequate for a grade school library may not be sufficiently sophisticated for a research laboratory library. An indexing or cataloging system that is highly expressive and compact may be so hard for some people to learn and use as to render it impractical. Languages that are unambiguous may also be unexpressive because of the need to insure that one term can never be mistaken for another, in any context. On the other hand, people are good resolvers of semantic ambiguity, even if computers are not, and they do not require that their languages be free of this characteristic, as is certainly demonstrated by the ambiguity of natural language.

6.2.3 Languages for Querying

Query languages, those used to express the criteria for selecting information from a store, must express more complex concepts than are required of either index languages or the compact codes used directly to store information. The principal difference is that the query language must be able to make conditional statements. It may also be called upon— and this is the trend in modern systems—to transmit instructions for some processing of retrieved data. An index language may simply state that a document is about subject a, was written by author x, has title y, etc. The query, however, must be able to express the searcher's interest in retrieving, for example, any material either on both subjects a and b, or on subject c, or anything written by x after date z. It may have to be able to do a calculation on retrieved data and then make a selection decision on the result. For example, we might want to retrieve the names of all bank customers who have made more than n deposits or have written more than m checks or have a balance greater than b during a given time period. Although this could be accomplished by having a running count of transactions stored as part of the client's statement, we cannot usually anticipate every possible calculation that a searcher may want. Thus it may prove more economical in the long run to enrich the query language with the ability to make these calculations as they are needed than to store the information, in advance, in every record.

Although the query language need not be identical to the index language, the two must be coordinated. If the vocabulary terms are not identical, they must be translatable back and forth. They should have about the same degree of expressiveness in regard to subject content, for it is pointless to have a query language capable of asking for the color of an object if there is no way to express this concept in the index language. Similarly, a search for documents on conservative economic policy in the United States in 1918 may have to be generalized to a search of economic history in many library systems.

Let us consider a few examples of query languages. Suppose we are interested in retrieving information from a library on this subject: the use of computers in tactical military operations. We would formulate a separate query for each different index language and structure in use by retrieval systems we might like to search.

If the library contained mainly books, we would approach the card catalog, or its mechanized equivalent, with a few subject headings in mind. If the query had to be submitted in writing, we might select from among the following Library of Congress subject headings concerning military operations:

> MILITARY ART AND SCIENCE
> MILITARY ENGINEERING (ELECTRONICS IN)
> TACTICS

We would like our book to be about military tactical operations and computers; hence we would also like one of the following terms to be applicable to the book:

> ELECTRONIC DATA PROCESSING
> ELECTRONIC DIGITAL COMPUTERS
> INFORMATION STORAGE AND RETRIEVAL SYSTEMS
> PROGRAMMING (ELECTRONIC COMPUTERS)

When composing the query, we should bear in mind that a chapter devoted to computers in a book on military operations will not necessarily cause the book to be indexed under computers. Therefore we may not want to insist that one term from each list be present in the book's catalog entry. If we do not so insist, we will get a lot of extraneous material about one subject or the other. Our query, then, might read as follows:

MILITARY ART AND SCIENCE

or

MILITARY ENGINEERING (ELECTRONICS IN)

or

TACTICS

or

ELECTRONIC DATA PROCESSING

or

ELECTRONIC DIGITAL COMPUTERS

or

INFORMATION STORAGE AND RETRIEVAL SYSTEMS

or

PROGRAMMING (ELECTRONIC COMPUTERS)

or, taking a chance on both subjects being prominent:

$$
\left[
\begin{array}{c}
\text{MILITARY ART AND SCIENCE} \\
\text{or} \\
\text{MILITARY ENGINEERING} \\
\text{(ELECTRONICS IN)} \\
\text{or} \\
\text{TACTICS}
\end{array}
\right]
\;\text{AND}\;
\left[
\begin{array}{c}
\text{ELECTRONIC DATA PROCESSING} \\
\text{or} \\
\text{ELECTRONIC DIGITAL COMPUTERS} \\
\text{or} \\
\text{INFORMATION STORAGE AND} \\
\text{RETRIEVAL SYSTEMS} \\
\text{or} \\
\text{PROGRAMMING (ELECTRONIC} \\
\text{COMPUTERS)}
\end{array}
\right]
$$

Another way to index documents, far more likely to be used in libraries that concentrate on research papers rather than books, is to prepare an abstract of the paper and enter the full text of the abstract into the computer as an index. As described in Chapter 5, the computer can make a concordance of the abstract, and retrieval can be done on the basis of the concordance representation of the document. This allows searchers to specify what words they want to find, and even in what relative positions the words must fall, but not to specify a subject classification, since this is not part of the abstract text. We could, then, request retrieval on the basis of the occurrence of one of the following words or phrases:

COMPUTER

COMPUTERS

DATA PROCESSING

appearing in the same document as one of these words (used to set the military environment) :

MILITARY

ARMY

TACTICS

and further require one of the following words to appear in the same sentence as one of the words of the first set:

TACTICAL

OPERATIONS

INFANTRY

ARTILLERY

ARMOR

Now, there is no guarantee that these sets of words would retrieve only the appropriate documents, and it is possible to construct a paragraph that uses them without actually being on the subject desired. But this is a reasonable place to start, and an examination of the actual material might indicate what changes should be made if a second query proved necessary.

Project DEACON,[2] it will be recalled (see Chapter 5), is one of several systems that aim for natural language communication between man and machine. In DEACON information is stored in the system files in a structured, artificial language, and queries may be addressed to the files in a form of natural language. A query that is valid in DEACON is in natural English, but not all valid English questions are meaningful to DEACON. Here are some samples of actual questions used to address a data base consisting of information on military personnel and organization:

> Who is commander of the 638th Battalion?
> What staff colleges has Lt.-Col. Parker attended?
> How many combat engineer companies have trained
>   at Ft. Irwin this year?

Finally, it is possible to query a natural language file in natural language. Such a technique is used by Williams and Perriens [11] to program a search of files of patent disclosure documents, without having to index the documents or to translate the queries into an artificial language.

We can see that the language selected for queries is heavily dependent on the indexing or file language and on the interpretive programs. In any query we must first identify the file or record to be examined. Very often this is implicit, for a retrieval system may offer no alternatives in regard to what file is to be searched. If our information spans such diverse topics as a company's personnel, inventory, library, and payroll, it is important to specify which file is to be searched, for the search of a library on an author's name, and the search of the personnel file on the same name, will obviously produce different results.

We do not always want to retrieve an entire record or document. This is particularly true when the actual information is stored in the file, not just an index to a document. When searching a personnel file, as shown in the DEACON examples, we do not want to retrieve all known information about Lt.-Col. Parker; we want to be selective. Indeed, one of the greatest advantages in using computers in general, and interactive systems specifically, is that the user asks for and gets exactly the information he wants, not an encyclopedic response that probably, but not necessarily, contains his specific datum within it. The query must be able to convey this requirement and enable a user to ask for the information he wants. The earlier queries we illustrated were aimed at retrieval of full documents, but the DEACON questions are directed at the specific facts illustrated.

If we can have the ability to specify the retrieval of individual items from a record, we often can also have the ability to perform calculations and other processes on these items. INFOL [9] allows limited computation to be performed under control of the query and the result of the computation to be used in the logic evaluating the relevance of a file record to a query. One could, for example, count the occurrences of some term in a record and use this count as a selection criterion. Other processes of interest to a retriever are sorting, editing, and temporarily storing.

Queries, then, must *identify* the information to be searched and the basis for selection, must *select* the information to be retrieved, and must also specify the *disposition* and *processing* of the selected information. They must do this in a language which is compatible with that of the index or data records, which can be learned and applied by users of the retrieval system, and which can be interpreted by the computer.

6.2.4 Search Programs and Strategy

We have now described files, file languages or structures, and query languages. A full comprehension of the retrieval process requires that we know the logic of the search program, for it imposes certain limitations on its users and provides capabilities that a conscientious searcher should know about. Regretfully, it is to the limitations that we must devote the most attention, for most query languages and search programs have built-in restrictions that may not be obvious to the casual user but nevertheless prevent him from asking certain questions or performing certain operations. The typical searcher is faced with the following situation when he wishes to use a retrieval system:

1. He has an incomplete knowledge of the contents of the files he wants to search. He does not know whether the information he wants exists. He does not know how much related information there may be. He does not know how careful he must be to discriminate between the information he actually wants and other, closely related but unwanted information. He does not know what alternative information he may be willing to accept if he cannot find what he primarily wants, for he does not know the possibilities.

2. He does not know the structure of the files he is going to search. Thus he does not know exactly what data elements are in each file, what he can and cannot retrieve from any single file, what is the most efficient way to search a file.

3. He may not know the file language; hence he will not know how to express his requirements precisely, how to get the program to separate wanted from unwanted information, how to specify that he wants *all* information, the *best* 10 documents, any 10 documents, etc.

4. He does not know what penalties the program imposes on various approaches to a search, what the cost-performance trade-offs are; how he can get the best information for his dollar or his hour of time.

The early mechanized information retrieval systems required that users submit a query and then await the output, perhaps a day later. The query was, of course, written in an artificial language, probably not familiar to the user, but the system had to operate on the presumption that he knew what he was doing—that he did know the answers to all the questions raised here. What possibility had he of getting high-quality, economical responses to his queries?

We cannot expect even the librarians who maintain files to have the answers to all these questions at hand. Some pertain to the mechanics of the system, but a part of the information is highly transitory and depends on what interpretation the requestor chooses to make of the fact that there are, say, 500 documents that seem to fulfill his needs. To some, this is too many, to others too few. Only the requestor can interpret this fact. Hence anyone using a retrieval system must operate to some extent under uncertainty. The programmer who designed the search program was also operating under uncertainty, for he could not know exactly what questions were going to be asked, or what types of questions were going to be asked with what frequency. We have, then, a situation in which strategy is called for—one in which decisions must be made with incomplete information, chances must be taken, and some trials must be made solely to obtain the information needed to proceed with the main effort.

Here is the great advantage of interactive systems. The searcher can use trial and error. He can make probes of the files to determine their structure or content. He can ask a few queries designed to find out the "lay of the land" and then use this information to formulate the query he hopes will bring him the information he actually needs. In other words, he carries on a dialog with the files and the search program. The dialog is aimed at circumscribing the problem, finding out first what difficulties exist in expressing information needs and how much information is in the files. Then the searcher begins work on how to separate what he wants from what he does not want, or to limit his output, or to change his stated requirements if forced to accept a substitute.

It is no more possible to set down a precise set of rules governing all search procedures, than to prescribe in advance the best military strategy for all situations. One can only teach principles, provide information, and describe the means of acquiring more information. What our searcher needs, at minimum, is a knowledge that he must make use of strategy and the mechanical facility to probe for information. Thereafter he should be able to learn from actual practice.

A frequent requirement in analytic work is to be able to conduct a search based on relationship between items in two different files. Although normally we expect to be able to ask for all items in an inventory file that have both the characteristics COLOR = RED *and* WEIGHT > 20, we usually implicitly assume that *color* and *weight* are fields in the same record. Now we want to consider what happens when the fields are in records of different files. Suppose we want to search a company's personnel files for all employees who attended colleges with enrollment greater than 1000 students. Such a question might be of interest to those planning a recruiting campaign but lacking the time to cover all the nation's colleges. Normally, we would not expect a college's enrollment to be stored with the name of the college in the employee's record. Hence we will have to look at one file to obtain data about colleges and another to find what colleges the company's employees have attended.

This kind of search, which we call a *multifile search*,[7] must be anticipated in advance, for many retrieval systems cannot perform it. One way in which it can always be done is to retrieve, first, the list of college names and then to compose a second query asking for all employees who attended college A or college B or . . . . If the list is long, though, this technique is impractical and may not even be expressible in the query language, which may well have a limitation on the number of terms that can be chained together in this fashion. What we would like to be able to do is make a two-part search and refer to the results of the first one parametrically in the second one. If the retrieval system is designed to permit this, it might allow us to ask, in part one of a query, for the retrieval of the list of college names. Part two would ask for retrieval of the names of employees who attended any college listed in the output of part one. Part two, then, does not give the list explicitly but rather makes reference to it and assumes the list has been stored somewhere during part one and can be made accessible during part two.

Note that a search operated in this manner does not require that the requestor know the names of the colleges he retrieves, and note also that the names of schools are not what he has asked to retrieve. He has asked for a list of the names of employees with certain attributes. To check the attributes another file search is required, but the requestor is freed of the task of looking at the output of this secondary search.

6.2.5 Maintenance

We gave a short example of the importance of file maintenance in Section 6.2.1. Here we shall use examples to illustrate further two aspects of maintenance: quality control and file organization. The former will show what kinds of difficulties we can encounter if we lack adequate quality controls, and the latter will indicate how much work or time may be required to provide these controls.

Consider a relatively simple file organization. Suppose our system consists of a file of document index records, each roughly the equivalent of a catalog card, and a cross index of subject terms. To make the example more interesting, we should have the subject terms be key words, rather than classification terms. Key words, of course, are just individual words, or sometimes short phrases, extracted from the text of a document and indicating something of the subject matter. There are usually far more key words in a document index than there would be classification terms or subject headings. We will assume an average of ten key words per document. The index record file is in order by document serial number, and the subject term file, of course, is in alphabetical order by key word.

When a new document is added to the library, an index record is prepared and added to the end of the file of index records. The key words in the index are extracted and are also posted to the individual records in inverted index files, each of which contains the name of a key word and a list of document numbers in which this key word has occurred. The first problem to consider is what happens when a key word appears in an index but is not to be found in the key word file. The program might simply assume the word is new and create an entry for it. Suppose the word were AIRCRAFT. This seems a reasonable enough word, and in general we would agree to open a new entry immediately. Suppose, however, the word were ARICRAFT. Should this misspelled word be automatically added to a list of accepted key words? If it is, we may be reasonably certain that the document in whose index it appears will never be retrieved by a search for AIRCRAFT. A somewhat similar question arises if we assume the synonym AIRPLANE was in the file when AIRCRAFT first arrived. Under this condition should we open a new entry for AIRCRAFT? There really is no fixed answer to the question. It is another of those that seem to call for human decisions to be made as the questions arise. In other words, when is a new word a synonym for an existing word? When is it simply a misspelling of an existing word? What is a genuinely new word? What can we expect the computer to do to answer these questions? We can see that the value of a retrieval system will degenerate if such questions are not resolved and resolved well.

Here, again, conversational capability could be used to allow the computer to call the librarian's attention to the arrival of a previously unknown word and to ask his decision on what to do with it. The librarian would probably want to scan the existing list of words to see if the newcomer is a synonym for any of them, or he might recognize an obvious spelling error and correct it immediately. Although mechanically simple, this kind of decision-making is not trivial, for the determination of what is a synonym may vary with context, as *memory* and *store* are essentially synonymous in the context of computers, but not in general usage.

The human thesaurus builder, then, may have the following options when a key word arrives that is not in the files. He can:

1. Change the word to a synonymous word that is in the file. This works both for spelling errors and for correctly spelled, true synonyms.

2. Choose to delete the word entirely. This option can be used, for example, with proper names that might be selected by an indexer but would swamp the thesaurus if allowed to accumulate.

3. Insert a *see also* reference, whose advisory nature might dictate that it be ignored by the computer, but which might be useful to human thesaurus browsers. Thus he might not officially equate *memory* and *store* but rather insert a reference between them for use by searchers.

The method of quality control we have illustrated here is not complicated or sophisticated. It is quite straightforward and can be implemented very easily. It can also break down completely if the thesaurus maintenance function is not properly handled. Actually, this is not primarily a programming problem but mainly one of human decision-making.

Now let us give some attention to the mechanical problems of maintenance. This time we assume a large file of information, say a personnel file, with many cross-reference files. The main file might contain records on the employees of an organization, in order by employee serial number. There may be cross references by department number (giving quick reference to all members of a department), by occupation, and by city and state of residence. The structure of this file system is illustrated in Figure 6.7.

When a new employee joins the company, a record is created for him and inserted into the file. Notations, or pointers, must then be set up in each of the cross-reference files pointing to the main entry. If the new employee is the first of his occupation or of residence in his town, a new record has to be created in the appropriate cross-index file. No decision-making is required here except to check on misspellings. Presumably, a coding scheme would be used for occupation, and any semantic problems about what a person's occupation is would be resolved before the record reached the computer. Entering new records, then, presents little problem, but it appears that the cost of entering a new record and making all the cross-reference entries is about n times the cost of entering the main record, where n is the number of cross references.

People change and their records change. What happens when an employee changes departments? Someone has to prepare a change notice for the computer. This should contain the employee's serial number and new department number. It may also give the old department number, or other redundant information, to guard against error. A key punch error in an employee number could lead to changing the wrong person's record, unless some redundant information serves as a "double check." To make the change it is necessary to find and delete the old department number. We say *find* even if the old number is given, because again it is best to play safe and guard against keypunch errors. Therefore the main employee record should be retrieved, and a check made that the recorded and the given old department numbers are the same. Then the program is reasonably sure that it has found the correct employee record. It must then (a) retrieve the old department record and delete the pointer to the main employee record, and (b) find the new department record and add a pointer to the main record. The latter is no different from any other add operation, but the deletion deserves some attention.

Figures 6.8 and 6.9 illustrate two possibilities for the state of the old department record when we retrieve it to delete the pointer to our

Employee File

Name
Dept. No.
Name
Dept. No.
Name
Dept. No.
Name
Dept. No.
Name
Dept. No.

Department File

Dept.No.	Manager's Name
	Name
	Name
	Name

Dept.No.	Manager's name
	Name
	Name

| Dept.No. | |

Occupation File

Occupation CHEMIST	Name
	Name
	Name

Occupation CLERK	Name
	Name
	Name
	Name

| Occupation | Name |

City File

City	State
Population	
	Name
	Name
	Name
	Name

Figure 6.7 Illustrative file system.

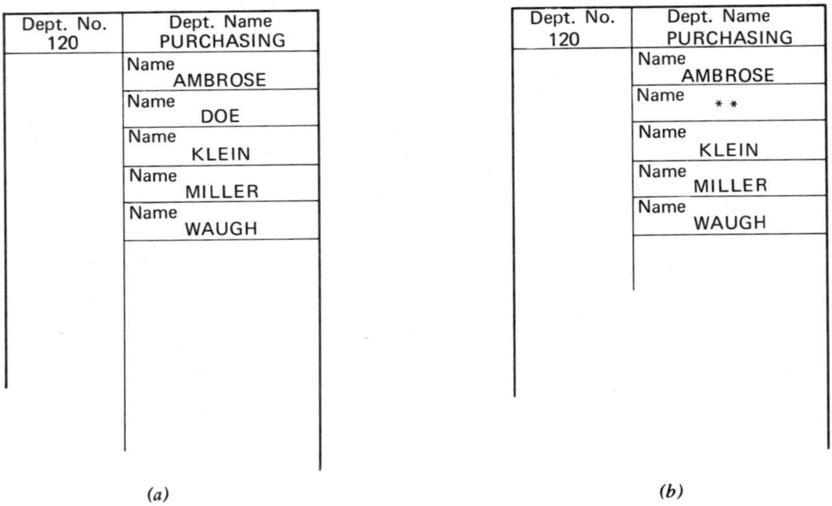

Dept. No. 120	Dept. Name PURCHASING
	Name AMBROSE
	Name DOE
	Name KLEIN
	Name MILLER
	Name WAUGH

(a)

Dept. No. 120	Dept. Name PURCHASING
	Name AMBROSE
	Name * *
	Name KLEIN
	Name MILLER
	Name WAUGH

(b)

Figure 6.8 Deleting an entry from a record. (*a*) Record before change. (*b*) Name deleted from record.

wandering employee. In the first case (Figure 6.8*a*) the pointer to employee Doe is amid several others. (We use the name itself as a pointer, but a serial or record number could serve as well.) We must first find the Doe pointer and then delete it. The computer program does not know that the pointer to Doe is second in the list. It has to look at each one until it finds the pointer that matches the Doe serial number. To delete this item, the program can either replace it with a symbol showing that this pointer is now deleted (Figure 6.8*b*) or it can move all the following pointers up a notch, as would be done with a manually maintained card index file. This alternative, as we have pointed out, is expensive for computers; it is cheaper and easier to use a code to denote that the previous value stored here has been deleted. If there is a great deal of activity, however, the file soon becomes cluttered with these notations, grows in size, and adds a heavy tax on every search. A compromise that the system designer might make is to use the delete notation but also go through the entire file occasionally, deleting the notations and repacking the file. This could be done at night when the computer is not otherwise in use. Whichever method is chosen, something must be done, and the wrong choice could affect system operations far into the future.

In case 2 (Figure 6.9), Doe is the only employee in the cross reference list for his department. When his pointer is deleted, therefore, the entire

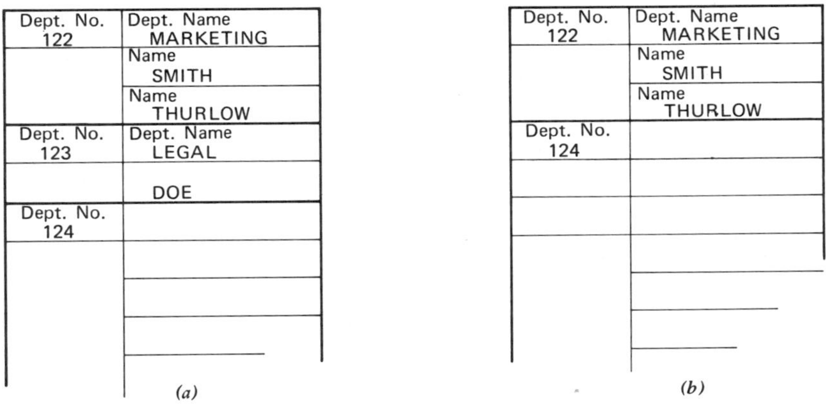

Dept. No. 122	Dept. Name MARKETING
	Name SMITH
	Name THURLOW
Dept. No. 123	Dept. Name LEGAL
	DOE
Dept. No. 124	

(a)

Dept. No. 122	Dept. Name MARKETING
	Name SMITH
	Name THURLOW
Dept. No. 124	

(b)

Figure 6.9 Deleting a vacant record. (a) Record before change. (b) Deletion of the only entry causes deletion of the entire record.

record should probably be deleted, although here, too, we have a choice of how to handle the situation. If we do not delete the department number record now, we face the possibility of accumulating a file full of empty cross-reference entries. If we adopt the practice of removing them, a little more time must be taken in each delete transaction to see whether the list is now empty and, if so, to erase the record. Although apparently insignificant, this little bit of extra time is added to each operation.

The worst situation comes when the management decides to change a department's number. These executives do not care who is in the department; they simply want department 12 changed to department 120. It is not enough to change the heading on the department number record. Each pointer to an employee record must be followed, and the department number in the employee record also changed, as shown in Figure 6.10.

What is the cost of such maintenance? Very roughly, a simple add or delete operation costs about as much as a simple search. That is, to find Doe's record, to delete it, or to add to it all cost about the same amount. To change department numbers costs considerably more than to find the department numbers or to find the list of members of the department. The real question, though, is, How often are maintenance transactions performed? This is a function of the using organization. In the library context, there is at least one maintenance transaction for each document indexed—the act of entering it into the system the first time. There is a similar-costing retrieval operation each time the index is re-

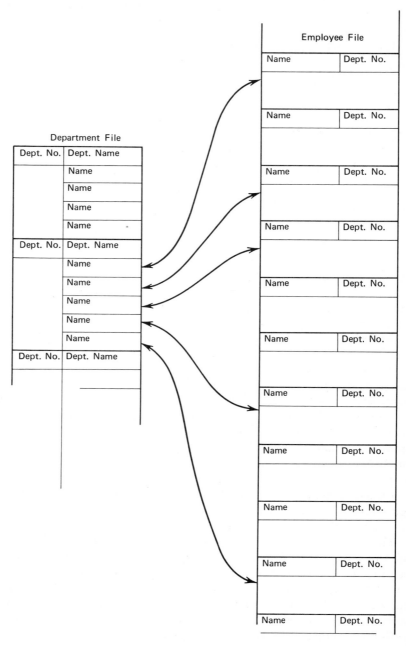

Figure 6.10 Cascaded record changes. To change the number of a department, the record of each member employee must also be changed.

trieved. How often is that? No fixed answer can be given, but experience tends to show that maintenance operations account for at least half the total cost of operating an information retrieval system.

6.3 INTERACTIVE RETRIEVAL

Most of what has been said in this chapter applies as well to interactive retrieval systems as to "batch," or preprogrammed, retrieval systems. We use the term *preprogrammed* to mean that the user must write a query, which is in effect a computer program, describing his requirements and his decision criteria in advance. The computer then executes this program for him, without further intervention on his part. A *batch* system is one that collects user queries and maintenance transactions and runs them whenever convenience and economy permit. For system users, this has a tendency to mean a 24-hour wait for results, although there is no logical reason why they cannot be forthcoming in five minutes. We shall consider, here, three questions about interactive retrieval: (1) What does it do for us? (2) What is the difference between interactive and batched or preprogrammed retrieval programs? (3) Is the difference worth the cost?

6.3.1 The Benefits of Interactive Retrieval

To a retrieval system user the most obvious benefit of interaction is speed. There are no middle men and no waits for a batch to be processed. A query is submitted directly to the computer through an on-line terminal, and search operations can begin almost immediately. In most cases intermediate results will be displayed and decisions will have to be made before the search can be completed. Thus, even if the complete search takes a long time, the user quickly sees some results and is soon brought into the process as an active participant. Although actual file searching is no faster in an interactive system, the requestor may be looking at the first retrieved record while the computer searches for the next one. Hence, from his point of view, the operation seems faster.

Also, because intermediate results can be shown immediately to the requestor, he can use them to make decisions regarding how the retrieval process is to be continued. The computer program, then, is required to do less complex decision-making. Because the requestor plays a large role in decision-making, he can exercise more control over the retrieval process. For a simple example, dictionary-searching can be improved (i.e., the requestor given more assurance he will get what he wants from it) if he is shown a segment of a dictionary and asked to select the words that match his search term, rather than letting the computer decide. If the computer must decide, it will make more mistakes and cost more. For example, if a requestor wants to search on JOHN PAUL JONES, he might be shown the contents of a "page" from the dictionary listing all the JONES entries whose first initial is either J or unspecified. Then *he* decides on which of the following he will want information:

> JONES
>
> JONES, CAPT.
>
> JONES, CAPT. JOHN P.
>
> JONES, COMMO.
>
> JONES, J.
>
> JONES, J. PAUL
>
> JONES, JOHN
>
> JONES, JOHN P.
>
> JONES, JOHN PAUL

Any purely mechanistic rule built into a search program for matching query names with dictionary arguments must, in the long run, give less satisfactory results than can be obtained if the only qualified expert, the requestor himself, makes the decision. It takes little of his time to read this list and indicate which names he accepts as matching his input term. A procedure similar to this has been implemented by Lockheed [10] in an experimental project for the National Aeronautics and Space Administration.

Use of this "menu" concept, in which a wide range of alternatives is presented to a requestor for his selection, reduces the searcher's need to preprogram difficult selection criteria. In other words, rather than make all his decisions beforehand by writing a computer program (or its equivalent in a query language), the user writes only simple statements and does his decision-making mentally, with the data actually before him. For the retrieval system user who is not a programmer or is not otherwise accustomed to mathematical-type notation, this is a great benefit, for his mind does operate along the lines of a computer program. This is a strange situation, and the results of his queries usually reflect both his distaste and his inexperience. Here we have in mind as a typical retrieval system user a lawyer, intelligence analyst, business manager, or journalist. The programmer who designs the retrieval programs and possibly also the query language is not the typical user, although he may be sorely tempted to employ only himself as a model searcher when fashioning his language.

The net gain from faster response, less complex language, and more direct involvement of the requestor in the search logic is, or should be, better retrieval. The requester should be able to avoid errors or to recover from them and quickly adapt to the reality of what is in the file. The reality may be that there is too little information for him, or too much at the level of generality on which he has chosen to ask; nevertheless, he works with the fact of what is there rather than a hypothesis about what might be available. Primarily, then, we look to interactive information retrieval to provide better-quality results—results closer to the needs of the user than can be achieved through preprogrammed retrieval requests.

6.3.2 The Requirements for Interactive Retrieval

In the abstract, there is not much difference between the functions performed by an interactive system and those carried out by a batch system. The primary difference is that the interactive system will involve the requestor at many different points during the process and defer many decisions to him. It will also offer him the option of stopping at an intermediate point, going back a step or two, and making a change. In our dictionary example above, if the requestor had chosen to accept JONES, JOHN PAUL as the only match for his query term, he might later have found insufficient information stored under this name. Then, when the list of recovered documents was displayed to him, he might have chosen to return to the dictionary search and change his match criterion, broadening his scope in the hope of picking up more useful data. With an interactive system this iteration would take only a few minutes. For a typical batch system, however, a full day might be required for each pass. Since the whole process might easily be repeated four or five times, the batch mode user obviously is called upon to exercise great patience.

In the mechanics of programming there can be great differences between interactive and batch retrieval systems. Interactive retrieval requires time-sharing or multiprogramming for efficiency—indeed, possibly for economic feasibility. We must realize that information retrieval involves relatively little calculation and that most of the computer time is occupied with input and output operations which leave the central processor idle. If we add to this the idle time caused by the requestor pondering over some intermediate output at his console, the percentage of actual processor usage decreases rapidly. Information retrieval users are not accustomed to paying a price for a search that would account for all this computer time, and libraries are rarely so well funded as to enable them to offer this service free to their clients. Hence time-sharing of some sort, to reduce the cost to each user to a negligible amount, is a clear requirement.

6.3.3 Costs versus Benefits

Instituting an interactive system, or converting to one, costs money, time, and patience (while all the persons involved learn a new way to do a familiar thing). Do the benefits justify the costs? At the present state of the art we think that interactive information retrieval is the only way to achieve the objectives usually claimed for a mechanized system—rapid retrieval, output tailored to the user's needs of the moment, minimum of requestor effort and time involved. Basically, information retrieval requires a sort of bargaining between the requestor and the files. He wants one thing; they may not have it to offer, at least not under the terms he originally specified. Hence he must be prepared to modify his requirements to suit the realities of the situation. From this point of view, interaction is clearly required.

On the other hand, there are limitations. There is no inexpensive, high-speed, remote printer. A remote user, then, is restricted in the volume of data he can obtain at an economical rate. Furthermore, if the information to be retrieved is not in machine-readable form (say, in book form), the user goes through an interactive process at high speed, but then has to wait for mail transmission or for photographic or other reproduction of the original documents. Another disadvantage is that interactive computer programs are actually not as sophisticated as those we hypothesize and, in practice, are more cumbersome to use than we like to believe when we talk about them. Many of the same people we strive to protect from having to preprogram their requests in mathematical notation are equally ill at ease working at a communications terminal that utters incomprehensible phrases and expects error-free input.

All these problems, though, can be overcome by technology. They do not seem to be problems of basic science or human behavior. Perhaps a good intermediate solution would be to form a team of the requestor and a reference librarian. The librarian would operate the equipment, make suggestions on search strategy, and interrupt output. The requestor would make substantive decisions about how to conduct his search.

6.4 AN EXAMPLE

Let us use a small retrieval system to show how a complete system would operate. Our example might consist of two files.

The first file contains all catalog records on documents stored in a library. Each record contains the bibliographic data, such as title, author, and publisher. It also contains subject descriptors, here in the form of key words taken from the text. Up to ten key words or short

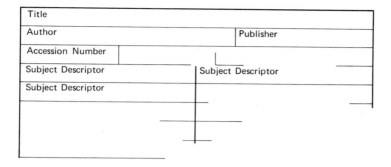

Figurs 6.11 A typical catalog record.

phrases may be used in any catalog record. A sample of a record is shown in Figure 6.11.

A second file is a cross index on all subject descriptors. Each record contains a key word and a list of all document accession numbers for which this key word was a descriptor. One of these records is shown in Figure 6.12.

6.4.1 System Requirements

With this file structure the query language that will be used to ask for information can take many forms. We have to decide what features we would like in the language and what ones we are willing to pay for. Let us assume that a survey of potential users has established the following requirements:

Subject Descriptor	
	Accession Number
	Accession Number
	Accession Number
Subject Descriptor	
	Accession Number
	Accession Number
Subject Descriptor	
	Accession Number

Figure 6.12 A typical subject cross reference.

1. Documents can be requested by subject descriptors, by title, by author, or by serial number.

2. The response to a query should be some intermediary form such as the index record, not the full document. Retrieval of the document itself should follow in a second step, after the requestor is sure that the documents represented by the catalog records resulting from his original request are really the ones he wants.

3. The query logic should be kept as simple as possible, since users are not trained in data processing. Simplicity will also hold down the cost of designing and implementing a search program.

4. The library staff does not want to restrict the key words that are used, but wishes to exercise quality control over the list of words in use.

6.4.2 The Proposed System

Here is a language that might have resulted from these specifications. It has some obvious deficiencies that we shall consider later. First, let us see how it would work.

A query will have four elements. The first specifies which file is to be searched, the full catalog file ordered on serial number, or the cross-index file ordered on subject descriptor. The next three terms specify the criteria for selection of records. The logic connecting these terms is always the same. A query, then, has this form:

FILE: (name of file)

TYPE, VALUE (TYPE, VALUE $+$ TYPE, VALUE)

where TYPE describes an information element, such as a key word, a title, or an author's name. VALUE is the particular title, author, etc., being sought. The other symbols mean that we are always requiring the presence of the first term *and* either one or both of the second two terms. We will allow any term to be missing; if it is, it will be ignored. Thus we can leave out the first term and have a query that calls for either one or both of the two terms given. Among the obvious deficiencies is the fact that we cannot ask for the occurrence of term A *or* B *or* C. *A search of any file will retrieve all records of this file that satisfy the search logic.*

6.4.3 Querying the System

Here is how the search program would handle queries. We will consider first a query directed to the main catalog file. The requestor would choose this file to search when he is concerned with elements other than subject descriptors, or with at least one element other than a search descriptor. Suppose he has asked for all works by John Doe published by the University Press. The important feature of this query is that it contains no information which will be of any help in locating the appropriate records of the catalog file. It will be necessary, then, to search every record of the file to be sure of recovering all possible answers to this question.

The search mechanics are simple but time consuming and expensive. A record is read from the catalog file, and the computer tests to see whether the author's name is John Doe. If not, the record cannot satisfy the query; it is immediately rejected, and another record brought into core memory. If this author's name matches the query, the publisher's name is tested and, if it also matches, the record is written out for the requestor.

Many variations are possible on the basic logic described here. The requestor could have used a request of the form AUTHOR, JOHN DOE (SUBJECT, MEDICINE). This retrieves all works by Doe on the subject of medicine. Since there may be more than one subject term in an index record, however, the search logic is slightly more complex. The program tests the author's name and, if it matches, begins a series of tests on subject. If the first subject descriptor tested fails to match the query, the record is not rejected. Each other subject term must be tested as well. The query says, in effect, that *any* subject term can be MEDICINE, not just the first one or the third one. When doing title or publisher searches, this problem does not arise, since there is only one such entry, although it may arise with authors. The file designer must decide which fields may occur more than once (i.e., in which cases there will be an array of fields) and must make the program aware of these so that it will search each occurrence.

Now let us see what has to be done in order to accomplish a subject search. Suppose the query is as follows:

FILE: CROSS INDEX

(KEY WORD, BODY + KEY WORD, SOUL)

which specifies that the cross-index file is to be searched and document numbers selected that are indexed under either BODY or SOUL or both.

The program first retrieves the BODY record, including its list of document accession numbers. It then retrieves the SOUL record. According to the query logic, we will accept any document whose number is in *either* list. The output to the requestor is this accession number list. The process is illustrated in Figure 6.13.

Had the query been of this form:

FILE: CROSS REFERENCE

KEY WORD, BODY (KEY WORD, SOUL)

it would have called for documents having *both* BODY and SOUL in their

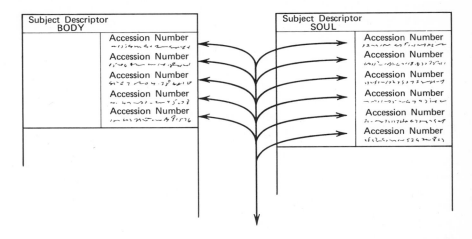

Figure 6.13 Retrieval from inverted files, I. Any document whose accession number is *in either* record will be retrieved.

indexes. The output to the requestor would have been the shorter list shown in Figure 6.14.

6.4.4 Search Strategy

The requestor obtains only modest value from a list of document numbers. However, according to the specifications given in Section 6.4.2, this is all we can directly provide him. That is, a search of the subject cross-reference file can only recover records that contain document accession numbers. If he wants the actual document indexes, he can request their retrieval by a query addressed to the catalog file, but he is restricted by the query language to asking for two of them at a time. Again, the limitation we arbitrarily impose on the query language is an irritant. Although real-life query languages have less obvious limitations, some are usually present.

Fortunately, a requestor can obtain some useful information out of a list of serial numbers. He gets a feel for how many documents this query will retrieve, and he may choose to modify the query on this basis alone if it is obvious that the yield will be far too many or too few. When the requestor feels he has a reasonable number of serial numbers, possibly after several tries at querying the cross-reference file, he often will prefer to see the catalog records before asking for retrieval of the documents themselves. In this way he can make an actual subject matter check, rather than a simple count, to see whether the material he is

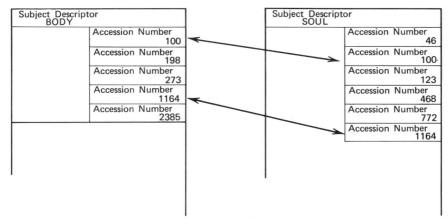

Figure 6.14 Retrieval from invested files, II. Any document whose accession number is *common to both* subject records will be retrieved.

retrieving seems to be truly pertinent to his problem.

Even this primitive retrieval system, then, offers opportunity for browsing or interactive querying, for the requestor to try more than one version of a request, and for him to see partial results before ordering retrieval of the full, hard-copy document. Without this capability, the requestor would have to try to be exactly right the first time, although he would normally have too little information to achieve this.

To summarize, the requestor doing a subject search through the cross-reference file has the following options, once he has received the output of his first query:

1. He can change the query, on the basis of the number of references printed out to him, making his new query either more or less restrictive than the first one.

2. He can request copies of the documents whose numbers are typed out to him, even though he is not sure of the degree of their interest to him.

3. He can query the catalog file to find more information on the documents whose numbers resulted from the first query.

Clearly, the requestor has a number of possibilities, and it is incumbent on him to select a strategy that accomplishes his objective with minimum cost or effort. There is no precisely determined sequence of events that can be preprogrammed and will be guranteed to work for all users in all cases. We take it as an axiom that relevance of documents is an individual matter, and that even the relevance of a given document to a given query will vary with the requestor and the particular circumstances of the search. The same person will make different decisions when doing an exhaustive research study and when casually trying to find some quick information on a topic. An expert in a field will be able to tell more about the value of a particular document from the name of the author, the publisher, and the date than will a novice, even if both are looking for exactly the same information.

Here, then, is the need for and the value of interactive searching. The search logic is no different from that used when the searching is done remotely in time. The difference is the system user's ability to see some results of a search immediately and to make any needed decisions as soon as these results are available.

Let us return, now, to, the question raised several times previously concerning the deficiencies in the query language. By deficiencies we mean here that the language is unable to express some concepts (for example, A *or* B *or* C), and the language can order some simple operations only cumbersomely (for example, the retrieval of the catalog records of the documents whose serial numbers were recovered in a cross-reference file search). In our example, we purposely chose a highly simplified language, both to clarify explanation and to show that this restriction exists and must be managed. Such restrictions must be coped with in most query languages, but they are usually far more subtle.

6.4.5   Query Language Problems

An index language and a query language both represent great simplifications of relatively complex ideas that may have been written into documents or are under consideration by a searcher. The search program may then impose additional restrictions that have the effect of further limiting the language, in this case the restrictions of being unable to retrieve automatically the indexes of documents whose serials have been recovered. Effective information retrieval demands that the system user understand the interactions among the languages, the search program, and the data being searched. Mere mechanical knowledge of the language of a query does not equip a person to make intelligent use of the total system—to be able to avoid excessively long searches, and the excessive and expensive retrieval of hard-copy documents before making full use of index files to reduce the set under consideration.

For effective retrieval, within the limitations imposed by the mechanics of any system, we need two things—knowledge of how the system operates and the ability to work interactively with it, to change our ideas on the basis of preliminary information retrieved. This is true of all systems, although the limitations imposed may vary. The need for interaction is also present, regardless of how well structured a query is, unless the requestor has full and complete knowledge of the contents of the files he is searching.

We have discussed in Section 6.2.5 the kind of maintenance operations that would be needed for the file system used in this example.

REFERENCES

1. Bush, Vannevar, "As We May Think," *Atlantic Monthly,* **176**, 1 (July 1945), 101–108.
2. Craig, James A., Susan C. Berezner, Homer C. Carney, and Christopher R. Longyear, "DEACON: Direct English Access and Control," *Proceedings of the AFIPS 1966 Fall Joint Computer Conference,* Spartan Books, New York, 1966, pp. 365–380.
3. Davis, Ruth M., "A History of Automated Displays," *Datamation,* **11**, 1 (January 1965), 24–28.
4. Doyle, L. B., "Semantic Road Maps for Literature Searchers," *J. Association Computing Machinery,* **8**, 4 (1961), 553–578.
5. Knuth, Donald E., *The Art of Computer Programming,* Vol. 1, *Fundamental Algorithms,* Addison-Wesley, Reading, Mass., 1968, pp. 228 et seq.
6. Meadow, Charles T., *The Analysis of Information Systems,* John Wiley, New York, 1967, p. 174.
7. *Ibid.,* p. 244.
8. Merritt, C. Allen, and Paul J. Nelson, "The Engineer-Scientist and an Information Retrieval System," *Proceedings of the AFIPS 1966 Spring Joint Computer Conference,* Spartan Books, New York, 1966, pp. 205–212.
9. Olle, T. W., "INFOL: A Generalized Language for Information Storage and Retrieval Applications," *Information Retrieval—A Critical View,* George Schecter, ed., Thompson, Washington, D. C., 1967, pp. 177–190.
10. Summit, Roger K., *DIALOG II User's Manual,* National Aeronautics and Space Administration, Washington, D.C., September 1967.
11. Williams, John H., Jr., and Matthew P. Perriens, "Automatic Full Text Indexing and Searching System," *Proceedings of the IBM Information Systems Symposium,* IBM Corp., Gaithersburg, Md., September 1968, pp. 335–350.

RECOMMENDED ADDITIONAL READING

1. Becker, Joseph, and Robert M. Hayes, *Information Storage and Retrieval: Tools, Elements, Theories,* John Wiley, New York, 1963.
2. Kent, Allen, *Textbook on Mechanized Information Retrieval,* 2d Ed., Interscience Publishers, a Division of John Wiley, New York, 1967.
3. Kochen, Manfred, ed., *The Growth of Knowledge,* John Wiley, New York, 1967.
4. Lefkovitz, David, *File Structures for On-Line Systems,* Spartan, New York, 1969.
5. Salton, Gerard, *Automatic Information Organization and Retrieval,* McGraw-Hill, New York, 1968.
6. Vickery, B. C., *On Retrieval System Theory,* Butterworths, London, 1961.

Chapter Seven

Information Acquisition

7.1 INTRODUCTION

Our subject in this chapter is the physical entry of data into a computer, with emphasis on the use of the computer as an active participant in eliciting the information from its human originator. When the man who initiates an information record is linked directly with the computer that will process it, several benefits accrue. The most direct and obvious is the speed with which new information gets into the computer's files. Less obvious and dramatic, but potentially of even more value, is the reduction of error that can be achieved by tying together the source and the processor of information.

7.1.1 Benefits of On-Line Data Entry

Let us take a quick look at some on-line data entry systems and see what advantages they offer. High's Dairy Products, a Washington, D. C., area grocery chain of 160 small stores, has its store managers place orders for new stock directly into a computer by means of a Touch-Tone® telephone. The chain has cut in half the delay between placing an order and the delivery of dairy products to its retail outlets. This reduces overstocks, outages, and spoilage, thus providing a direct, practical benefit to the company.

Carson, Pirie, Scott and Company, a Chicago department store chain, has reduced from an average of 2 minutes to 30 seconds the time required to check a customer's credit standing when processing a charge transaction. The company uses the same data entry techniques but

182

has a computer-driven voice answer-back service. This results in solid benefit in customer relations and permits more effective use of both sales department and credit department personnel. The latter devote more of their time to difficult cases and have been able to reduce defaults significantly.

In airline reservations systems, such as American Airline's SABRE System, the reservations agent enters a customer's name, telephone number, and so on, as soon as a sale is made. All other agents have immediate access to the information that a given seat has been sold. The customer data are immediately available for reconfirmation or any other transaction between the customer and the airline. Here, it is to the mutual benefit of the airline and its customers to know that a sale has been recorded in a certain name and that the complete transaction has been processed—there is no middle man to misplace a reservation. Customers are more certain of their space, and the company knows with a greater degree of precision what it has for sale.

In each of the cases just cited, speed has been the major advantage gained. The critical time between creation of a record and its receipt by the computer that will act upon it is reduced. If this record contains an error, however, we have created an uncertain situation: the computer may be unable to act upon the data, or it may take an undesirable or unforeseen action. The effect of a null or an undesirable action may vary from none at all to paralysis of the computer system or to the failure of a larger system in which the computer is a part.

We may roughly classify input errors into either of two categories— (1) errors of content or judgment, as classifying a book under the wrong heading (e.g., the mathematical discipline *game theory* under *recreation*), and (2) transcription errors, including spelling errors, typographical errors, and format errors. The first type of error is made by the human originator of a data record; the second can be made by him or by any of the (frequently, many) intermediary people who transcribe the originator's data before machine entry. These include keypunch operators, teletype operators, and computer operators (cards can be dropped).

It is hard to categorize what happens when an input error is made because systems vary so widely, but the general situation is as follows. From the time error-laden data enter a computer until the record is corrected, we are in a position between two extremes. If the error is detected, the entire record or perhaps only some portion of it may be rejected. Either way, we must do without some of the information until the correction is made. If the error is not detected, the file contains errors that may then propagate. Some operations can cope with or tolerate this situation, but others cannot. A single error in listing a man's salary may be tolerated by a system handling census data, but the same transcription error will not be tolerated by a payroll system that is subject to audit. We cannot resist the editorial comment that, although the extent to which input errors are detected and corrected in different systems is expected to vary, it is distressing how often the very possibility of their existence is allowed to go unnoticed.

The traditional way to put data into a computer involves a man writing down his information, having it transcribed by a keypunch or paper tape punch or teletype operator, having another transcription operation following the first for verification purposes (or a proofreading function intervening), and then entering the data into the computer. What happens when data so entered are found to be erroneous? The entire record or the offending part of it must find its way back to the originator or other person qualified to make the modification needed. The time required to find out who this person is, transmit the error-containing record, have the person make the correction, and reinitiate an input entry process can be quite lengthy. By contrast, in a conversational data entry system the originator works through a console or terminal and is directly and immediately informed of any errors detected in his data. The correction process then requires only a few seconds. Thus the human time for correcting errors is negligible; the computer time is comparable to that required with a batched input system. When selecting between on-line and traditional data entry techniques, then, we must weigh the benefit of higher-quality files against the high initial installation cost of an on-line system.

7.1.2   Costs of On-Line Data Entry

Let us briefly consider these on-line costs. When entering nontext data (i.e., mostly numbers and codes), rough figures indicate [1] that the periods of time required for block lettering (the typical mode of filling in paper forms), keypunching, and hunt-and-peck typewriting are about the same. We specify nontextual data because the ability to scan a source document and remember a long sequence of words will materially speed typing or keypunching. Verifying, a process by which the keypunching of cards is duplicated as a check on errors in the original punching, takes the same amount of time as keypunching. We may assume that proofreading of nontext data is also comparable in this respect.

The cost, then, of entering a set of symbols into a computer involves the analytic time for the originator to decide what data to enter, the transcription time for him to record them on paper, a second transcription time for this record to be keypunched, and a third time for it to be verified or proofread. If there are variations in this process, such as the originator typing his material, or the use of paper tape instead of punched cards, the timing is not materially affected. Also involved, of course, are the costs of the two transcription operations beyond the first one and the cost of their transcribing machinery, that is, the originator must create the record, but it is possible to eliminate the other operations by having the originator go on-line. To balance this is the cost of the on-line terminals and the multiplexing equipment and communications control programs operating within the computer.

As an example, assume that an input operation involves an originator who splits his time, half on analysis and half on transcription. In this case, he must be backed up by half a keypunch operator and half an editor or verifier. If we can do away with the latter two functions by transferring them to the originator and the computer, we have saved the equivalent of one clerical salary, plus the cost of transcribing equipment. At current prices, this would mean on the order of $400-$500 per month for a salary, ignoring overhead, which varies considerably, and another $50-$100 per month for keypunch machinery. This amount of money will more than pay the monthly rent on most alpha-numeric CRT or typewriter-type terminals and will provide for some computer time as well. Therefore, although we cannot be very specific because it is difficult to allocate costs to a single terminal, it can at least be seen that a large sum of money is potentially available and that this amount is within the range of what remote data entry equipment costs.

There are, of course, opposing factors—possibly high initial expense, technological unemployment, and the problem of low reliability resulting from reliance on a single system. We do not, by any means, imply that on-line data entry is desirable for all users. We do suggest that it may be financially within the reach of most users who have large numbers of people and a considerable amount of computer time devoted to input operations.

7.1.3 Long-Term Effects

One result of the need to reduce errors in computer input has been extreme rigidity in the design of data forms and input records. Often such forms restrict the degree of choice of individuals or limit the processing that can be done to simplify the procedure. As any applicant for employment in a large organization or for registration at a university will attest, the number of different forms that call for repetition of the same information can be staggering. Restrictions and redundancies in the design of forms have grown as a self-defense measure. Without them the orderly processing of the forms, either by manual means or by unsophisticated computer programs, is impossible, and without the forms pay checks are missed and diplomas not awarded. For example, I recall an incident during a prolonged stay at a hotel not specializing in long-term guests. The cashier knew of no way he could give me my bill, *to date,* unless I checked out of the hotel. We went through the ritual of checking me out and then in again, as a guest in the same room, so that I could be enabled to pay my accumulated charges while remaining in the hotel.

The excerpts below, taken from the *General Electric Forum,* anticipate some social benefits from improved information entry means:

"Ninety or ninety-five per cent of all computer-based information systems today depend on the assumption that somebody is taking piles of paper and key-punching a Hollerith card." [4]

" . . . the general trend is toward the gradual abandoning of traditional punched and printed media in favor of new advanced techniques which allow direct introduction into the computer from source documents or processes." [3]

"In today's society we face a certain amount of conformity simply because if there weren't such conformity we wouldn't be able to manage the situation; we wouldn't be able to schedule things, we wouldn't be able to plan. Now all this can be changed substantially by better means of information processing. In other words, in an information-rich society, the individual will have much more freedom of choice because society will be able to stand much more diversity among its members without the results being chaotic." [5]

We may, then, look to this new way of communicating with a machine as a return to flexibility and to individuality in our personal dealings with large organizations. The power of the computer can be harnessed toward this end, rather than that of institutionalizing man's communication in order for him to be able to exchange information with computers.

7.2 MODES OF ACQUISITION

We shall discuss three broad approaches to direct man-machine data entry. Although our interest is focused primarily on interactive systems, we start with a set of one-way communication systems or, more precisely, systems in which most of the information flows one way and only error indications go the other way. We shall consider next a rather stereotyped approach to a conversational system, one that follows a relatively strictly prescribed format in accomplishing its objective. Finally, we shall consider a fully interactive approach in which the man and the machine converse freely, somewhat as equals.

7.2.1 One-Way Communication

In a one-way communication system, we must presume a low probability of error, or at least of detection of error. Since the computer is very limited in its ability to respond to the originator of information, there is no way to explain the nature of an error or even, necessarily, to identify the specific datum that is at fault. As we shall see, it is occasionally possible to go outside the basic communications system when a serious error is involved.

A one-way communication system exists when a sales clerk uses a cash register, particularly the large variety that prints information on a bill or receipt. Not all the information printed is displayed to the clerk, and, although the number of buttons is limited, there is no error checking on those that are depressed. In a supermarket operation, the price of each item is displayed so that both the clerk and the customer can see it, but often the entry of items is too fast for the customer to keep up. Although the printed tally can be checked at home, probably few people take the trouble. Therefore an error on the part of the clerk is likely to go undetected, unless it is very large, say entering $99. instead of $.99. Each item entered into a supermarket cash register is classified as grocery, tobacco, nonfood, etc. Here, too, it is unlikely that an error will be detected and even less probable that it will be corrected, for it hardly matters to the customer and probably concerns the store only for statistical purposes. In short, most errors on a retail food bill are not critical, even if they are small price errors. For this reason both the store and most of the customers are willing to operate on a no-check basis.

In the High's Dairy system mentioned earlier, the local store manager enters his order to the warehouse through the Touch-Tone® telephone. Each item has a code number and he enters this plus the quantity desired. The data go directly into a computer without being checked further. The information originator can cancel a line or call the operator at the computer when he needs help. He initiates one of these actions by use of the eleventh and twelfth buttons on the telephone. Some cursory validity checks are made as data are entered, but no one verifies that an order for bread was indeed meant to be bread, not butter. There are checks made on illegal codes, however, and on numbers far out of the normal range. When an error is detected, a tone signal can call for a retransmission. A coding error on the part of the manager will result in a wrong delivery, but this happening is rare enough, apparently, for High's to be willing to take this chance. Of course, the same kind of error can be made in a manual system as a result of illegible handwriting, and High's is finding a net reduction in errors of this type through use of the telephone system. This means that managers are making fewer mistakes with the numeric coding than resulted from poor handwriting before.

Another kind of one-way communication is found in such applications as factory scheduling. Here, each piece making its way through a series of factory operations is accompanied by a punched card. Whenever the piece reaches a new work station or is completed at one station, its card and another one identifying the station or workman are entered into a remote card reader, such as the IBM 1030 data collection system. A preprinted card, of course, conveys relatively little information. But the timeliness of the information enables a central computer to schedule work flow through the factory, to monitor the status of the entire plant, and to spot trouble situations as they arise. Because the input messages are extremely simple, the error rate can be held down.

7.2.2 Prescribed Format, Two-Way Communication

Adding a remote display device to an on-line data entry system enables the computer to provide active assistance to the originator of the information being entered. One important accomplishment is that the originator can see what he is posting to the files and can do his own proofreading. If the computer detects an error, it can indicate which field of information is at fault.

Displaying the information also permits the originator to vary the sequence of data entry, a feature that may be a convenience to him, and allows the computer to ask for specific fields that may have been omitted previously. A typical technique is for the computer to display the equivalent of a form on a cathode ray tube, with boxes set aside for the entry of specific fields. The computer may then use some highlighting devices, as in Figure 7.1, to indicate which field the responder is to fill in next, or instead the responder may take the initiative and position a cursor to indicate which field he is about to enter.

In this mode, it is also possible for the originator to add information to an existing record. The computer can retrieve a record identified by the originator and display whatever information already exists in this record. The originator then enters his new information, as in Figure 7.2.

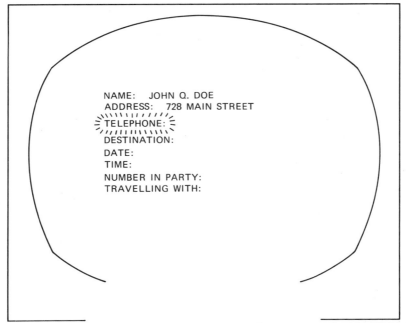

```
NAME:     JOHN Q. DOE
ADDRESS:   728 MAIN STREET
TELEPHONE:
DESTINATION:
DATE:
TIME:
NUMBER IN PARTY:
TRAVELLING WITH:
```

Figure 7.1 Entering a data record. The computer can be programmed to highlight the name of the data item it wants the console operator to supply next. One such highlighting technique is to make the name of the item flash on and off.

Here is an excerpt from a prescribed-format conversation that might ensue in an airline reservation system.[6, 8] Our example is a combination of information retrieval and data entry, but in a system of any complexity this will be a common situation.

The message A 10MAY DCA 400P asks a reservation system for information about space availability (A) on flights from the city where the message originated to Washington, D. C. (DCA), on the tenth of May, around 4:00 P.M. The computer responds with fare and schedule information, somewhat as follows:

        10 MAY F 21.00 Y 17.00
    1. 123 F6 Y1   LGA DCA 400P 442P DC9 S 0
    2.   45 F0 Y2   LGA DCA 430P 515P 727 S 0

This message tells the reservation clerk that on the tenth of May the first-class fare is $21.00, tourist class $17.00. There are two flights, numbers 123 and 45. Flight 123 has available 6 first-class and 1 tourist-class seats. It leaves New York's LaGuardia Airport for Washington at 4:00 P.M., arriving at 4:42 P.M., making use of a DC-9 aircraft, serving a snack, having no intermediate stops.

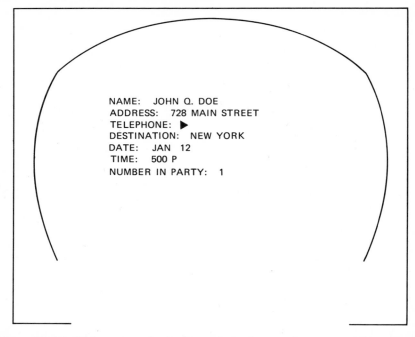

Figure 7.2 Modifying a record. At times, it is the console operator who takes the initiative. First, he calls for the record he wants and then uses a cursor to indicate which data item he wants to fill it. Here, a reservation agent has recalled a passenger's record and is using the cursor (the triangular shaped character after TELEPHONE) to inform the computer that he is about to supply, or modify, the passenger's telephone number.

The ticket agent may select flight 23 by entering three elements: 1, for line one, meaning that he wants the first flight displayed; Y for tourist class; and ss1 for sell one seat. The computer confirms this request with the following message:

1 123 Y 10 MAY LGA DCA SS1 400P 442P

This confirms that a ticket for flight 123 has been sold for May 10, from New York to Washington, one seat sold, leaving at 4:00 P.M., and arriving at 4:42. The computer now wants information on the passenger, and this may be typed in, in any order, by the clerk, who must identify each item of information. Thus:

—WRIGHT/W*   (—denotes passenger's name,
                            *ends the field)

9GA4—6700B*   (9 means telephone number,
                            B means business phone)

The computer might, at this point, retort
HOME TELEPHONE MISSING
and the clerk would then elicit this information from the customer and enter it as

9372-7383H*

Now that the passenger's full description is available, it can be retrieved at any time, as can the record of his seat purchase.

We have called this a prescribed-format conversation, even though the clerk is allowed to vary the sequence of inputs, because the number of items of information to be recorded and the number of questions that an agent can ask are quite limited. We can see that, in spite of the relative simplicity of the conversation, this method gets all relevant information into the computer quickly. The flight inventories can be immediately updated. If a passenger in Los Angeles wanted to book a connection with flight 123 immediately after Mr. Wright made his reservation, the clerk would know that no tourist-class seats remained. (Note line 1 of the display on page 189, which shows only one seat left before Mr. Wright bought.) Similarly, if Mr. Wright were to cancel his reservation, this news would be made available to all reservations offices throughout the country, as soon as they requested information on this flight. With any other basic approach to data entry, both the customer and the airline are left in some doubt as to whether Mr. Wright's reservation has been duly recorded and will be both retrieved and honored at flight time. (Note that it does little good to retrieve 101 reservations if there are only 100 seats on the airplane and the flight has been oversold.) There can be many variations on how this conversation is carried out; we refer here to the fact of the on-line conversation.

Another example of a limited-range conversation is one of those mentioned in Section 7.1.1, which combines use of the Touch-Tone® telephone and a computer-driven voice response unit. At Carson, Pirie, Scott and Company sales clerks can enter a customer account number and the proposed amount of purchase through the telephone and receive a voice response from the computer authorizing the transaction or denying permission. The advantages here are speed and the reduction of human effort. Actually, no changes are made to files through this conversation. It is entirely a query system. The same technique is used in banks for checking the status of accounts before checks are cashed.

We can see, from these brief examples, some of the power of on-line data entry. We can also begin to have an inkling of the limitations, principally that the human conversationalist is talking to a very restricted intelligence. He is unable to ask other than routine, predetermined questions, and he can get back only limited replies. With Touch-Tone®

input, the human being has no immediate check on the accuracy of his transcription; and, although some checks can be made, one can visualize significant problems if this method were used to compose a customer's bill in a large department store. The far more elaborate airline systems provide greater protection against simple errors, but mistakes are still possible and system users may be lulled into a false sense of security. Again, though, we must recognize that errors were plentiful before mechanized reservations systems were adopted. On the whole, the airline systems reduce errors by providing the agent with a written record of all transactions. Although the Touch-Tone® systems provide no such record, their conversations are faster and the equipment is less expensive.

7.2.3 Unstructured Conversation

We stretch a point somewhat with the title for this section. It is meant to be a relative term. In a sense, any conversation is structured and is governed and limited by the interests, vocabulary, and articulation of the participants. We shall now consider man-machine conversations in which each partner is far more free than in our previous examples to select or suggest the next element of conversation, and in which the entire conversation is oriented toward an overall goal. The path to this goal is not very important. Such an unstructured conversation may be indicated whenever the information to be provided to the computer is highly variable in form or content.

Representative of such a structure is a U. S. federal income tax form, with all its possible attachments and schedules. There is a basic form, not all parts of which are applicable to any one taxpaper, and there are also seemingly innumerable other forms that may be attached, depending on whether the taxpayer has sold a house, achieved capital gains or loss, engaged in his own business, and so on. The sequence of entry of data items on such a form depends on the content of answers to certain questions; not all questions are answered by all taxpayers. Hence, filling out the form is something like designing a computer program. At many points, the information originator must make a decision on what to do next, and this decision is often based upon the response to the last question or to a combination of responses to earlier questions.

Except in the most trivial sense, this situation did not arise in our earlier examples. Each answer to a question was complete in itself, or made an implicit reference to other information elements. For instance, this was done by selecting a flight by line number, rather than flight number, and that decision, in turn, depended upon the order of selection of flights for display. In the tax form we are moving into a new dimension **altogether.**

Another example of unstructured conversation arose in a research project that had as one of its objectives the elicitation of programming documentation from the programmers.[11] Here a generalized report structure was used, questions were asked of the programmer through a console, and his answers became entries in a report. However, not every report is structured in exactly the same way. There may be an input section and an output section for all reports, but the number of inputs or outputs described will vary. Different fields of information will be obtained for different kinds of programs and for different types of data items (for example, if a data item is described as a fixed-point integer, we want to ask different questions about it from those that will apply if it is described as an alphabetic field). Some programs or portions of programs are designed entirely for error handling, and these often have a special importance in documentation. To further complicate the problem, what one person calls an error program may be an output program for another. The author of a message-transmitting program may not consider it to be an error-handling program, but a second author whose program branches to the first one to send an error message to the operator does consider it to be an error routine. So we must expect that the same program system may be differently described by different people.

In interrogating programmers on their designs, then, it appears unfeasible to ask a rigid set of questions and expect each programmer to have all answers ready on demand. We have to recognize that he does not know some answers, even while acknowledging that the question is legitimate. Other questions may not pertain to a particular program. Not all programs have output routines, for example, and the documentor should be free to indicate this, rather than have to reply DO NOT KNOW when asked. Also, programs vary in structure and require different levels of detail for an adequate description. And, certainly, programmers are in a position to document different parts of a program at different times. Finally, there is a requirement for programmers to retrieve information about what they have previously put into the files, as well as what other programmers have entered. For example, two different programmers may use the same file, and it is important for both of them to verify that they are making the same assumption about the structure and composition of this file. An interrogation program that is to benefit programmers by reducing the amount of work required of them in documentation must recognize these many points of variability, and not only cope with them but also carry on a smooth conversation with each programmer in spite of them.

Another example, this one hypothetical, of an unstructured conversation would be involved in on-line book cataloging. This is by no means a "straight line" process of completing a standard form or a standard number of entries on a catalog card. For one reason, the number of separately identifiable fields that could appear on a Library of Congress card (the one most generally used in the United States) is over 100.[2] This is not to say that there are more than 100 entries on one card, but that the entries on any card are selected from this number of possibilities. Another reason for variability is the uncertainty of what to enter into any given field. Even the author's name may entail a file search before the new entry can be made, to determine whether this name has appeared in the catalog before and, if so, in what form. In the assignment of classification codes and subject headings the cataloger may have to do fairly extensive research to find how similar books were cataloged in the past. In fact, it has been estimated [7] that Library of Congress catalogers spend up to 60 per cent of their time doing searches in conjunction with their cataloging operations.

Here, then, is a truly complex data entry operation. It is complex because a great deal of human judgment must be exercised and because consistency is needed among many people performing similar activities. There must be a continual interaction between the information originator and the existing data files, as well as with the program that is eliciting information.

7.3 PROGRAMMING FOR CONVERSATIONAL DATA ENTRY

The demands on program design for the three levels of complexity in respect to information acquisition vary considerably. In one-way transmission, once the computer has been interrupted and the processing program brought to bear (or the incoming message queued for processing when convenient), the program expects a simple message in a prescribed format. If an error is detected in the input, a simple message may be returned to the sender. This may be in the form of a distinct tone in a Touch-Tone® telephone system, a bell on a teletype, or a verbal message. In any case, it will ask for retransmission of the last input message. This kind of program requires little more versatility than one that reads data from punched cards stacked in the computer's card reader.

Dealing with a true two-way conversation, even with a limited data structure, is more of a problem. Generally, the sequence of operations is as follows. The originator informs the computer he wants to enter data. The computer presents him with some form of guidance, varying, as we have said, from asking for single items in sequence (for example, NAME _____, RANK _____, SERIAL NUMBER _____), to displaying a complete data form and indicating what item is requested next, to telling the originator to indicate what data item he wants to enter. In many cases (airline reservations or book cataloging, for instance) the computer is then required to retrieve some existing information relevant to the originator's request. Hence the program must elicit a proper identification of the records being sought before the elicitation of new information begins. This loop—identification of a record, retrieval of the record, elicitation of new information—may be repeated more than once during any transaction. The main difference between this form of acquisition program and a one-way system is variability. The acquisition program must be able to respond in different ways to different kinds of inputs. Some of these input messages will be provided by the data originator, some by retrieval from existing files, and some from the program's own error-detecting routines.

As we begin to consider programs for unstructured conversation, we can see that they must be less rigidly constructed. An unstructured conversational program may do relatively little processing of data, but it will probably do a great deal of decision-making. It will be expected to be able to recognize small differences among inputs and to assess its own status to help decide how to interpret any given message. In other words, context now becomes important. We no longer ask the originator to specify explicitly the context of any conversation. The context may be discernible, by a sensitive program, as a function of earlier conversation.

Whenever the computer has asked a question of the data originator, the program must then be able to:

1. Recognize, within reasonable limits, whether the answer is a valid input or not. For example, if the datum is an address, we would not expect a program to be able to verify every possible street address in the world, or even all within any one major city.

2. If the input is not valid, be able to take appropriate action, normally informing the originator of the invalidity and the reason for it and asking him for new data.

3. Be able to recognize and act upon certain nonresponsive answers. These we define as messages that are transmitted after a question has been asked of the human responder but that, rather than answering the question, direct the computer to do something different. For example, a data originator might answer a question with BACK to indicate he wants to go back to the last question and give a different answer, or with QUERY to indicate he wants to ask a question about information stored in files, or GO TO _____ to indicate he wants to talk about a different subject.

For each recognizable situation or state, the program must have a predetermined action or place in the program to branch to. The action may, of course, be expressed parametrically. Having determined that an error has been detected, the programmer could give his action decision in terms of, say, the amount of traffic the system is handling or the number of mistakes the originator has made this day. He need not specify a separate action for one error per day, for two errors per day, etc. Here, then, is where the diligence of the author of the data acquisition program can pay off. The more conditions he can recognize and the more meticulously he can discriminate between different but similar answers, especially erroneous answers, the better—that is, the more meaningful and productive—his conversation can be.

Articulation of the conversation is not the sole objective, however, and we may consider the *Eliza* program of J. Weizenbaum,[14] described in Chapter 5, as an example of a program that can carry on a remarkably sophisticated conversation with a man, yet need not have or work toward a defined goal. Excerpts from *Eliza* conversations were illustrated in Figures 5.7 and 5.8. This progarm makes use of a syntactic analyzer to insure that it can rephrase the originator's statements into meaningful English sentences.

7.4 AN EXAMPLE

We shall take as our example a simplification of a generalized program for use in interrogating people, primarily for information acquisition purposes. It is called computer-assisted interrogation (CAINT) [9] and is a

"system of computer programs for use in man-machine communications. Its principal function is to enable a computer to elicit information from a man by interrogating him—asking him a program of questions where the program follows a logical course depending both on information available before the interrogation started and on that gained during the interrogation. The information acquired is intended to be put to immediate practical use, in updating a data base, generating reports, or driving other interrogations.

"During the course of an interrogation, the interrogee will be given information as well as asked questions, and he may ask his own questions, as well as provide answers. Thus, a CAINT interrogation is truly conversational, with information and questions flowing in both directions. The conversation, particularly in the machine-to-man direction, is somewhat stereotyped, the machine's versatility being limited by a repertoire of generalized, fragmented statements which are particularized and assembled for use as needed. The conversational range of the computer, then, depends upon a system user's versatility in designing these statements—a process somewhat akin to computer programming.

"CAINT permits an item of information arriving in a data base to be presented to a man, and enables the system to ask a set of questions about the datum. These are tailored to that datum in the context of the overall data base as it stands at the moment. In other words, different questions might be asked, in response to the same stimulus, given a different data base environment. For example, in a management reporting system [for a computer programming project], a conversation between CAINT and a programming group leader might be, in part, as follows:

Machine Statements	*User Responses*
Your responsibility is: Tracking Program. Estimate your completion date.	1 DECEMBER 1966

"The machine then responds to this estimate depending upon the history of the original assignment and responses to this question when asked in previous interrogations. Possibilities include:

Your estimate indicates adherence to original schedule.	(NO RESPONSE REQUIRED)
Your last estimate indicated 1 October 1966. What is the reason for the delay?	DESIGN CHANGE PROMULGATED IN PROJECT MEMORANDUM NO. 123 INCREASED COMPLEXITY OF THE PROBLEM."

7.4.1 The Structure of an Interrogation Program

We call the basic unit of an interrogation program a *step*.[10] This is the set of program language statements concerned with the presentation of a message and the elicitation of, and analysis of, a response to the message. There are four major subdivisions on a step: *heading, text, response analysis,* and *ending.* They are concerned, respectively, with initializing bookkeeping items used by a program, presenting the message and asking a question, analyzing the answer received to the question, and performing another series of bookkeeping functions at the conclusion of response analysis, before going to the next step. It is only from the ending section of a step that a transfer can be made to a point *outside* the step. If the decision to branch is made elsewhere, the desired address must be recorded and the transfer deferred until the ending is reached.

The step, as a unit of programming, is restricted to eliciting only one element of information, although an element may vary in complexity from a single number to an array of numbers or a natural language text. This is done to keep the overall program modular and to make it easy to change. It is actually possible, within this rule, to have more than one conversational exchange between program and responder in a step. If a data originator fails to give a recognizable answer, an arbitrarily long conversation may ensue by continually looping back to the beginning of the step from the point where the answer is declared unrecognizable. But these unrecognizable replies are not treated as new information for the data base.

The logic of CAINT imposes no limit on the nature of the response given by an information originator. The main limitation to be considered is the ability of the program author to analyze or recognize a response, which means his ability to direct CAINT how to analyze it. For programming purposes, we classify responses as follows: multiple choice, item, structure, array, phrase and text, (natural language). These are defined and discussed below.

Multiple Choice. Logically the simplest of all response types, multiple choice gives the responder a limited selection of possible answers, typically on the order of five or six. Special cases are *true/false* and *yes/no* responses. It is obviously easy to write a computer program to recognize these responses as well as variations, such as *Yes* or even *Y*. It is also possible to allow more than one answer to be given and more than one to be correct (e.g., "Select two out of the following six. . . ."). The author is free to decide which answers are correct or acceptable and which are incorrect, or to make no judgment on the acceptability of an answer.

Item Responses. An item is a single number or alphabetic or alpha-numeric field. It is possible to limit the responder to a small set of choices (e.g., "Which candidate do you favor?") but not possible to physically restrict him to remaining within the set in the author's mind. Generally, then, use of item responses implies more elaborate analysis of answers than is needed for multiple choice. The author should be able to recognize correct or acceptable answers and highly probable wrong or unacceptable ones, and must also analyze unrecognizable replies to try to determine what the trouble is. He might, for example, have to make sure that the responder was using only numbers if the question called for this form of reply or that no illegal characters were embedded in his alphabetic reply.

Structures. In this context, a structure is a set of items, not necessarily identical in form, in a prescribed order or format. The interrogation program should be able to decompose the structure into individual items and proceed essentially as if it were an item response. A common example is the entry of dates, with DAY, MONTH, YEAR to be entered as prescribed, perhaps in the form DDMMYY, with each field numeric. If a responder enters June 1, 1968, in reply to a question calling for the six-character numeric form, his answer will not be recognizable by arithmetic checking programs. Without going to the extreme of testing for all possible forms of date entry, the program might have been written to test for a leading alphabetic character and, if found, reject the reply with instructions to pay more attention to format. When the next response is received, it can be tested for correctness as to value.

This (elicitation, rejection with explanation, re-elicitation), by the way, is an example of a multipart conversation that elicits only one information element. The structure being sought could always be elicited by a series of item questions. The main reason for combining them is to speed communication and simplify the responder's work. It can become very tedious for him to enter a data structure in small increments and in response to a series of short questions when he is able to grasp a more complex question and has enough familiarization with the subject matter to give a single structure response when asked.

Array Responses. We may want to elicit an array of responses from a responder. Examples of such usage are "List all inputs to your program," "List the principal exports of Peru." An array-eliciting question is the same as an item question except that after each response another one is expected until the responder signals he has completed his list. The author must make provision for recognizing a special end-of-list response and taking appropriate action.

Natural Language Responses. There are circumstances in which it is not possible or convenient for the author to plan for all possible user replies. Some questions do not have precise answers, some require an explanation of why the responder selected the reply that he gave, some elicit a comment to be used later for analysis of the program or for the responder to amplify the answer. When an author elicits a natural language response, he must realize that he cannot be precise in analyzing it, although much can be done.

A description of work in the analysis of natural language inputs to a computer is found in Chapter 5. In early work done with the CAINT system natural language responses were not analyzed but were accepted, stored, and made available for retrieval or report generation. It was left to the CAINT programmer to so program his questions that there was complete agreement between the responder and the program as to what the subject matter of a text response should be. In this way the programmer can virtually make the computer available to any input the originator wants to enter.

7.4.2 Nonresponsive Answers

The theory behind CAINT is that the program author anticipates the kinds of answers he should or could get to his question and hence can reduce the complexity of response analysis to recognizing which type he has, in fact, obtained. We expect and require that the responder be responsive to the question. But he is not always able or willing to follow the line of conversation specified by the author. We restore some balance in the interaction between man and machine by providing the responder with a set of *nonresponsive* commands which he can use in place of the reply requested by the program.

These nonresponsive commands serve primarily to allow the responder to change the sequence of interrogation or to interrupt it temporarily. The following commands have been used experimentally:

GO TO n causes transfers of control to step n. This is primarily a debugging aid and requires the responder to know the program well enough to work directly with step numbers.

BACK transfers control to the question asked immediately prior to the present one. This is not necessarily step n - 1 if used at step n, for n might have been branched to from anywhere in the program. BACK enables a responder to recover from an erroneous answer that he discovers after having transmitted it.

SIGN OFF terminates the interrogation session, saving necessary information for resumption at a later time.

QUERY enables the responder to have access to an information retrieval system and to retrieve information from the data base. After execution of the query, the interrogation program resumes where it was interrupted.

REPORT enables the responder to have a standard report produced from information in the data base. This is useful in very complex situations, where the responder may need periodic reviews of what he has entered thus far.

The following responses are used as conventions, and must be explicitly recognized by the author in his response analysis section of a question:

NO means that the responder does not want to answer the question or is presently unable to answer it. It has the effect of stating that a question does not apply or that no answer is available now.

END indicates the end of a list of inputs, all requested by the same question. If the question asked for all schools attended, for example, END would follow the name of the last school on the list.

7.4.3   Unrecognizable Answers

Deciding how many answers to anticipate and make explicit plans for is a matter of programmer skill and diligence. The more precisely defined the question, presumably, the more precise will be the possible responses. But precise questions are not always possible or even desirable. When a question is vague or general, particularly when it calls for a natural language response, response recognition becomes a formidable problem. For example, Slack and Van Cura[12] report that in a medical patient-interrogation system even simple *yes*/*no* questions had to make provision for responses indicating "don't know," "don't understand," and "don't want to answer."

The author who can detect and act upon erroneous or partially erroneous answers will probably achieve greater rapport with his responders and accomplish more with his programs. However, performing such detailed analysis, even with the aid of CAINT, is a great challenge. Even routine responses of the multiple choice type are susceptible to error, and the range of possible mistakes is such that it is not worthwhile checking for all possible errors. If, for example, a question calls for a *true*/*false* response, the author can anticipate a few variations on these replies (such as *T, t, TRUE, True,* and *Tru*); but, if none of the anticipated variations is found, the author must go to a generalized unrecognizable answer routine, just as he must if he is unable to decipher a text response.

The general approach taken in early experimentation with CAINT was to inform the responder that his answer was unrecognizable and to ask for a new one. He was allowed three consecutive unrecognizables; then he was assumed to be either fooling or hopelessly confused and was cut off. In a multiterminal system operating with a proctor, the proctor could be alerted to the trouble and asked to check on the responder.

With each successive unrecognizable answer, a different message was transmitted to the terminal, with successive messages generally becoming increasingly peremptory in tone. The responder was branched back to the point in the question where another answer was elicited, and then he tried again. The program author was allowed to supply the messages to be printed out; all else was provided by CAINT.

7.4.4   A Sample Interrogation Program

We shall illustrate a hypothetical computer program used to interrogate hospital patients as they are admitted, in order to elicit from them the following information:

> NAME
> ADDRESS
> INSURANCE COMPANY
> POLICY NUMBER
> HAVE BEEN A PATIENT HERE BEFORE?
> DOCTOR'S NAME

This is a far more simple information structure than CAINT was designed to handle, and it would not necessarily be the best approach to acquiring this information in an actual application. The information elicited is obviously not enough for a meaningful patient record, but, as usual, our intent is to indicate how a function works, not to show it in its full operational complexity.

The illustrative program is written in the programming language PL/I,[13] but not all the bookkeeping code required of a PL/I program is shown. The program should not be difficult to follow even with no prior knowledge of PL/I. A flow chart is shown in Figure 7.3. In reading the chart, bear in mind that the flow of control from step to step is not shown. To follow the branching logic, the reader must use subroutine NEXT to determine what step would be executed next.

Program statement	*Comment*
1. S (1) : CALL INIT (1) ;	s (1) is a label, or symbolic address of the beginning of the program. INIT is a subroutine that handles administrative functions.
2. MSG = 'ENTER YOUR NAME';	MSG is the address of the character string to be transmitted to the terminal. Here we set up the first question in MSG.
3. CALL ASK;	ASK is a subroutine that transmits the contents of MSG to a terminal and asks for a response.

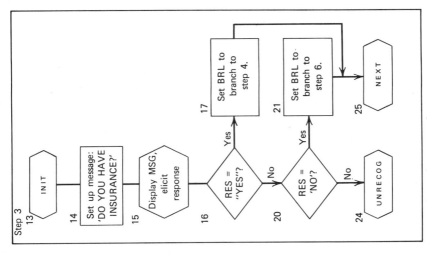

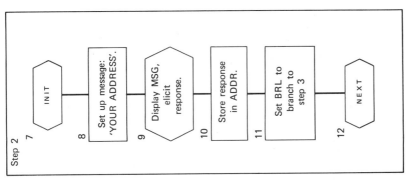

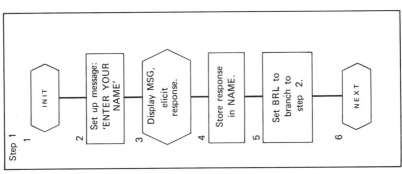

Figure 7.3a Flow diagram of interrogation program. Figures correspond to line numbers of program in text.

203

Program statement	Comment
4. NAME = RES;	RES contains the originator's response to the question. Here we transfer this response to location NAME, which is part of the patient's record, and clear RES for later use. If the responder had answered BACK or given some other non-responsive reply, ASK would have recognized it and taken appropriate action.
5. BRL = 2;	BRL indicates the step to which we want to branch next (it stands for branch label).
6. CALL NEXT;	NEXT is the subroutine that decides where to branch to next. Its coding starts at line 78.
7. S (2) : CALL INIT (2) ;	
8. MSG = 'YOUR ADDRESS';	The patient's address is elicited and stored in
9. CALL ASK;	location ADDR of the patient record.
10. ADDR = RES;	
11. BRL = 3;	
12. CALL NEXT;	
13. S (3) : CALL INIT (3) ;	
14. MSG = 'DO YOU HAVE INSURANCE?';	
15. CALL ASK;	
16. IF RES = 'YES' THEN DO;	Here we have our first response analysis. If the patient claims insurance,
17. BRL = 4;	we want to find out something about his policy,
18. GO TO SE (3) ;	which we will do in step 4.
19. END;	Branching is done by going through subroutine NEXT, not by a direct branch to a new step.
20. IF RES = 'NO' THEN DO;	If the patient has no insurance, we skip the insurance data acquisition.
21. BRL = 6;	
22. GO TO SE (3) ;	
23. END	
24. CALL UNRECOG;	Having asked an obvious *yes/no* question, we provide for action in either eventuality, but prudence dictates that we also make some provision for the patient's failure to answer properly. This subrou-

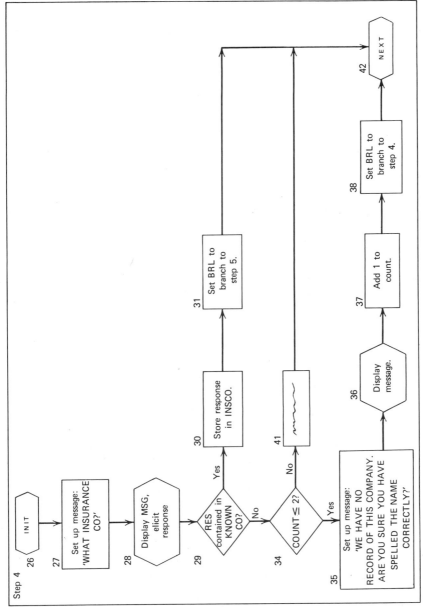

Figure 7.3b Flow diagram of interrogation program. Figures correspond to line numbers of program in text.

Program statement	*Comment*
	tine will tell him his answer is unacceptable, tell him why, and ask him to reply again. His problem may be purely one of mechanical difficulty in coping with the terminal, so we allow him several tries. If he persists in giving unrecognizable answers, we must interrupt the interrogation and call for help.
25. SE (3) : CALL NEXT;	We need a label on this statement (SE denoting the end of the step) because we branch to it from lines 18 and 22.
26. S (4) : CALL INIT (4) ;	
27. MSG = 'WHAT INSURANCE COMPANY?';	
28. CALL ASK;	
29. IF MEMBER (RES, KNOWNCO)	Here we are using a *function*, called MEMBER, which executes a subroutine and then assumes a value. This function compares our response with each member of an array, KNOWNCO, of insurance company names. If the patient's company is on the list (known to the hospital), the function MEMBER has the value 1, otherwise 0.
30. THEN DO: INSCO = RES;	If the company is known, its name is stored in the patient's record.
31. BRL = 5;	Preparation is made to branch to the next step.
32. GO TO SE (4) ;	
33. END;	
34. IF COUNT $\leqslant$ 2 THEN DO;	Count will be initially 1. See line 37 for explanation of its use.
35. MSG = 'WE HAVE NO RECORD OF THIS COMPANY. ARE YOU SURE YOU HAVE SPELLED THE NAME CORRECTLY?';	If the company name, as given, is not known, our first reaction is to give the patient another chance to reply, on the assumption that the failure to match may have been caused by a misspelling.
36. CALL TELL;	We use TELL here, because we really are not asking for a reply. What we are going to do is repeat the step that originally asked the question.

	Program statement	Comment

	Program statement	**Comment**
37.	COUNT = COUNT + 1;	Before doing so, we see how many times we have done that. If twice or more, we assume the name is truly unknown, the mismatch not being due to spelling error, and proceed accordingly.
38.	BRL = 4;	Set BRL for the step to be repeated.
39.	GO TO SE (4) ;	
40.	END;	
41.	ELSE DO;	Here would be the coding to be used when the patient has an insurance company unknown to the hospital.
42. SE (4) :	CALL NEXT;	
43. s (5) :	CALL INIT (5) ;	Start of the step eliciting further details on the insurance policy.
44.	MSG = 'WHAT IS YOUR POLICY NUMBER?';	
45.	CALL ASK;	
46.	POLICY = RES;	Store the policy number.
47.	BRL = 6;	It is not possible for the hospital to keep a list of all valid policy numbers. Hence the information must be accepted at face value, so no checks are made.
48.	CALL NEXT;	
49. s (6) :	CALL INIT (6) ;	
50.	MSG = 'HAVE YOU EVER BEEN A PATIENT AT THIS HOSPITAL BEFORE?';	Now we are getting ready to make use of any information already on file for this person. The medical history of the patient is useful; hence we will retrieve any available. Outdated insurance data, however is of no value, so a completely new set of insurance information was collected earlier.
51.	CALL ASK;	
52.	IF RES = 'YES' THEN DO;	If the patient has been here before, we want to retrieve his record from the files. The GET subroutine will retrieve a record stored under the name previously provided.
53.	CALL GET (NAME) ;	
54.	BRL = 7;	
55.	GO TO SE (6) ;	
56.	END	
57.	IF RES = 'NO' THEN DO;	If he has not been here before, we will need to establish a patient number and create a new record.

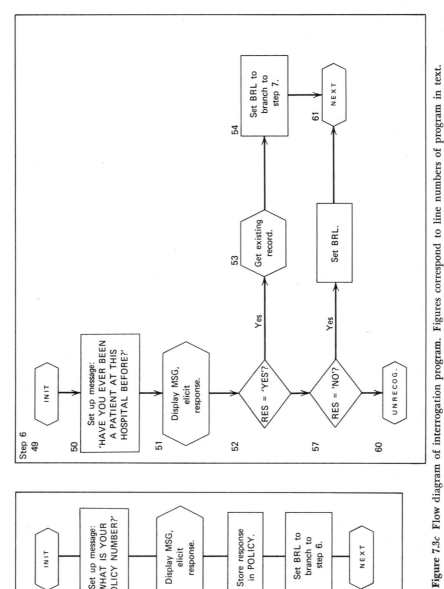

Figure 7.3c Flow diagram of interrogation program. Figures correspond to line numbers of program in text.

Program statement	Comment
58. BRL = ——;	Coding for this is not shown.
59. GO TO SE (6) ;	
60. CALL UNRECOG;	
61. SE (6) : CALL NEXT;	
62. S (7) : CALL INIT (7) ;	
63. IF FOUND = 1 THEN DO; • • •	We assume the retrieval subroutine, GET, sets an item called FOUND to 1 if the record being sought was found, and to 0 if not found. If the record was found, we will add the recently elicited information to it. The details of this are not shown.
64. END;	
65. MSG = 'NO RECORD FOUND UNDER' ‖ NAME ‖ 'COULD YOU HAVE BEEN ADMITTED UNDER A DIFFERENT NAME?';	The composition of this message illustrates the use of previously stored information in a message. The ‖ means *concatenate,* or attach one string of characters to another. Here the patient's name, as he typed it in, is embedded into the message shown.
	The use of this message illustrates another provision for input error. The patient may misspell his own name, particularly if he is not an experienced typist. A woman may have married since her last admission and forgotten that her previous admittance was under her maiden name. We use the same approach as with the insurance company name—first see whether failure to match was caused by a simple typing error.
66. CALL TELL;	
67. MODE = REV;	We are now preparing to operate a previous step (number 1) as a subroutine of this step to try again on the name. The controls for doing this are described under subroutine NEXT, line 78. We will inform CAINT that we are in a review mode, and tell it where to start the review and where to end. In this case, only one step is involved, so START = END.
68. START = 1;	
69. END = 1;	

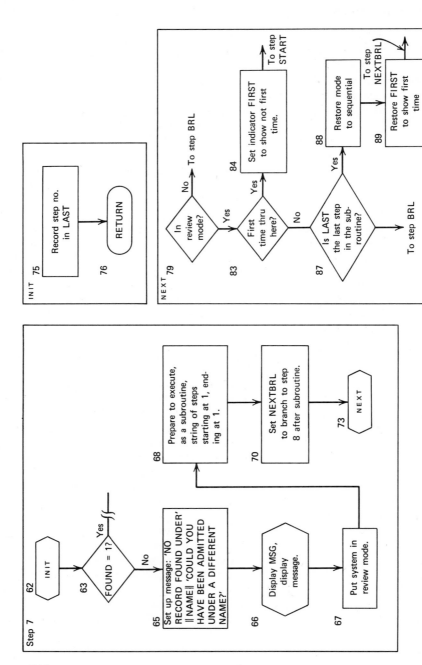

Figure 7.3d Flow diagram of interrogation program. Figures correspond to line numbers of program in text.

Program statement	Comment

70.   NEXTBRL = 8;

Set NEXTBRL to show what step is to be executed after the subroutine is completed.

71.   GO TO SE (7) ;
72.   END;
73. SE (7) :   CALL NEXT;

This is as far as we shall go in illustrating data acquisition. The remaining portions of the program are some of the subroutines referred to earlier.

74. INIT (STEP) :   PROC;

INIT, in this example performs only the task of recording the number of the latest

75.   LAST = STEP;

step whose execution has begun. This number is stored in LAST.

76.   RETURN;
77.   END;
78. NEXT: PROC;

NEXT decides where to go next. If not in review mode, this is a trivial decision, since branching would always be to the step indicated by BRL.

79.   IF MODE = REV THEN DO;

If in the review mode, branch to REVIEW.

80.   GO TO REVIEW;
81.   END;
82.   GO TO S (BRL) ;

If not in review mode, branch to indicated step.

83. REVIEW: IF FIRST = 1 THEN DO;

FIRST is an indicator having the value 1 (true) if this is the first time we have come here for a given review, 0 (false) otherwise.

84.   FIRST = 0;

If it is the first time, reset FIRST to a false value (not the first time any more) .

85.   GO TO S (START) ;

Branch to the step indicated as the beginning of the set of steps to be executed as a subroutine.

86.   END;
87.   IF LAST = END THEN DO;

We come here if we have reached the ending of a step after having started to execute the subroutine. We first check to see whether the step just executed was the last one we were required to execute.

88.   MODE = SEQ;
89.   FIRST = 1;

If it is the end, reset MODE to sequential and resume operation of the interrogation program in the original sequence.

Program statement	*Comment*
90. GO TO S (NEXTBRL) ;	Item NEXTBRL was set by the step that called the subroutine to show where to
91. END;	resume sequential operation.
92. ELSE DO;	We come here when we are neither at the beginning nor at the end of the subroutine.
93. GO TO S (BRL) ;	
94. END;	
95. END NEXT;	

7.4.5   The Conversation

In Figure 7.4 we show how the interrogation program just presented would appear to a user. Only a few of the many possible trails have been followed in the program, but two points should be evident. (1) A great deal of programming is required to carry on even a short conversation, notwithstanding that this program was written in a high-order language specially adapted for such applications. (2) The programmer must constantly keep in mind what the user will see in order to get statements to fit together grammatically and contextually when these statements may not have been written sequentially in the program. Note how this has been done at lines 6 and 7 of the illustration and again at lines 12 and 13.

From the author's experience in working with programs such as these, it seems certain that significant progress will come in this field only when the process of writing programs is made considerably simpler or the programmer is given far more machine assistance in writing them.

As you read this example, a few of the problems of the composers of such interrogations may become apparent. One such problem is that the program has to serve for many different interrogees and, of course, not all people are equally quick at comprehending the questions or adapting to a new way of communicating. If everything is explained in full detail, there is the danger that the reader will be bored to distraction or so confused as to be worse off than before. If inadequate instruction is given, the program must be able to cope with the variety of ways in which various people will answer the same basic question. For example, on line 9 of the illustration the patient is asked if he has ever been a patient at this hospital before. In human conversation the answer "in 1958" is completely comprehensible and acceptable. However, the computer in this case has been programmed only to look for a yes/no answer, intending to ask for the date in a separate question. There is no fixed solution to such problems. It is a constant compromise between the amount of time required to write a program versatile enough to handle all desirable cases and the cost at information acquisition time in terms of the interrogee's time and the quality of the data elicited from him.

A similar problem may occur when one person is to use the interrogation program over and over again for a long period of time. The question on line 9 contains 53 characters, including punctuation, spaces, and a nonprinting carriage return. On a teletype this would require more than 5 seconds to print. If a message of this length were to be presented every few minutes (as might happen in interrogating an airline ticket agent), this would seem an intolerably long time, especially since the user knows from the very first word exactly what the message is, and then he must wait the full 5 seconds to respond to it. One solution [10] to this is to use different versions of a question, having the program select the desired version as a function of the number of times the question has been used in this particular interrogation session. For example, after asking "Have you ever been a patient at this hospital before?" one or two times, an alternate form such as "Been here before?" may be used. Again, the cost in terms of programming time must be balanced against the cost in terms of time saved in operation.

Machine Statement	Patient's Response	Comment
1. ENTER YOUR NAME	jane a. doe	This message generated by step 1.
2. YOUR ADDRESS	123 45th ave., new york, n.y.	Step 2.
3. DO YOU HAVE INSURANCE?	yes	Step 3. The program will inquire further only if the patient claims insurance.
4. WHAT INSURANCE COMPANY?	mutual	Step 4 asks for the company name.
5. WE HAVE NO RECORD OF THIS COMPANY.		The system is unable to find this name on its list of known companies. The possibility of a misspelling is suggested.
6. ARE YOU SURE YOU HAVE SPELLED THE NAME CORRECTLY?		Note that the patient is not really expected to answer this rhetorical question.
7. WHAT INSURANCE COMPANY?	mutual enterprise corp.	Now step 3 is repeated, the name again requested.
8. WHAT IS YOUR POLICY NUMBER?	123456	This time the name was found, and we go on to ask for the policy number at step 5.
9. HAVE YOU EVER BEEN A PATIENT AT THIS HOSPITAL BEFORE?	in 1958	The program now wants to know if it should look for a previous hospital record. This answer, possibly understandable to a person, is not understandable to the program.

10. YOU MUST ANSWER YES OR NO

The unrecognizable subroutine is used.
Then the question is repeated.

11. HAVE YOU EVER BEEN A PATIENT AT
    THIS HOSPITAL BEFORE?   yes

12. NO RECORD FOUND UNDER JANE A.
    DOE COULD YOU HAVE BEEN
    ADMITTED UNDER A DIFFERENT NAME?

No record has been found under this name.
The patient is first asked whether he or she might have used a different name (possibly he has misspelled his own name, through a typing error).
Our patient gives her maiden name, under which she previously entered.

13. ENTER YOUR NAME   jane allen

Figure 7.4 The interrogation program as seen by the user.

REFERENCES

1. *A Guide to Office Clerical Time Standards,* Systems and Procedures Association, Detroit, 1960.

2. Avram, Henriette B., John F. Knapp, and Lucia J. Rather, *The MARC II Format: A Communications Format for Bibliographic Data,* Library of Congress, Washington, D.C., January 1968.

3. Beltrami, Ottorino, quoted in *The General Electric Forum,* **X,** 4 (Winter 1967–68), 29.

4. Coe, Jerome T., quoted in *The General Electric Forum,* **X,** 4 (Winter 1967–68), 29.

5. Fano, Robert M., "The World at Our Fingertips?" *The General Electric Forum,* **X,** 4 (Winter 1967–68), 5.

6. *Introduction to Programmed Airline Reservations System (PARS),* Form E20–0298, IBM Corp., White Plains, N. Y., 1967.

7. King, Gilbert W., et al., *Automation and The Library of Congress,* Library of Congress, Washington, D.C., 1963, p. 80.

8. Martin, James, *Design of Real-Time Computer Systems,* Prentice-Hall, Englewood Cliffs, N. J., 1967, pp. 92–100.

9. Meadow, Charles T., and Douglas W. Waugh, "Computer Assisted Interrogation," *Proceedings of the AFIPS 1966 Fall Joint Computer Conference,* Spartan Books, New York, 1966, pp. 381–394.

10. Meadow, Charles T., Douglas W. Waugh, and Forrest E. Miller, "CG–1, A Course Generating Program for Computer-Assisted Instruction," *Proceedings of the 23rd National Conference, ACM,* Brandon Systems Press, Princeton, N. J., 1968, pp. 99–110.

11. Meadow, Charles T., Douglas W. Waugh, Gerald F. Conklin, and Forrest E. Miller, *Evolutionary Systems for Data Processing,* Report ESD–TR–68–143, U. S. Air Force, Electronic Systems Command, Bedford, Mass., 1968.

12. Slack, Warner V., and Laurence J. Van Cura, "Patient Interviewing," *Postgraduate Medicine,* **43,** 3 (March 1968), 68–74, and 4 (April 1968), 115–120.

13. Weinberg, Gerald M., *PL/I Programming Primer,* McGraw-Hill, New York, 1966.

14. Weizenbaum, Joseph, "ELIZA—A Computer Program for the Study of Natural Language Communication Between Man and Machine," *Communications of the ACM,* **9,** 1 (January), 36–45.

RECOMMENDED ADDITIONAL READING

The literature on this subject is rather sparse. Most books or papers tend to discuss the specific application involved or the hardware mechanics, not the conversational techniques of information acquisition, with the result that we find it difficult to see how the author designed his program. Several of the items listed below have already been cited as references in this chapter but are repeated for lack of other choices.

1. Feingold, Samuel L., "PLANIT—A Flexible Language Designed for Computer-Human Interaction," *Proceedings of the AFIPS 1967 Fall Joint Computer Conference,* Spartan Books, New York, pp. 545–552 (for the composition of conversational programs).

2. Hughes, J. L., *Programmed Instruction for Schools and Industry*, Science Research Associates, Chicago, 1962 (for an insight into the problems of linking together conversational elements).

3. Martin, James, *Design of Real-Time Computer Systems*, Prentice-Hall, Englewood Cliffs, N. J., 1962 (for the mechanics of programming and communications).

4. Orr, William D., ed., *Conversational Computers*, John Wiley, New York, 1968 (for a general treatment).

5. Weizenbaum, Joseph, "ELIZA—A Computer Program for the Study of Natural Language Communication Between Man and Machine," *Communications of the ACM*, **9**, 1 (January 1966), 36–45 (for the problems of language interpretation).

Chapter Eight

Instruction

8.1 INTRODUCTION

This chapter is about programmed instruction and its implementation with the aid of a computer. Programmed instruction (PI) is a means of presenting instructional material to students in small units called *frames* and sequencing the frames according to some logical plan.

The unit of presentation of material in PI is called a _____.

The **FRAME** is the unit of presentation. When we put a set of frames together into a logical sequence we call it a _____.

A **PROGRAM** is the organized set of frames, carefully sequenced by the author to present material gradually and meaningfully.

This is a short example of programmed instruction, a relatively new concept in education that is becoming both popular and effective and may lead to a revolution in teaching methods. Programmed instruction is not without its problems and defects, however, some of which are reduced and some compounded when a computer is used as the means of presenting programmed instructional material to the student. Because PI, even without the participation of a computer, may be unfamiliar to many readers, we shall begin our treatment of this subject with a lengthy discussion of what programmed instruction is and a description of some of its history, problems, and effects. Then we can see what the computer can contribute to the process and how PI can be augmented in this way to produce computer-aided, or computer-assisted, instruction.

8.2 THE BASIC CONCEPTS OF PROGRAMMED INSTRUCTION

For programmed instruction, as for any relatively new concept, several formal definitions are in common use. It is well to begin by stating one, but we must not let any formal definition constrain our thinking on what PI is or might become through further understanding or development. Lysaught and Williams[10] call instructional programming "... the process of arranging materials to be learned in a series of small steps designed to lead a student through self-instruction from what he knows to the unknown of new and more complex knowledge and principles." A learning program they call "... the completed route to mastery of the subject for which it has been prepared—ordered and ready for the student to follow."

An almost universal feature of PI is frequent reinforcement, testing a student's comprehension and giving him feedback on his performance. The feedback helps him remember what he has learned and, when he does well, motivates him to continue to do so. Psychologists use the term *reinforcement* to describe a process that increases a tendency to repeat a behavior pattern when the behavior results in a reward or the absence of a punishment. Indeed, it is from studies of reinforcement and stimulus-response theories that the concept of PI evolved, largely through the work of B. F. Skinner[15] and S. L. Pressy.[13]

The usual characteristics of a PI course are these:

1. Instructional material is presented in small units, usually called *frames.*

2. The sequence of presentation is based on logical development of the material being taught, frames building up on a base of material learned in previous frames.

3. Students are tested for comprehension in almost every frame, and immediate feedback based on their answers is provided.

4. The students work either without a teacher or with little direct assistance; hence PI is usually thought of as being self-instruction.

5. As a consequence of the auto-instructional characteristic, students are able to move at their own speed and are neither held back by a pace adjusted to the mean of a large class nor pushed too quickly through material they are not grasping.

Combining these features into one outstanding attribute, we might summarize PI as amounting to customized or personalized training. Neither textbook nor lecture nor recitation session, however well planned or conducted by the teacher or author, can give each student the personal attention to his own particular difficulties that PI can. Furthermore, PI potentially offers each student the individual, even though vicarious, attention of the best teachers and authors and thus helps to make our utilization of outstanding teachers more effective.

Excellent summaries, comprehensible to the layman, of the history of the development of programmed instruction may be found in Lysaught and Williams[11] and Hughes.[2] We shall review a few highlights here and then refer the reader to these texts or to the original research papers on the subject[9] for further information. Two key studies influenced the development of the subject. Skinner,[15] working on problems of learning in animals, discovered that quick reinforcement speeded the learning process. Pressy[13] developed an apparatus for giving tests. Using multiple choice logic and giving an immediate grade to the student on each answer, he discovered that students learned while taking the tests, and that those who did not know some of the answers learned them as a result of the feedback and, on being retested, showed an increase in comprehension.

Although there have been many teaching machines (this expression generally refers to machines other than computers) on the market, probably the most effective presentation device developed to date is the book. The machines generally do little more than present a frame (on a sheet or page of paper or a frame of microfilm), elicit an answer to a question, in all but the simplest cases have the student himself compare it with the right answer, and branch accordingly. With material printed in book form, these functions can be performed for a much lower cost than is possible with most hardware. Also, no positive or negative motivational complications caused by the use of a machine, or the need to operate it, as part of the learning process are introduced. We shall see that this aspect of book presentation falls on both sides of the ledger when considering what the computer has to offer to programmed instruction.

There are two general approaches to the presentation of material and feedback to the student. These are called *intrinsic* and *extrinsic* programming. Extrinsic programming, also called *linear* or Skinnerian after its originator, is characterized by having the sequencing of frames determined by the author, not the student. In this form of programming, the questions asked at the end of a frame call for a constructed response rather than a choice among multiple given answers. Proponents of this form of programming feel that the student remembers better when he must positively state an answer than when he simply recognizes the right response among other candidates. Even more valuable is the self-discovered, constructed response, one given by the student when the particular fact called for has not been explicitly stated in the course, but the author has written the material with the intent that the student be able to reach the desired answer and thus discover it for himself. The second question (third frame) at the beginning of this chapter is an example. The correct answer PROGRAM has not yet been defined in the course. In an extrinsic course, the student proceeds to the next frame in sequence, regardless of his response. The succeeding frame may review the previous response, to reinforce or correct the student, but there is no branching to another location or portion of the course. The short program at the beginning of this chapter is an extrinsic, or linear, course.

An intrinsic, or branching, course presents the student with a choice of answers and, on the basis of the particular one he selects, branches him to a different frame to continue the course. This technique was developed by Pressy[13] and N. A. Crowder.[1] In this approach to course writing, the actual sequence of frames may be different for each student. The author decides on the possible successors to any frame, and the condition for branching there, but it is the student's actual choice of a response that determines which branch is followed. An example of such a form is

```
                    If  X = 3 x 2
                    then X = ?
if your answer is  a.  5  go to frame _____ on page _____
                   b.  6   "   "     "    _____ on page _____
                   c.  1   "   "     "    _____ on page _____
                   d.  none of these
                       go to frame _____ on page _____
```

Intrinsic programming enables the author to anticipate the kinds of mistakes his students may make and to prepare remedial material specific to each predictable error. If the student in this example answered *a* or *c*, he might be chastised for failure to read the operation sign correctly. If *d*, he might be made to review all his arithmetic lessons; if *b*, he can go on to more advanced work.

Clearly, there is no sharp boundary between these methods, for a student can be asked to fill in a blank (construct an answer) and then be presented with a table of successor frames as a function of his answer. The problem is that there is no physical limitation to the number of different constructed answers, and these tables may grow quite large, presenting a very practical problem for the authors and publishers of books. Generally, the extrinsic form permits more abstract questions to be asked and gives the student more latitude in comparing his own answer against the given one. For example, in a course on computer programming, once the point is reached where the student is writing small programs, it is almost impossible to predict all the possible forms he might use and still be correct. To overrestrict the question avoids the issue. Hence authors give a correct answer, and the student must compare it with his own solution and decide whether the two are essentially in agreement. This has the weakness that the student may either be fooling himself or be missing some subtle point.

The two greatest criticisms leveled against PI are (1) that it is too impersonal, that students are deprived of the benefit of a live, concerned teacher, responsive to their needs or even just aware of their existence as individuals; and (2) that PI is not well suited to advanced or abstract subjects. Both charges have some truth in them, but do not tell the whole story.

Certainly it is true that self-instruction through PI is less personal. Its advocates point out, however, that this may be better instruction, that a teacher with 30 students is not giving much attention to most of them, and that the student with a serious learning problem may never have it recognized and diagnosed and be given appropriate remedial instruction. Furthermore, there is often a choice between PI, or self-instruction, and none. Consider the student who is handicapped or otherwise barred from the classroom, such as military personnel on remote assignments with time on their hands. Actually, most advocates of PI in the regular school situation support the continued presence of the teacher in the classroom. He and PI do not conflict, but rather can work together to produce better education for more students.

As to PI's effectiveness in abstract subjects, there appears to be a strong argument here. K. O. May[12] has done a study of PI in advanced mathematics and has reached a negative conclusion on its application there. The problems involved in breaking down a difficult, abstract subject into neat little frames, asking a trivial question at the end of each, and proceeding are too much for the world of complex ideas, at least so far. Today PI seems to be better fitted to well-structured material that can be decomposed into precise, small units for which questions of the right-or-wrong type can easily be formulated.

Another weakness of PI, from the economic viewpoint, is that several times as many pages are required to cover a given amount of material as are needed to cover the same ground in a conventional text. Many PI courses are in the form of bound books that are twice the size of conventional texts and still do not cover all the ground. This costs the student or the school more money. Also, the PI text is of little value as a reference book during or after the course; hence the student desiring such a reference work encounters another economic disadvantage of PI.

Just how effective is programmed instruction as a pedagogical technique? There is no short answer. Some persons have raised doubts about the retentiveness of students who study this way, although no evidence exists on which to base a conclusion derogatory to PI. There is simply insufficient evidence in its favor. Unquestionably, students usually go through programmed material faster than they do conventional material.[3] This is not surprising since a classroom presentation must be aimed at some midpoint between the best and the worst students and, for safety's sake, often favors the weaker ones. Those who do not do well in a conventional course are missing some part of it, essentially not completing the same course as the better students, so that, in a fixed amount of time, they do less work. Also, the speed of PI may simply be attributable to the individual approach, rather than to the programmed form of presentation. Again on the positive side, surveys taken by researchers after testing students with PI courses indicate that most of the students would like to have more of their work presented in this way.[4] Significantly, however, very few would like to be taught exclusively by PI. We may conclude, rather qualitatively, that PI offers a faster approach to teaching, that it can be at least as effective as ordinary teaching, that students would not like to see their teachers disappear, and that PI offers a means of exposing students to the best teachers in a somewhat personalized way.

8.3 PROGRAMMED INSTRUCTION AND THE COMPUTER

The role of the computer in assisting in the presentation of programmed instruction has, somewhat harshly, been described as "simply a page turner." This is no more fair or accurate than to describe the computer's role in science as "simply an adding machine." The computer brings a great potential to programmed education, one that is not yet fully realized and may not be realized for many years to come, but that is evident nevertheless.[16]

Basically, computer-assisted instruction (CAI) enables the teacher to communicate with his students in a highly personalized, although dehumanized way. The well-written CAI course enables the teacher to anticipate many possible student answers, to analyze complex responses, and to route the student in many ways through the course. So many and varied are the possibilities that the conventional lecturer may never achieve the results in an hour that a CAI course can. The use of a computer or of PI does not, of course, imply dismissing the teacher, even the classroom teacher; but it changes his role and can make him more effective because he can have available the results of a degree of diagnostic work never possible in the normal schoolroom.

Let us consider what new characteristics the computer can bring to programmed instruction. First, there is speed of reaction, of page turning, if you will. The delay between the end of a student's answer and the computer's (teacher's) reaction to it can be reduced to the point of being imperceptible to the student. One of the weaknesses of book presentation of PI, particularly when the scrambled text method is used, or when there is much supporting material such as illustrations or test sheets, is that the student can be distracted by the inordinate page-turning time. The computer offers the opportunity, available nowhere else except through a private tutor, to feed a student new information as fast as he indicates he can take it and can demonstrate that he comprehends it.

Although programmed instruction is usually self-instruction, the computer can serve as a surrogate teacher that actually converses with the student and shows an awareness of his particular answers and his overall pattern of responses. One valuable way in which this is so lies in the computer's ability to analyze a student's answer. Book-form PI courses must limit the number of multiple choices open to the student, or must leave it to him to decide for himself if his answer is right or wrong. The computer gives the teacher a powerful capability to analyze the student's answer, piece by piece if that is appropriate, and to find what part is wrong and what is right. The teacher can have an answer decomposed and then use exact matching, as he would in an intrinsically programmed course, or he can call for constructed responses; in either case, he programs the computer to *analyze* the answer, not just match it. If the teacher calls for a date, he can tell which part of the date is right or wrong, forgiving minor errors but not necessarily forgetting them, or he can separate a number from its dimensional label and separately grade the student's choice of value and label.

In the field of natural language analysis, although computer interpretation is still relatively weak, the example shown in Figure 5.8 on p. 126 indicates a promising future for this approach to teaching. In teaching computer programming for example, the teacher can cause a student's program to be executed and can tell that it is right if it produces the correct result. The problem here is that there are many ways to write an acceptable program to accomplish a given task, and to list them all in a multiple choice question is impossible. Consequently, many PI courses oversimplify the questions to ease comparison and branching, somewhat short-changing the student in the process.

By attaching a variety of peripheral equipment to the teaching computer, its versatility can be greatly enhanced. There is no need to stay only with the printed page. One can use the traditional typed output to talk to the student, photographs (usually slides or microfilm images projected on a small screen), cathode ray tubes for both text and graphic output generated by the computer, or audio output in the form of prepared messages recorded on a program-addressable tape recorder. These variations afford the teacher more flexibility in holding the student's interest, in explaining difficult concepts, and in demonstrating sounds. Showing a student a colored photograph and describing it with a voice recording can be quite effective a way to teach art or the recognition of skin diseases.

Student input can be typed, transmitted through special switches or keys, entered through a light pen, or voice-recorded on tape (this for later analysis by the teacher, for practical computer recognition of speech is not yet a reality). Additionally, student input can be through almost any mechanical or electrical device that can be attached to the computer.

The computer's memory can be used by the course author or teacher to achieve better analysis of student response patterns and more sophisticated branching and remedial instruction. It is difficult, at best, to use a pattern of student response to make branching decisions in a printed PI course—to remember, for instance, that a specific student tends to forget there are two square roots of a number or to use incorrect tenses of verbs. With CAI, this is quite simple, for the teacher can program the storage of the type of error made at each frame and can analyze and summarize this information at any time in the course. He can, for example, end a session with a student by printing out a statement that most of his errors are caused by using the wrong tense, by unfamiliarity with a particularly useful formula, or by lack of knowledge of a class of diseases. This can help the student (and the teacher) and can be used as the basis for remedial work that is specific, not just to a single error but to a recurring pattern of error. Also, student answers can be stored and recalled for self-analysis; a review of his unbroken chain of present-rather-than-future-tense verbs may make more of an impression on a student than any live or programmed lecture, however specifically tailored.

Three important features of computer-assisted instruction are related more to the teacher or the course author than to the student, but they can have great effect on teaching technique and effectiveness. First, the teacher need not be over concerned with keeping to a pure linear- or pure branching-type course. Although he need not be a purist in writing printed courses either, the mechanical problems of book layout reinforce the tendency to be uniform. The computer, however, makes branching easy to keep track of, and it is a simple matter to use constructed responses and still check them and branch as a result of the response. Regardless of the technique selected, the computer plays no favorites and is equally well adapted to either the linear or the branching type or to compromises.

Second, the author's ability to have the computer maintain complete records of student responses and progress is useful, not only in evaluating his students, but in evaluating his own course material as well. Such feedback is just not available from ordinary teaching methods. Indeed, one of the advantages of programmed instruction is that it forces the instructor to recognize the weak points in his text and to do something about them. Hence programmed texts may surpass ordinary ones because they have had the advantage of more meticulous attention in their composition.

Third, correlative with the author's review capability is his course modification capability. Here is the single point on which the computer most significantly outstrips the book form of presentation. A computer course can be modified in little more time than it takes to type the text of the change. Once this is done, it is complete, and the change has been made for all students who take the course from this point forward. To change a paragraph in a published book, however, would require at least a handmade change to each copy, and to alter the logic or the sequence of presentation of material calls for a new edition. This ready change capability of CAI can be used not only for correcting course errors but also for gradual implementation of ideas and techniques into a course. In early drafts, for example, the teacher can use minimum checking of student responses and can gradually expand his analysis of each answer, becoming more precisely diagnostic as he proceeds. Also, he can turn over some of the mechanics of response analysis to assistants while he retains full control over the presentation of text and the logic of branching.

In summary, the computer is a versatile machine for presenting information to a student, for recording the student's answers, for enabling the author to review both his own and the student's performance when a course is taken, and for modifying the course when needed. Properly used, the computer is not a replacement for the classroom teacher but rather a device to relieve him of much generalized lecturing and to provide him with a level of diagnosis of each pupil's performance that is not practical in the traditional classroom.

8.4 EFFECTIVENESS AND PROBLEMS OF COMPUTER-ASSISTED INSTRUCTION

The effectiveness of computer-assisted instruction is hard to evaluate, apart from the effectiveness of such component factors as programmed instruction, well-written material, individualized instruction, and the special motivation that goes with being a part of experimental work in a new field. Even if, as has been done,[14] a course is given in the traditional way, then the course material is programmed for CAI presentation, and students taking the course in different ways are given the same test, the results alone are not sufficient to tell how well CAI performed. How does the experimenter remove the effect of heightened interest of students in this new way of teaching? It could well be that the novelty alone accounted for the difference in performance, and this might wear off soon. As a generality, the studies that have been done, both in PI and CAI, tend to show that students do better with these methods than with traditional ones, that they like them, but that they do not want to see the teacher removed from the classroom.[5, 14]

In one of the few industrial trials of CAI, IBM's Field Engineering Division used the technique to provide field engineers with a uniform background on fundamentals before bringing them together for more advanced classroom training.[8] As a practical matter, such an application, aside from the effectiveness of CAI as a teaching method, reduces the cost of training by giving the personalized remedial instruction to each individual at his own office, cutting travel costs and time away from the job, and enabling the main training courses to be scheduled more effectively.

The field of CAI, however, is not utopian. There are problems, some concerned with the machinery, or hardware, and some with the computer programs and instruction programs, or software.

Hardware problems include the very existence of the student terminal, for to some it is an interesting gadget and could replace the course as the object of attention. Computer-assisted instruction systems tend to depend heavily on typewriter input from the student; and although there is usually no need for high speed or expert typing, a high price can be paid for typing errors or lack of purely mechanical skill in using the keyboard. Also used are pictorial displays, CRT displays that enable the student to respond by using the light pen to point to a selected answer, audio instruction, and audio responses. Good use and mixing of these devices can help reduce the dependency on mechanical skill on the part of the student, at the risk of overwhelming him with gadgetry.

In all these devices response time is a problem. How quickly should a computer respond to a student answer? How fast should the computer be able to type? How quickly should it change pictures or frames of pictorial display? The ideal answer is that response should be as rapid as possible or as rapid as the student wants it, but reaction speed plays a large role in determining the cost of the computer system. We wish, then, a response and output rate that minimizes interference with the student's thought processes, but enables the computer to stay within a price the school can afford. Attempts to fix these parameters are confounded by the consideration that students can adapt, given time, to devices and performances that seem intolerable on first encounter. We also find that the prices schools can afford vary considerably. Industrial and military training instructions, for example, include in their costs the salary of the student, whereas scholastic and collegiate institutions do not.

In regard to software, the biggest problem is course writing. How do we get courses that can take best advantage of the power of the computer? Compared to book writing, CAI course writing is in its infancy, with only a comparatively small number of people ever having written a course, and few having taken one. No one has used CAI throughout his educational career and thus become as familiar with these courses as most of us are with books. Writing a CAI course is roughly comparable to writing a textbook on the subject, in terms of the author's time and effort, and there is not yet the incentive for the best teachers to present their material in this way. Also, computer programming is an unfamiliar art to most instructors, and they are unable to make as lucid and interesting a presentation through the intermediaries of a program and a computer as they can in face-to-face interaction with students in the classroom. This further militates against authors who are not directly involved in PI or CAI research devoting themselves to programmed courses instead of standard texts (and standard royalties).

We are given no choice but to wait and watch the software of CAI develop, to encourage more authors to try this mode of expression, and to find ways of capitalizing on work done by others. In fact, one almost wishes, as this is written, that hardware development would be arrested for a few years while teachers concentrated on seeing how well they could prepare material for the machines at hand.

8.5 MECHANICS

To demonstrate how computer-assisted instruction works, we shall present a much simplified version of the Coursewriter I language developed by IBM, in several forms, for its CAI systems.[7] This language is the medium of communication between the course author and the computer. The author uses the Coursewriter language to give his instructions to the computer on how to present course material and how to react to student answers. The computer interprets these instructions and communicates with the student. The language used by the author is not the language directly understood by the computer. Authors' statements must be interpreted by another program, and each author command may generate a large number of machine operations. The Coursewriter commands can either be *compiled* (the entire course translated into machine instructions first and then executed) or run *interpretively*, in which case each author command is examined, translated, and executed in its turn, before the next is considered.

We shall describe a *subset* of the Coursewriter language used with the first commercially available IBM CAI system. By a subset we mean only a few commands selected from the complete authors' repertoire, but enough to constitute a meaningful and operable language. The complete language is described in Reference 7. We shall first describe the individual commands, then discuss how they are used, and conclude with an example of a CAI course written in this language. Although more advanced versions of Coursewriter are now available, they have tended to progress in the direction of greater logical power, not necessarily ease of use.

8.5.1 The Commands

There are two classes of commands, *major* and *minor*. Major commands are those directly concerned with presenting instructional text and testing the student's reply to a question. Minor commands are essentially satellites of the major commands, and whether or not they are performed depends on the result of matching or failing to match some replies that have been anticipated by the author. Major commands have an implicit branching logic associated with them, minor commands normally are followed by the next instruction in sequence [except for the branch *(br)* command, which is a minor one but changes the normal course sequence].

qu (text)

The *qu* command is a major one. It includes a line of text, generally unrestricted in composition. The command is used to ask a question, and it instructs the computer to print the associated text to the student. This is the basic command of a CAI language; it can be used to present the instruction material and then ask a question about it. Most of the remaining commands are concerned with interpreting the student's reply to a *qu*.

ca (text)

The text part of this major command contains an answer that the author anticipates the student may give. The author can anticipate as many answers as he wishes, using this command and others to do so. The computer is directed to compare the text of this command with the student reply and to take one action if they are the same, another if they differ. The name *ca* is derived from *c*orrect *a*nswer and is normally used by the author to indicate an answer he feels is correct; but, as we shall show, it also has other uses.

cb (text)

This is a minor command that tells the computer to take the same actions if the student gives the answer contained in the text field of this command as it did for a *ca* that *must* have preceded the *cb*. If there are several things to do, this is a shorthand way of saying, "Repeat all action commands associated with the last *ca* in case of this (text) as an answer."

wa (text)

This major command is normally used to anticipate a *w*rong *a*nswer. It is similar to the *ca* except that the action to be taken includes asking for another reply to the question by the student.

wb (text)

This bears the same relationship to *wa* as *cb* does to *ca*.

un (text)

This command is used when the author wishes to specify an action to be taken for any student response that is *un*recognizable after all the *ca*'s, *cb*'s, *wa*'s, and *wb*'s have been tried. It is a major command. Normally, the author specifically anticipates all the replies he can think of or wishes to recognize. For any other result, he will follow the path that starts with this command. In this case, the text part of the command is not used for matching; it is a message printed out to the student (possibly "Your answer is unrecognizable, try again"). After a *un* is executed, the student is expected to try again unless the author causes another action to be taken.

br (label)

This is a minor command that an author can use to change the normal sequence of commands. It causes the computer to ignore the commands that follow, and to pick up the sequence at the command specified by the label. This is equivalent to providing a location of the next command to be executed. If the *br* occurs following a *wa* or *un*, it will override the feature of the *wa* or *un* command that requires another student answer.

ty (text)

This minor command causes the message contained in the text field to be typed out on the student's console typewriter. Unlike the *qu,* also a message-printing command, *ty* has no functions other than typing.

8.5.2 Use of the Commands

Let us review the commands with an eye to how they are used and how they are interpreted by the computer. In this simplified language, the *qu* command must always be used to start a new frame. The text portion is printed, and the computer awaits a response. Actually, if another *qu,* a *ty,* or a *br* is encountered before the first *ca, cb, wa, wb,* or *un,* the new instruction is executed without waiting for a reply to the first *qu.* Hence the computer will stop and await a reply only if an answer is anticipated by use of a *ca, wa,* or *un.*

If the course reads:

```
qu  How much are 2 + 3?
ca  5
```

the computer will stop at the *ca* command and await a response. If it reads:

```
qu  How much are 2 + 3?
qu  You should know this quite well.
```

the computer does not stop before typing the second line of text.

If a *ca* is used in connection with a *qu,* and there is a match between its text field and the student's reply, the computer executes all following minor commands until the next *ca, cb, wa, wb,* or *un* is encountered, which stops the sequential execution of minor commands. When the next *qu* is met, it is executed. We can see that there is nothing peculiar to "right" answers in the *ca* logic. The command is really used any time the author wants to go on to the next frame without having his question answered again. It could also be used to recognize an answer so woefully wrong that the student obviously needs remedial work, not repeated questioning. For example:

```
qu   Are you ready to go to the next command?
ca   Yes
br   (next frame)
ca   No
ty   Then you should review the last two pages.
```

There is no "right" or "wrong" answer to this question. There is only a student ready or not ready to go one way or another.

The *cb* command, it will be recalled, repeats the logic of the *ca* to which it is attached. We can illustrate this by repeating the last example.

```
qu   Are you ready to go to the next command?
ca   Yes
cb   yes
cb   y
br   (next frame)
ca   No
cb   no
cb   n
ty   Then you should review the last two pages.
```

The author has decided to allow the responses *Yes, yes,* and *y* to be treated as acceptable affirmative replies, and *No, no,* and *n* to be accepted as negatives.

The *wa* command is used when the author wants the student who has given a wrong answer to reply again. Use of this command enables him to anticipate usual error situations and to provide some needed hint or remedial remarks before the next student reply. For example:

```
qu   What is the value of y if y = 3 x 2?
ca   6
ty   Right, now we'll try a harder one.
     (Automatic branch to next qu)
wa   5
ty   Check the operation sign and try again.
     (Automatic branch to point just after last
     qu, to test new answer)
un   Read the question carefully and try again.
     If you don't understand, ask for help.
```

Here the author assumes an answer of "5" means that the student added instead of multiplying, rather than that he did not know how to find the product of 3 and 2. He need not put in a *br* command after the *ca* and *wa* because the program automatically branches for him.

This example also illustrates the use of *un*. The author cannot anticipate all the possible ways a student can go wrong, so at some point he must put in a catch-all, or suggest the student review the instructions or ask for help. Again, no *br* is needed because the course automatically loops back to try again. Note that the *ty* is executed before branching, following the *ca* and the *wa*.

Let us now summarize the control logic of this abbreviated language.

After a *qu*	execute the next sequential instruction.
After a matched *ca*	execute any associated *ty's* or *br*'s. If not diverted by a *br*, upon encountering the first major instruction, skip ahead to the next *qu*. (That is, after executing the minor commands, bypass all other *ca, cb, wa, wb,* or *un* commands and go to the next frame.)
After a matched *cb*	same as *ca*
After a matched *wa*	same as *ca*, except that, instead of going to the *next qu, go back to the last*, so the student can try another answer to the question. The text of the *qu* is not repeated.
After a matched *wb*	Same as *wa*.
After a *un*	Same as *wa* except that, if there is more than one *un*, the first is used with the first unrecognizable answer, the second with the second, . . . (The differences between the *un* and *wa* commands do not lie in their control logic.)
After a *ty*	go to the next sequential command unless the logic of one of the major instructions overrides this. (For example, if a *ty* follows a *ca* and precedes a *wa*, the *wa* is not executed. If a *ty* is followed by a *br*, the *br* is executed.)
After a *br*	go to the location in the course designated in the text portion of the *br*.

Before proceeding to a more lengthy example of the use of this language, we should point out an important technique of author strategy that is not so readily illustrated in this reduced language. We have mentioned the teacher's ability to diagnose patterns of student response and to branch to different course segments accordingly—to carefully selected remedial work, to more advanced work, or perhaps to more review or practice of what has just been covered. In the command set we have illustrated, the author has only the last student response to use for analysis, making it more difficult, but by no means impossible, for him to collect student patterns. There are two ways in which an author might do this.

In one method, the student is branched through a hierarchy, or tree structure, of questions; when he arrives at the end of any particular branch of the tree, the author knows he got there only by means of a certain sequence of correct responses, or of failures to respond correctly. A conclusion regarding the student's overall pattern is reached implicitly, since the author need never have written down explicitly the patterns he is looking for or, as a totality, the criteria for making a decision about overall performance. This technique can be implemented in the language described, as we shall illustrate presently.

The alternative is to record the response to each question as it is made, and analyze the set of responses after completion of the set of analytic questions. In this approach, decision-making is done by a direct analysis of the complete set of responses up to the decision point, a mode requiring that the author make explicit his classification criteria. The illustrated language subset does not have the facility for this technique, but the reader should be aware that in actual practice it is available.

In general, the instructions we have omitted from the Coursewriter language can perform the following functions:

1. Store a response or other information that the author may designate in an area of memory set aside for records on each student.

2. Branch conditionally to a different frame, that is, use the contents of a memory location to decide whether a *br* command will be carried out or ignored.

3. Perform arithmetic with the contents of the memory, enabling, for example, an author to count the number of right and wrong answers as the course proceeds, or the number of a certain kind of question the student gets wrong, or the number of times the student must repeat the answer to any given question before he gets it right.

4. Record the student's responses, or a subset of the responses. The subset to be recorded can be only right answers, wrong ones, unrecognizable ones, all answers, etc. These recordings are made on magnetic tape or disk and cannot be analyzed by a Coursewriter program, but are printed out for the author's use later.

5. Insert small programs written in "machine language" to perform any function or process desired on the student's response. Simple examples are the stripping out of case shift and punctuation characters to make a long response easier to check against a stored standard. (For

example, *The Quick Brown "Fox"* can be made to equal *the quick brown fox* or *thequickbrownfox.*)

6. Control the use of audio and pictorial presentation devices attached to the student's console. These commands are logically similar to the *ty,* directing the computer to present a particular slide from the projector or recorded message from the tape recorder.

8.6 AN EXAMPLE

The following is a simplified example of how the abbreviated instruction language we have described could be used to teach a topic in elementary algebra.

Label	Instruction	Text	Comments
A1	qu	A quadratic equation has the general form ax2 + bx + c = 0, where a, b, and c are constants and x the variable. Do you know how many roots a quadratic equation has?	This command presents the instructional material and asks the question.
	ca	2	Two correct forms are anticipated, but still more are possible (e.g., Two). If correct, the student is congratulated. Next command executed is in the next frame, at label A2.
	cb	two	
	ty	Good	
	un	Your answer is not right. Since this is your first CAI course, you may have made a typing or procedural error. Check for a typographical error and try again.	The student is given the benefit of the doubt and is asked to answer the question again. He gets this message after his first unrecognizable answer. If he enters another unrecognizable reply, the next un is operated.
	un	There are two roots, or solutions, to a quadratic equation.	Assumption is made at this point that the student does not know the answer. He is told and then branched to the next frame.
	br	A2	
A2	qu	In the equation 3x2 + 2x + 1 = 0 what is the value of a?	A simple test of the student's knowledge of the general form of a quadratic equation. If the answer is right, he is congratulated, and he proceeds (without need of a *br* command) to the next frame.
	ca	3	
	ty	Good	

Label	Instruction	Text	Comments
	wa	2	Either of these answers implies an actual failure to grasp the material, rather than a typing error. The student is given a hint and the chance to try again.
	wb	1	
	ty	Remember, a is the coefficient of x2 in the general form of the equation. Recheck the general form and try again.	
	un	Your answer corresponds to neither a, b, nor c. Call the instructor if you need help or try again.	Since his answer is not one of the obvious wrong ones (and also is not right), he may be in serious trouble. He might feel better asking for help from his instructor.
	un	Perhaps you'd better ask for help.	Two unrecognizable answers in a row certainly imply something is wrong, and the student is cut off the machine.
A3	br	END	
	qu	b?	He must have given the value of *a* to get here. We now ask him about *b*.
	ca	2	It would have been nice to know whether he got the previous answer on the first try or not, and to word the machine's response here differently if he did not. This would require the memory briefly referred to above. Particularly, it maght have been desirable to type (ty), "Good, that's two in a row" (if this were the case) or "Now you're getting it" (if there had been an error in the first try at the last frame, but none here) or a simple acknowledgment if both frames required two tries.
	ty	Good	

Label	Instruction	Text	Comments
	wa	3	We now have some information, implicitly, on this student's history. He had to have answered frame A2 correctly or he would not be here. Hence we can use this knowledge to give him a very specific comment on his last answer.
	ty	But you just said, and correctly so, that a = 3. Then what is b?	
	wa	1	The teacher's (author's) patience is running out. A terse hint is given, and the student will have another chance.
	ty	b is the coefficient of x. Try again.	
	un	Your answer is not correct. Try again or call for help.	If his answers are still unrecognizable, he is probably having trouble with the mechanics of the system.
	un	Consult with your instructor.	There is no point in continuing with this student until an instructor can look at the record of his performance and find the source of the trouble.
	br	END	
A4	qu	Then c must be ———?	Again, the author knows the student has answered all questions correctly (even if not on the first try) to get here, so the question is worded in this context.
	ca	1	This answer transfers the student to the next frame.
	ty	Right	
	wa	2	
	wb	3	

Label	Instruction	Text	Comments
	ty	You have given this answer to a previous question. c is the constant term in the equation. Try again.	If there are two *un*'s, the first is executed after the first unrecognizable answer and the second after the second unrecognizable answer. This gives the instructor a chance to be increasingly firm or to give more hints as the student continues to miss.
	un	Your answer is not recognizable. Ask for help or try again.	
	un	Your answer is still unrecognizable. Ask for help from your instructor.	
	br	END	
A5	qu	The roots of a quadratic are $$x = \frac{-b \pm (b2 - 4ac)1/2}{2a}$$ If the roots are denoted r_1 and r_2 and if $$r_1 = \frac{-b + (b2 - 4ac)1/2}{2a}$$ fill in the missing information for r_2: $$r_2 = \frac{-b \ ? \ (b2 - 4ac)1/2}{2a}$$	The student has been through a review of the meaning of a, b, and c. Now this notation is freely used in new instructional material.
			Presumably, the author would have preferred a more sophisticated way of testing the student's comprehension here. Entry by the student of an equation even this simple is a problem on a typewriter however, and might cause more confusion than it cleared up.

Label	Instruction	Text	Comments
	ca	—	Accordingly, the author used a simplification of the question he really wanted to ask— "What is the expression for r_1?"
	cb	minus	
	ty	Very good	
	wa	+	
	wb	plus	
	ty	If this were correct, what would be the difference between r_1 and r_2? Look over the general expression for the roots and try again.	
	un	Your answer is not correct. Try again.	
	un	Your answer is still wrong. Ask for help before resuming.	
	br	END	

Once again, the student can reach the next frame in this course only if he answers A5 correctly, however, many times he tries. We have not illustrated remedial frames within this course, but their use is indicated, especially when there is evidence of repeated failure to answer correctly the first time. Incidentally, good PI technique dictates [6] that the questions be so worded that most students will get an overwhelming majority of them right. A PI course is not an examination, and there is no need to make every question difficult to answer. Correct answers help a student's morale and improve his motivation for future work.

We conclude this chapter with a view of the illustrative course as it might have appeared to a student, in this case one of modest accomplishment. Student replies are underlined.

Conversational Text

Comment

A quadratic equation has the general form $ax^2 + bx + c = 0$, where a, b and c are constants and x the variable. Do you know how many roots a quadratic equation has?

<u>yes</u>

The student's literal answer indicates the author should revise the question.

Your answer is not right. Since this is your first CAI course, you may have made a typing or procedural error. Check for a typographical error and try again.

<u>2</u>

Good

In the equation $3x^2 + 2x + 1 = 0$ what is the value of a?

<u>2</u>

Remember, a is the coefficient of x^2 in the general form of the equation. Recheck the general form and try again.

<u>3</u>

Good
b?

$$\underline{2}$$

Good
Then c must be _____?

$$\underline{2}$$

You have given this answer to
a previous question. c is the
constant term in the equation.
Try again.

$$\underline{1}$$

Right
The roots of a quadratic are

$$x = \frac{-b \pm (b - 4ac)^{1/2}}{2a}$$

If the roots are denoted r_1
and r_2 and if

$$r_1 = \frac{-b + (b - 4ac)^{1/2}}{2a}$$

fill in the missing information for r_2:

$$r_2 = \frac{-b \ ? \ (b - 4ac)^{1/2}}{2a}$$

$$\underline{minus}$$

Very good

REFERENCES

1. Crowder, Norman A., "Automatic Tutoring by Intrinsic Programming," *Teaching Machines and Programmed Learning*, A. A. Lumsdaine and Robert Glaser, eds., National Education Association, Washington, D. C., 1963, Part IV, pp. 286–298.
2. Hughes, J. L., *Programmed Instruction for Schools and Industry*, Science Research Associates, Chicago, 1962.
3. *Ibid.*, Chapter 5.
4. *Ibid.*, p. 45.
5. *Ibid.*, Chapters 4, 5 (pp. 39–56).
6. Ibid., p. 72.
7. *IBM 1401, 1440, or 1460 Operating System; Computer Assisted Instruction*, Form C24–3253–1, IBM Corp., White Plains, N. Y., 1965.
8. Long, H. S., and H. A. Schwartz, "The Potentials of Computer-Assisted Instruction in Industry," *Training Director's Journal*, September 1966.
9. Lumsdaine, A. A., and Robert Glaser, eds., *Teaching Machines and Programmed Learning*, National Education Association, Washington, D.C., Part IV, 1963.
10. Lysaught, Jerome P., and Clarence M. Williams, *A Guide to Programmed Instruction*, John Wiley, New York, 1963. p. 2.

11. *Ibid.,* Chapter 1, pp. 1–28.
12. May, Kenneth O., *Programmed Learning and Mathematical Education,* Mathematical Association of America, Committee on Educational Media, San Francisco, 1965.
13. Pressy, S. L., et al., "Pressy's Self-Instructional Test-scoring Devices," *in* Lumsdaine and Glaser, *op cit.,* Part II, 1960, pp. 32–93.
14. Schurdak, J. J. *An Approach to the Use of Computers in the Instructional Process and an Evaluation,* Research Report RC–1432, IBM Research Division, Yorktown Heights, N.Y., July 6, 1965, pp. 28–31.
15. Skinner, B. F., et al., in Lumsdaine and Glaser, *op cit.,* Part III, pp. 94–256.
16. Suppes, Patrick, "The Uses of Computers in Education," *Scientific American,* September 1966, pp. 207–220.

RECOMMENDED ADDITIONAL READING

1. Bushnell, Don D., and Dwight W. Allen, eds., *The Computer in American Education,* John Wiley, New York, 1967.
2. Caffrey, John, and Charles J. Mosmann, *Computers on Campus,* American Council on Education, Washington, D.C., 1967.
3. Hickey, Albert E., and John M. Newton, *Computer-Assisted Instruction: A survey of the literature,* 2nd Ed., Intelek, Inc., Newburyport, Mass., 1967 (AD 649 335).
4. Silberman, H. F., and R. T. Filep, "Information Systems Applications in Education," *Annual Review of Information Science and Technology,* Vol. 3, Encyclopaedia Britannica Co., Chicago, 1968, pp. 357–395.

Chapter Nine

Editing Text

9.1 INTRODUCTION

The activities of composing, editing, and preparing a text for publication present ideal targets for the developers of interactive computer systems. Typically, a manuscript is changed and transcribed many times as it progresses from an idea in the mind of its author to a page of professionally printed copy. The author may make several versions himself, starting with a very rough draft, refining this by posting changes directly on the original page, and retyping whenever the density of alterations makes the copy illegible. The final manuscript then goes to an editor, who perhaps makes or suggests other changes and adds notations providing instructions to the printer or typesetter. The author reviews all the editor's notes and may make further changes. Finally, if the text is typeset and printed (as opposed to being typewritten and reproduced by photography, or offset), galley proofs are prepared; these call for another round of author and editor changes, both as to content and as to layout. Finally, page proof is prepared and is followed by another round of changes. This description fits the production of a book but may be somewhat modified for the production of technical journals or newspapers.

Figure 9.1 shows a rough, typewritten draft, prepared by the author from even more rough, handwritten notes which, in the case illustrated, would have been in telegraphic style, not proper English, and probably illegible to anyone other than the author. In Figure 9.2 we show corrections posted to the rough draft. It may be noted that not all errors have

been caught—for example, in the third line from the bottom, the paren-
thetical expression should read $2^4 = 16$. Figure 9.3 shows the results of
the next typing, this time by a professional typist, and in Figure 9.4 this
copy has been marked by a copy editor for typesetting. Some errors are
still undetected! The galley proof is shown in Figure 9.5, and the
proofreader's marks indicate how many errors reached this stage of production. The actual, published version appears in Figure 9.6.

What stands out, in preparing material for publication, is the
number of people who have some hand in creating the final copy—
whether the printed page or a typescript—and the number of changes
that typically are made before the text is in final form. Too many
changes may necessitate retyping or the resetting of type; both processes
are expensive and time consuming.

If we consider the many typings and annotations, whether for change
or for printer instruction, to be processes performed on a basic text, we
become interested in the cost of the processes, their mechanical nature,
and the extent to which they are "creative" functions. Not all the
creative work is done by the author. Editing the text to conform to a
style, detecting and correcting errors, and laying out the page for both
utility and attractiveness are also in the realm of creative work. The
aim of an interactive computer system should be to help both writers
and editors to perform their tasks.

We can apply computers to text preparation and editing to (1)
reduce retranscription, the repetitive recopying of text solely for the
purpose of making it look neater, (2) assist in the mechanics of page
layout, and (3) simplify the posting or application of changes to a text,
to affect either content or format. In this chapter, we shall consider
these functions in two stages. First, we shall consider computer aids to
the author in initially recording his material, making changes, and
creating draft copies; and then we shall discuss problems of page layout,
including both modification of the text to fit prescribed limits and allocation of space to different types of material. Finally, we will present an
example of an interactive text acquisition and editing system.

9.2 CREATING AND EDITING THE TEXT

The IBM Administrative Terminal System (ATS) ,[8,10,11] which will
be used as the basis for discussion here and in the more detailed example
in Section 9.4, is a data-processing system having as its principal function
the acquisition of copy, the processing of changes to it, and the production
of edited, well-formatted typescript. In this section we shall concentrate

If a probability is zero then p_1 log p_1 = 0 and noinformation

reaults. If a probability is K 1, p_i log p_i = o and, again, no informatin

results. ~~IXXHMXX~~ Since both 0 and 1 probabilities represent certainty

an event either can not happen or always happen s - we find a mathematical

representati n of our intuitive idea that information is the dispelling of

uncertainty, and if there is no uncertainty, there can be no information.

IN Figure 7-1 we show a plot of the p $\log_2$ p.

If we use logarithms to the base 2 two, the units of H are called <u>bits</u>,

or binary digits. Fro example, there are 32 (25) letters in an alphabet

each equally likely to occur, the formula says that five bits of

information are representaed. A bit, as a unit of measure shpuld

not be confused with what we moght call a <u>physical bit</u>, a magnetized

area on magnetic tape or a single magneticcore in a computer memory, which

can have value zero or one. Each physical bit does not necessarily

convey a bit of information. When we use a six physical bit computer code

(capable of representing 2^6 = 64 symbols) only for the ten decimal

numeric symbols, there is obvious redundancy in our coding dow to the

use of only four bits, still represent eveery decimal digit (2^4 - 16)

and still have some redundancy. Figure 7-2 shows how an alphabet of

32 symbols are coded using five bits.

Figure 9.1 An author's self-typed draft typescript.

on function, and leave most of the detail for the example.

The basic concept of ATS, viewed as a computer program, is that each user (and there may be as many as forty simultaneous users) is given an area of memory called a *workspace,* wherein he enters his text and executes various processes upon it. The use of workspace is illustrated

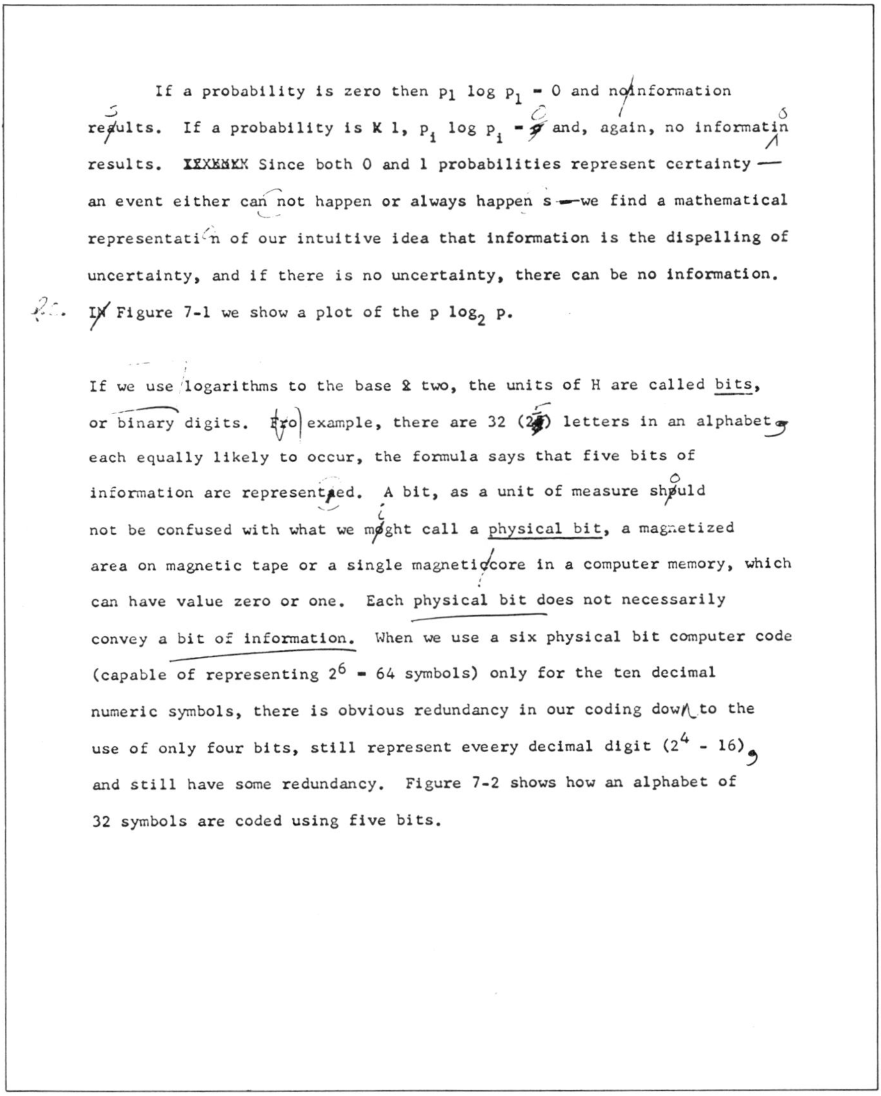

If a probability is zero then p_1 log p_1 = 0 and no information

results. If a probability is K 1, p_i log p_i = 0 and, again, no informatin

results. Since both 0 and 1 probabilities represent certainty —

an event either can not happen or always happen s — we find a mathematical

representation of our intuitive idea that information is the dispelling of

uncertainty, and if there is no uncertainty, there can be no information.

In Figure 7-1 we show a plot of the p $\log_2$ p.

If we use logarithms to the base 2 two, the units of H are called bits,

or binary digits. For example, there are 32 (2⁵) letters in an alphabet,

each equally likely to occur, the formula says that five bits of

information are represented. A bit, as a unit of measure should

not be confused with what we might call a physical bit, a magnetized

area on magnetic tape or a single magnetic core in a computer memory, which

can have value zero or one. Each physical bit does not necessarily

convey a bit of information. When we use a six physical bit computer code

(capable of representing 2^6 = 64 symbols) only for the ten decimal

numeric symbols, there is obvious redundancy in our coding down to the

use of only four bits, still represent eveery decimal digit (2^4 - 16),

and still have some redundancy. Figure 7-2 shows how an alphabet of

32 symbols are coded using five bits.

Figure 9.2 The author's typescript corrected.

in Figure 9.7. The author also has the option of permanently storing
text; if he elects to do so, he can later retrieve it from permanent storage.
All processing is done in workspace. To print or otherwise process a
document in permanent storage, it must first be retrieved and placed in
a workspace. No document can be permanently stored unless it has

If a probability is zero, then $p_1 \log p_1 = 0$ and no information results. If a probability is 1, $p_i \log p_1 = 0$ and, again, no information results. Since both 0 and 1 probabilities represent certainty--an event either cannot happen or always happens--we find a mathematical representation of our intuitive idea that information is the dispelling of uncertainty, and if there is no uncertainty, there can be no information. In Figure 7-1 we show a plot of the $p \log_2 p$.

If we use logarithms to the base two, the units of H are called <u>bits</u>, or binary digits. For example, if there are 32 (2^5) letters in an alphabet, each equally likely to occur, the formula says that five bits of information are represented. A bit, as a unit of measure should not be confused with what we might call a <u>physical bit</u>, a magnetized area on magnetic tape or a single magnetic core in a computer memory, which can have value zero or one. Each <u>physical bit</u> does not necessarily convey a <u>bit of information.</u> When we use a six physical bit computer code (capable of representing $2^6 = 64$ symbols) only for the ten decimal numeric symbols, there is obvious redundancy in our coding down to the use of only four bits, still represent every decimal digit ($2^4 - 16$), and still have some redundancy. Figure 7-2 shows how an alphabet of 32 symbols are coded using five bits.

Let us consider this from another point of view.*
Suppose the alphabet to be used in communicating between two points

---

*See Cherry [2] for a fuller treatment of this approach.

Figure 9.3 Final, typed copy.

first been placed in a workspace. Thus ATS creates an electronic copy of the embryo document. All changes to it, whether to revise or to edit for final printing, are made on this copy by the computer. There is never a need to retype a document just to clean it up or revise its format.

The author types his material, much as he would in ordinary draft

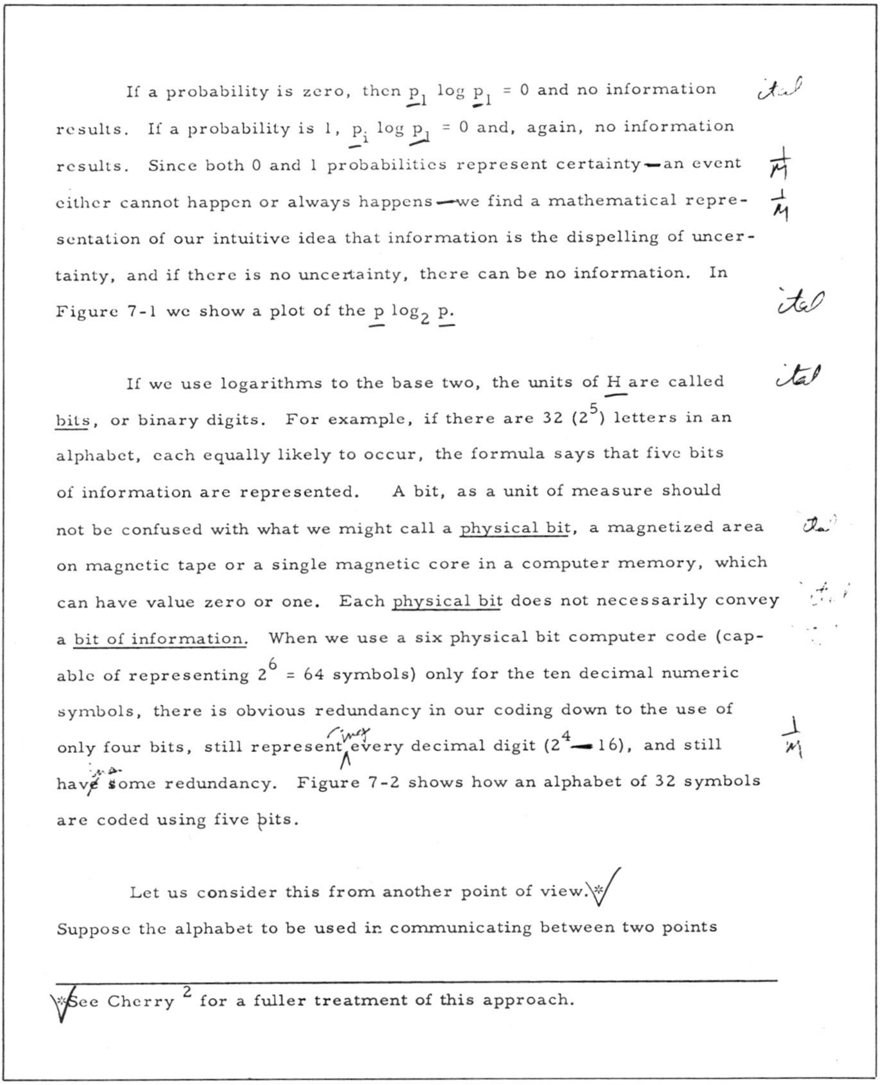

If a probability is zero, then $p_1 \log p_1$ = 0 and no information

results. If a probability is 1, $p_i \log p_i$ = 0 and, again, no information

results. Since both 0 and 1 probabilities represent certainty—an event

either cannot happen or always happens—we find a mathematical repre-

sentation of our intuitive idea that information is the dispelling of uncer-

tainty, and if there is no uncertainty, there can be no information. In

Figure 7-1 we show a plot of the $p \log_2 p$.

If we use logarithms to the base two, the units of H are called

bits, or binary digits. For example, if there are 32 (2^5) letters in an

alphabet, each equally likely to occur, the formula says that five bits

of information are represented. A bit, as a unit of measure should

not be confused with what we might call a physical bit, a magnetized area

on magnetic tape or a single magnetic core in a computer memory, which

can have value zero or one. Each physical bit does not necessarily convey

a bit of information. When we use a six physical bit computer code (cap-

able of representing 2^6 = 64 symbols) only for the ten decimal numeric

symbols, there is obvious redundancy in our coding down to the use of

only four bits, still represent every decimal digit (2^4 ─ 16), and still

have some redundancy. Figure 7-2 shows how an alphabet of 32 symbols

are coded using five bits.

Let us consider this from another point of view.

Suppose the alphabet to be used in communicating between two points

---

See Cherry [2] for a fuller treatment of this approach.

Figure 9.4 Copy editing on the manuscript.

typing, except that he divides it into *units* of arbitrary length. A unit
may be a line of type, or it may be a sentence or paragraph, that is, a
grammatically defined entity. Each unit is numbered by the computer
and thereafter becomes the basis for retrieval and modification. The
author may recall or delete a unit by number, make an insertion after

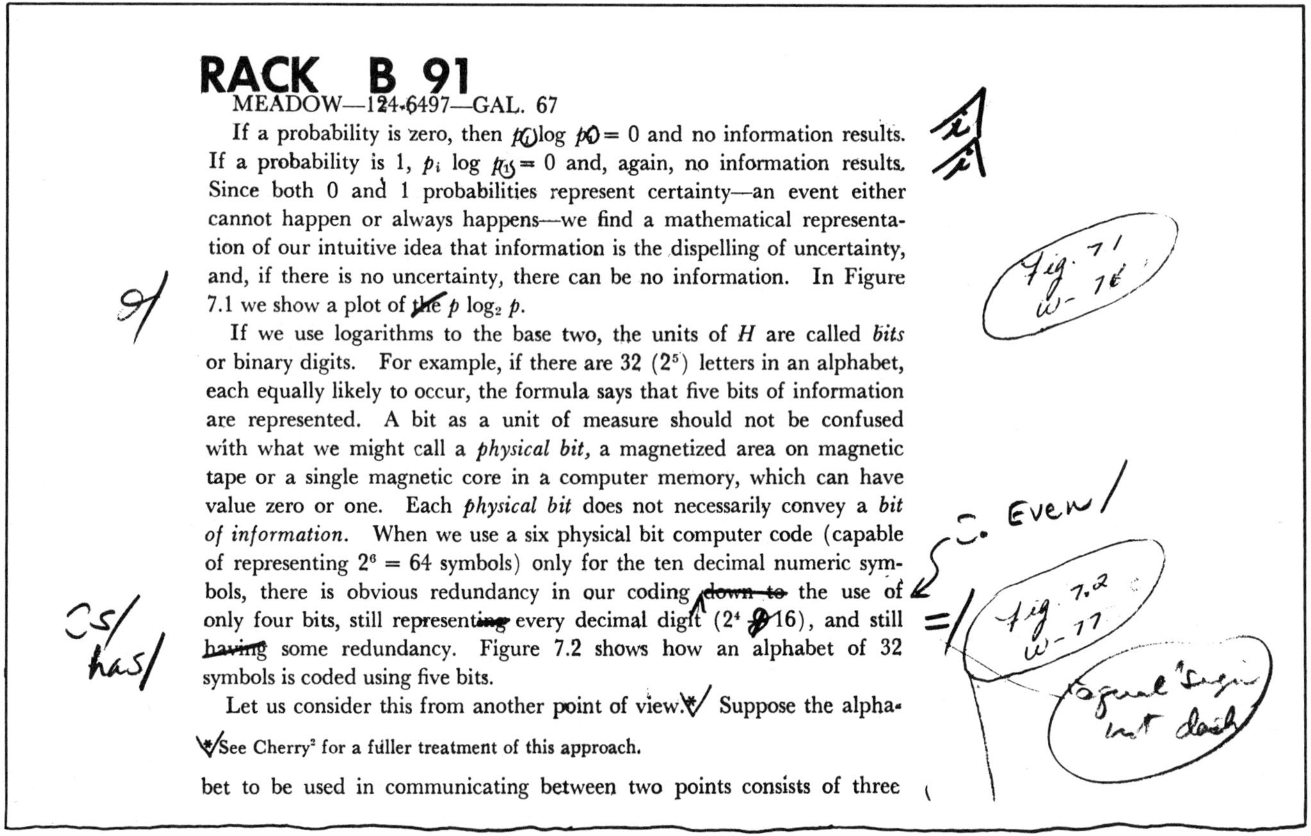

RACK B 91
MEADOW—124-6497—GAL. 67

If a probability is zero, then $p \log p = 0$ and no information results. If a probability is 1, $p_i \log p_i = 0$ and, again, no information results. Since both 0 and 1 probabilities represent certainty—an event either cannot happen or always happens—we find a mathematical representation of our intuitive idea that information is the dispelling of uncertainty, and, if there is no uncertainty, there can be no information. In Figure 7.1 we show a plot of the $p \log_2 p$.

If we use logarithms to the base two, the units of H are called *bits* or binary digits. For example, if there are 32 (2^5) letters in an alphabet, each equally likely to occur, the formula says that five bits of information are represented. A bit as a unit of measure should not be confused with what we might call a *physical bit*, a magnetized area on magnetic tape or a single magnetic core in a computer memory, which can have value zero or one. Each *physical bit* does not necessarily convey a *bit of information*. When we use a six physical bit computer code (capable of representing $2^6 = 64$ symbols) only for the ten decimal numeric symbols, there is obvious redundancy in our coding down to the use of only four bits, still representing every decimal digit ($2^4 = 16$), and still having some redundancy. Figure 7.2 shows how an alphabet of 32 symbols is coded using five bits.

Let us consider this from another point of view. Suppose the alphabet to be used in communicating between two points consists of three

See Cherry[2] for a fuller treatment of this approach.

Figure 9.5 A galley proof with corrections marked.

If a probability is zero, then $p_i \log p_i = 0$ and no information results. If a probability is 1, $p_i \log p_i = 0$ and, again, no information results. Since both 0 and 1 probabilities represent certainty—an event either cannot happen or always happens—we find a mathematical representation of our intuitive idea that information is the dispelling of uncertainty, and, if there is no uncertainty, there can be no information. In Figure 7.1 we show a plot of $p \log_2 p$.

If we use logarithms to the base two, the units of H are called *bits* or binary digits. For example, if there are 32 (2^5) letters in an alphabet, each equally likely to occur, the formula says that five bits of information are represented. A bit as a unit of measure should not be confused with what we might call a *physical bit*, a magnetized area on magnetic tape or a single magnetic core in a computer memory, which can have value zero or one. Each *physical bit* does not necessarily convey a *bit of information*. When we use a six physical bit computer code (capable of representing $2^6 = 64$ symbols) only for the ten decimal numeric symbols, there is obvious redundancy in our coding. Even the use of only four bits still represents every decimal digit ($2^4 - 16$) and still has some redundancy. Figure 7.2 shows how an alphabet of 32 symbols is coded using five bits.

Let us consider this from another point of view.* Suppose the alphabet to be used in communicating between two points consists of three symbols: a, b, and c. We do not wish to have to transmit the full Morse or Hollerith letter representations, as this would be a waste of

Figure 9.6 The final, published form. *Copyright, 1967, John Wiley & Sons, Inc.*

or within a unit, or add new units.

When entering text into the system, the author or typist will make errors ranging from simple typing mistakes that can be left for correction during a later editing operation, to more serious errors such as omitting

Figure 9.7 The concept of workspace. The user directs ATS to operate on data in a *workspace*, an area of memory temporarily assigned to him during one session of working on the computer. If he would like his text kept on file in the system, he orders the system to keep a copy in permanent storage. He can cause text to be moved back and forth between workspace and permanent storage.

a line or repeating one, or organizing work poorly (especially if original composition is done directly with the system). The latter types of mistakes call for large-scale corrections and, in conventional typing, might require the retyping of at least one full page. The computer, however, gives the author a repertoire of text modification commands that enable him to minimize the amount of retyping needed to recover from errors, however heinous. Some of these commands are described in detail in Section 9.4, and a glance ahead to the illustrations in Section 9.4.6 will give the reader a picture of ATS functions.

After a draft has been completed, the author may have the computer retype it to provide him with a clean, legible copy. He may then make whatever changes he desires, all through use of the modification commands, and create additional clean, new copies at will. Finally, he can order the preparation of an edited copy that can be fed directly to a reproducing machine to make his final document. The electronic copy of the text can be retained in permanent storage and used for making new copies or for later modification, as needed.

We have not described the process of storing and retrieving the text in much detail, since, as we hope is obvious, this is merely a combination of the processes of information acquisition and retrieval described in Chapters 7 and 8. Let us emphasize this point—the basic functions of a text-editing computer system are the acquisition of information, in much the same way as any data-handling system acquires input from its users, and the later retrieval of this information, either in totality or in specified parts. What distinguishes an editing system from these others is the range of processes that may be performed upon the data, once they are acquired by the computer. These, we describe in the next section.

9.3 COMPOSING AND FORMATTING A PAGE

The most commonly performed editing processes are justification, hyphenation, layout of the page (counting lines, inserting page headings, footings, and page numbers), and space allocation—deciding, for example, how much of the raw material available will be published in an edition of a newspaper and where it will be placed. It is interesting to note that each of these functions has an esthetic aspect, so that whatever results are produced by the computer cannot be judged or accepted solely on the basis of speed or economy. They also tax the ability of systems designers to state the esthetic requirements to a programmer. What, for example, determines whether a page is acceptably laid out?

9.3.1 Justification

Justification means to adjust the spacing in a line of type or print so that it will begin and end at specified points. If all lines are justified, they are aligned vertically. We may also speak of *left justifying*, in which the lefthand edges of all lines of print are aligned (commonly done by a typewriter), and *right justifying*, in which the righthand ends of the lines are aligned. Fully justified print is more pleasing to the eye and is preferred whenever attainable.

When type is set by a printer, not only does each letter have a different width, but also a variety of spacing widths is available. On a conventional typewriter, all letters and spaces have the same width. In typesetting, a printer selects and sets the type and then, in a separate operation, prints it. Hence he can pause, while setting the type, to look at it and make adjustments in spacing before printing. Or he can easily revise his print after looking at a proof copy. When typing, of course, there is no practice run unless the typist wants to type out each line, count the spaces, make whatever adjustments are necessary, and then retype it on a different sheet of paper. In either case, justifying is a process that is carried out when a text is otherwise all ready for publication, since changes in the text may induce spacing changes that could require the entire document to be retyped or reset. We shall consider here only the problems of justifying typewritten copy. This is somewhat more simple, since the number of variables is fewer, but the basic concepts are the same.

One way to insure that typewritten copy lines up at both sides of the page would be to move the last word on the line to the specified right margin and put all the excess space just before this final word. While mechanically simple, this solution is esthetically unacceptable. Proper technique calls for spreading the excess space fairly evenly throughout the line. Here is one way to do this. Where n is the number of spaces in a line, we take n characters (including interior spaces) of the text to be printed. If the $(n + 1)$st character is a space, we have an even line and no justifying is necessary. If the $(n + 1)$st character is not a space, we are in mid-word, and in the absence of a hyphenation scheme (see the next section) we must go back to the space preceding the last, or incomplete, word. This justification scheme is shown in Figure 9.8. The number of characters thereby removed from the line equals the number of spaces we must sprinkle somewhere into the line.

To distribute the spaces, we scan backward through the line, putting an extra space where each existing space now exists. If we come to the left edge of the line before running out of spaces to insert, we start over

NOW IS THE TIME FOR ALL GOOD MEN TO COME TO THE AI

····|····|····|····|····|····|····|····|····|····|

    5   10   15   20   25   30   35   40   45   50

D OF THE PARTY.

····|····|····|····|····|·

    55   60   65

To arrive at a 50-character, justified line, we would take the first 50 characters, discover that the fiftieth (I) is not blank, and count back until the first blank is encountered. The number of positions counted determines the number of blanks that must be embedded in the text.

NOW IS THE TIME FOR ALL GOOD MEN TO   COME   TO   THE

····|····|····|····|····|····|····|····|····|····|

    5   10   15   20   25   30   35   40   45   50

AID OF THE PARTY.

····|····|····|····|·

    5   10   15   20

Figure 9.8 Justification of text.

again at the right and continue until all spaces are disposed of. Clearly, this method will always put more space on the right side of the page whenever space is unevenly distributed. To overcome this tendency, we can alternate starting on the right and on the left sides with successive lines. The idea is to avoid "rivers" of white space on the final page.

The typesetter follows the same basic plan, but, having variable size spaces, he can insert space between the letters of a word as well as between words. This is hardly ever done with typing although it may be desirable, particularly with narrow columns, where otherwise the space between words may be as large as, or larger than, the adjacent words.

In Figure 9.9, we show the entire process in greater detail. We have a text to be printed in lines 50 characters wide. The first step for the justification program is to count forward (left to right) 50 characters, adding some fixed number of spaces for each tabulate character we encounter. The tab (⟨T⟩) is used to indicate paragraph indenting. The amount to be indented must be set into the justification program, and the tabs must be physically set to corresponding positions on the typewriter where the final typing is to be done. Assume the left tab is set at position 10. Then the justification program counts the tab character as 10 spaces and will pick up only 40 more. Making this substitution, the 50th character is the E in the word FATHERS (line 5 of figure 9.9) and, of course, is not a blank or a space. The program now counts back to the first space or, actually, to the last character immediately preceding

```
....|....|....|....|....|....|....|....|....|....|
    5   10   15   20   25   30   35   40   45   50
```

1.　ℐ"FOURSCORE AND SEVEN YEARS AGO OUR FATHERS BROUGHT
2.　FORTH ON THIS CONTINENT A NEW NATION, CONCEIVED IN
3.　LIBERTY AND DEDICATED TO THE PROPOSITION THAT ALL
4.　MEN ARE CREATED EQUAL."

5.　*bbbbbbbbbb"FOURSCORE AND SEVEN YEARS AGO OUR FATHERS

6.　bbbbbbbbbb"FOURSCORE AND SEVEN YEARS AGO bOUR
7.　bbbbbbbbbb"FOURSCORE AND SEVEN YEARS bAGO bOUR
8.　bbbbbbbbbb"FOURSCORE AND SEVEN bYEARS bAGO bOUR
9.　bbbbbbbbbb"FOURSCORE AND bSEVEN bYEARS bAGO bOUR
10.　bbbbbbbbbb"FOURSCORE bAND bSEVEN bYEARS bAGO bOUR
11.　bbbbbbbbbb"FOURSCORE bAND bSEVEN bYEARS bAGO bbOUR

12.　FATHERS BROUGHT FORTH ON THIS CONTINENT A NEW NATION,

13.　FATHERS bBROUGHT FORTH ON THIS CONTINENT A NEW
14.　FATHERS bBROUGHT bFORTH ON THIS CONTINENT A NEW
15.　FATHERS bBROUGHT bFORTH bON THIS CONTINENT A NEW
16.　FATHERS bBROUGHT bFORTH bON bTHIS CONTINENT A NEW
17.　FATHERS bBROUGHT bFORTH bON bTHIS bCONTINENT A NEW

* The symbol b represents a blank inserted by the justification program.

Figure 9.9 Detail of justification.

the first space, which is the R in OUR. The number of characters traversed, 6, is the number of spaces that must be inserted into the line to move OUR to the right margin.

To insert the spaces, the program goes back from the end of the line to the next space, inserts one blank (line 6), reduces the count of blanks remaining, and continues (lines 7 through 11) until either the left end of the line is encountered or the count of spaces to be inserted reaches zero. In the latter case, the process is finished and the program goes on to the next line. If the program reaches the left end of the line, however, it must return to the right side and begin again to insert extra spaces in existing spaces, now expanding each space between words to three spaces. The process is repeated until all spaces are disposed of.

Now the program is ready to begin the second line of print. It skips the space character and starts the second line with the first letter of FATHERS. Again it counts 50 characters, this time ending with the I in NATION (line 12). Counting back from this letter to the last character

```
· · · · | · · · · | · · · · | · · · · | · · · · | · · · · | · · · · | · · · · | · · · · | · · · · |
    5      10     15     20     25     30     35     40     45     50
```

```
          "FOURSCORE  AND  SEVEN  YEARS  AGO    OUR
FATHERS  BROUGHT  FORTH  ON  THIS  CONTINENT A  NEW
NATION, CONCEIVED IN LIBERTY AND DEDICATED TO   THE
PROPOSITION THAT ALL MEN ARE CREATED EQUAL."
```

Figure 9.10 The fully justified text.

preceding the first blank gives 5 spaces to the w in NEW. This time the program begins to insert extra space from the left side, and the resulting line of print is shown in lines 13 through 17 of the illustration. The completed text is shown in Figure 9.10.

9.3.2 Hyphenation

Hyphenation is used, in general, to make a page of justified text look better by reducing the number of embedded spaces. Clearly, if we can go farther into a word before terminating a line, we have fewer spaces to insert, but we create for ourselves the problem of finding out where it is permissible to break the word. If we are trying to put a very long word into a very narrow column, such as a partial column alongside a picture on a page, as shown in Figure 9.11, we may find

```
          "FOURSCORE        AND
SEVEN   YEARS   AGO OUR FATHERS
BROUGHT    FORTH    ON     THIS
CONTINENT   A    NEW    NATION,
CONCEIVED  IN   LIBERTY    AND
DEDICATED   TO THE PROPOSITION
THAT   ALL   MEN   ARE   CREATED
EQUAL."
```

(<u>a</u>)

```
          "FOURSCORE AND   SEV-
EN   YEARS    AGO   OUR   FATHERS
BROUGHT FORTH ON THIS    CONTIN-
ENT A NEW NATION, CONCEIVED IN
LIBERTY AND DEDICATED   TO   THE
PROPOSITION   THAT   ALL MEN ARE
CREATED EQUAL."
```

(<u>b</u>)

Figure 9.11 Using hypenation to improve justification. *(a)* A narrow column justified without hyphenation *(b)* The same narrow column with hyphenation.

that without hyphenation the word size exceeds the available space and there is no way to use the space. Of course, when we are dealing with typescripts averaging about 60 characters in width, there is little chance of encountering words that will not fit on an entire line. Even so, in the literature of organic chemistry we might find cumbersome pages resulting from the use of long, unhyphenated words.

How to hyphenate, then, becomes the problem. There seems to be general agreement that no universally accepted procedure exists.[4,9] One approach would be to maintain a dictionary showing, for each entry, all possible break points. This causes two problems. First, every form of a word would have to be shown, for often it is the endings and the prefixes that delimit the preferred break points. Even in a large standard dictionary all of these are rarely shown for a given root; hence the list would be long and expensive to search. Second, the dictionary would have to include rarely used words, such as chemical or proper names, for these may be the most critical ones to hyphenate. Rather than being restricted to most commonly used words, the dictionary would have to be extensive. Of course, a possible alternative would be to store only, say, one thousand frequently used words and let these be the only ones that can be hyphenated.

Another approach is to provide a hyphenation program with a set of rules that it can use for computing the break point in a word. One example of such a rule is: break between double consonants (as let-ter). We could also store a list of common prefixes and suffixes, a far shorter list than that in a full dictionary, and allow breaks between the root and the prefix or suffix. Unfortunately, whatever the rules, they lead to eventual gaffes that are highly attention-getting on the printed page. Danielson[5] lists these among other errors made by automatic hyphenation programs:

> per-imeter
> param-ount
> sto-ry
> Gol-dwater

It would seem that the more computer time and space that is devoted to the hyphenation problem, the more effective can be the solution, in the form of better dictionaries and more subtle word analysis programs. However, these cost money, and other approaches must also be considered. Two extremes are possible.

The first is the approach that we illustrated in Section 9.3.1, hyphen-less justification. Bozman[3] shows a more effective use of this technique with typeset material, where the size of the line of type is varied to compress or expand a line without any hyphenation. The lines are permitted to vary as much as ½ point (a point is about $\frac{1}{72}$ inch) in either direction. The difference is not readily apparent to the reader's eye.

A second approach is to return man to the problem and to present words that exceed some minimum length to an editor or author for his decision in regard to division. This can be done through a small console and need not take his full attention. The computer, of course, will be delayed in its processing, but if time-sharing methods are used the delay is not costly in terms of machine time, for the computer will be busy on some other task while awaiting the editor's decision. The net result is to lessen the cost of computer justification with hyphenation. Such an approach is reported by Borthwick[2] for the Reading, England, *Evening Post*.

9.3.3   Layout and Page Composition

To assemble justified text into pages requires more than counting the number of lines on a page. A page, in a book or a typewritten report, consists of heading material (usually a title or running head, possibly a security classification or other special notation, perhaps a page number), and a page footing, which may also have special notation, such as a security classification or a page number. Required to lay out a page are the following: well-planned margins, special provisions for titles and subtitles, specifications for tables and other material that should not be broken across two pages, and rules about starting new paragraphs or major subsections of a chapter near the bottom of a page.

The ATS system permits authors or editors to specify any heading and footing messages they may wish to use, to request the computer to count and print page numbers, and to specify the number of lines of print on the page, the length of each line, and various special conditions. Among the special points that the editor can recognize are places where the typewriter should be stopped to change the print element, allowing a font change to be made and thereby making it possible for titles, captions, and the like to be typed with a different print style from the main body of text. The editor can also specify that n lines are to be skipped, leaving on the page a space that will either remain blank or be occupied by graphic material added later; or that no paragraph may begin unless at least m lines remain within the established text area of the page; or that a new page is to begin regardless of the number of lines remaining. In addition, he can order typing to be done in either single- or double-space mode.

Most of these functions are quite routine. A count is maintained of each line of print generated, and this count is compared with the total number of lines permitted. When this number is reached, the page is changed. Changing pages may require printing a footing, printing a heading on the next page, incrementing and printing the page number, skipping the requisite number of lines between heading and start of text, and resuming the printing of the text. All the parameters, statements of whether or not headings or footings or page numbers are to be used and whether single or double spacing is desired, must be entered before the page is printed. Other commands, telling when to stop, when to change to a new page, and so on, are embedded into the text and executed whenever they arise.

Only the "look-ahead" commands are unusual. For example, the author or editor may have specified that a new paragraph is not to begin unless at least 5 lines remain on the page. To verify this, when a new paragraph begins, the program must tentatively add 5 to the current line count and see whether the total remains under the page maximum. If it does, the line count reverts to its previous value and the lines are typed out one by one with the knowledge that the page will not be overrun. If the command has been to leave, say, 15 spaces for later insertion of an illustration, the program must look ahead again. In this case, if there are not 15 spaces on the current page, the page must be terminated and the program must remember that all 15 spaces must be reserved on the next page. A desirable refinement would be to allow the program to substitute text if, say, 10 lines remain on a page where the editor wants to insert a 15-line picture. The picture can be put on the next page, and the first 10 lines of text that would normally have followed the picture can go on the current page.

Similarly, an editing system could plan for footnotes. Each use of a footnote would have to require an indication of where the footnote was stored (what its ATS unit number is). The editing program would have to make a diversion to find this unit, edit it, count the number of lines it uses, test whether that many lines are available on the current page, and, if not, plan to continue the footnote on the next page. We occasionally find books with a large number of long footnotes, and these pose a special problem, as much to the printer as to any program that expects to lay out the text automatically. Footnotes *can* be one or more pages long. There can be several footnotes in the main body of text on a page. Although every footnote should begin on the page where the reference is made, all cannot necessarily end on the same page, and editors do not like to allocate a complete page to footnotes. Therefore an excessively long footnote may have to be continued at the bottom of each of several pages running, and this, in turn, may cause trouble with the footnotes that originate on these pages.

Some esthetic problems of automatic page layout can be alleviated by composing an entire page, or perhaps several pages, in advance of printing. When all the material for a page is available, decisions about spacing can be made. When printing a stored document, ATS edits and types a line at a time, and, of course, lines once started cannot be cancelled. If a page is terminated because of insufficient room to start a new paragraph, there may be some extra space at the bottom of the page. With printed material adjustment is made by moving the entire body of text within the page, centering it and thereby minimizing the effect on appearance of lack of the usual number of lines. An automatic typing system could do the same thing, but has to compose the complete page first, discover that this adjustment is needed, and then insert the appropriate number of spaces and print.

The same form of adjustment offers help with footnotes. Suppose a footnote is called for that uses all but five of the remaining lines on a page. If, on the fourth of the remaining lines, another footnote reference occurs, a space allocation problem is created. What can be done, however, is to delete the last line of text, leaving the current page two lines short and shifting both the new footnote and its reference onto the next page. By inserting a single extra space at the top of the page, between heading and text, the page is adjusted for the missing two lines and retains a good appearance.

The same look-ahead features can be used for the required spacing between headings or titles and the following text. Look-ahead algorithms may even be authorized to make minor changes in the spacing requirements in the interest of overall good layout, such as increasing or reducing by a small amount the required spacing between titles and text to expand the material on a page or to accommodate an extra line or two of text.

9.3.4 Type Font Variations

The ATS system makes use of a form of IBM Selectric® typewriter as a terminal. This has an easily replaceable type element that permits different fonts to be introduced at the will of the author or editor. Whatever font is used, the horizontal space required for a character remains constant and the vertical distance between lines of print also remains constant, so that none of the spacing calculations are affected by a change in type style.

Today, computers are used to prepare copy for typesetting machinery, as well as for typescripts. Usually, this is done by preparing a punched paper tape used to drive a composing machine that assembles the actual type or photographic images. Material set in this way almost always has font variations, both in style and in size. Such variations require no profound changes in any of the functions described heretofore, but they increase the complexity because each letter may have its own height and width.

Typewritten final reports generally imply low-budget operations, and typeset copy conversely suggests a higher budget. Therefore, more computer time can be afforded to do the extra processing needed to prepare typeset copy; in fact, this extra computer time may be amortized by savings in the time and labor normally required to perform the same functions manually. Within the information-processing world, one of the best-known applications of computer-prepared copy is in MEDLARS,[7] a system of the National Library of Medicine, which produces the *Index Medicus,* a guide to current medical-related literature. A tape is prepared by computer and fed to a device called GRACE[1] (Graphic Composing Equipment), which produces the copy shown in Figure 9.12.

9.3.5. Space Allocation

An interesting complement to the physical layout and composition of a page is the use of a computer to decide, or to help decide, what goes onto a page. Danielson and Briggs[6] report on a program that helps the editor of a newspaper decide what copy to include in an edition. The system uses paper tape input, containing news stories transmitted by an Associated Press teletype, together with an editor's general decision on how much space he wants to allocate to each class of story. The program counts the number of lines of copy available and compares these counts with space availability figures. It then makes adjustments when more space is needed or insufficient copy is available.

The program has some capabilities similar to those of ATS in that it can add to, or delete material from, a story. Stories may be transmitted by AP in fragmented form, with additions, deletions, and corrections following the main story after a time lapse. The editing program must be able to associate new fragments with existing stories and then make the changes called for. Stories are stored on magnetic tape, accessible to the computer. The space allocation program can then always have available the latest figures whenever it is called upon to plan an edition.

In using the initial version of the program, a story selected for publication might have been cut off in midparagraph; the program would have selected exactly the same number of story lines as it had space available. The usual practice of news writers, however, is to prepare copy essentially as a series of ever-more-detailed repetitions of the basic

CUMULATIVE INDEX MEDICUS

Leoni E: La mononucleosi infettiva
Gazz Int Med Chir 68:2209-21, 15 Nov 63 (65 ref.) (It)
Leoni GC, Taglieri G: Rilievi siero-epidemiologici in un campione della popolazione dell'Asmara (Eritrea). III. Ricerca degli anticorpi anti-O-streptolisinici.
Arch Ital Sci Med Trop 45:189-98, Apr 64 (It)
Leoni L, Tecce G: Azione della rifamicina SV sulle reazioni della sintesi proteica in vitro.
Chemotherapia (Basel) 7:194-9, 1963 (It)
Leoni R: Un nuovo farmaco a largo spettro di azione per il trattamento delle vaginiti.
Riv Ostet Ginec 19:106-8, Feb 64 (It)
Leoni R see **Battaglia GB**
Leonida D see **Bashe WJ Jr**
Leonoris SM: Simplicity: key ingredient of a successful diaster plan. Hospitals 38:84-8, 16 Jul 64
Leonov BV, Lomova MA, Rudakov IA: Sviaz' radiochuvstvitel'nosti krys s antiokislitel'noi aktivnost'iu kostnogo mozga i soderzhaniem neésterifitsirovannykh zhirnykh kislot v ikh krovi pri sostoianii "stress". Radiobiologiia 3:518-22, 1963 (Rus)
Leonov BV, Lomova MA: Izmenenie soderzhaniia obshchikh zhirnykh kislot v kul'ture tkanei posle gamma-oblucheniia. Radiobiologiia 4:72-5, 1964 (Rus)
Leonov VM: Osnovnoi obmen i likhoradka pri tifo-paratifoznykh zabolevaniiakh.
Arkh Pat 25:75-81, 1963 (Rus)
Leonov VM: Izmerenie temperatury arterial'noi i venoznoi krovi u cheloveka.
Lab Delo 10:245-7, 1964 (Rus)
Leonova AG see **Pavlov PV**
Leonova EV see **Kravtsova EE**
Leonova LA: Kozhnye temperatury i potootdelenie u shkol'nikov, obuchaiushchikhsia professii tkacha.
Gig Sanit 28:43-7, Sep 63 (Rus)
Leonova NA see **Burobin VA**
Leonova VG: Prenatal'naia dinamika kachestvennogo sostava krasnoi krovi cheloveka.
Pediatriia 42:3-9, Oct 63 (Rus)
Leonova VI: K voprosu ob allergicheskikh i tobsicheskikh reaktsiiakh pri primenenii antibiotikov.
Vestn Otorinolaring 25:83-7, Sep-Oct 63 (Rus)
Leonovich AL see **Krasnikova Ela**
Leonovich AL see **Markov DA**
Leont'ev VIa: Fizicheskoe razvitie detei, stradaiushchikh khronicheskoi pnevmoniei i bronkhial'noi astmoi.
Vop Okhr Materin Dets 8:40-3, May 63 (Rus)
Leont'eva GR see **Govyrin VA**
Leont'eva KA see **Kogurova MI**
Leont'eva NS, Pokrovskii: O funktsional'nom sostoianii pochek pri koarktatsii aorty.
Ter Arkh 35:45-50, Nov 63 (Rus)
Leont'eva NS, Pokrovskii AV: O pechechnom krovoobrashchenii i mechanizme gipertonii pri koarktatsii aorty. Sovet Med 27:31-5, Sep 63 (Rus)
Leont'eva NS see **Kolesnikoz SA**
Leontiuk LA: Obrazovanie dopolnitel'nykh istochnikov psycho-prophylactique à l'accouchement.
Vie Med Suppl25-6, 1963 (Fr)
Lepage F, Michelon B: Incidences obstetricales des myopathies.
Med Infant (Paris) 70:413-6, Aug-Sep 63 (Fr)
Lepage F, Sureau C, Galula M: De la stérilisation chirurgicale à la stérilisation médicamenteuse temporaire. Maternite 13:87-95, Apr 64 (Fr)
Lepage F see **Michelon B**
Lepage G, Grondin P: Le sang et ses substituts en chirurgie cardiaque.
Un Med Canada 93:577-8, May 64 (Fr)
Lepage G see **Gilbert G**
Lepage G see **Grondin P**
LePage GA: Basic biochemical effects and mechanism of action of 6-thioguanine.
Cancer Res 23:1202-6, Sep 63
LePage GA see **Brink JJ**
LePage GA see **Kimball AP**
Lepage M: The separation and identification of plant phospholipids and glycolipids by two-dimensional thin-layer chromatography.
J Chromatogr 13:99-103, Jan 64
Lepage M see **Paquin R**
Lepe A see **Castro M**
Le Pecq JB, Bourgoin D: Etude théorique et expérimetnale des conditions d'utilisation de la viscosimétrie pour la détermination de l'activité désoxyribonucléasique I.
Biochim Biophys Acta 80:173-82, 17 Feb 64 (Fr)
Le Pecq JB see **Le Talaer JY**
Le Pecq JB see **Paoletti C**
L'Epée P, Lazarini HJ: Le problème de la mort pendant le travail. Arch Mal Prof 25:245-6, Apr-May 64 (Fr)
L'Epée P, Lazarini HJ, Campet L: Armes à feu dangereuses d'un type inattendu.
Ann Med Leg (Paris) 43:570-1, Nov-Dec 63 (Fr)
L'epée P, Lazarini HJ: Quelques problèmes relatifs à la syphilis en médecine légale et en médecine sociale.
J Med Bordeaux 140:1431-4, Sep 63 (Fr)
L'Epée P, Texier L, Lazarini HJ: Manifestations cutanées, à type de kératodermie palmaire, voisines des troubles nerveux réflexes extenso-progressifs de Barré. Ann Med Leg (Paris) 43:571-2, Nov-Dec 63 (Fr)
L'Epée P see **Dervillée P**
Le Peltier: 17 lésions artérielles fémoro-poplitées traitées par reconstruction immédiate.
Bull Soc Med Milit Franc 57:251-8, Jun 63 (Fr)
Leperchey F, Gaultier M: Intérêt du cyclarbamate par voie rectale en pratique courante chez l'adulte.
Vie Med [Med Ther] 45:635-8, Apr 64 (Fr)
Leperchey F see **Gaultier M**
Lepeschkin E: The electrocardiographic diagnosis of bilateral bundle branch block in relation to heart block. Progr Cardiov Dis 6:445-71, Mar 64
Lepeschkin E, Surawicz B: Correlation between the atrial and ventricular trans-membrane action potential and the electrocardiogram in electrolyte imbalance.
Lepintre J see **Seringe P**
Lepisto VE, Holland RW: Dacryocystorhinostomy. With polyethylene tubing. Amer J Ophthal 57:668-70, Apr 64
Lepková V see **Běhounková L**
Lepkovsky S, Nalbandov AV, Dimick MK, et al: Growth and reproduction of depancreatized chickens.
Endocrinology 74:207-11, Feb 64
Lepkovsky S see **Han PW**
Lepkowski A: Zdolność wyczuwania drgań w zakresie tonów slyszalnych przy badaniu audiometrycznym przewodnictwa kostnego.
Otolaryng Pol 17:163-6, 1963 (Pol)
Lepkowski M, Turski C: Leczenie chirurgiczne choroby torbielowatej pluc. Gruzlica 32:355-60, Apr 64 (Pol)
Leplat G: Léo Weekers (1881-1962)
Ann Oculist (Paris) 196:965-6, Sep 63 (Fr)
Lepley D see **Stengel BF**
Lepley D Jr, Bormes W, Kayser K: An electronic device for accurate identification of the cardiac conduction system. Its development and use in open heart surgery. Amer J Surg 106:933-7, Dec 63
Lepley D Jr see **Dawes RB**
Lepley D Jr see **O'Connor T**
Leplus R: Virus et hémopathies.
Vie Med 45:271-5, Feb 64 (Fr)
Lepoire J, Montaut J, Bouchot M, et al: Anévrismes artério-veineux intrafrontaux vascularisés par l'artère ethmoïdale antérieure. A propos de trois observations.
Neurochirurgie 9:159-66, Apr-Jun 63 (Fr)
Lepoire J, Larcan A, Montaut J, et al: Le syndrome de retention chloro-sodee avec hypertonie osmotique en neuro-chirurgie.
Ann Med Nancy 2:1233-45, Sep 63 (Fr)
Lepoire J, Montaut J, Renard M: Méningites a répétition par fistule ostéoméningée congénitale de l'étage antérieur révélée par un traumatisme.
Ann Med Nancy 2:1497-508, Nov 63 (Fr)
Lepoire J, Montaut J, Renard M: Hematome sous-dural spontane chronique au cours d'un traitement anticoagulant prolonge.
Ann Med Nancy 2:1246-56, Sep 63 (Fr)
Lepoire J, Montaut J, Medot A: L'empyème sous-dural spontané. Maroc Med 42:876-85, Nov 63 (Fr)
Lepoire J, Tridon P, Montaut J, et al: Thrombose de la carotide interne chez une enfant de deux ans.
Arch Franc Pediat 20:1234-8, Dec 63 (Fr)
Lepoire J see **Chalnot P**
Lepoire J see **Kissel P**
Lepoire J see **Neimann N**
Lepoire M: La circulation extra-corporelle et l'hypothermie profonde dans le domaine de la neuro-chirurgie.
Transfusion (Paris) 6:413-7, 1963 (Fr)
Lepore PD, Siegel PB, King KW: Proximate and amino acid composition of eggs and chicks from growth-selected lines of White Rocks.
Life Sci 8:584-93, Aug 63
Lepori R see **Balestra E**

Figure 9.12 An example of computer-composed text.

story, for just this kind of eventuality, that is, so editors can cut wherever convenient. Hence this weakness is not too serious. A relatively minor adaptation of this technique can provide an allocation method that uses only integral numbers of paragraphs. This leaves the embryonic page with gaps or slight overages. On average, however, the amounts of overruns will balance the underruns; and, when the two are not in balance, fillers and space allocation variations can be used to make up the difference.

With such a program a news editor could compose a complete newspaper by computer. The machine could take copy from the wires, edit it, and decide how much and what to use. The man would classify the articles and decide on location—what stories to place where in the paper—or he could assign this function also to the computer, again presuming that he classifies stories by importance and classifies space by importance or subject matter. For example, in American journalism the righthand column on the front page is traditionally reserved for the most important news story of the day, and it is clearly a human function to determine what story rates this classification. Likewise, the third page might be reserved for sports, the fourth for financial coverage, and so on. Assigning stories or groups of stories to specified locations in the newspaper, rather than simply selecting a specified number of lines from each group of stories, is somewhat like doing page layout with variations in type font, compared to being restricted to one fixed size of type. The basic program logic is not much different, but it requires more information and more time for the calculations.

The significance of programs such as these, together with others we have described, is that writers and editors can be enabled to communicate directly with the computer at a high level of abstraction. The editor still makes the decisions as to what subject coverage mix there will be, what stories are important, and what constitutes attractive layout. He can communicate these decisions easily to a computer and see the results far faster through these means than otherwise. Possibly he will want to experiment with several approaches and select the one that looks best to him, an option rarely available to a time-pressed news editor. This is the essence of man-machine interaction. Man decides, classifies, and makes esthetic judgments. The machine implements his decisions.

9.4 AN EXAMPLE

In this section we present, in more detail than before, the mechanics of a text entry and editing system. The system outlined is patterned roughly after the IBM ATS *but is not the same.* The differences are all in the direction of simplification. In short, what we present here is simpler than ATS and, if implemented, would do less for the user. We shall try to introduce features in approximately the order that a user might encounter them, and then offer some explanation of how each feature is or could be implemented.

We postulate a user who is the author of a technical report to be typed in draft form, edited, and finally published as a reproduced type-script. It should be realized that the author will probably not do his basic, creative work on-line, but that he will have prepared extensive notes, or possibly a handwritten rough draft, before he begins to use the terminal. This is probably true even if he is an accomplished typist, for the terminal makes demands on his attention that might inhibit his creative work. In the following sections we describe the functions of signing in, or informing the computer of the presence of a user; entering data; preparing a draft copy; entering corrections to the draft; and print-ing the final document.

9.4.1 Signing In

The first step in using an editing system is for the user to identify himself and, by implication, to request that the computer reserve an area of memory for him. It will be recalled that we said earlier the system will open an area of "working storage," which is held for the user until he signs off this terminal. If he leaves the terminal with the intention of returning later, he must store his document in permanent storage, an act that the computer will perform for him on demand. The area of working storage is on a disk, just as the area of permanent stor-age may be; but when a document is in working storage, portions of it may be moved in and out of core memory as new material is added or old material is recalled or changed. Material in permanent storage, on the other hand, may not be changed or its units individually addressed. The entire document has to be transferred to working storage first. Only a limited number of working storage areas are available, whereas the number of permanent storage areas can be far greater. We need only one working storage area for each terminal or input line to the system, and the amount of material in core storage at one time, for any user, need not be more than one unit (line, sentence, etc.) . These storage relationships are illustrated in Figure 9.13.

A working storage area is assigned to the terminal through which the user communicates. Permanent storage is assigned to the *user,* not the terminal, and may be retrieved at any terminal connected to the

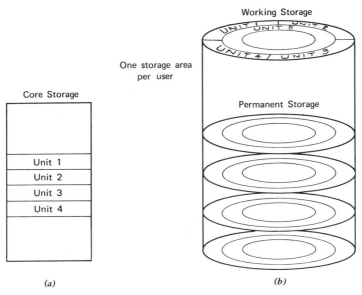

Figure 9.13 Storage areas. (*a*) One region in core storage is made available to each terminal in actual use. The regions may be smaller than the working storage regions on the disk. (*b*) The disk has a virtually unlimited number of storage units for each user and can accommodate a large number of users, even though the number of people who can use the system at any one time is limited.

same computer if the operator at this terminal knows the correct storage-area numbers. A system of coded storage-area designations provides a form of security to system users, to prevent unauthorized use or modification of their information.

9.4.2 Data Entry

Having set up a working storage area, the author is ready to begin typing his report into the computer. He must define the kind of basic information unit he wishes to use, in this case a line or a grammatical structure. For most typing it will be the latter, usually a sentence. As long as the author is not using the line as a unit, he is free to choose whatever structure he wants, including arbitrary end points for units. In other words, a unit ends when the author says it ends and he may say this at any time. Units are automatically numbered sequentially, on entry into the computer. The end of a unit (see Figure 9.14) is indicated by a single carriage return if line units are used, and by two carriage returns if arbitrary units are used (in the latter case, a single carriage

12   This is the first unit of our text. It is not intendedcr
to be a paragraph but appears so in the first draft.crcr

13   The double cr signifies the end of a unit. The characterscr
cr, of course, do not actually print.crcr

14   We can start a new paragraph by typing in somecr
spaces or a tabulate character.crcr

This is the first unit of our text. It is not intended
to be a paragraph but appears so in the first draft.
The double cr signifies the end of a unit. The characters
cr, of course, do not actually print.
     We can start a new paragraph by typing in some
spaces or a tabulate character.

Figure 9.14 Text units as originally entered and as printed.

return may occur within the unit, whereas in the former case, by definition, it cannot). In this way, the copy of the text that is produced during
data entry looks fairly ordinary, except that each unit starts a new line.

All typists make mistakes, and since we are assuming the report
author is doing his own typing from rough notes, we must assume a
relatively high error rate. Here is where the computer performs one of
its most important timesaving functions, for it is not necessary to retype
a full page or full unit when a mistake is detected. The author has a
range of error-correcting commands at his disposal. We shall discuss two
of them here, and defer the others until later. Our present interest is
concentrated on correction techniques for material while it is being
typed, not for retroactive changes or major revisions of a text.

The terminal through which the author works has one key on it
called the *attention* key, which we shall henceforth abbreviate attn, and
which transmits a signal to the computer but does not print any symbol
on the page in the typewriter. This key, in effect, switches the computer
from a mode wherein it is accepting data to one wherein it is expecting
a command from the user. If the author is typing a line and he discovers
an error he wants to correct now, he strikes the attn key, alerting the
computer that the next signal is a command, not a continuation of the
unit of text.

The simplest correction command consists of a backspace character
(bksp). All characters that the author backs over are erased. The
author may resume typing wherever he leaves the carriage. On the
printed page the correction is typed on top of the original, but in the
computer's memory the original has been erased. If the author strikes
attn bksp he has just erased the last character he typed before striking
the attn key. The next character after a backspace is treated by the
computer as a return to data entry mode, so this character replaces the
last one just erased. Thus A attn bksp B is equivalent to having typed
just the character B, even though the page in the typewriter shows the
two letters superimposed. A backspace correct operation is illustrated
in Figure 9.15.

```
NOW IS THE TKME
            ₿₿₿
            IME FOR ALL GOOD MEN
```

This shows the effect of the backspace key. Actually, all three lines shown
here would be superimposed, and the misspelled and corrected word TIME would
be illegible, but the computer sees the character string illustrated here. Its
interpretation of this message is

```
NOW IS THE TIME FOR ALL GOOD MEN
```

Figure 9.15 The backspace correct operation.

Although no precise figures are available, the probability is relatively high that, if a typist makes a one-character error, he will discover it before typing the next character. In other words, when experienced typists strike the wrong character, they usually know it almost immediately. To correct these errors requires only three key strokes: <u>attn</u>, <u>bksp</u>, and the correct character. Still, there are times when an error is discovered only after half or three quarters of a line has been typed, or even a line or two later. Instead of an error, there might be simply a desire to change what was said, regardless of whether it was right or not. To make a change *within the unit currently being typed,* regardless of how far into the unit, the user need only type <u>attn</u> _ cr. Here the _ character signifies that the entire unit currently being entered is to be erased. The author must then retype the complete unit, making the correction as he does so. The carriage return (cr) following the combination <u>attn</u> _ signies the start of the new text o fthe unit. Figure 9.16 shows the results of use of this command.

NOW IS THE TKME FOR ALL GOOD MEN <u>attn</u> _ <u>cr</u>

This sequence cancels the unit that is being entered and signals for the start of a new one. To correct the misspelling of TIME here, the typist chooses to start the entire unit over again. He next types

NOW IS THE TIME FOR ALL GOOD MEN

Figure 9.16 Correcting by deletion of a unit.

We have shown two correction commands. One allows the user to erase selectively, by moving from right to left, everything passed over. The other erases all of the current unit. Both apply only to the current unit. Mistakes discovered after a unit has been completed require other commands, but the programming required to perform these two functions is relatively simple. The backspace erase requires only that a single address be modified, so that the next character received goes to the new location, instead of the original location; that is, if the next position in which a text character is to be stored is 100 and, instead of a printable character, <u>attn bksp</u> is received, the address of the next character is reset to 99 and the system is postured to accept data again. To handle the unit erase, the program need only branch to the point within itself where receipt and storage of the new unit starts, and receive it all over again.

With these commands, then, an author can prepare a draft of his copy. Although this will probably still have errors in it and there may be many parts he wants to change, a large portion of the purely typographical errors can have been removed.

9.4.3 Preparing a Draft Copy

When a complete copy of the text has been entered into the computer, and some of the corrections are applied on the way, a fairly clean copy is stored electronically. The hard copy produced at the terminal, however, may be quite messy. It has overscores wherever corrections have been made, and commands to the computer are interspersed with the text. It is not a script that will be convenient to use for proofreading and polishing. For these purposes the author needs a clean copy, which he can now obtain with very little additional work on his own part. What we have assumed he would like, at this stage, is something like a galley proof. He is not overconcerned with precise page layout, although he might like an idea of how the final document will look, but he does want clean copy and wide margins for making annotations. He would also like to have the unit numbers printed beside the unit text. This is important because future changes in the text will have to be made by first identifying the units involved.

Here are the commands he may use for this purpose. Each must be preceded in use by the nonprinting <u>attn</u> key.

The command <u>attn</u> p x <u>cr</u> will print (*p*) the document, using a page width of *x* characters. This command assumes that the number of lines on a page has previously been communicated to the computer. This information is sent before the print command, in the form <u>attn</u> ! y <u>cr</u>, where ! means "set the page length" and *y* is the number of lines per page. Since the page length command stays in force until rescinded, it need be given only once, at the beginning of the series of commands that order a document to be printed.

If we affix the letter *n* to the print command, <u>attn</u> pn x <u>cr</u>, we have asked the computer to print unit numbers beside the text.

The sequence

<u>attn</u> ! 50 <u>cr</u>
<u>attn</u> pn 30 <u>cr</u>

causes our document to be printed, 50 lines to the page, each page having 30 characters across it. Unit numbers will be typed in the right-hand margin.

9.4.4 Corrections to the Draft

We may now assume our author has printed for himself a clean copy of his draft report, with the appropriate number attached to each unit. He has reached the point where he begins to consider corrections he has not previously posted, as well as major changes to the text. The complete document having been printed, there is no longer any question of posting corrections only to the current unit, for no current unit exists. All units have been acquired, stored, and printed out again. Henceforth, the author will have to identify the unit involved whenever he wants to make a change. The following are the commands he may use.

Delete. The sequence <u>attn</u> d x <u>cr</u> instructs the computer to delete (d) unit x. Since ATS has the characteristic that all units are immediately renumbered after such a command, the printed unit numbers on all other units are no longer exact. If an author wants to delete units 51 and 53, for example, and he first deletes 51, he must then ask for deletion of 52, for all units beyond 50 will have been renumbered; that is, with 51 deleted, the former 52 is now 51, the former 53 is now 52, and so on. It is a good practice to delete the higher-numbered units first, when more than one is to be deleted, to make it easier to keep track of unit numbers.

Although immediate renumbering has obvious disadvantages to the user, not renumbering also has disadvantages. If he deletes units 51 and 53 and the system does not renumber, we must then have the computer program keep track of all deleted unit numbers lest the system user accidentally name one of these units in a future command. If we do not do this, what shall we ask the program to do when, after having deleted unit 51, the author later asks for unit 51 to be printed, deleted again, or modified? It is, of course, possible to ignore the command or to inform the user that no such unit exists. If his own bookkeeping is in error, however, and he thinks there should be a unit 51, this bland statement does not help him resolve his problem.

Of course, we could have the program keep a history of units, noting all transactions and the date of the action. Then, any request for the processing of a nonexistent unit could lead to a retrieval of the history of this unit, showing why the command cannot be executed. But this puts a heavy extra burden on the program, whereas immediate renumbering puts a relatively light burden on the user.

Print a Unit. The command <u>attn</u> x <u>cr</u> requests that unit number x be retrieved and printed. This might be done by an author after he has made an extensive revision to a unit and wants to see the unit in clean form. Also, one way to help overcome the confusion involved in renumbering units is to select a single unit, ask for it to be printed, by number, and then check that the expected unit was printed. This helps the author verify how renumbering has taken place. This printing does not permit line width and page length controls, as does the attn p n cr sequence. The shorter form is used primarily to generate proof copy.

Insert. The author may wish to add new material as well as delete old. If he wants to create a complete new unit, he may do so with an insert command. The sequence <u>attn</u> i x <u>cr</u> informs the computer that the author wants to enter a new unit, to be inserted immediately *after* existing unit *x*. Once again, units are renumbered and, if a series of such commands is to be given, the highest-numbered unit should be changed first, working toward the beginning of the document, to reduce the effect on the author's bookkeeping of unit number changes.

Moving Units. A common requirement of authors is to reorganize large blocks of their material. To enable this to be done without re-typing, two commands can be used together that have the effect of taking units from their original positions and inserting them in given positions behind named units. The first command is an insert, <u>attn</u> i x <u>cr</u>. The second, given in lieu of a new unit, is <u>attn</u> y z <u>cr</u>. Here, *y* designates the first of a set of contiguous units and *z* the last of the set of units, all of which are to be moved to a new position immediately following unit *x*, specified in the first of the pair of commands.

Changing Units. To make minor changes in the content of a unit, the author has available a set of commands that enable him to accomplish his changes with the minimum amount of typing. Two of the commands are similar to those used during the composition of the unit. The author first calls the unit he wants to change by issuing a print unit command. After the printing is done, this unit is still "current" and available for modification. He may use the backspace erase technique if the error is near the end of the unit. It operates just as it did before, except that it always starts from the very end of the unit, not from the point where the error was discovered. The sequence

<u>attn</u> x <u>cr</u>
<u>attn</u> <u>bksp</u> <u>bksp</u> <u>bksp</u>

causes the system to be ready to accept new text, starting at a point three characters before the end of the original form of unit *x*. The author then types as much text as he wants into the newly constituted unit.

To make changes near the beginning of a unit, the author may identify a word within the unit and ask for all subsequent text to be deleted and the system readied to accept new text from the indicated point on. To change a unit, the author might type in the sequence

<u>attn</u> x <u>tab</u> changes <u>cr</u>

This would cause the system to print out the first line of unit *x* (for identification) and then to erase everything after the word *changes* and to be prepared to accept new text following this point.

Still another variation permits the replacement of words or phrases, without erasing everything following the changed text. To do this, the author enters

<u>attn</u> x <u>cr</u>
<u>attn</u> word1 <u>tab</u> word2 <u>cr</u>

These cause unit *x* to be typed out and then cause word2 to be inserted into the unit in place of word1. Either "word" could actually be a phrase, and there is no need for the two to be the same length. Note that the revised unit is not automatically printed. To verify that the correction was properly posted, the author must enter another <u>attn</u> x <u>cr</u>.

By repetitive use of these commands and the commands used to print a draft, an author or editor can change and rechange a document, printing new drafts whenever needed or convenient. The complete text is never retyped by hand, however many changes are made.

9.4.5   Publication

When the document is finally ready for publication, the author and his editors will have printing requirements different from those used in copy preparation. They may want to change margin settings, to suppress the printing of unit numbers, to add page headings and page numbers, and to justify the type. They may also want to be able to stop printing occasionally to change the type element on the typewriter (hence the type font used), to leave space for illustrations, or to change paper in the typewriter (final copy may be desired on something other than continuous form paper).

First, the author must specify the length of a page. We have stated earlier that this can be done with command <u>attn</u> ! n <u>cr</u>, where *n* is the number of lines per page. This command will remain in force until changed. To invoke the mode of operation wherein a heading will be printed on each page, the author, also before printing starts, enters <u>attn</u> h and follows it with the text of the heading he would like. The system then prints this heading on every page without further effort by the author. Hence <u>attn</u> h EDITING TEXT <u>cr</u> will cause the title EDITING TEXT to be printed at the top of every page.

Heading material is entered as a single-line unit, the positioning of which is not under user control. If, within this line of text, the author enters <u>attn</u> <u>attn</u> page, the page number will be computed and printed at the position in the line where these characters appeared. Thus <u>attn</u> h EDITING TEXT <u>attn</u> <u>attn</u> page <u>cr</u> causes the title to be printed as a heading, with an automatically computed page number immediately following.

The command <u>attn</u> <u>attn</u> is treated as a stop code, and causes the system to stop printing until an <u>attn</u> message is received. It occurs within a unit of text. At this time, the system user can change type fonts, reposition paper, or change paper. Thus <u>attn</u> h <u>attn</u> <u>attn</u> EDITING TEXT <u>cr</u> will stop the typewriter just before the page heading is printed. Typing will resume when an operator transmits <u>attn</u> to the computer. In this case, the heading could be typed in a font different from that used for the body of the previous page.

The command <u>attn</u> + m causes *m* lines to be skipped on printing. This command, like the stop code, must be embedded into a line unit.

Finally, printing can be justified, if the character *j* is used in place of *p* in a print command. The format is the same as for typing drafts, except that the *n,* for unit numbers, is omitted. Hence <u>attn</u> j 50 <u>cr</u> instructs the system to begin printing, under control of any previous commands specifying page length, heading control, and so on, justifying the type and using a column width of 50 characters.

9.4.6 Illustrative Text

The following illustrations show the effects of applying the commands we have described.

attn c

Clears a work space for the operator at this terminal. The cleared work space is associated with the terminal, not with the operator.

Fourscore and sevn

The author begins preparation of his copy. He gets this far and discovers he has misspelled the word *seven*. He stops and will correct it now.

attn bksp

The computer has erased the last character, now has in its memory *Fourscore and sev*, and is ready for new text immediately after the *v*.

en years ago our fatherscr
brough forth on this continentcr
a new nation, conceived incr
liberty and dedicated to thecr
proposition that all men arecr
created equal."crcr

The margins used in typing at this stage have no relation to those that may appear in final copy.

Now we are engaged in a greatercr
civil war, testing whether thatcr
nation or any nation so conceivedcr
and so dedicated can long endure.crcr

The author ends his unit with a double carriage return. He is ready to begin the next unit. A second unit is entered.

attn ! 50 cr
attn pn 40 cr

Now the author wants a draft copy prepared. His draft will have 50 lines per page and 40 characters per line (approximately) and will have unit numbers printed.

```
Fourscore and seven years ago our
fathers brough forth on this continent
a new nation, conceived in liberty and
dedicated to the proposition that all
men are created equal."                    1
Now we are engaged in a great civil war,
testing whether that nation or any
nation so conceived and so dedicated can
long endure.                               2
```

There are some errors here. We have a set of quotation marks at the end of the first paragraph, but nowhere else. There is a misspelling, *brough*, in unit 1, and there should be a comma after the first occurrence of *nation* and after *dedicated* in unit 2.

We decide to insert quotation marks and a tab character for indentation at the very beginning, and omit them at the end of the first unit. The commands to accomplish this and the other changes are as follows:

```
attn 1 cr
```
This causes unit 1 to be printed (printing omitted here).

```
attn bkspcr
```
The final character of unit 1, the quotation mark, is erased.

```
attn Fourscore tab"Fourscore cr
```
This replaces the first word, *Fourscore*, with the same word preceded by a quotation mark.

```
attn brough tab brought cr
attn 2 tab nation
```
The misspelling *brough* is replaced.

We call unit 2 and ask that everything after the first occurrence of the word *nation* be erased and the system made ready to accept new text after that point.

Now we are engaged in a great civil
war, testing whether that nation   , or cr

any nation so conceived and so dedicated, cr
can long endure.crcr

attn 2 cr
Now we are engaged in a great civil
war, testing whether that nation, or
any nation so conceived and so dedicated,
can long endure.

attn h GETTYSBURG ADDRESS cr

attn j 50 cr

The system types this portion of the unit for us. The erasure has been made, and the machine is ready for us to continue.

We complete the unit, making both our pending corrections as we do.

We wish to verify the corrections.

The unit is correctly typed.
We are ready for final printing.
We will print with the title shown at the top of each page.

We order the computer to begin printing justified text, 50 columns wide. The page length remains as previously set, also at 50.

```
        "Fourscore  and  seven  years  ago   our
fathers  brought  forth  on  this  continent a new
nation, conceived in liberty and dedicated to  the
proposition  that  all men are created equal.  Now
we are engaged  in  a  great  civil  war,  testing
whether that nation, or any  nation  so  conceived
and so dedicated, can long endure.
```

Here we see the final, justified copy with the two units run together. Although not as pleasing as typeset printing, this paragraph looks better than conventional, unjustified typescripts and resulted from typing only a first draft and then a few corrections.

REFERENCES

1. Austin, Charles J., "Experience with the GRACE System," *Automation and Electronics in Publishing*, Spartan Books, New York, 1965, pp. 61–70.
2. Borthwick, J. M. B., "Multi-access On-line Computer-assisted Typesetting," *Advances in Computer Typesetting*, The Institute of Printing, London, 1967, pp. 196–199.
3. Bozman, William R., "Computer-Aided Typesetting," *Advances in Computers*, Vol. 7, Academic, New York, 1966, pp. 195–207.
4. Danielson, Wayne A., "The Man-Machine Combination for Computer-Assisted Copy Editing," *Advances in Computers*, Vol. 7, Academic, New York, 1966, pp. 183–187.
5. *Ibid.*, pp. 183–185.
6. Danielson, Wayne A., and Bruce Briggs, "A Computer Program for Editing the News," *Communications of the ACM*, 6, 8 (August 1963), 487–490.
7. Karel, Leonard, Charles J. Austen, and Martin M. Cummings, "Computerized Bibliographic Services for Biomedicine," *Science*, 148, 3671 (May 7, 1965), 766–772.
8. Savides, Peter, *ATS Self-Instruction Manual*, Report TR 00.1591, Systems Development Division, IBM Corp., Poughkeepsie, N. Y., April 1967.
9. Strunk, William, Jr., and E. B. White, *The Elements of Style*, Macmillan, New York, 1959, p. 31.
10. *1440/1460 Administrative Terminal System, Application Description*, Form H20–0129, IBM Corp., White Plains, N. Y. (undated).
11. *1440/1460 Administrative Terminal System (ATS), Terminal Operator's Manual*, Form H20–0185, IBM Corp., White Plains, N. Y. (undated).

RECOMMENDED ADDITIONAL READING

1. Hattery, Lowell H., and George P. Bush, eds., *Automation and Electronics in Publishing,* Spartan Books, New York, 1965.
2. *Introduction to Datatext,* Form Y20–0035, IBM Corp., White Plains, N. Y., 1966.
3. Lee, R. W., and R. W. Worral, eds., *Electronic Composition in Printing,* NBS Special Publication 295, National Bureau of Standards, Washington, D.C., 1968.
4. Matthews, M. V., and J. E. Miller, "Computer Editing, Typesetting and Image Generation," *Proceedings of the AFIPS 1965 Fall Joint Computer Conference,* pp. 389–398.
5. Stevens, Mary Elizabeth, and John L. Little, *Automatic Typographic-Quality Typesetting Techniques, A State-of-the-Art Review,* NBS Monograph 99, National Bureau of Standards, Washington, D.C.; 1967.

Part III Advanced Applications of Interactive Systems

Chapter Ten

Interactive Programming

10.1 INTRODUCTION

In interactive programming a programmer is in direct communication with the computer through a remote console (Figure 10.1). He can enter his program through the console, change it, ask for it to be run, and, on the same console, see the output his program has generated as well as messages sent from the compiler or monitor. A program can be run immediately (or very shortly) after being composed, and the results of its operation are immediately available to the programmer, who can then change the program and rerun it if necessary. Segments of a program may be run in the same way, so that each segment can be debugged before others are begun. Hence this mode of operation is truly interactive.

There are frequently two modes of operation of commands, *direct* and *stored*. In the direct mode a command is executed immediately on being received and interpreted by the computer. For example, the command Type 2 + 2. in the JOSS language results in the computer typing 2 + 2 = 4. In the stored mode, the programmer writes and stores a program, much as conventional programmers do, but he can call for its execution whenever he pleases. Thus he can type 1.1 Type 2 + 2. Do step 1.1. and the computer will recognize the second command as an order to execute the first one, which, because it was prefixed with a step number, was stored as received and not executed. Although many interactive systems operate in approximately this way, work has been done on other techniques, including a graphic means of entering pro-

Figure 10.1 Working with an interactive programming system. *Photo courtesy C. L. Baker.*

grams into the computer.[10] Eliminating the direct mode can reduce the cost of operation of a time-sharing system, and this is frequently what is done in the less expensive systems.

The direct mode of programming enables the computer to be used as a high-performance desk calculator, for making quick tests of a proposed program idea and for temporary patching of an existing program during debugging. The stored mode is more satisfactory for a program that is long or is to be used repetitively. The combination enables the programmer to write part of a program, test it, make needed changes, try the result again, and repeat until he is satisfied.

On-line programming is one of the most successful of man-machine functions, or at least one of the most often acclaimed functions. Although the reasons for this popularity are not universally agreed upon, they will provide an insight into other man-machine endeavors. First, most of the time users have a free choice of either using an on-line system or following conventional procedure. Those who elect on-line programming, then, are presumably predisposed to favor it and to forgive some of its weaknesses. Furthermore, these users will probably understand what the alternative is and be appreciative of the reduced time required to complete a programming task in this manner.

Second, on-line programmers are not dealing with an abstraction. They are *programming,* and in doing so they perform the same steps they would perform if writing code on paper for later keypunching. The difference is that new tasks are added; old, familiar ones are not replaced. The experienced programmer, then, has hardly any relearning to do.

Third, the working relationship between man and machine is probably smoother than in many of the other applications. The interactive computer introduces fundamental changes into the programming process. Perhaps its greatest contribution is that it provides immediate feedback to the programmer. Of course, so do many of the other interactive processes described in other chapters. In this case, however, we are not simulating the action of the computer; the computer is actually executing the program while we wait. If a mistake has been made, the programmer finds out *immediately,* while the program is fresh in his mind. If he is not sure of the best way to solve a problem, he can try several ways, *right now.* It is also beneficial to be able to write the program in small steps and check out each step as it is written, then gradually test all the components together. Although this approach is theoretically possible with off-line, or batch, programming, it is not always used because the programmer, not wanting to be idle while waiting for segment one to be run on the computer, writes segment two while waiting. Then, if an error is found in segment one, this may require that he modify segment two as well. The more steps into which he divides his program and the greater elapsed time between runs on the computer, the greater is this hazard of a chain reaction of program modifications. With on-line programming, it is usually more convenient to check out the first component before going on to the next.

The time required to submit a request for a program to be run, wait one's turn, and finally receive results is called *turn-around time.* With time-sharing, turn-around time is near zero. In batch-processing systems (users queue up for access to the computer), on the other hand, turn-around time is frequently 24 hours.

On-line programming does not logically require a time-shared computer, but time-sharing is mandated for economic reasons. Indeed, this is the primary application of time-sharing, and many times these two expressions, on-line programming and time-sharing, are used interchangeably. They are not the same, though, and either can exist without the other. G. E. Bryan,[1] in an analysis of user patterns with RAND Corporation's JOSS, found that an average user spent 45–50 minutes in a session at his console. During this time he used an average of 6.6

minutes of actual computer time. Even this latter figure is significantly influenced by a few heavy users. The median amount of computer time actually used was 50 *seconds*. We can see, then, that on-line programming without time-sharing is an expensive proposition, since for more than 98 per cent of the time the computer is not working productively for the particular user. Most of the time unaccounted for will be spent in thinking or typing.

The impetus for on-line programming came mainly from universities and large scientific laboratories, notably MIT, Dartmouth, the RAND Corporation, and the Bell Telephone Laboratories. A common problem for such organizations is trying to accommodate a very large number of computer users with scientific-type problems. These people, whether scientists or students, are not primarily professional programmers and are interested in results for use in some other project, that is, the program is not the end in itself. They are impatient of any time necessary for debugging. The user, if he is a student, may have a fixed deadline 2 or 3 days hence, when his class next meets, and 24-hour turn-around time is incompatible with this condition.

A number of on-line programming systems are in use today. Among the best known are BASIC [7] (developed at Dartmouth College, and made popular by General Electric), JOSS [2] (developed by the RAND Corporation), QUIKTRAN [4] (IBM), and APL [8] (IBM). Each of these is primarily a mathematical programming language, and each has a number of restrictions as compared with a general-purpose programming language. Typical restrictions are the following. Variables must be numeric (i.e., no variable can have the *value* CHICAGO). Even numeric variables may be restricted to floating-point form only, or fixed-point form only, the choice not being under the control of the using programmer. Also, these languages usually restrict the programmer to the use of a fixed amount of core memory with no (or only limited) control over auxiliary memory, so that he cannot move data in and out of his allotted core area at will.

BASIC and QUIKTRAN are dialects of FORTRAN, that is, the former languages are similar in construction to the latter but are simplified. BASIC, since its original appearance at Dartmouth, has now emerged in a variety of forms. MIT's Project MAC [3] is still more general in nature, offering its users more languages and more flexibility in using these languages. The IBM Computer-Assisted Instruction [5, 6] system has within it the equivalent of an on-line, time-shared programming system for use by authors in writing new courses. A CAI system, as we have learned, imposes severe logical restrictions on the kind of programs that can be written.

In summary, we see that on-line programming almost inevitably requires some sacrifice on the part of the user. He gains better rapport with the computer. He may save money in the long run. But he must usually surrender some logical power, accept some reduction in capability, so that the programming system can operate with reasonable efficiency. So long as the users are fairly homogeneous in their computer requirements, however. and there is a good fit between their needs and the provisions of the language in use, on-line programming will be popular and profitable.

10.2 REQUIREMENTS AND ENVIRONMENT FOR ON-LINE PROGRAMMING

We have already stated that a major requirement for a successful on-line programming operation is that the inevitable system restrictions and capabilities match the needs of the users. We cannot present a meaningful set of requirements that are met by all on-line programming systems. We shall describe, then, in general terms, a mathematically oriented system, typified by JOSS, BASIC, APL, and QUIKTRAN.

10.2.1 The Computing System

Time-sharing is a practical requirement. If a computer system costs $200 per hour and has 20 simultaneous users, the cost to each is $10 per hour, which is less than the average cost per hour of a programmer's time, if overhead is considered. Use of a time-shared, on-line programming system for an hour's work may well save at least an hour's additional work on the part of the programmer, although figures to support such a supposition are obviously hard to find.

A simple programming language is needed for several reasons. Primarily, this will hold down the requirements on the time-sharing monitor and interpreter which have to process program statements. Simplifying the language reduces the time required for the system to carry out commands. A simpler language also reduces the number of programmer errors, thus increasing further both overall system efficiency and responsiveness.

The advantage of having two modes of program entry, direct and stored, cannot be overestimated. If there is only the stored mode, as in the early BASIC, the on-line system is little more than a remote job entry system, one through which the programmer can transmit a program, or a modification, and a request to operate a program, though turn-around time is only a few seconds. In the direct mode he can initialize data (that is, assign initial values to data items), change the effect of a program, simulate the action of a program, vary his starting and ending points, and selectively survey the contents of memory while debugging. These capabilities, of course, are in addition to the user's ability to operate in a desk calculator mode, whereby he can directly perform calculations. But the importance of the direct mode is far greater in its impact on programming than in its ability to do rapid calculations. Included in direct mode operations is usually a set of commands (insert, delete, replace) for modifying a stored program, commands not usually available to a programmer operating in an off-line or batch mode.

When operating off-line, a programmer usually changes his programs by physically replacing cards in a deck and then re-entering the entire deck. Incidentally, those who argue against on-line programming because of the inherent inefficiency of an interpretive system may forget the high cost of repeated recompilation of conventionally submitted programs. When a programmer must recompile a program because he made a single punctuation error and consumes 15 minutes of computer time in doing so, there is a high overhead charge that is not always recognized as such.

A compiler translates commands written by a programmer into the detailed programming language understandable by the computer. Traditionally, a compiler works on an entire program at once. If the original (or *source*) program is changed, to whatever degree, the entire program must be recompiled. An interpreter performs the same basic functions, but does so on one command at a time. It does not store the results of its translation. As a command is translated, it is executed and the record discarded. If the same command is to be executed again by the program, it must be retranslated each time. On the other hand, if a change is made in the source program, no compiling or interpreting function is triggered or required until the new command is actually ready for execution. Hence the compiler carries out a high-cost operation that then enables the object program to be run efficiently, at high speed. The interpreter is a slower-operating program that has no "entrance fee"—costs are not incurred before the execution of the source program. However, the object program operates more slowly and at a higher cost. The use of a compiler imposes long delays between the submission of a program for a compilation and its availability for execution.

An interpreter has an added advantage of great importance for time-sharing: it requires very little memory for the storage of object programs. Source language statements can be brought into core memory a few at a time. When a source program is compiled, larger blocks of core must be set aside for storage of pages or other subdivisions, and moving these blocks about in memory requires the expensive relocation process.

When a program is to be run in "production," that is, to be executed with real data in operational use, probably consuming a large amount of computer time, it is almost always more efficient to compile it and run it at full speed. Once a program is debugged, the compilation process need not be repeated. Interpreting is more efficient for a program that is being debugged, that will almost certainly have to be recompiled before each use, and that runs only for a short period with small amounts of test data.

Unfortunately, few computer systems offer a free choice of method. Once the choice of system is made, different languages are usually imposed on the user, and he cannot freely decided to operate by interpreter one day and by compiler the next.

Provision should also be made for putting both programs and data files in common, or library, areas where they can be freely used by anyone, to the advantage of all. Once a computational program has been debugged, for example, it should be put into the system library and made available to any other user needing a similar function performed.

An on-line computing system, particularly in a school, may have many users working on similar programs. We usually want to provide protection for each programmer against having his programs modified by others, accidentally or otherwise. Similarly, if the system allows for the storage of data, the "owner" of these data will want to prevent others from modifying them without authorization. To provide this protection, each user is usually identified by a code number, and allocation of memory and access to programs or data are based on this code. Any user knowing a particular code can access the program or data stored under its protection. A provision has to be made for enrolling and disenrolling users at a central, or command, station to keep adequate control over the system. Ordinary users will not have access to the list of authorized users; hence, even if one user knew someone else's number, he could not remove this person from the rolls or enter himself on them.

None of the features listed above is unique to on-line computing. Even the use of an interpreter instead of a compiler could conceivably be justified in a batch processing system that has a large number of small jobs, with a requirement for fast turn-around time. The problem of protecting data files tends to occur only with on-line systems; but, as we find increasing use of large files permanently stored in the computer on disks, the desirability of protecting them against encroachment by other programs is worth considering.

What we have done, then, is to assume a set of attributes of computing systems all of which favor rapid execution and hence provide rapid response to the programmer. In meeting these requirements, a number of simplifications in the programming language may have to be imposed.

10.2.2 The System Environment

Perhaps the most important environmental consideration for on-line programming is that the population of users be people whose time is highly valued (being highly paid is *not* the same). There must be the assumption that the productivity of these people can be improved and that it is important to achieve this improvement. A prime example is a research laboratory whose staff is interested primarily in its major field of endeavor. To these people, time spent programming, while necessary, is time spent away from their main objective. Similarly, a student, although he draws no salary, must be given enough free time to do assignments in subjects other than the one requiring use of the computer, and must be able to complete assignments within the schedule of the class. He cannot, in other words, be given a semester's assignments and be told only that all should be completed by the end of the term.

Also, the type of program most commonly written by the users must fit comfortably within the constraints imposed by the programming language. Here is the major reason why on-line programming is found so seldom in professional programming laboratories. People writing compilers, information retrieval systems, or the like for broad commercial distribution find that the constraints of BASIC or JOSS are excessive and that recourse must be had to a more powerful and generally used language, whatever the cost in individual programmer efficiency.

Third, there must be enough users to keep the computer system busy a reasonable portion of the time. This is mainly a problem for so-called dedicated systems, which are able to operate only the on-line programming system. Some modern multiprogramming systems allow an on-line computer system to be operated simultaneously with batch processing. With this arrangement, whenever on-line usage is slack, more of the computer's resources can be shifted to the accomplishment of the batched tasks, and vice versa. An on-line programming system should be available during a large part of the work day, to be most beneficial. Operating in the on-line mode for two or three separate and short periods of the day, such as, 8–10 A.M. and 1–3 P.M., puts the user somewhat in the position of a programmer operating in a batch mode with short turn-around time.

Again, because use of on-line programming represents a conscious choice of one form of operation over another, the attitude of users is an important consideration. On-line programming offers advantages to users only if they want these advantages and will utilize them. This technique is still new and is not necessarily comfortable to all people. Furthermore, some people feel that giving programmers "free" use of a computer encourages wastefulness, fostering a tendency to replace careful thought with hastily conceived solutions. This argument we do not accept, and instead challenge its proponents to offer some evidence that 24 hours rather than 24 seconds of reaction time induces more thought or leads to a better product.

An argument less easy to counter is that many people are not comfortable working through a typewriter and under a form of time pressure wherein a system is constantly waiting for the programmer to make the next move. The pressure really is not supposed to be there, since idle time costs little, if anything. (The actual charge depends on the accounting system used to allocate costs among users, but thinking time is inexpensive on almost any on-line system.) The unfamiliarity of the typewriter, though, is real. Newer terminals, such as those incorporating cathode ray tubes, seem to be making no particular progress toward ease of use by amateurs. It would appear that competence with a typewriter is going to become increasingly important in the computing profession and may even, in spite of its absence of intellectual content, become a prerequisite for a programming career.

A powerful argument in favor of on-line systems is that a programmer must otherwise spend long periods relearning a program after a 24-hour separation from it. When a programmer has made a correction in a program and submitted it for recompilation and running, the next day, when the results come back, he may have to pore through his work for an hour to try to recall what he was trying to do, and how the program logic works in the particular area he was testing. Designing a program or making changes in one shown to be in error is an intellectual process that requires the programmer to keep in mind a complex structure of program logic and data and to be able to visualize how the program will operate on the selected test data. When a day's delay intervenes, he must carefully rebuild this structure in his own mind and will not always do so with perfect accuracy. It is not uncommon, in my experience, to be baffled the next day in trying to find an explanation for an action that seemed obvious the day before.

The counter argument is that the delay provides an opportunity for a "fresh" look at the problem and helps to prevent a programmer from continuing down a wrong path he may have stumbled onto at some time while hastily revising a program. Stepping away from a problem, it is true, can give valuable insight.

Regardless of the attitude of the reader toward on-line programming, no written description of it is adequate. On-line programming provides a different relationship between a man, a complex structure called a program, and a complex organism called a computer. It is difficult to portray this relationship in words. Professor Joseph Weizenbaum of MIT has compared on-line programming with psychoanalysis, pointing out that one cannot appreciate it without trying it.

10.2.3   Capabilities of a Typical System

Presented below are the general features of an on-line programming system that is oriented primarily toward mathematical programming. Everything mentioned here is compatible with the JOSS system; and, since our example in Section 10.3 will be based on JOSS, the reader can consider this an introduction to that language.

The user first identifies himself to the system and provides a key number. The name and the number must be acceptable to the system, or the user is not permitted to continue. It is also possible that the system is fully occupied at this time and cannot allow even a legitimate used to "go on." Most systems will permit more users to enroll than can actually work simultaneously.

Once signed on, the user operates in either the direct or the stored mode. When the keyboard is opened, that is, when the user is allowed to transmit, if he precedes his message with a number of appropriate form, this number is taken as the line number of a program statement and the computer assumes he is entering a program in the stored mode. If the user's message does not contain a line number, it is treated as a direct command and will be executed immediately by the computer. *JOSS commands are not checked for validity until ready for execution.* Hence a stored command that is invalid is not detected until the program of which it is a part is executed. A direct command that is in error, however, will be caught at once since the computer attempts to execute it immediately.

We may broadly classify the commands as those ordering the execution or halt of a program or portion of one, those concerned with storing and retrieving data (including programs), those ordering the execution of a single command, assignment statements that perform arithmetic operations and store results, and conditional statements. We shall not give here the complete repertoire of commands, but in the next section will introduce a few of them as they are needed in the sample program.

If a program has been stored, the command DO, with some indication of what is to be done, causes the designated program to be executed. DO may call for an entire program or a single statement. There are other commands for stopping or interrupting a program or for resuming after an interrupt. Basically, they are all concerned with giving the programmer control over what is executed and the conditions under which execution is to be suspended.

As new programs are written or data defined, these elements are kept in a working storage. They may be filed in more permanent storage and later retrieved selectively on command of the programmer. Thus he may work for an hour on a program, writing it, changing it, testing it with different data. When he is finally satisfied, he can have the last version of the program stored for his use at other programming sessions. Stored material, whether in temporary or permanent storage, can also be deleted at will. Beside this capability, the programmer may call upon previously written functions made available to him as if they were basic system commands. For example, there is a square root function whose use may be programmed as easily as if root extraction were one of the basic arithmetic operations.

The programmer may enter a single processing command for direct execution. He may say x = 3 with the result that the value stored for *x* is immediately set to 3. He may also ask for a datum to be typed, either a data item or some part of a stored program. Thus Type x. results in the computer replying x = 3. If he asks for a program to be typed, he receives a transcript of the program as stored.

Finally, the programmer can enter commands for storage. He does this by affixing a step number to each command. Hence 1.1 Type x. tells the computer to store the command Type x., tagged with a step number of 1.1, for later use. If we look upon the step number as a command, the entry of stored commands is done by giving a command to store the command that follows. The command *to store* is executed immediately. The command *to be stored* is, of course, deferred. A stored command can be replaced by typing in a new command, using the same step number as before. The sequence 1.1 Type x. 1.1 Type y. results in a command to type variable *y* in step 1.1.

The list of commands that can be executed by a program is long and is summarized in Section 10.2.4. As we shall see in Section 10.3, it is not necessary to learn or make use of all commands to benefit from JOSS.

On-line debugging is the major advantage of on-line programming. Some services toward this end are provided automatically by the system, and others must be supplied by the programmer for himself. The main service provided by the computing system is a syntactic analysis of the command. If the command is invalid, the programmer is informed and the command is not executed. Typical errors are simple omissions of punctuation or misspellings. It is possible, however, to make reference to a data item for which a value has never been established. If we say Set x = y + 2. the computer will respond y = ? ? ?, meaning no value has yet been assigned to this variable. The computer could have made use of whatever value is in the actual memory location referred to, but this introduces chaos into the program and can lead to much frustrated debugging. A program that uses a data item before specifying at least its initial value will produce different results each time it is run. This is not good practice.

The extent to which the system's analysis of an illegal command is presented to the user varies. JOSS, unfortunately, merely reports the error. Thus 1.1 Typd x. would trigger the machine reply Eh? But, in order for the computer to know this command is illegal, it has to have more information than it has passed on. It knows that Typd is not a legal command. It is very easy for a programmer to miss this and to look for address or format errors instead.

Even this question of how much error diagnosis the system should pass on is controversial. The programmer would usually like full information on what he has done wrong. A syntax analysis program, however, does not always know *what* is wrong, even when it is sure *something* is wrong.

Here is an example. Suppose we have a program that uses the variables *n, i,* and *m.* We assume *n* was previously used to refer to an array, any individual member of which is normally identified as *n(i).* JOSS permits the usage Type n. and takes it to mean to type out all stored values in the array. It also permits the usage Type n(i). and takes this to mean to type out only the *i*th value of *n.* JOSS also permits the usage Type a,b,c., where *a, b,* and *c* are any variables which will then be typed out sequentially. Now consider the statement Type n(i,m. This is invalid, but why? Has the programmer omitted the right parenthesis immediately after *i,* or has he typed a left parenthesis instead of a comma? He could, quite validly, have meant to insist either a right parenthesis after *i* or a comma after *n,* and there is no way JOSS (or anyone else) can tell his intentions. JOSS is faced with the choice of issuing an error message that makes a possibly meaningless assumption or simply saying

Eh? which tells the programmer to look carefully for the trouble. The decision was made not to mislead, even at the risk of not informing.

Finally, we must remember the restrictions imposed by an on-line system. There is usually a restriction on memory used, but not necessarily any way for the programmer to tell how much he has used. There is usually a restriction on the type of variables used and perhaps on the names that may be assigned to them. For example, JOSS limits the name of a variable to a single letter. BASIC permits a single letter followed by a single digit, if desired. The PL/I programming language allows up to 31 characters for a datum name. These considerations are important for large projects, not for small programs. Both JOSS and the early BASIC restrict variables to numeric values only. That is, in these languages we cannot refer to a variable that will have a letter for a value. Other, more subtle limitations are imposed by any system, and the user must find them and be sure he can operate within them.

10.2.4   Summary of JOSS Language[9]

The tabular summary on pages 295-298 is reproduced with the kind permission of the RAND Corporation, originators of JOSS.

10.3   AN EXAMPLE

The problem we wish to solve is that of finding the smallest number in a set of numbers. If there is more than one occurrence of a smallest value in the set, the number of such occurrences is to be listed. The numbers in the set are to be typed in on demand, and the program is to type out the smallest value in this set and number of occurrences. The dimension of the set, that is, the number of numbers to be scanned, is arbitrary.

We will organize our program in four parts, illustrated in Figure 10.2. Part 1 will be a control section, calling other parts into operation as needed. It first calls part 2, which will contain the programming steps needed to acquire the set of numbers from the user. Part 3 will first call part 4, wherein the smallest value is found. Part 3 then causes the smallest value and count to be printed. Hence part 1 starts by calling part 2, to acquire the data. Then it calls part 3. Part 3 calls part 4 to find the smallest number and then prints out the necessary data.

The program on page 299 has several intentional errors in it, some logical and others procedural. It does not use all available JOSS facilities,

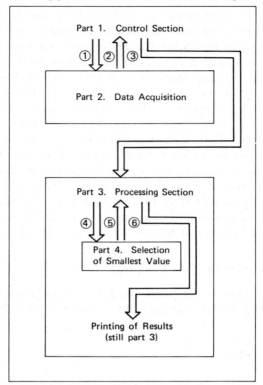

Figure 10.2 Program organization.

but it adequately illustrates on-line programming technique. In the programming statements to follow, numbers on the extreme left identify lines for reference purposes only. These numbers would not appear on the page typed at the console. Step numbers, of the form 1.2, however, would appear. Machine-generated messages are shown with a gray background. Man-generated messages are in regular form. JOSS can vary the color to help the user separate his input from the machine's output.

Because the fully annotated program is so long, we have inserted an unannotated program listing at several points. This is a convenience to the reader, but the working programmer would have to remember to ask for it when he needs it; it would not be produced automatically.

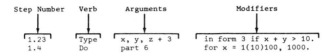

Step Number	Verb	Arguments	Modifiers
1.23	Type	x, y, z + 3	in form 3 if x + y > 10.
1.4	Do	part 6	for x = 1(10)100, 1000.

DIRECT COMMAND: Step number not present; command is executed immediately.

STORED COMMAND: Step number present; command is stored in order of step number.

STEP: A stored command; step number is limited to 9-digit number ≥ 1.

PART: A group of steps whose step numbers have the same integral part.

FORM: A pictorial specification of literal information and fields to be filled with values, for formal output. Fields are indicated by strings of underscores (with optional decimal point) or strings of periods (for a tabular form of scientific notation):

Form 7:

I = __.___ amps.   V = ... volts

NUMBERS: Nine significant digits; $10^{-99} \leq |value| \leq 9.99999999 \cdot 10^{99}$ or *value* = 0.

SYMBOLS: Single-letter identifiers, upper- or lower-case. May identify decimal values, logical values (true, false), formulas, and arrays of values.

FORMULAS: May have up to ten formal parameters (distinct letters) or none (see *Let*).

ARRAYS: May have up to ten, integer-valued indices in the range [-250, 250].

ARITHMETIC: Addition (+), subtraction (-), multiplication (·), division (/), exponentiation (*), and square root (*sqrt*) give true results rounded to nine significant digits. Zero is substituted on underflow.

RELATIONS: < > ≤ ≥ = ≠ (extended relations permitted; e.g., a < b ≤ c).

LOGIC: and   or   not

GROUPERS: ( )   [ ]   used interchangeably, in pairs.

IMPLIED GROUPINGS:

$$3 + 1/2 + 1/4 \cdot 5 \;\rightarrow\; (3 + 1/2) + (1/4) \cdot 5$$

$$-2*3 \cdot 4 - 5 \;\rightarrow\; [-(2^3) \cdot 4] - 5$$

$$2*3*4 \;\rightarrow\; (2^3)^4$$

a or b and not c or d   →   a or [b and (not c)] or d

Set	Assigns a value. *Set* and final period may be omitted on direct commands. Set x = 3. Set a(5, x) = y + 3•z - x☆2.
Let	Defines a *formula* of up to ten parameters. Let f(x, y) = x☆2 + 10•x - 6•y. Let h = (b - a)/2. Let D(f, x) = [f(x + d) - f(x)]/d.
Delete	Erases values, parts, steps, forms, formulas. Delete x, part 3, all forms. Delete all values, all formulas. Delete all.
Type	Types quoted text, or types blank lines (_), values, parts, steps, etc. Type "The quick brown fox". Type x + 3, D(sin, 0), _, all steps. Type all.
Demand	Types identification and equals sign, then waits for user to input value. Treats blank input lines as interruptions. Demand a(3, i). Demand t as "temperature".
_Do_	Initiates execution of step or part (step by step beginning at first step of part), repeatedly if modified by a *for* or a *times* phrase. Do part 6 for x = .1, 2(2)10, 100•a + 2•b.
_(Do ...)_	Interprets direct *Do* as a stored *Do* (i.e., does not cancel before execu- tion), but returns to user when done. (Do part 3.)
Done	Terminates execution of current *Do* for current repetition.
Quit	Terminates execution of current *Do* for all repetitions.
Cancel	Terminates execution of all *Do*'s.
(Cancel.)	Direct only! Terminates execution of last *(Do ...)*.
_To_	Alters step-by-step sequencing. Continues at indicated part or step. To step 3.5.
Stop	Suspends step-by-step execution to await instructions from user.
_Go_	Continues execution after *interrupt*,[†] error message, or *Stop* command.

[†]Pressing the INTERRUPT button on the console.

Page	Advances paper to next page.
Line	Types a blank line.
Form	Identifies (by an integer) and stores the form typed on the next input line. Form 3: x = ____.___ y = ____.___ z = ...
Use	Prepares to use indicated file for all subsequent file actions. Use file 107 (*code*).†
File	Stores an item in the file. File part 3, x, z as item 7 (*code*).
Recall	Retrieves an item from the file. Recall item 3 (*code*).
Discard	Erases an item from the file. Discard item 3 (*code*).
if	Modifies any command. JOSS carries out command if condition holds. Type x if 0 ≤ x < 5. Set y = 3 if x ≤ 10 and x·y = 10.
for	Modifies *Do* only. JOSS executes part or step repeatedly for specified set of values. Do part 3 for x = 1(1)10(10)100, 1000. Do step 1.2 for x = .01, .03, .1(a)b.
times	Modifies *Do* only. JOSS executes part or step specified number of times. Do part 4, 43 times. Do step 7.3, n + 1 times.
in form	Modifies *Type* only. JOSS types values in fields of specified form. Type x, y, z*2 in form 3.
sparse	Modifies JOSS's treatment of missing array elements. JOSS treats them as zeros and they require no storage. Let A be sparse.
item-list	A summary of items in the file being used. Type item-list.
time	Time of day at RAND. Type time.
users	Number of consoles being serviced by JOSS at the moment. Type users.
size	Number of storage units currently occupied by user's program and data; about 1900 are available.
timer	Time in minutes and hundredths since log-on or last *Reset timer*.
$	Current line number (1-54) on typed page.

---

†Codes, if used, are composed of no more than 5 letters and/or digits; no distinction between upper- and lower-case.

sqrt(x)	*square root, $x \geq 0$*		sgn(x)	-1, 0, +1 for x < 0, x = 0, x > 0	
sin(x) ⎫ cos(x) ⎭	*|x in radians| < 100*		ip(x)	*integer part*	ip(100.5) = 100
			fp(x)	*fraction part*	fp(100.5) = .5
log(x)	*natural log, x > 0*		dp(x)	*digit part*	dp(100.5) = 1.005
exp(x)	e^x		xp(x)	*exponent part*	xp(100.5) = 2
arg(x, y)	*angle (see figure) in radians,* arg(0, 0) = 0.		|x|	*absolute value for decimal values*	

$|true| = 1$

$|false| = 0$

```
        sum[i = a(b)c: f(i)]          sum(x, y, z + 10)
        prod[i = a(b)c: f(i)]         prod(x, y, z + 10)
        min[i = a(b)c: f(i)]          min(x, y, z + 10)
        max[i = a(b)c: f(i)]          max(x, y, z + 10)
        conj[i = a(b)c: P(i)]         conj(x < y ≤ z, y > 3, P)
        disj[i = a(b)c: P(i)]         disj(x < y ≤ z, y > 3, P)
```

first[i = a(b)c: P(i)] *gives first value of i for which* P(i) *is true*

tv(P) *= 0 if* P *is false, = 1 if* P *is true,*
= false if P *is zero, = true if* P *is nonzero*

$$(P_1: E_1; \ P_2: E_2; \ldots; \ E_n)$$

where: P_i are expressions for logical values,

means: If P_1 is true use E_1, otherwise if P_2 is true use $E_2,\ldots,$ otherwise use E_n.
Set x = (0 < y ≤ 5: 0; y < 10: y*2; 5).
Let P(x) = [x = 0: 1; prod(i = 1(1)x: i)].

298

1. Delete all.cr

This deletes any previous information in the working area of memory. Its use is a precaution that old programmers learn to take. The character CR represents a carriage return, which actually does not print. Since CR is the end-of-message symbol for JOSS, we have indicated it whenever used.

2. 1.1 Do step *cr

We begin to enter the program in stored mode. The first requirement is to execute (Do) the part of the program that will elicit data from the user. We made a mistake here and typed Do step instead of Do part. The * indicates that the line should be ignored. A carriage return is sent and the program step repeated, this time correctly.

We ask for the execution of part 2 (wherein the numbers are typed into the computer) repetitively, iteration being governed by a variable i, which is to have value 1 initially and then be increased by 1 until the value m is reached. m is the number of numbers in our set.

We then want part 3 of the program executed, the part that finds and prints the smallest number. This command has been typed incorrectly. Note that the computer does not reject it at this point because it is to be stored, not executed immediately.

The command Demand tells the computer to ask the operator of the console, at the time the command is executed, for a value for the variable named. This command will result in a message being typed to a user saying n(i) =, and he will type in a value.

3. 1.1 Do part 2 for i = 1(1)m.cr

4. 1.2 do part 3.cr

5. 2.1 Demand n(i).cr

6. **3.1 Do part 4.c̲r̲**

We show that we have begun part 3 by simply changing the first digit of our step numbers. We first ask for execution of part 4.

7. **3.2 Type s,c in form 1.c̲r̲**

Now, we assume part 4 has found the smallest number, called s, and has counted the number of times s occurred and called the count c. We ask for s and c to be printed, embedded in a sentence that we will shortly provide, called form 1.

8. **Form 1:c̲r̲**

We now state that we are about to prescribe form 1.

9. **There are _____ occurrences of smallest value _____.c̲r̲**

This is form 1. The blank spaces will be filled in, in order of occurrence, by the variables named in the type command.

10. 4.1 Set $s = n(i)$ if $n(i) \leq s$.<u>cr</u>

11. 4.2 Set $c = c + 1$ if $n(i) \leq s$.<u>cr</u>

We now begin part 4, where we will actually find the smallest number. We will assume the numbers being tested are called $n(1)$, $n(2)$, . . , $n(m)$; therefore the ith number is called $n(i)$. If the ith number is less than or equal to the current value of s, replace s with this value, so that s always is less than or equal to the current n. The form of this command says to make the replacement only if $n(i) \leq s$. Otherwise the command has no effect.

Now, if $n(i)$ was less than or equal to s, add 1 to the counter. Again, if s was greater than $n(i)$, the command has no effect. We have now finished part 4.

We glance back at our program and see a mistake. We have asked for execution of part 4 only once, whereas it should be executed once for each member of n. Hence, we make this change, by retyping with the same step number. In the process, we struck the e key instead of the 4 key. A simple error such as this can be corrected by backspacing and retyping.

To assure ourselves, we ask for the changed step to be typed out.

We verify that the correction was made properly. We have now entered our entire program and are ready to begin debugging.

12.   3.1   Do part 4 for i = 1(1)m.

13.   Type step 3.1.cr

14.   3.1   Do part 4 for i = 1(1)m.

See Figure 10.3 for a listing of the program at this point.

1.1 Do part 2 for i = 1(1)m.

1.2 do part 3.

2.1 Demand n(i).

3.1 Do part 4 for i = 1(1)m.

3.2 Type s,c in form 1.

Form 1:

There are _____ occurrences of smallest value _____.

4.1 Set s = n(i) if n(i) ≤ s.

4.2 Set c = c + 1 if n(i) ≤ s.

Figure 10.3 Current listing of program, I.

Since part 1 calls parts 2 and 3, and part 3 calls 4, we can run the whole program by asking only for part 1.

Here is the first of our diagnostic aids. In step 1.1 (see the revised version, line 3) we made reference to m, the number of numbers to be tested, but have never assigned a value to m. This will be easy to fix, but in order to get on with the program, we will force in a value and patch the program later.

This command directly assigns a value of 3 to m. The command is not part of the program we have written, but it will do to get us started.

We ask, again, for the program to execute part 1.

15. Do part 1.cr

16. Error at step 1.1: m = ???

17. m = 3cr

18. Do part 1.cr

305

Here are the requests for the three numbers, in response to our <u>Demand</u> n (i) command. The <u>demand</u> has been executed for $i = 1$, 2, and 3. The values we entered have been stored for future use.

The computer is now trying to execute the command we purposely typed illegally in step 1.2 (line 4). We note that we get no assistance in figuring what went wrong, but in this case it is obvious.

We type the command correctly, again identifying it as step 1.2.

There has been a communications error. The computer did not receive a valid first character, although we typed it correctly. Probably the trouble was caused by noise on the telephone line (the computer, when this program was actually written, was 250 miles away).

19.   n(1) = 3cr

20.   n(2) = 2cr

21.   n(3) = 1cr

22. Error at step 1.2: Eh?

23. 1.2 Do part 3.cr

24. #.2 Do part 3.

25. Sorry. Say again:

The computer types what it received, with the illegible character replaced by a #, and then tells us to repeat the last message.

We repeat the message, and it appears to have been accepted this time.

We ask only for execution of part 3. Part 1 requires re-typing the *n*'s, and we know they remain correctly stored as last entered by us.

Another unacceptable com-mand. No value of *s* has been defined. We now realize that no initial value of *c* has been defined either, and this means that we have failed to initial-ize three variables: *m*, *s*, and *c*. Hence we had better revise the program right now.

26. 1.2 Do part 3.<u>cr</u>

27. Do part 3.<u>cr</u>

28. <u>Error at step 4.1: s = ???</u>

The number 1.01 is smaller than 1.1, so this command will be inserted ahead of step 1.1 by the computer. Instead of just demanding m, we will ask the computer to send us a message stating what the number is for. This usage will result in the machine sending us the message *Length of array to be searched* instead of $\underline{m =}$.

We set s and c to be zero.

Now we try the entire program again.

Here is our request for the value of m, asked for in terms of the message we provided earlier.

We elicit the values of $n(1)$, $n(2)$, and $n(3)$ again.

---

29. 1.01 Demand m as "Length of array to be searched".<u>cr</u>

30. 1.02 Set s = 0.<u>cr</u>

31. 1.03 Set c = 0.<u>cr</u>

32. Do part 1.<u>cr</u>

33. Length of array to be searched = <u>3cr</u>

34. n(1) = <u>3cr</u>

35. n(2) = <u>2cr</u>

36. n(3) = <u>1cr</u>

The program runs to completion and gives us an unexpected result. Now it is up to us to examine the program we have written and find what was wrong. It is clear that something has gone amiss.

37. There are   0 occurrences of smallest value   0.

See Figure 10.4 for a listing of the program at this point.

38. 3.01 Set s = n(1).<u>cr</u>

We have it! We set s initially to zero, then never encountered an n that small. Hence we never changed s and never counted any new lows. So s and c retained their initial values. We can change this by initializing s to the value of any one of the n's guaranteeing that it is at least as big as one of them, and hence not smaller than all of them. We have to be careful to do this *after* we elicit the n's, so we put this new command in part 3.

1.01 Demand m as "Length of array to be searched".

1.02 Set s = 0.

1.03 Set c = 0.

1.1 Do part 2 for i = 1(1)m.

1.2 Do part 3.

2.1 Demand n(i).

3.1 Do part 4 for i = 1(1)m.

3.2 Type s,c in form 1.

Form 1:

There are _____ occurrences of smallest value _____ .

4.1 Set s = n(i) if n(i) ≤ s.

4.2 Set c = c + 1 if n(i) ≤ s.

Figure 10.4 Current program listing, II.

39. Do part 1.cr

Now we try the whole program again.

40. Length of array to be searched = 3cr

This is going as before, but we have put in values for n of 1, 2, 3 instead of 3, 2, 1, which should make no difference.

41.   n(1) = 1cr
42.   n(2) = 2cr
43.   n(3) = 3cr

44. There are   1 occurrences of smallest value   1.

The answer seems right. The smallest number is 1, and it occurs only once. We cannot be too complacent, though, for it is still possible the program will fail under other conditions. Hence we will try again, with a different array of input numbers.

45. Do part 1.cr

We ask for the program to be executed again, set up for an array of five numbers, and enter the array as before. This time we have used a negative number, but there is still only one occurrence of the smallest value.

46. Length of array to be searched = 5 cr

47.   n(1) = 0cr
48.   n(2) = -1cr
49.   n(3) = 2cr
50.   n(4) = 0cr
51.   n(5) = 4cr

52.
```
There are        -1 occurrences of smallest value    2.
```

What's this? Both s and c are wrong! Some more musing shows us that the numbers are reversed. We have printed s where c should be, and vice versa. See step 3.2 and form 1. We asked for s to be typed first, but the first number indicated in the form is the count, c. This will be easy to fix. If we mentally make the change, we find we are not so badly off as it seemed at first. We did find the smallest value, -1, although our count is off by 1. In order to help in scanning the program, since we have made several changes, we would like to print it all out, in clean form.

53. Type part 1.gr

54.
```
1.01  Demand m as "Length of array to be searched".
```

Here is the program, together with the commands.

55. 1.02 Set s = 0.
56. 1.03 Set c = 0.
57. 1.1   Do part 2 for i = 1(1)m.
58. 1.2   Do part 3.
59. Type part 2.cr
60. 2.1   Demand n(i).
61. Type part 3.cr
62. 3.01 Set s = n(1).
63. 3.1   Do part 4 for i = 1(1)m.
64. 3.2   Type s,c in form 1.
65. Type part 4.cr
66. 4.1   Set s = n(i) if n(i) $\leq$ s.
67. 4.2   Set c = c 1 if n(i) $\leq$ s.

68.

We decide we cannot see immediately what is wrong with our counting logic, so we will do a trace on the program. At the start of part 4 we will have the machine type out the current values of $n(i)$, s, and c. As we watch these change, we should get an idea of what is wrong. Remember that the type-out will be *before* a test is made comparing s with $n(i)$.

Here is the form for typing out the trace data.

69. Form 2:

70. For n(i) = _____ s is _____ and c is _____ .

See Figure 10.5 for a listing of the program at this point.

71. Do part 2.cr

We start the program again, from part 2 bypassing the request for a value of m; hence m stays at 5, and we retain the old values of $n(i)$.

1.01   Demand m as "Length of array to be searched".

1.02   Set s = 0.

1.03   Set c = 0.

1.1   Do part 2 for i = 1(1)m.

1.2   Do part 3.

2.1   Demand n(i).

3.01   Set s = n(1).

3.1   Do part 4 for i = 1(1)m.

3.2   Type s, c in form 1.

Form 1:

There are _____ occurrences of smallest value _____.

4.01   Type n(i), s, c in form 2.

Form 2:

For n(i) = _____ s is _____ and c is _____.

4.1   Set s = n(i) if n(i) $\leq$ s.

4.2   Set c = c + 1 if n(i) $\leq$ s.

Figure 10.5 Current program listing, III.

72.

```
For n(i) =      0 s is      0 and c is      2.
```

Here are the values of $n(1)$, s, and c. The first two are correct, since we have just set s to $n(1)$. However, c is wrong. In fact, since we did not do part 1 this time, c retained the value it had at the end of our last debug run. This was a strategic error on our part, but we can still make use of this run.

73.

```
For n(i) =     -1 s is      0 and c is      3.
```

After the first test, ready for the second. $n(2)$ is -1, s remains at zero, and c is 3. This is reasonable, too. Since $n(i)$ is a new low, it is appropriate that we increment c (which should have been initially 0) by 1.

Now ready for the third test. $n(3)$ is 2. s was correctly replaced last time by -1. c has been incremented again. Here is the cause of our problem. Each time we find a new low or a tie with the previous low, we are incrementing c. We should start the count over again with a new low, not add to the old value of c.

We get a partial confirmation of our theory here. When there is no new low, we do not increment c.

The answer line, while wrong, is consistent with our hypothesis. We must remember to interchange s and c in the type command.

It will be easier to erase all of part 4 and rewrite it.

74. For n(i) =   2 s is   −1 and c is   4.

75. For n(i) =   0 s is   −1 and c is   4.
76. For n(i) =   4 s is   −1 and c is   4.

77. There are   −1 occurrences of smallest value   4.

78. Delete part 4.cr

We will calculate c this time before changing the value of s, so that we can be sure we can tell whether the n is less than the current s or equal to it. If n is less than s, we have a new low and want to reset c to 1.

If $n = s$, we have a tie with a previous low, and want to add 1 to c.

Now we make the comparison of n with s and replace s if n is lower.

We finally make the change affecting the order of typing s and c.

We rerun the entire program, putting in a new test array, this time with two occurrences of the low value.

79. 4.1 Set c = 1 if n(i) < s.cr

80. 4.2 Set c = c + 1 if n(i) = s.cr

81. 4.3 Set s = n(i) if n(i) ≤ s.cr

82. 3.2 Type c,s in form 1.cr

83. Do part 1.cr

84. Length of array to be searched = 5cr

85. n(1) = 1cr

86. n(2) = 0cr

87. n(3) = -4cr

88. n(4) = 5cr

89. n(4) = -4cr

90. There are   2 occurrences of smallest value   -4.

The resulting print-out is correct! We should test the program with still more data, but this sample illustrates all the main points in using the system and in the strategy of on-line debugging.

Figure 10.6 shows the final form of the program. The following is an unannotated transcript of the material just covered.

1.01　Demand m as "Length of array to be searched".

1.02　Set s = 0.

1.03　Set c = 0.

1.1　Do part 2 for i = 1(1)m.

1.2　Do part 3.

2.1　Demand n(1).

3.01　Set s = n(i).

3.1　Do part 4 for i = 1(1)m.

3.2　Type c,s in form 1.

　　　Form 1:

　　　There are _____ occurrences of smallest value _____.

4.1　Set c = 1 if n(i) < s.

4.2　Set c = c + 1 if n(i) = s.

4.3　Set s = n(i) if n(i) ≦ s.

Figure 10.6 Final listing of program.

Head.
14:05   7-09-68   py   (1)

Delete all.

1.1   Do step *
1.1   Do part 2 for i = 1(1)m.
1.2   do part 3
2.1   Demand n(i).
3.1   Do part 4.
3.2   Type s,c in form 1.
Form 1:
There are _____ occurrences of smallest value _____.
4.1   Set s = n(i) if n(i) ≦ s.
4.2   Set c = c + 1 if n(i) ≦ s.

3.1   Do part 4 for i = 1(1)m.

Type step 3.1.
3.1   Do part 4 for i = 1(1)m.

Do part 1.
Error at step 1.1: m = ???

m = 3
Do part 1.
         n(1) = 3
         n(2) = 2
         n(3) = 1
Error at step 1.2: Eh?

1.2   Do part 3.
#.2   Do part 3.
Sorry. Say again:
1.2   Do part 3.

Do part 3.

Error at step 4.1: s = ???

1.01   Demand m as "Length of array to be searched".
1.02   Set s = 0.
1.03   Set c = 0.

Do part 1.

14:13   7-09-68   py   (2)

Length of array to be searched = 3
        n(1) = 3
        n(2) = 2
        n(3) = 1
There are   0 occurrences of smallest value   0.
3.01 Set s = n(1).
Do part 1.
Length of array to be searched = 3
        n(1) = 1
        n(2) = 2
        n(3) = 3
There are   1 occurrences of smallest value   1.
Do part 1.
Length of array to be searched = 5
        n(1) = 0
        n(2) = −1
        n(3) = 2
        n(4) = 0
        n(5) = 4
There are   −1 occurrences of smallest value   2.

Type part 1.
1.01 Demand m as "Length of array to be searched".
1.02 Set s = 0.
1.03 Set c = 0.
1.1 Do part 2 for i = 1(1)m.
1.2 Do part 3.

Type part 2.
2.1 Demand n(i).

Type part 3.
3.01 Set s = n(1).
3.1 Do part 4 for i = 1(1)m.
3.2 Type s,c in form 1.

Type part 4.
4.1 Set s = n(i) if n(i) $\leq$ s.
4.2 Set c = c + 1 if n(i) $\leq$ s.

4.01 Type n(i), s, c in form 2.
Form 2:
For n(i) = _____ s is _____ and c is _____.

14:17   7-09-68   py   (3)

```
Do part 2.
For n(i) =          0 s is          0 and c is        2.
For n(i) =         -1 s is          0 and c is        3.
For n(i) =          2 s is         -1 and c is        4.
For n(i) =          0 s is         -1 and c is        4.
For n(i) =          4 s is         -1 and c is        4.
There are          -1 occurrences of smallest value        4.

Delete part 4.

4.1  Set c = 1 if n(i) < s.
4.2  Set c = c + 1 if n(i) = s.
4.3  Set s = n(i) if n(i) ≦ s.

3.2  Type c,s in form 1.

Do part 1.
Length of array to be searched = 5
         n(1) = 1
         n(2) = 0
         n(3) = -4
         n(4) = 5
         n(5) = -4
There are          2 occurrences of smallest value       -4.
```

REFERENCES

1. Bryan, G. E., *JOSS: 20,000 Hours at the Console—A Statistical Summary,* Memorandum RM–5359–PR, The RAND Corp., Santa Monica, Calif., August 1967.

2. Bryan, G. E., and E. W. Paxson, *The JOSS Notebook,* Memorandum RM–5367–PR, The RAND Corp., Santa Monica, Calif., August 1967.

3. Fano, R. M., "The MAC System: The Computer Utility Approach," *IEEE Spectrum,* **2,** 1 (January 1965), 56–64.

4. *IBM QUIKTRAN: A New Dimension in Conversational Computing,* Form 520–1518, IBM Corp., White Plains, N. Y., 1967.

5. *IBM 1500 Instructional System, System Summary,* Form CAI–4038, IBM Corp., White Plains, N. Y. (undated).

6. *IBM 1500 Operating System, Computer-Assisted Instruction Coursewriter II,* Form CAI–4036, IBM Corp., White Plains, N. Y. (undated).

7. Kemeny, John G., and Thomas E. Kurtz, *BASIC Programming,* John Wiley, New York, 1967.

8. Pakin, Sandra, *APL/360 Reference Manual,* Science Research Associates, Chicago, 1968.

9. Smith, J. W., *JOSS: Central Processing Routines,* Memorandum RM–5270–PR, The RAND Corp., Santa Monica, Calif., August 1967, pp. 169–172.

10. Sutherland, W. R., *On-Line Graphical Specification of Computer Procedures,* Technical Report 405, Lincoln Laboratory, Massachusetts Institute of Technology, Lexington, Mass., May 23, 1966 (AD 639 734).

RECOMMENDED ADDITIONAL READING

1. Fano, R. M., and F. J. Corbato, "Time-Sharing on Computers," *Information,* W. H. Freeman, San Francisco, 1966, pp. 76–95.

2. Greenberger, Martin, et al., *On-Line Computation and Simulation,* The MIT Press, Cambridge, Mass., 1965.

3. Kemeny, John G., and Thomas E. Kurtz, "Dartmouth Time-Sharing," *Science,* **162,** 3850 (Oct. 11, 1968), 223–228.

4. Orr, William D., *Conversational Computers,* John Wiley, New York, 1968, especially pp. 13–41.

5. Scherr, Allan Lee, *An Analysis of Time-Shared Computer Systems,* The MIT Press, Cambridge, Mass., 1967.

6. Shaw, J. C., "JOSS: A Designer's View of an Experimental, On-Line Computing System," *AFIPS Conference Proceedings,* Vol. 30, Thompson, Washington, D.C., 1967, pp. 455–464.

Chapter Eleven

Design

11.1 INTRODUCTION

We might define a *design* as a plan for assembling a set of components into a whole, or system, usually in a new way or to accomplish some new end. Designing a machine is not building it; it is specifying what elements shall be combined, in what way, to accomplish the intended objective. Because the components do not have to be manipulated physically and instead can be treated symbolically, design is a function that can be performed with the aid of a computer. There is very little restriction on the kind of design implied by this statement. We can design computer programs, textile patterns, steel structures, automobiles, or electronic circuits. We can handle this diversity of applications because, in each case, the activity is resolved into one of telling the computer which component is to be included in the system and how it relates to other components, already chosen.

We shall treat the problem of computer assistance in design primarily as one of language processing. The designer must be able to communicate with the computer at a level of abstraction and in a vocabulary that is meaningful to both. A design language must be capable of describing enough detail of the application for which it is used to get the job done, yet must also allow the designer to talk in generalities. For example, as we shall see later, a design language may allow a man to construct a polygon by indicating the points he wants to use as vertices. He can even construct a polygon inscribed within a circle, by picking points on the circumference of the circle. Having constructed his figure by a series of detailed commands to the computer, he can then address the figure as a whole. He can order the computer to make it a regular polygon, by making all the component lines of equal length. He can rotate the polygon. He can order that one of the sides be made parallel to some other, specified line. He can enlarge the polygon or contract it. He can order it reduced so that its altitude matches that of another figure drawn earlier.[6]

With this kind of command repertoire, the designer can alternate between detailed work and abstract work, can configure a fully detailed microstructure and then perform macroscopic functions or analyses. Thus the computer provides access at two levels, something every designer needs—the ability to do detailed work and then "back off" and examine the product as a whole. If the recording of the details or the making of a change or the applying of a function takes too much time or effort, the designer loses "touch," loses his "feel" for the work as a whole. Using the computer enables him to be closer to his work, to have more detailed information and more different views of the results at his fingertips.

Here, briefly, is what the computer does for a designer. It can quickly produce a drawing (Figure 11.1) or graphic image or a list or file. It can easily modify any previously assembled image or file, thereby not only reducing the cost of errors but also offering trial and error as a feasible design approach. Also, the computer can present the information it has stored as part of a design to other computer programs, which will act upon this information. Hence other computer programs can predict the performance of a system being designed, and this information can be immediately fed back into a redesign or modification process. We mean *performance* literally. If the system being designed is an electronic circuit, the computer can predict the electronic properties of this circuit. Thus the designer is given a third view of his product. Not only can he view and work with the microstructure and the macrostructure, but also he can "view" performance and can make direct use of performance data in the design process.

A computer system that can perform these functions, as we have described them so far, comes closer than has any of our other manmachine communication systems to Licklider's concept of man-machine symbiosis.[3] Smooth, effective communication at these different levels requires immense amounts of software support and, often, special hardware, beyond what is typically found attached to a computer.

In the discussion to follow, we shall concentrate on man-machine communication in geometric terms: how we indicate where we want a line or a point, or that a polygon is to be rotated. We will also consider what information the computer program needs to be able to perform

Figure 11.1 An engineering drawing produced through a CRT. *Photo courtesy IBM Corp.*

its duties in this context. We defer until the end of the chapter any further discussion of the applications of this technology, for the reader will need a better understanding of how much work the computer must do to appreciate what can and cannot be accomplished with such methods.

11.2 BASIC ELEMENTS OF GRAPHIC DESIGN

A difficulty with representing geometric structures in a computer is that they can be defined in more than one way. A point, for example, can be specified by a set of coordinates. It is also the intersection of two lines, the center of a circle, or the centroid of an irregular figure. A line segment is not just the shortest path between two given points. It may be a perpendicular passing through a point, a tangent at a point, or the intersection of two planes. A bridge or an automobile is a collection of a great many points, lines, and curves connected in carefully defined ways and with each having physical characteristics in addition to its geometric characteristics.

Therefore a computer-stored representation of a point must include not only the point's coordinates but also a description of the relationship between this point and other relevant points, lines or curves. Every line must be associated with the points within it and with other lines with which it intersects or has any specified relationship. When we order the computer to rotate a large structure, the computer must act like the staff of an army and translate our command into thousands of more detailed commands to each subordinate element, down to the lowliest point. For, if a polygon is to be rotated, every point within it must be rotated and all relationships among the components of the polygon must be preserved as the overall change takes place.

We shall consider six aspects of graphic data handling: (1) The representation and storage of points, (2) the representation of lines and simple curves, (3) the entry of elements into the computer, (4) interactions among elements, (5) performing functions on assemblages of lines and points, and (6) tracking, a method by which the designer can enter the lines and curves he wants drawn.

11.2.1 Points

There are two logically equivalent and very simple ways to "enter" a point into a computer, that is, to inform the computer that it is to create, or *open*, a record for this point and to display it on a screen. The designer can indicate the point on the face of the cathode ray display tube with a light pen and have the new point displayed there. Alternatively, he can enter the coordinates digitally, through a keyboard. Probably he would start any completely new figure by entering a single point, even if only to establish the starting place of a more complex figure. After he has used points to build up lines and has indicated relationships among the lines, however, he needs other ways of indicating points. Suppose that he has defined two pairs of points, that the computer has constructed lines between them, and that the lines intersect. Suppose he now wishes to construct a third line, originating at the intersection of the first two. He has not explicitly entered the point of intersection, and his light pen is not accurate enough to single out this one point and distinguish it from an adjacent one. (Remember that all figures in a display are constructed from a finite number of points on the face of the tube. Here, unlike the world of Euclidean geometry, we have the concept of the *next* point.)

Let us go back and follow our designer, as he builds his structure, and see what information we would have to record in order to enable him to make reference to the point of intersection of the lines. First, he enters one point, via the light pen. The computer has the coordinates of the point and neither has nor needs any other information to establish a record in its files for this new point. Then he indicates a second point. Again a record is established containing only this pair of coordinates. Next the designer tells the machine to connect these two points with a line segment. In addition to establishing a line record, which we describe in the next section, the computer must add to each point record the notation that it is a terminus of line 1. This really consists of two distinct items of information—that the point lies *on* the line and that, within the line, its special position is at the end.

The same procedure is required for the second line, with the result that we quickly have four point records as shown in Figure 11.2. As the computer draws the second line, it can test mathematically whether the two lines have any points in common. In this case there is a common point, and the coordinates of this point are derivable by calculation. Therefore a fifth point record is initiated, and it indicates membership in two lines. Its special position, in both cases, is *point of intersection*.

We should pause here and consider what information we want in a point record. Clearly, we want the coordinates of the point, relative to some fixed location on the face of the scope. We also want a list of

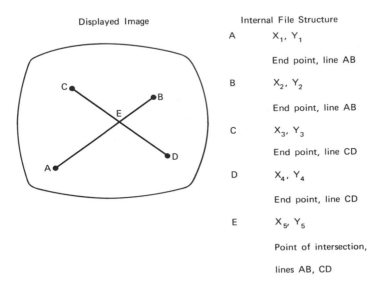

Displayed Image	Internal File Structure
	A X_1, Y_1
	End point, line AB
	B X_2, Y_2
	End point, line AB
	C X_3, Y_3
	End point, line CD
	D X_4, Y_4
	End point, line CD
	E X_5, Y_5
	Point of intersection, lines AB, CD

Figure 11.2 Representation of intersecting lines.

the higher-order structures of which it is a member; but, since points are in lines (or curves) and lines are in polygons and polygons are in other structures, we might restrict ourselves to showing only the next-higher-level geometric entity. For a point, the next level is a line or simple curve. For each one, we need the identification of the structure (e.g., line 1) and the role that this point plays in it (e.g., *end point, center of circle*). If the line or circle is a member of some other structure, we can let the line record show this fact.

We also want to name each point by some other means than its coordinates. In this way, once a record has been set up, we allow any of its elements to change. We could, for example, draw a circle with Point E (of Figure 11.2) as its center, add the circle to the set of curves of which E is a member (or related), and then erase the two intersecting lines that defined E in the first place. The name of the point and, in this case, the coordinates would not have changed, but we would strike out the two lines as containing structures and add, instead, the circle.

A typical structure for a point-defining record is illustrated in Figure 11.3. It contains a name, a set of coordinates, and a set of containing figures and the role played in each.

11.2.2 Lines and Curves

From our work with points we have implied that, at minimum, a record descriptive of a line must contain an identification of the line

---

Name of point

X coordinate

Y coordinate

⌈ Structure of which the point is a member

⌊ Role of point in structure

⌈ · · ·

⌊ · · ·

·

·

·

Note: once a point is defined, say by specification of its coordinates, its position can be changed without specifying new coordinates by, for example, rotating a line on which the point lies.

Figure 11.3 Structure of a point-defining record.

(a line number or name) and a list of the components of itself. In this case, the components are the points that are on the line and have a point record established. We do not need to have a record for *each* point that comprises a line. Although this would be physically possible because the line consists of a finite number of points, it is very expensive and quite unnecessary.

By analogy with the point record, we should consider alternative ways of defining a line and allow for variation in the way any given line is specified. For example, a line (or, more properly, a line segment) is defined by two points or by a point, a slope, and a distance. Any of these parameters may be specified indirectly. The slope of a line may be given, not in degrees, but by stating that the line is to be parallel to or perpendicular to another line. The length of the segment may be specified as half the length of segment A, and so on.

We have now identified the following information to be kept in a line record:

Line identification. This consists of a name, number, or arbitrary tag that uniquely identifies the line.

Line definition parameters. Every line segment has beginning and end points, a slope, and a length. Not all of these are needed to define a line, but all can be computed once the line is specified by any required set of them. For example, if a line is defined and later extended somewhat in length, the new length can be computed from the new end point.

Points contained. This is a list of all the points that fall on the line segment and for which there are point records. The number of such points will vary as the design changes and may increase or decrease by, for example, adding or deleting intersecting lines, without necessitating any changes to the line in question.

Relations to other lines. A line may be specified as parallel or perpendicular to any other line or as intersecting it at some given angle. The designer may want these relationships preserved if he changes the related line. For example, if line A is parallel to B and the designer rotates A, he might expect the computer to rotate B for him, since he has previously fixed this relationship. On the other hand, he may initially specify A and B as parallel, and then change his mind, so he would like to be able to impose or remove this relationship at will. The record should indicate whether or not the relationship is binding. Each relationship that we want our system to recognize must be separately identified.

Containing structures. Just as with points, we will want to record the names of larger structures of which our line is a member.

To generalize this record organization from lines to other curves, we must decide what curves we will store and what the parameters of these curves are. For circles or arcs of a circle, we replace the line-defining parameters with a center and radius definition. Then, if only an arc is wanted, the angular length of the arc and possibly, for convenience, the linear length of the arc may be stored. It is actually easier to store *only* arcs, with a full circle being an arc of 360 degrees. Other curves could be stored as sets of circular arcs and lines or as separately defined curves. A record structure for lines and circular arcs is illustrated in Figure 11.4.

Line			Arc		
Beginning point:	X_1, Y_1*		Center of curvature:	X_1, Y_1*	
End point:	X_2, Y_2*		Radius of curvature**		
Slope †			Beginning point of arc		
Length †			Arc length**		
Structure of which a member			Structure of which a member		
Points contained			Points contained		

$$\left\{ \begin{bmatrix} \text{Role} \\ \text{Coordinates*} \end{bmatrix} \begin{bmatrix} \cdot\ \cdot\ \cdot \\ \cdot\ \cdot\ \cdot \end{bmatrix} \vdots \right. \qquad \left\{ \begin{bmatrix} \text{Role} \\ \text{Coordinates*} \end{bmatrix} \begin{bmatrix} \cdot\ \cdot\ \cdot \\ \cdot\ \cdot\ \cdot \end{bmatrix} \vdots \right.$$

* Can be specified by reference to a point record.

† Can be specified by reference to another line, for example, slope = slope of line CD.

** Can be specified by reference to another arc.

Figure 11.4 Record structure for storing lines and arcs.

11.2.3 Entering Elements into the Design

A point may be entered into a design by using the light pen to show where the point is to go. In addition to indicating the coordinates, the designer must tell the computer what he is doing and what he wants.

He states that the point indicated by the pen specifies the coordinates of a new point for which a record is to be created and stored and that a dot is to be displayed at the indicated point. We shall provide greater detail in the example in Section 11.3.

To enter a line by specifying its end points, the designer has to specify two points and *make known that he is defining a line*. This action on his part will result in creation of two new point records and a line record. If we have programmed the computer to detect all points of intersection with existing lines, creating the new line may result in more than two new point records, but the designer need take no explicit action regarding these additional points.

To enter an arc, several parameters are needed (see Figure 11.5): the center of the circle of which the arc is a part, the radius of the arc, the angle of the arc, and its starting point.

All the information required for any of these figures could be entered digitally through a typewriter keyboard; but if we were to insist on entering geometric data in this way, we would hardly have an interactive system within our frame of reference. Here, then, is where the light pen is most valuable—for specifying position information. As position data are entered, correlative information can be entered through a keyboard, instructing the computer how to interpret the light pen's actions. Each key, or switch, on a keyboard might be assigned a special meaning when used in conjunction with the pen. Two examples are as follows: "The next point indicated by the pen is to be entered into the design as a new point" and "The next two points specify a line. Create new records for the two points and for the line." There are many ways in which switches can be coded to accomplish essentially the same objective. We provide a more detailed example in Section 11.3.

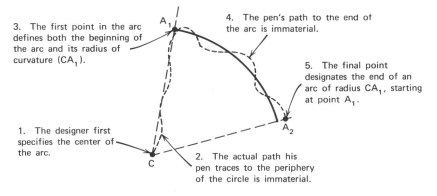

3. The first point in the arc defines both the beginning of the arc and its radius of curvature (CA_1).

4. The pen's path to the end of the arc is immaterial.

5. The final point designates the end of an arc of radius CA_1, starting at point A_1.

1. The designer first specifies the center of the arc.

2. The actual path his pen traces to the periphery of the circle is immaterial.

Figure 11.5 Entry of an arc.

It is possible to arrange for the entry of far more complex curves and structures than we have described here. One common technique is to allow the designer to specify that any of a predetermined set of standard figures is to be placed on the screen at a point indicated by the pen, and then recorded as being part of the display. In this way, an electronic circuit designer can ask for a symbol representing a resistor or a ground to be put into his drawing at a point specified. Although these symbols are relatively simple to construct, they can be made a part of the system's repertoire if they are going to be used often, as they would be in circuit design.

Occasionally, the designer may want to enter a complex curve for which no prepared model or prototype exists in the system. If this requirement is anticipated, he could be allowed to sketch the curve freehand with the light pen; the program would record the track made by the pen and then approximate the track with a series of lines and circular arcs. The line and arc records would be automatically created and stored without the designer having to participate in the approximation process. Finally, the designer might want to enter such a freehand curve and then specify a certain segment of it as being a straight line or a circular arc. A program can allow him to do this if he will specify the boundaries of the curve segment in question and indicate the type of curve to be fitted to each segment.

11.2.4   Interaction of Lines and Points

Let us consider how these record structures interact when the designer wants to make a change in an existing design or to add to it. Suppose the designer wants to enter a structure as shown in Figure 11.6. He first enters point A, by use of his light pen, and a record is established for it. At this time, only its coordinates are known. Then he enters point B, and a similar record is established. Next the points are connected with a line. The designer has now established line AB.

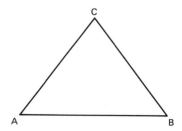

Figure 11.6 A structure to be designed.

	Point Records before Entering Point c		Point Records after Entering Point c
A	X_1, Y_1 Member of AB End point	A	X_1, Y_1 Member of AB End point
B	X_2, Y_2 Member of AB End point	B	X_2, Y_2 Member of AB End point Member of BC End point
		C	X_3, Y_3 Member of BC End point

Figure 11.7 Modifying records as new points are added.

The second line may be entered by initiating point c and then telling the computer to connect B and c with a line. Now, the program must create the BC line record, which contains the same information items as the AB record. But he must also modify the point B record to show its membership in two lines (Figure 11.7). He can add the third line, CA, by telling the computer to connect points c and A, and again creating the new line record and modifying the A and c point records to show membership in new lines.

Now, suppose he wants to change the overall structure to the irregular figure ACBD shown in Figure 11.8. Note that he can not simply establish point D and tell the computer to move A to it, because that would shorten line CA as well as rotating AB. Point A serves two functions,

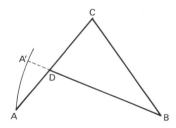

Figure 11.8 Modifying a structure. The designer wants to change the original structure, ABCA, to produce ACBD.

and the designer must make clear to the computer that he wants it moved *only in its capacity as the terminus of line* AB and not as terminus of CA. He must have a way of transmitting this message to the computer. This emphasizes our assertion (Section 11.1) on the importance of a language that adequately expresses the needs of the user. If the designer cannot make the computer understand the difference between moving point A in *both* its capacities and moving it in only *one* of its roles, he will find this automated design system a frustrating tool to use. On the other hand, artificial languages of programming and man-machine communication must be interpreted by a computer program and are not as expressive as natural language. Hence the designer of the program system must make decisions balancing simplicity and complexity in his language, the ease of use of the system and full service to all users, system cost and system performance. Within any given man-machine communication system, the language elements are usually fixed. With suitable programming, however, the vocabulary and functions can be changed to meet the requirements of different applications.

Returning now to Figure 11.8, we may postulate that we have made provision for discriminating among the roles of point A and can direct the computer to move A (as terminus of line AB) to the position shown as A'. Then the designer could tell the system to terminate AB where it intersects CA, at point D. Again, we said in an earlier statement that the system could be programmed to compute all intersections whenever a new line is created, to create point records for them, and to list these points in the line record. Therefore the system knows where this intersecting point is, can establish it as the new terminal point, discard the old terminal at this end, and recompute slope and length. The point D will also have to be added to line AC as a constituent point but plays no defining role in this line. These file changes are indicated in Figure 11.9.

11.2.5 Functions of Structures

We may define a *structure* as any set of points or lines. They need not even be connected. Any of the configurations in Figure 11.10 could be considered single structures, just by the designer so specifying. Having built one of these structures by the methods just described, the designer may now manipulate them at the macroscopic level and watch the performance of his structure as a whole.

Here are some simple geometric examples. Given the structure shown in Figure 11.11a, consisting of a set of unconnected points, the designer can order these to be rotated, say 45 degrees. Without going into the mathematics of the transformation, this can be accomplished

Before		After	
A	X_1, Y_1	A	X_1, Y_1
	Member of AB		Member of CA
	End point		End point
	Member of CA	B	X_2, Y_2
	End point		Member of BC
B	X_2, Y_2		End point
	Member of AB		Member of BD
	End point		End point
	Member of BC	C	X_3, Y_3
	End point		Member of BC
C	X_3, Y_3		End point
	Member of BC		Member of CA
	End point		End point
	Member of CA	D	X_4, Y_4
	End point		Member of BD
			End point
			Member of CA
			Point of intersection, CA BD

Figure 11.9 Change in point records after a change in design structure.

by the application of quite standard formulas. Since there are no lines, we need only recompute the coordinates of each point to perform the required function. Slightly more complex would be a rotation about some point other than the center of the viewing screen, as shown in Figure 11.12. Here we are rotating the structure around a point at the center of the bottom of the screen. Actually, we could rotate around points not even on the screen by using a keyboard to specify the center of rotation. The basic concept remains the same, but increasingly more information must be provided to use other than the most obvious centers of rotation.

Suppose we had a line in the structure, as in Figure 11.13. Since the line is just a set of points, if we rotate each point in the line we accomplish the rotation of the line. An easier way is to rotate only the defining points of the line and then redraw the line. In this case the defining points can be assumed to be points A and B. But, before the program begins its rotation work, it has to decide, for itself, what it is going to rotate. In the earlier example (of rotating a cross), only points

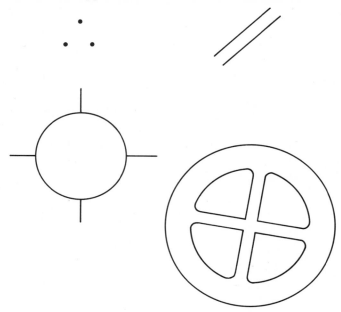

Figure 11.10 Some examples of structures.

were involved and the order of working on them was of no consequence. They were unrelated except for structure membership. Now the program must start with the structure record, recognize that there is a line in it as well as a point, and then look at the line record to find the points involved It must remind itself to return to the line record after having rotated the points.

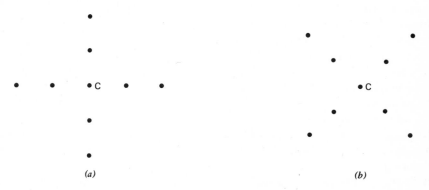

(a)   (b)

Figure 11.11 Rotating a structure. (a) Original structure. (b) Structure rotated about its center point.

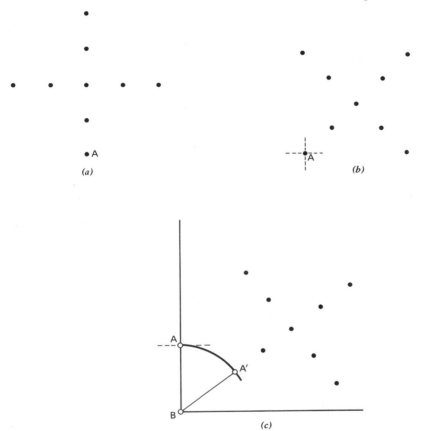

Figure 11.12 Additional forms of rotation. (*a*) Original structure. (*b*) The structure rotated about point A, a member of the structure. (*c*) The structure rotated about point B, outside the structure.

Hence, to rotate the structure of Figure 11.13, the program first looks (Figure 11.14) at the structure record, finds there is one line and one point, looks at the indicated line record, and finds that the line is defined by two points and has no other relations indicated. The defining points are rotated, the line record is then updated (the positions of the defining and contained points and the slope have all changed), and finally the independent point c is rotated. We hope that even readers not familiar with computer programming can appreciate how much programming is required for these simple functions.

These rotations (as well as expansions, contractions, and lateral shifts) constitute the first step in letting the designer evaluate the per-

Figure 11.13 Rotating a structure containing lines and points.

formance of his design. So far, of course, performance has meant only how the structure looks to the designer's eye, albeit from several points of view. But, if the structure had been, not just a point and a line, but a three-dimensional representation of an automobile body, the designer could turn the drawing in all directions. Within a few minutes he could view the design from many angles, something he would otherwise not be able to do without creating a spatially accurate three-dimensional model of the new design. Hence he can, even at this level, evaluate esthetic performance.

If some significance other than geometric is ascribed to the members of a structure, other kinds of evaluation can be performed. For example, if the lines of a structure are to be treated as steel beams and certain weight and stress characteristics are assigned, a complete stress analysis

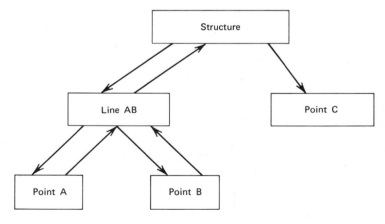

Figure 11.14 Tracing interconnections among structural elements. To rotate the structure, the program must trace through each constituent element, and elements of the elements, to be sure all component records are found and appropriately modified.

Figure 11.15 Start of a circuit design. The designer starts with the positioning of a single symbol, actually a structure that was previously constructed.

of the resulting structure can be computed directly from the drawing or, more precisely, from the descriptive data stored in files.

To do this kind of analysis, we really should construct our figures with components more nearly resembling those of the system we are designing. For example, if we are going to design an electronic circuit, we define a set of basic circuit elements and use these rather than points and lines to assemble the structure.[2] Figure 11.15 shows the designer beginning a circuit that consists, at this point, only of a single resistor. If the designer now adds a power source and closes the circuit (Figure 11.16), he can ask the computer to make certain calculations on the performance of the circuit. He may identify two points, A and B, and ask for calculation of the voltage drop between them.

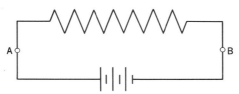

Figure 11.16 A minimal circuit design. The designer has completed a simple circuit and identified two points, A and B, about which he will later want some information.

With the more complex circuit of Figure 11.17a, the designer may use his light pen to construct a curve representing an input to the circuit and ask the computer to calculate the resultant output wave. By simple switch manipulation, the designer can modify the shape and hence the electrical characteristics of the simulated input curve (Figure 11.17b) and can immediately see the change in the resultant output curve. Thus he achieves a degree of interaction with his circuit that he could normally obtain only after actually constructing the circuit and conducting live tests or performing lengthy calculations. Here he sees at the design stage what circuit performance will be and makes any changes while it is still easy and inexpensive to do so.

Of course, the validity of this procedure depends on the validity of the circuit analysis program. If the analysis program does not accurately represent the circuit performance, the designer is not seeing the actual situation and his final product may not perform according to specifica-

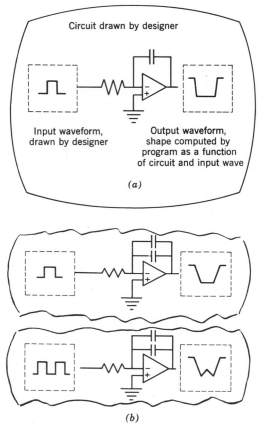

Figure 11.17 Interactive electronic circuit design and analysis. (*a*) The designer sketches a circuit and "tries it out" by having the computer simulate the circuit's action on a given input. Here the designer decides he must change the circuit. (*b*) A change is made in the circuit, and the input waveform is again "tested." It appears to be correct, so another input waveform is tried.

tions. The same comment holds for all analysis programs. If the analysis is inaccurate or oversimplified or if the designer fails to input the proper characteristics of his structure, he cannot expect valid results.

Figure 11.18 shows the process of testing a circuit in more detail. *Top left:* By pointing an electronic light pen at a display of control program statements, the engineer indicates to the computer the sequence of steps to be executed. *Top right:* The system then displays a sub-program that will enable the engineer to retrieve an electrical circuit from the computer. An initial value of resistance in ohms is being

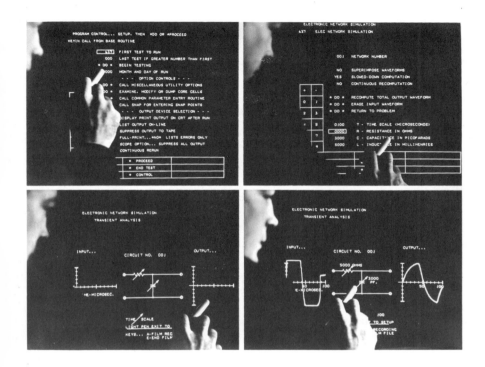

Figure 11.18 Using a computer-aided circuit design program. *Photo courtesy IBM Corp.*

entered on the display. *Bottom left:* Under computer control, a schematic of the electrical circuit on which the engineer is working is displayed. *Bottom right:* Using the light pen, the engineer has drawn an input wave form at the left of the display. Values of the various circuit elements appear in the center. On the basis of the input wave form and the circuit values, the computer determines the characteristics of the output wave form, and this is displayed at the right. To redesign the circuit, the engineer can change the value of its various elements by pointing his light pen at the vector arrows on the display (as shown). The computer adjusts the values by predetermined increments.

11.2.6   Tracking

One of the most useful services an automated design system can perform is allowing a designer to "draw" a figure with his light pen and then "fix up" the resulting figure according to his specifications.

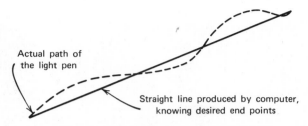

Actual path of
the light pen

Straight line produced by computer,
knowing desired end points

Figure 11.19 Drawing a line with the light pen.

For example, to draw a line, he would like to be able to place his pen on the surface of the screen (Figure 11.19) and sketch the line just as he might do with a pencil on a piece of scratch paper. Probably, the curve he draws will not really be a straight line, but our design system needs only the end points and the information that the curve drawn is supposed to be a line. Sometimes the designer wants the actual curve he draws entered into the structure as a series of approximating lines and arcs. To accomplish these and other tasks that involve following a movement of the light pen, the computer must be able to track the pen's motion.

One way that this is done involves the use of a *tracking cross*. This is a cross-shaped structure on which the designer can call, just as he can call on any other predetermined, specially shaped structure. If the light pen is placed at the center of the cross and then moved, a program will cause the cross to follow the pen's motion. The resulting track of the cross's center can be displayed as it is generated, or just the end points can be recorded, the latter being all that is necessary for straight line drawing. The area on the face of the screen that is sensed by the pen is much larger than a single point. In fact, the user cannot normally position the pen so accurately as to hit a single point.

Tracking is done by having the computer sense which quadrant of the cross the pen is in, and then moving the center of the cross into this quadrant (Figure 11.20). Even if the pen starts in position exactly over the center of the cross, as the designer moves toward the point he ultimately wants to reach he moves it off center, toward the target. As it moves, the computer senses the correct quadrant and repositions the cross. Thus the cross follows the motion of the pen with a slight lag. At any point along the track, the designer can stop, lift the pen, and indicate by switch action that the last position of the cross is to be recorded as the terminus of the curve.

What may appear, even to the designer, as if the pen were leaving

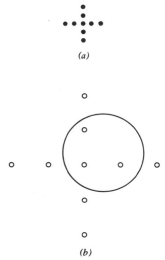

(a)

(b)

Figure 11.20 The tracking cross. (*a*) The tracking cross may be a pattern of dots. (*b*) This enlarged view shows the particular set of dots "illuminated" by the pen. With these three points illuminated, the program will move the center of the cross into what is now the upper right quadrant.

a legible trace on the face of the screen, is actually an interactive process, repeated many times, of the computer sensing the position of the pen and moving the cross toward it, possibly displaying dots on the screen to indicate previously detected positions as it moves. The interaction between the pen and the tracking cross and its supporting programs is illustrated in Figure 11.21.

11.3 AN EXAMPLE

In this example we shall first define the features of a hypothetical automated design system and then follow through a short exercise in the use of the system to compose a simple geometric structure.

We will make provision for storing four kinds of elements: points, lines, circular arcs, and structures, with a structure being defined here as any set of one or more of the basic elements or of other structures. We shall store the information listed below about each element, with the record designs being those illustrated in Figures 11.3 and 11.4. The term *pointer* means a cross reference to another record.

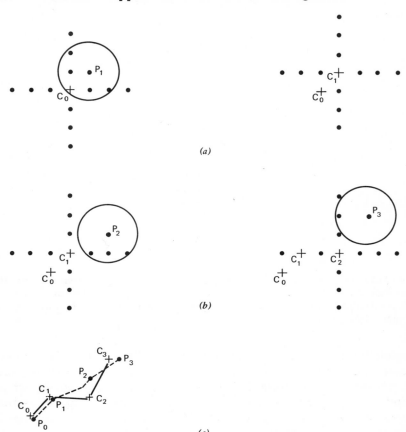

Figure 11.21 Tracking logic. (*a*) c_0 is the initial center of the tracking cross, positioned there by the light pen. P_1 is the center of the area illuminated by the pen as it moves away from the initial point. (*b*) c_1, the new cross center, is positioned at or near P_1. As soon as the cross reaches P_1, the pen moves to P_2, the cross following. (*c*) The sequence of cross center points approximates the track of the light pen.

Element	Information Stored About Element
Point	A name, or identification, of the point. The coordinates of the point. Pointers to higher-order elements of which the point is a member (lines, arcs, structures).
Line	Identification of the line. For each point on the line that we want to take note of, the role of this point and a pointer to its point record. The minimum required points are *start* and *end*, these being defined as roles played by points. Other possible roles are *intersection point, midpoint, etc.* For each

Element	Information Stored About Element
	intersecting point, a pointer to the intersecting line or arc is also needed. Pointers to any structure of which the line is a member.
Arc	Identifier. Coordinates of the center and radius. Starting point, angular length, and constituent points as for lines, that is, points of intersection with other arcs or lines. List of structures of which a member.
Structure	A list of pointers to constituent members, whether points, lines, arcs, or other structures. Pointer to structure of which a member (if any).

For equipment, we will assume a cathode ray output device with a light pen, a matrix keyboard, and a typewriter keyboard for input. The matrix keyboard will have switches for use in conjunction with the light pen. We can assign meanings to keys as follows:

Key Designation	Meaning
Enter a point	If this key is depressed, the computer will assume that the next use of the light gun will mark the coordinates of a new point to be entered.
Enter a line	The computer will display the tracking cross, which will then follow the light pen to a designated point. The next designated point will be recorded as the initial point of the line, the next after that as the terminal point.
Enter an arc	As in line entry, the computer will expect the first point entered after this key is depressed to be the center of a circle, the second point to be on the periphery of the circle, and the third point also to be on the periphery. As was shown in Figure 11.5, the first and second points, taken together, define the radius of the arc, the second point defines the start, and the third point denotes the end of the arc. The path taken by the pen from A to B to C is irrelevant.
Define a structure	Use of this key will be followed by the depressing of a point, line, or arc key, which will, in turn, be followed by use of the light gun. If the designer depresses a line key and then points to a line, this line will be considered to have been included in the structure now being defined.
Define a curve	When this key is used, the tracking cross will appear and may be moved to a starting position that is recorded by use of the *enter point* key. The cross can then be moved over any path to a second point, also

Key Designation	**Meaning**
	designated by use of the *enter point* key. The resulting track is traced on the screen, and a program will approximate it by a series of lines and arcs. All these will be stored in the files, and the entire curve will be designated a structure.
Delete	If followed by one of the four keys listed above, *delete* indicates that the element next pointed to by the light gun is to be removed from the file and from the display screen.
Move	The tracking cross appears and is then positioned by the designer on an element he selects and identifies by an element switch. The designer then moves the tracking cross, and when he next indicates a point entry, the entire element is translated by the amount indicated, retaining its original orientation.
Expand	The next point indicated with the light pen is treated as the center of a new display. This display replaces the original one at twice the previous scale. It shows, however, as much of the original as fits on the screen. The display is temporary. It can be removed by a *delete* key and will be replaced by the original display.
Contract	This operates similarly to *expand* except, obviously, that the display is temporarily *reduced* in scale by a factor of 2.
Rotate	The next point indicated with the light pen is the center of rotation. The tracking cross will appear above this point. The next two points to which the cross is then moved indicate the amount of rotation desired, as is done in defining an arc.
Position	The tracking cross appears and may be moved. When the next *enter point* key is depressed, the cross is positioned exactly at the closest existing point.

Clearly, several of these functions make use of keys that can be ambiguous or even meaningless if used in the wrong context. For example, if the last command was *expand,* as we have defined it, the only meaningful next commands are *expand,* which further enlarges the display, or *delete,* which restores the original display and is a prerequisite to any further operations. If *expand* and *contract* were not considered temporary commands, the large- or small-scale figures they produce would have to be made into structures. Then file entries would have to be made so that, instead of creating a temporary structure, we would have to have the ability to store the original structure temporarily in order to shift back and forth between the enlarged and the regular-scale structures.

The tracking technique will be that described in Section 11.2.6. To review our proposed method of operation briefly, the designer works with both matrix keyboard and light pen, using the former to show what meaning is to be attached to the points indicated by the pen. Different keys or switches will impart different meanings to light gun action.

This system does not perform all possible design functions. It is ample, however, to demonstrate the techniques involved in this application.

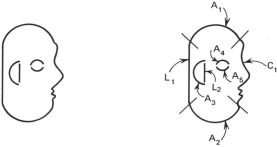

Figure 11.22 A structure to be assembled from lines and arcs.

Now assume we want to draw the figure shown in Figure 11.22. This consists of two straight line segments, five arcs, and one other curve that we will find easier to enter as a light pen track and have the computer approximate for us with lines and arcs.

A

B

Figure 11.23 Starting the figure.

In Figure 11.23, we draw the first line, which will be the back of the head. This takes the following commands:

Designer's Light Pen Action	Key Used	Computer's Action
	Enter a line	Tracking cross appears.
Move cross to A	*Enter a point*	Top of line entered as start point.
Move cross to bottom, point B	*Enter a point*	End of line entered into computer—entire line appears on screen.

In Figure 11.24 we add the top of the head, as an arc connected to the vertical line. Use these commands:

Figure 11.24 Adding an arc.

	Enter an arc	Tracking cross appears.
Pen indicates center of circle, C.	*Enter a point*	
Move pen to point D .	*Enter a point*	Pen moves to point D to define start of arc.
Move pen to point E	*Enter a point*	Pen moves to point E to define end of arc. Smooth arc appears as soon as point E has been entered.

Figure 11.25 shows the addition of the chin, another arc, entered just as the first one was.

Figure 11.26 shows the insertion of the face, an irregular curve that the designer wants to draw freehand. He enters the following:

Figure 11.25 A second arc is added.

Figure 11.26 The face is drawn as a freehand curve.

	Define a curve	The tracking cross appears.
Move cross to point F	*Enter a point*	Computer is ready to accept a new curve.
Face is drawn	*Enter a point*	The track described is entered into the computer, a series of approximations is worked out, and the whole is automatically designated a structure.

The ear and the eye are added by a line and two arcs, and the first draft of the head is now complete. The designer then designates the entire drawing as a structure:

	Define a structure	
Pen touches line 1	*Enter a line*	
Pen touches arc 1	*Enter an arc*	
Pen touches the curve	*Enter a curve*	
	•	The remainder of the elements are identified with the new structure.
	•	
	•	

Now the designer would like to examine his handiwork. This is possible, and he does so in Figures 11.27 through 11.29.

	Expand	Tracking cross appears.
Move cross to expansion center	*Enter a point*	Computer records the point and expands the display around it, Figure 11.27.
	Delete	Original face is restored, Figure 11.28.
	Contract	Tracking cross appears.
Move cross to a point on the image	*Enter a point*	Image contracts, Figure 11.29a.
	Delete	Original is restored, Figure 11.29b.

Figure 11.27 The final face enlarged (×2 scale).

Figure 11.28 The original scale of the structure is restored.

(a)   *(b)*

Figure 11.29 The figure is contracted (*a*) and restored again (*b*).

At this point the designer decides he does not like the face he has drawn. He wants to erase it and redraw it. He uses the following:

	Delete	Tracking cross appears.
Move cross to a point on the face	*Enter a curve*	The curve is indicated as the element to be deleted. Face disappears, Figure 11.30a.

(a) *(b)*

Figure 11.30 The freehand curve is deleted *(a)* and redrawn *(b)*.

	Define a curve	Tracking cross appears to start new face.
Move cross near point F	*Enter a point*	Cross is superimposed on point F.
Pen traces new face	*Enter a point*	Last position of cross indicates end of curve, and the new face is shown in Figure 11.30*b*.

11.4 APPLICATIONS

So far we have illustrated only simple geometric problems. Simple as they may be, however, they would require large and complex programs for implementation. We have established the following general characteristics for an on-line design system: (1) the ability to enter the smallest components of a design by first identifying a component and then indicating its position within the overall structure, (2) the ability to group components into structures or to remove components from a structure, (3) the ability to move or modify a structure in its entirety by directly addressing the complete structure rather than each individual component, and (4) the ability to process structures or to compute some function of the structure and its components.

These capabilities give the designer the chance to build the structure he wants and then to work with this assemblage as a single entity. He can easily change the structure or erase it and start over. Although we have restricted our examples to two-dimensional structures, three-dimensional ones are possible.[1]

To assess the applicability of these techniques to practical problems, we must consider what kinds of design activity are appropriate and what the current state of the art is for each type, that is, how far advanced are the programs and the equipment used in this kind of work.

11.4.1   Characteristics of Automated Design Systems

Matching the qualities we specified for on-line design systems, we would expect a design activity that could benefit from mechanization to have the following characteristics:

1. It must involve a limited number of basic components that can be designed beforehand and then called into use in any design by switch action. It is not actually necessary for all components that will ever be used to be standardized beforehand, but most of them should. Otherwise the creation of the basic elements by the overall designer becomes tedious, and he loses much of the potential value of using the computer. For example, the composition of natural language text (the "design" of a paragraph or article) would benefit little from automated design because system users would have to either learn a code for each of the more probable words or enter the full word each time. Either alternative places a heavy burden on the composer, who might then just as well be working through a typewriter or nongraphic input terminal. We do not intend to imply that composers of natural language text should not use interactive systems. We do mean, though, that the method of selecting predefined components (words) is more awkward than simply typing in the words desired, one letter at a time. This makes the *letter* not the *word* the fundamental unit.

2. Although the majority of elemental components should be switch-selected, what constitutes an elemental or basic component may vary. Hence it should be possible to design these basic components by essentially the same process as that used for the larger structure. Perhaps, as in the case in a large engineering design activity, different people would be responsible for designing components, assemblages of components, larger modules, and so on to the final, complete product. It should be possible, then, to incorporate the product of anyone's design in another design by a simple call-up action.

3. The relationships among components of the design must be apparent in a two-dimensional, essentially black and white presentation. This requirement covers most structural problems, where even three dimensions can be represented. (Color-generating terminal devices are now beginning to appear.) A musical composer could use such a system to save him the considerable amount of work involved in preparing a properly drawn and annotated musical script, but he cannot expect the computer to evaluate the score for him. It can make certain mechanical checks, such as for beats in a measure, but it cannot, in general, assess the quality of the music. An on-line design system can be used for layout and editing of verbal text, where the important activity is moving

words within a sentence, inserting and deleting, and forming a visual pattern of the page.

4. To earn its high cost, the computer should be capable of evaluating the design. Evaluation programs need not replace the human evaluator, but they should reduce the amount of routine, time-consuming work required to test the validity of the overall structure or the manner in which it is assembled. In a structural design application, we would not expect the computer to evaluate the esthetics of a new building design, but we would require it to evaluate the stress on all members.

5. There is a frequent need to switch the level of discourse from evaluation of the final result of the design process to the details of a single lowest-level component.

How effective has the mechanization of design processes been? Although we seem to be on the verge of making automated design not only a reality but also the standard way to do the job, we are not yet there. It is not always possible to pin-point specific reasons why a concept has not gained general acceptance; however, in this case some reasons might be the following:

1. High cost of equipment. Both the graphic display devices and the amount of computational capability needed for graphic processing are expensive. If the equipment delivered the increase in productivity suggested as possible, this high cost would probably be justified. We cannot, then, blame the problem on price alone, although the high cost may account for a certain reluctance to experiment.

2. Lack of standardized programs and procedures. As was characteristic in the early days of many major applications within the programming profession, we find a tendency for new installations to like to write most of their own programs rather than borrowing existing ones from other organizations. For example, although the concept of the tracking cross is in general use, many minor variations on the same theme employ slightly different shapes and tracking logic. Of course, for sophisticated design problems, a new user will probably have to be prepared to write most of the programs himself, and this returns us to the cost consideration as a deterrent to general usage.

3. Limitation on the designer's field of vision. Even the largest cathode ray tubes have a viewing area about the size of two sheets of ordinary typing paper. Resolution is such that the images cannot be too small. Hence there is a limitation on how much of the design the designer can see at one time, and this imposes an unfamiliar constraint on him. Working at his own desk or drawing board, he can cover a large sheet of paper with a series of sketches and his eye can dart from

one to the other rapidly as he tries to assimilate them. This darting of eyes must be replaced with a positive action to recall a particular page if he works through a console, and the time required in the latter case is significantly greater. Imagine a bridge player who, in order to arrange and bid his hand, was permitted to see only one or two of his cards at a time. Although he could train himself to remember the unseen ones, it would be a bother to do so; and the resulting irritation, as well as the disruption in thinking caused by trying to recall the entire hand, would certainly introduce errors into his bidding and playing.

4. Change in habits required. Aside from the particular ways in which it is manifested, there is the general problem of the unfamiliarity of this way of working (i.e., through a console) and the discarding and replacement of the accumulated habits of a lifetime. Although people can adapt to the new ways, many are reluctant to do so; even among those who make the change, the initial reaction will probably be that the old ways were better. This kind of reaction can be overcome only by persistence or by concentration on younger people, who may have less resistance to change.

With these requirements and limitations in mind, let us now look at two applications of on-line design to practical problems.

11.4.2 A Textile Design Application

The basic problem addressed is to reduce the excessive amount of time required to translate an artist's sketch for a textile pattern into a weave design, that is, a detailed pattern of interlocking threads. The resultant fabric is essentially a mosaic that can vary in color and texture. The discernible pattern is made by varying the color threads in use and by varying the number of threads a given thread passes across in the weave. To achieve a particular shape on the resulting fabric, many possible weaves that have different textural and structural properties can be used.

Figure 11.31 shows a simple contrast in two weaves. The first is the simplest basket weave (one over, one under). If this were woven in black and white, it would make the fabric seem gray. The second shows how, by varying the number of vertical threads traversed by a horizontal thread, a striped pattern can be made. Translating an artist's sketch into such a weave pattern can take several man-weeks, since the placement of each thread relative to every other one must be specified. The objective of automating weave design is to reduce this time lag and cost, rather than to affect the weaving process or the quality of weave

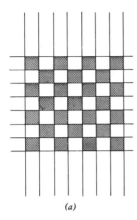
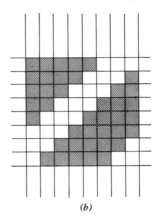

(a)   (b)

Figure 11.31 Basic weaving patterns. (a) Simple "one over, one under" weave. Each row and column represents a single thread. (b) By varying the number of threads traversed by a given thread, striped patterns can be achieved.

design. Each designer may have a repertoire of several thousand weaves and must select from among these the few he will want to try out.

A solution worked out by J. R. Lourie [4] is to enter the artist's sketch into the computer by use of a light pen. Different color or texture areas can also be indicated by light pen. A computer program examines these data and sharply delimits the areas of like tone, somewhat like constructing a paint-by-the-numbers form (see Figure 11.32). The designer can select a weave for each area (Figure 11.33), have the computer simulate the use of this weave on this pattern, and view the results on the CRT (Figure 11.34). Weaves are represented by subroutines that process pattern data in a certain way and are stored in a library accessible to the designer. If a designer is not satisfied with any of the library weaves, he may design his own weave and enter it into the library. Thus he has the flexibility to work with individual threads and design a structure called a weave, and then to use this weave as a component of another structure, the design of a particular fabric.

One of the structure-processing programs makes checks against certain forbidden practices, such as having any given thread pass over too many other threads. Even this restriction will vary with the type of fabric being designed. A tapestry or drapery may be structurally far weaker than a football uniform.

The results of this design process can be directly used to control a loom. Hence the designer produces not only a design but also the actual means of communicating this design to the implementing tool.

This system exhibits all the features we specified earlier for an on-

Figure 11.32 The artist's sketch ready for selection of a weave. *Photo courtesy J. Lourie.*

line design system, except that the machine performs only a limited amount of evaluation. Except for the structural evaluation, which the computer does perform, the evaluation of a weave design is largely esthetic. The process offers a considerable saving to the user, however, in the sheer amount of time required to compose a design.

11.4.3   An Architectural Design Application

A program for architectural design is reported by W. M. Newman [5] (Figure 11.35), then of Imperial College, London, which incorporates most of the features we have described so far. The program enables an architect to design buildings with certain constraints. There is a limit to the overall dimensions, there can be no more than four stories, there must be supporting columns at specified places, and all structural features (walls, doors, windows) must lie parallel to a set of grid lines that appear in subdued light on the screen.

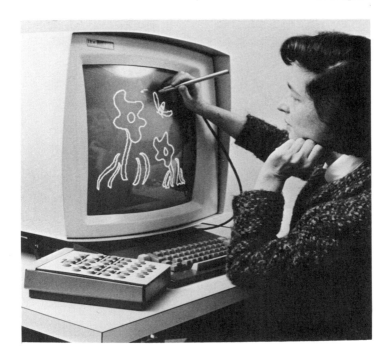

Figure 11.33 The designer uses the keyboard to indicate the desired weave and selects the area in the sketch by light pen. *Photo courtesy J. Lourie.*

The system provides the architect with a set of basic building elements: wall sections, doors, etc., which may be called up by keyboard action and then positioned by the light pen. Because all components must lie along grid lines and because they must abut each other, the designer need only bring the new component near the one he wishes to attach it to, and the computer "drops" it exactly into place, as shown in Figures 11.36 and 11.37. A combination of the keyboard and the light pen can duplicate, move, or rotate any element.

Because the building being designed may be far larger than will fit on the screen at one time, the system has a feature that provides the effect of a camera panning across the entire floor plan. The designer can ask for the display to shift across the existing floor, even though the entire floor can never be seen at once. Similarly, other floors can be recalled and displayed. Of course, provision is made for revising any previously designed floor or component.

Figure 11.34 The weaves have been selected and now the thread patterns are displayed on the artist's sketch. *Photo courtesy J. Lourie.*

A unique feature of this system is its ability to display two floor segments simultaneously, one of them with a lesser intensity, having the appearance of a gray line in an otherwise black and white image. This feature can be used to compare corresponding portions of two different floors to insure that windows, doors, and load-bearing members are positioned correctly with respect to each other.

The system is able to compute floor areas (see Figure 11.38) and to maintain an inventory of the components incorporated into a building design. As originally reported, the program did not perform other calculations but was apparently meant to be extended to provide this capability.

Figure 11.35 The architect entering a drawing into the computer. *Photo courtesy W. M. Newman.*

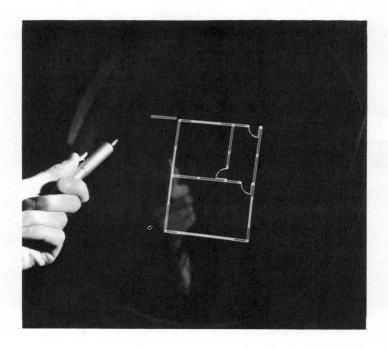

Figure 11.36 The designer places a new member near an existing one. *Photo courtesy W. M. Newman.*

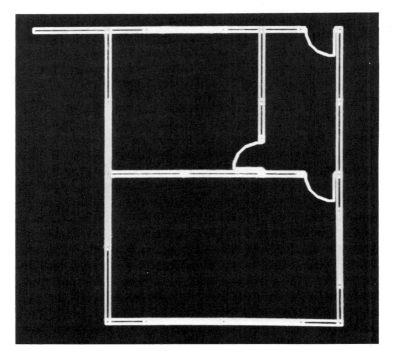

Figure 11.37 The program assumes the designer meant to attach this member to the existing structure and "drops" it into place. *Photo courtesy W. M. Newman.*

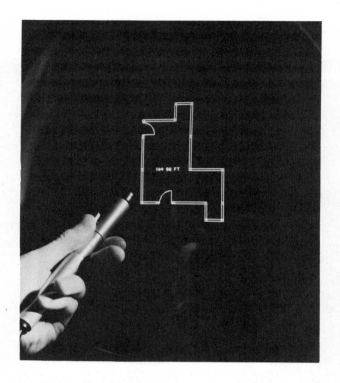

Figure 11.38 Upon request, the program computes and displays floor areas for the designer. *Photo courtesy W. M. Newman.*

REFERENCES

1. Johnson, Timothy E., "Sketchpad. III, A Computer Program for Drawing in Three Dimensions," *Proceedings of the AFIPS 1963 Spring Joint Computer Conference,* Spartan Books, New York, pp. 347–353.
2. Kendler, James, "Computer Aided Circuit Design," *EEE,* **15,** 6 (June 1967).
3. Licklider, J. C. R., "Man-Computer Symbiosis," *IRE Transactions on Human Factors in Electronics,* **HFE–1,** 1 (March 1960), 4–11.
4. Lourie, Janice R., John J. Lorenzo, and Abel Bomberault, "On-Line Textile Designing," *Proceedings of the ACM National Meeting, 1966,* pp. 537–544.
5. Newman, W. M., "An Experimental Program for Architectural Design," *Computer Journal,* **9,** 1 (May 1966), 21–26.
6. Sutherland, Ivan E., "Sketchpad, a Man-Machine Graphical Communications System," *Proceedings of the Spring Joint Computer Conference, 1963,* Spartan Books, New York, pp. 329–346.

RECOMMENDED ADDITIONAL READING

1. Gruenberger, Fred, ed., *Computer Graphics Utility/Production/Art,* Thompson, Washington, D.C., 1967.
2. Jacks, Edwin L., "A Laboratory for the Study of Graphical Man-Machine Communication," *Proceedings of the Fall Joint Computer Conference, 1964,* Spartan Books, New York, 1964, pp. 343–350.
3. Orr, William D., *Conversational Computers,* John Wiley, New York, 1968.
4. Prince, M. David, "Man-Computer Graphics for Computer-Aided Design," *Proceedings of the IEEE,* **54,** 12 (December 1966), 1698–1708.
5. Sutherland, "Sketchpad" (see Reference 6). Much of this pioneering article will be beyond the beginning reader, but an equal amount will be comprehensible. It is worth trying.

Chapter Twelve

Management
Information Systems

12.1 INTRODUCTION

The frequently used expressions *Management Information System* (MIS) and *Command/Control System* are sometimes assumed by the uninitiated to imply management or control *by* a computer. Actually, these systems, which we shall generally call simply MIS, are often nothing more than combinations of the kinds of systems we have described in preceding chapters. Basically, a MIS is an information retrieval system, but it has some other critical functions. For effective management, data must be "good"—timely, complete, and accurate; hence successful MIS's will often contain data acquisition systems. A good manager will want to experiment with more than one approach to a problem. Hence he will want his MIS to do much processing of structures—performing calculations on a complex information structure to permit a system user to see the data in a new perspective. In the management world, this will often be called *modelling* or *simulation*. In these ways a MIS reduces the amount of work required to interpret the data, but does not replace the manager as the principal decision-maker. The really difficult decisions that managers and commanders are called upon to make tend to be too complex even to formulate in mathematical or algorithmic terms, let alone to delegate to a computer program.

Because we view a management information system as a composite of other systems and processes, rather than explain the fundamentals again, we shall concentrate on providing some insight to the problems of management and the reasons why a computer can be of such great assistance. We remind the reader that we are describing *interactive management systems,* not MIS's in general.

12.2 THE NEEDS OF MANAGEMENT USERS

Let us look at an information retrieval system from the point of view of a user. He may be a research worker, but he also has a decision to make. He needs to know how much experimentation done by others to repeat, which approach to his problem he should take, what his chances of success appear to be. He uses the retrieval system (or library) to provide data on related work done by others, which will become the basis for his decision. We generally expect that he will assimilate all the available information in a professional manner and evaluate it on the basis of his training and objectivity. We fully recognize that this is not a mechanical process, that it requires subjective analysis, and that it is not a matter of selecting one choice from a small number of clearly defined alternatives, but rather of choosing one or more approaches from a host of imprecisely defined possibilities.

The business manager is perhaps the most frequently analyzed decision-maker. John Dearden describes three levels of management functions: [1] *strategic planning,* which has to do with setting corporate objectives and policies; *management control,* which is concerned with accomplishing the objectives by subdividing and delegating them, along with the resources needed to accomplish the assigned tasks; and *operational control,* which is fairly direct control of the men and equipment that carry out a plan. He points out that the boundaries between these levels are not distinct and that several layers of organizational structure may be involved in each of the management levels. The top level he describes somewhat as we have described an information retrieval system used by a researcher. The user of the system deals to a large extent with intangibles. Speed, Dearden says, "is practically never vital . . . it is not usually possible to determine values precisely and . . . complete accuracy of results is neither possible nor necessary." [2] This is by no means an attempt to derogate the role of a manager. Indeed, it is a recognition of how complex this role is.

If we turn to the two lower levels of management, management control and operational control, we find people concerned more with figures and with quantifiable information in general: schedules, budgets, man-hours, production schedules, and the like. Here we do find the computer aiding in decision-making and even making decisions. These tend, however, to be decisions that represent a function of many variables, difficult for a man to make but based on known information. In short, these decisions, many of which can be made by use of mathematical programming [10] techniques, involve matters not of grand strategy but of detailed planning at a tactical level—the allocation of available resources to tasks at hand. Examples of such decisions are selecting product mixes to be manufactured and scheduling operations in a machine shop.

In light of these definitions, we might define a decision-making system for managers or commanders as one that assists them in planning for future operations. This planning activity is not research, in the sense that it is not a search for already-existent information generated by others that might tell what a decision should be. Nor, for our purposes, is planning a matter of computing a function of a set of known variables to optimize some activity. The manager needs to know, in general, what is going on in his business, what is going on in his business environment (the market, the competition, the regulatory agencies), and what is going to happen. He is particularly interested in questions that begin, "What would happen if . . ."? Many of these questions, particularly those involving the prediction of the future, do not have quantitative answers, do not have answers that are stored in a data base waiting to be retrieved, and are not computable from data that are there. Given an estimate of a possible situation in the future, though, the computer can be programmed to extrapolate present conditions into this version of what is to come. A manager might, then, ask his computer to calculate the effects of a price rise (change in present price), based on existing market research data (estimate of future market conditions).

Hellner [4] suggests, and perhaps in doing so points out most succinctly what is missing from the typical MIS, that a military intelligence system cannot be just a passive retrieval system but must also draw, or help draw, inferences from the data. In other words, although many management systems exist that can make optimizing decisions, they tend to start from the premise that the state of the system is completely defined. Hellner says we do not necessarily know the situation; we know only a set of alleged facts. Although in military intelligence it is well accepted that we do not know the true situation, the same thing is probably also true, even if not so well accepted, in business. Basing a decision on these alleged "facts" is not good management. It is certainly not the role of top management as defined by Dearden. Management should be thinking about what other situations could also lead to the same set of reported facts, what other information is needed and how it can be obtained, perhaps what can be done to change the "facts." This, then, is decision-making as it should be at the higher levels and is the true job of a manager. A data-processing system that does not recognize the existence of this kind of activity (the need to doubt, refute, and build on the data base) is both passive and blind. It cannot make key decisions because it cannot see what decisions need to be made.

We are not sure that any data-processing system such as we have just described exists. Furthermore, many computer systems that are called management information systems or command control systems, while existing, are not interactive. We must return to our own objective, then: to describe interactive management or decision-making systems. In the absence of a body of existing systems that meet our requirements (interactive, inference-drawing), most of what we shall have to say will be speculative.

12.3 COMPONENTS OF A MANAGEMENT INFORMATION SYSTEM

An interactive MIS, according to our definition, should have five major components.

1. An Information Acquisition System. Whether or not this system is interactive depends on the nature of the data, but the information contained in the MIS must be timely and complete. The system must allow for partial, or incomplete, information and for conflicting versions of "facts" and speculative information. Speculative information consists of data entered into the system for the purpose of evaluating their relationship to other information—basically to help with the question, "What would happen if . . . ?"

2. An Interactive Information Retrieval System. The information contained herein, called the system's *data base,* and its search and maintenance programs must be available to and *used by* all levels of the organization. Lower-ranking members of the organization, those closer to the day-to-day operation and to quantified information, would have the responsibility to review the data base, keep it "clean," monitor errors, detect and act upon information gaps. They would make recommendations up the line on the information aspects of their findings (why data are wrong, what can be done, etc.) and on the substantive aspects (e.g., what current information seems to imply, what caused certain situations). The higher ranks look to the system for a broader view: trends, conditions, situations conducive to certain actions.

The query language for the system must allow for differences among the users.[3] Those who design data sets and files need a language rich in detail with which they can originate and modify files. Those concerned with data entry and with operating-level information retrieval, however, probably need only a simple language that can be highly symbolic. Finally, those concerned with strategic-level management need a language that can express the ideas on which they wish to search, ideas not readily expressed in highly symbolic, mathematical languages. Correspondingly, the data base must be a flexible organism. It must be changeable in structure without major upheaval. It must allow for interaction among files, multifile retrieval, or retrieval based on correlation between one file and another.

3. A "Command Design" System. This is analogous to a graphic design system, but the objective is to construct, not a graphic image, but a schedule, organization, or other organization-related entity. It is a way of entering a decision into the computer when the decision is recognized, not as a statement of *yes* or *no,* but as a complex set of information. One example is a PERT-like schedule,[8] representing a manager's decision on the way he wants to conduct his project; a second is an organization chart for a new division; a third, a diagram of a plan of attack for the military. In these cases there should be structure-manipulating programs, such as one for calculating the critical path in the PERT network, or the probable cost of the new division, or the time to execute a military maneuver. One of the reasons for wanting to be able to input speculative information into the system is so that it can be operated upon by these processing programs, just as the regular data base is.

The command design system must be interactive if it is to be of maximum value. It must encourage its users to experiment, and it must not penalize them too much for doing so (i.e., no excessive charges for machine time, or demands upon their own time for preparing hypothetical data for a trial). In short, it must encourage users not to rely solely on their official data base. The whole idea is not only to draw inferences directly from the data, but also to consider, after Hellner, what else could have caused this information to show up in the data base.

4. Information-Processing Programs and Models. One of the ways in which a MIS is distinguishable from an information retrieval system is that users of a MIS often want first to retrieve data from a file and then to do something with them, other than just reading them. It may be a matter of operating a cost analysis program on existing data under the assumption that a new salary plan for employees will go into effect. Or it might be a test of a proposed new product against a model or simulation of the retail market. A model,[6] in this sense, is a computer program that represents certain attributes and interactions of the real world, possibly the extent to which the retail buyers can be swayed by a given investment in a particular type of advertising, or the effect on luxury buying of a price rise. Although such models have the appearance of being predictive, they usually are intended only to show *typical* outcomes or to indicate a range of results that are most likely to occur. Models do not replace management decision-making, but they can sharpen it.

Models can be used on an interactive basis, also. War games or business games are typical examples. Here the commander or manager receives a stream of messages, as he might in the actual situation. He replies (makes and promulgates decisions or asks for more information) also by sending messages. The computer simulates the action of the world around him. If, in a military game, the commander decides to engage in a battle, the computer will weigh the strengths of the opposing forces, probably introduce some random variation (the underdog sometimes wins), and produce an outcome in terms of casualties and positions held or lost. Again, this kind of model does not predict the real world, but it does get a commander used to the kind of decision-making eventually expected of him, as well as the kind of results he may anticipate from certain kinds of actions on his part. If the model is sophisticated enough, it can point out to its user the consequences of acting on incomplete information (when complete information was actually available at the time but had not been requested) or of overcaution (waiting for information that may never materialize).

5. *Some Aids to Inference Drawing*. Being realistic, we admit that data processing has little to offer in this area now. We might, however, characterize the use of models as an aid to inference, for it offers an easy way for the user to draw inferences and have the computer help him with evaluating them. But the computer is not a full partner, able to make original suggestions. Rather, it serves as an eager assistant, carrying out plans and testing ideas.

Another way the computer can help is to compare the output of a model, or structure-manipulating program, with current information in the data base. This would be of assistance in projecting a hypothetical action and then seeing what changes would have to be brought about to fulfill the projection. For example, if a particular schedule is proposed, the computer could study and present its findings on the increase in personnel—or the new facilities or the additional purchases needed to accomplish the proposed action. It could go further. Taking personnel build-up as an example, it could not only compute the probable numbers of new people needed in each category, but also look at historical figures, population growth figures, etc., and assess the possibility of actually accomplishing this build-up. Are the additional people available? What will it take to get them? What will be the effect on the business of taking the necessary steps? A real example is what happens to present employees' salaries as higher starting salaries are paid to newcomers— salaries that must be paid to attract recent graduates in an ever more competitive situation. Can the company afford to raise all salaries? Can it afford not to? Just such pressure was in large part responsible for the merger of the American and National Football Leagues; a major business decision was triggered by the competition for player personnel.[5] To what extent a MIS can really answer these specific questions, we cannot say. But we feel they are the kinds of questions that need answering.

Finally, we can take a big jump and look forward to the day when machines can scan a data base and initiate suggestions to the manager, perhaps reversing the roles described above. The machine might get the ideas and ask the man to check them for reasonableness. We cannot underestimate the difficulty of this, at any practical level. Readers who have uncomfortable feelings about "thinking machines" taking over our lives and replacing man may take some comfort from the fact that a true inference-drawing program of this magnitude is a long way off.

12.4 THE DIFFICULTIES WITH MANAGEMENT INFORMATION SYSTEMS

Let us look closer at the shortcomings of a typical management information system and the reasons why it is difficult to implement a true decision-making system.

1. Low-Quality Data Base. When a data base is to be used as the foundation for decision-making, we must consider the extent to which it accurately represents the world it is supposed to represent. There is an unfortunate tendency for people to accept whatever comes out of a computer as true, although, precisely because this output is coming through an unfamiliar channel, it ought to be subjected to greater scrutiny than other information.

More insidious than errors are oversimplifications. These may be made at the time that data enter the system, when a coder or clerk is required to make a judgment about some fact and enter only a highly condensed, possibly not representative, version of the fact. We also build in oversimplification when we design a data base. When we design an information retrieval system to permit only one subject classification term, we are oversimplifying. When we record a student's performance in a course with a single grade, we are oversimplifying.

When a far more sophisticated decision-maker tries to resolve a question for himself, he may find that the computer and its data base are unable to respond to him in the discriminating terms he needs to use. For example, a receptionist in a business office exercises a decision-making function at one level when she refers visitors to members of the staff. When the visitor's stated interests are unfamiliar to the receptionist, she "classifies" him as best she can and passes him on to someone else. If this first-level decision has been wrong, subsequent "processing" of this "transaction" may become increasingly confused, as the visitor accosts members of the firm who are not involved in public relations and whose technical specialties are narrow enough to make them even less adept at classification than the receptionist. In short, the visitor is lost in the organizational structure.

The same sort of thing can happen from the other direction. Management wants to know why sales are lagging or recruiting has dropped off or the enemy keeps winning, and no one at the contact level (with customers, recruits, or enemies) has collected data in sufficient detail for the analytically-minded person to answer his question. What is involved, in this case, is not a failure of information retrieval. It is a matter of the information never having been recorded in the first place.

2. *Lack of Appreciation for the Quality of a Data Base.* However well designed and maintained it is, a data base cannot represent all aspects of reality. It simply cannot portray a complex social situation with all the nuances that a trained, competent person can. This kind of insight, a perception of reality and a grasp of all the important aspects of a situation, may be the single quality most responsible for elevating the decision-maker to his present position of authority. When such a person relies solely on an oversimplified, possibly out-of-date computer file, he is brought down to a common denominator. In real life, not only does the principal manager or executive have this keen perception, but also he relies, and is in the habit of relying, on a staff whose perceptions he trusts and which serves him as a filter for information. To entirely replace this staff with a computer data base may impose too severe a constraint on his customary way of operating and will probably cause the loss of much valuable information in the process. If the decision-maker lacks the technical background to appreciate the strengths and failings of a MIS and its data base, he ensnares himself in this trap.

3. *Lack of Inferential Capability.* We have dealt before with this principal weakness of the MIS. A system without inference-drawing ability cannot make creative suggestions, but merely recirculates old data. It does not point out what is missing, but relies only on the items of information predefined as part of the data base. It cannot indicate which item of information is suspect if there is a conflict among the stored items.

4. Lack of Ability on the Part of Managers and Their Staffs to Use the Tools Available. To obtain the full measure of benefit from a MIS requires a high degree of understanding of the languages used, the content and structure of the data base, and the logic of the processing program. Although beneficial use can be made without this detail, doing so amounts, again, to oversimplifying. In addition, there are always errors in a large system, possibly logical design errors or data base errors of content or structure. Again, we point out that the top managers, who achieved their prominence on the basis of their ability to spot such weaknesses in a complex organization and to see what had to be done to correct them, probably have no idea what is wrong with their computer system or how it can be corrected.

We have been quite critical and skeptical, even negative, about management information systems, in a book devoted to advanced computer applications. Why is this? The primary reason is that there are big gaps between information retrieval and inference-drawing, between computing a strategy, given a full set of well-defined variables, and deciding on the basis of ill-defined objectives and unknown factors. Much of management consists of predicting and controlling human behavior, and this is not an activity we can quantify with any great degree of success. Although some persons believe that behavior can be quantified and predicted, our quarrel is mainly with those who do not realize the difficulty of doing so. Worse, these people may not recognize when, or the extent to which, the significant variables bearing on an organization's behavior have been quantified and recorded.

On the positive side, we present two quotations that help to explain why, even though computers may not do much actual management decision-making, a computer-based MIS can be a valuable management tool. Daniel Melcher* has written in the *Library Journal:*

"And I've always liked the story that was told of one of the larger corporations. Back in the days when you couldn't hold up your head in big corporation circles unless you had a computer, they went right along with the rest. But they were unusually well-advised on procedure

---

* Reprinted from *Library Journal*, March 15, 1968, published by the R. R. Bowker Co. (a Xerox company) © 1969 R. R. Bowker Co.

and they recruited and trained an inside team of systems analysts and gave them a full two years to prepare the way for the computer. At the end of that time the company was able to report that the computerization program had already shown greater savings than had been anticipated, even though the computer itself had not yet arrived." [7]

And Daniel A. Roblin, Jr., is quoted in the *General Electric Forum:*

"We . . . formed a committee of operating people who analyzed every piece of paper in use in the entire corporation—an exercise that would have been useful in itself if we'd never bought a computer. . . . The people assigned to this committee, several of whom were at first skeptical about the advantages of a computer, began to think in terms of what it could do to streamline the communication system of the company to make it more efficient and productive." [9]

12.5 AN EXAMPLE

For the basis of our example we shall take a computer programming organization, one that has about 200 people and might be a large project group, a small company, or a division of a larger company. We assume all members of the group are involved on one project; hence most of their problems concern the operations of this project. However, we will assume the group also has a marketing or entrepreneurial, function, soliciting new business so that the group's income can continue on completion of the current project. We will describe a MIS that might be used by such an organization, and our emphasis will be on the user's point of view, not on program logic. Most of the programs required of such a system have been described elsewhere. The important thing here is how they are combined and made available for use to the organization. Again, we stress that the important point about a MIS is what it does for its users. Ease of use or sophistication of programs is secondary to this consideration.

12.5.1 The Organization

The organization we propose to serve is shown in diagram form in Figure 12.1. The functions of the organizational elements are described below.

The *Project Manager* is responsible for the entire project—performance of technical objectives, management of personnel, meeting deadlines and staying within budget limitations, customer relations, and

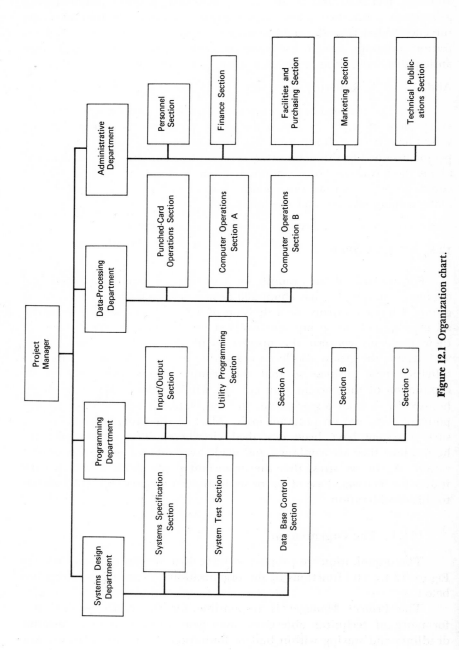

Figure 12.1 Organization chart.

winning new business for his group. His time is spent mostly on administrative matters, and he is not greatly involved in the day-to-day technical decisions affecting his project.

The *System Design Manager* not only handles the administrative functions of managing his department, but also is the person to whom the project manager delegates the principal responsibility for monitoring the technical progress of the project and for assuring adequate system design. The *System Design Department* has three sections:

1. *System Specification* is a small group of senior systems analysts who are responsible for the initial design of the system, for making design changes when the customer-supplied system specifications change (regrettably, the word *when* is the appropriate one, not *if*), and for insuring that the programs produced actually meet the stated specifications.

2. *System Test* is responsible for designing program tests that will demonstrate whether the completed programs meet specifications. The people in this section must work closely with the System Specifications Section and with the Programming Department and will have to revise plans as design changes are made. Their testing plans may have a major effect on overall system scheduling because of their possible requirements to test programs in a certain sequence that may require program A, for example, to be available in order to test program B.

3. The *Data Base Control Section* is responsible for the overall coordination of all data used by any programs. This group must insure that all programmers using the same data elements are assuming the same characteristics of the data, calling them by the same name, etc. Since programmers are constantly changing their programs, this group must continually monitor all programming activity for these purposes.

The *Programming Department* is responsible for the writing and debugging of all project programs. It has the majority of the personnel of the project organization, and the overwhelming number of these workers are programmers. This department is provided with design specifications by the System Specifications Section and is expected first to produce a program design to conform with the specification given it, then the program, then an individual program test plan. (Programmers test their own programs. The function of the System Test Section is to test assemblies of programs as a system or as subsystems.) There are five sections within the Programming Department devoetd to specialized programming: the *I/O Section* is concerned with inputs and outputs, the *Utility Programming Section* is responsible for general programs that are used by other programs in the system and require a greater degree of expertise in programming technology than do the applications programs, and, finally, three sections are devoted to producing the programs that perform the functions of the overall system. We have called these simply *Section A, B,* and *C,* for their detailed roles are not of interest to us. These are, though, the key production people of the entire project organization. It is their schedules, their personnel problems, and their needs for computer time and other services that create most of the administrative problems.

The *Data-Processing Department* operates the computers and provides keypunching and other off-line services for programmers and others. This department is also responsible for liaison with the computer manufacturer and his service personnel. The department has three sections, one for keypunching and miscellaneous tabulating operations, and two for main computer operations on each of two shifts.

The *Administrative Department* is a service organization. It includes a *Personnel Section,* which takes charge of hiring people and the administration of employee records and programs, and a *Finance Section,* whose duties are primarily to monitor expenses and keep management informed of performance with regard to budget and to estimate costs on future or proposed work. A *Facilities and Purchasing Section* handles the maintenance of the office space and all purchases made from outside companies. The *Marketing Section* maintains customer liaison, mainly for the purpose of soliciting additional business from established sources and actively searches for new business from other prospects. A *Technical Publications Section* is responsible for the editing, production, and art work on all reports and other documents issued by the project organization.

It would be possible to draw a formal chart depicting the flow of information among these groups. However, the formal lines of flow of information in an organization do not necessarily represent the actual paths, and basing an information system on them may well result in solving the wrong problem. Rather, we have an enlightened management that recognizes the need for informal channels of communication. For example, when the System Specification Section is considering a change in system specifications, the members may want to talk informally with several programming groups, the Data Processing Department, and a cost accountant before making a decision. These conversations will be by direct contact or telephone, not by transmission of a formal document requesting information.

12.5.2 Management Reports

Some information is routinely collected on a periodic basis, and some is obtained only when needed. Here is a list of the regularly scheduled reports required of members of the organization.

1. Each manager, each programmer, and some of the other professionals (e.g., salesmen) are expected to turn in a weekly progress report on the activities under their control. For a programmer, this will give the status of his program, anticipated completion date, expected amount of computer time needed to complete it, and so on. For a manager, the report will consist of aggregate information and will be stated in terms of milestones listed in a formally constructed project schedule.

2. Each person responsible for a periodic report is also expected to make an additional report whenever there is a major change in status. For example, if a program is completed on Tuesday, the programmer will not wait for Friday to report this to the MIS. Similarly, an unexpected computer failure requiring a day to fix will be reported immediately.

3. Formal reports of hours worked are turned in by each employee every week; these include a project or task number to which the person's time is charged for project accounting purposes. These reports, of course, contain errors and are always subject to revision. Similar reports are submitted by Data Processing for computer time used, by Purchasing for any materials purchased, and by anyone who travels, to cover his expenses for transportation, meals, lodging, and business entertainment.

4. Technical management files contain a schedule, composed of milestones or objectives, with assigned personnel, expected costs, and completion dates. Also included are narrative descriptions of all programs or specifications for programs and data files that comprise the operational system. These elements are not entered on schedule, but changes are posted as they occur. Each person responsible for a milestone is expected to make a periodic report verifying that the schedule is still correct or, alternatively, changing it.

Each department manager has a terminal in his office for querying the MIS or for entry of data. Subordinate managers and programmers have terminals readily available. About twenty terminals are in use in the entire organization. Incidentally, the number of hours of actual use of each terminal and the number in use simultaneously at any one time are vital system parameters that are not easy to predict unless experience from a similar arrangement is available on which to base the estimates. There are few such cases; hence the designers of this MIS will have to expect a fairly wide deviation from predicted figures.

Each person who contributes information to the system is permitted to query it, although some access restrictions are imposed on certain files, notably personnel and financial data. Thus any programmer can retrieve information about his own schedule or specifications, about related programs or data files, or about overall system objectives. Any group leader can retrieve financial or personnel information about his own group, but only an authorized manager can retrieve personal information and confidential cost data.

12.5.3   The Files

Before we can consider what the people who are faced with these problems can or should do, we must decide what files and processing programs are available. We can assume the following files.

Program Design Specifications.   This file will include a description of the purpose and logic of each program; a list of the subprograms contained in any program; a list showing the control structure of a program—that is, for each subprogram, the other subprograms to which the first one may transfer or branch; and a list of all data items or files used by a program.

Data Specifications.   For each file or individual item or record used by any program within the system, there should be a description of this data element, its specifications, and the programs with which it is used.

Project Schedule.   A list of the specific tasks to be accomplished during the project will include, for each program to be written, the following information: program testing, documentation, and integration with other programs. For each task, there will be stored a planned start date, planned completion date, estimated elapsed time required, person responsible, number of man-months required, prerequisite tasks, and resources required (e.g., computer time). For the purposes of composing a PERT network, each task should have three completion estimates: most probable, optimistic, and pessimistic.

Computer Schedule.   Based on assumed model of computer usage as a function of the programming activities being performed (debugging, system testing, etc.), an estimate of the computer time required can be calculated from the current project schedule. Since the latter will change often, the computer usage prediction model (i.e., the program representing the relationship between programming activity and computer utilization) will be run often and may feed back information that causes further revision of the schedule. The model will be based on average computer usage figures for a programmer working at a given stage of a program. Each person will be assumed to use x minutes of computer time per day during stage 1 of program production, y minutes per day during stage 2, etc. The stages are to be defined but will probably cover writing the program, debugging by the programmer, formal testing by the programmer, system testing of groups of programs together, and revision of programs after system testing has uncovered an error. Estimates of time would have to be made in terms of maximum, minimum, and most probable. Such a model is needed so that design or other changes can quickly be converted into computer time demands and these compared with available time.

Organization File. This contains a record for each department, section, or smaller group. It includes the name of the manager or supervisor and either the members of the group or the names of subordinate groups. It also includes the names of all programs or other tasks assigned to the group and historical data on the group's performance in the past, that is, a comparison of scheduled task completion dates with actual data.

Personnel File. This contains a record for each person in the organization, with personal and payroll information about him, his present assignment, a history of his assignments, his performance on them, and his occupational specialty.

Manpower Distribution. This shows the number of people assigned to various categories of work or status. For example, it will give the number of job applications now being processed, the number of people now engaged in tasks on the project, and the number needed in the next few time periods. Each list of people is broken down by occupational specialty and, if possible, gives the names of the individuals. Such a file enables planners to find out how many new employees may be available in a few weeks, how many people currently on the project have assignments that may end within the next month, and so on.

Business Prospects. This is a file of all known future projects or customers, together with descriptions of sales activity regarding each, an estimate of the requirements for the project if won, and a projection of the probability of winning.

The Budget. This shows, on a week-by-week basis, the amount of money available for each task on the official project schedule (administrative tasks included) and the amount actually spent, as determined by labor vouchers, expense accounts and purchase orders, and computer utilization figures. It includes an extrapolation to the end of the project, based on planned expenditures and expected computer and manpower usage as shown in the project schedule. A change in project schedule will necessitate a new budget projection, which may also create feedback requiring a further revision of the schedule.

Obviously, these files are highly interconnected. Equally obviously, none is of any use unless the information it contains is up to date and correct. We have indicated that the file-handling system can be programmed to detect conflicts or duplicate entries. Hence a proposed change in a project schedule that results in planning for more people than are actually available, for example, could be at least flagged by the file-handling program.

Many times, managers or others in an organization may propose to take an unwise action that, in the absence of a management information system, could be made because there was no one to say nay. With a MIS, this action can be blocked because a program will point out any inconsistency. In the long run, this is going to have one of several effects. (1) The most beneficial result would be that everyone concerned did a better job of planning, making full use of information never before available to him. (2) It is possible, however, that continued rejection by the computer of decisions like those a manager was accustomed to making before MIS was adopted would result in abolishing the system, whether or not justified. Alternatively, the manager's superiors might decide that it was he who lacked the judgment needed for the job. (3) Finally, it is possible that the weakness being discovered here lay not in the managers' judgments but rather in the models used to project requirements into the future. Here we return to our earlier point about the representation of reality. If the model, which may have seemed reasonable as a mathematical approximation to a complex phenomenon, does not truly represent the situation, it may begin rejecting valid decisions on the part of its users. In any conflict between the users and the computer, then, we must recognize the possibility that it is the computer program that is lacking in judgment.

We have mentioned briefly how these files are to be maintained and need not discuss this subject again. Since enough terminals are assumed so that every professional employee has ready access to one, it is only a matter of discipline whether or not these terminals are used and the files are kept current and accurate.

12.5.4 The Problems

We shall discuss some management information problems in terms of the ability of the proposed MIS to aid in their solution.

1. During the early stages of the project, when there is not a full

complement of people aboard, the design section is piecing together the technical plan for the project. As new ideas are suggested, they must, if apparently plausible, be integrated into the existing design (which cannot yet be very detailed), and all implications developed. Implications of a design include the time required to implement it, the number and type of people required, the amount of computer time, the data files required of the program, and other programs that may be needed to assist in accomplishing the task. Less senior people, many of them from the Programming Department, are assigned to develop these details; and, as the System Specification Section makes changes or as the programmers discover the need to revise a design, a substantial communications problem is created. Although incompletely developed information is flowing in all ways, delays in typing and internal mail can negate its value by late delivery, or it may even be misplaced and never reach its destination.

2. After the system design has been set and the production of programs begun, a change is requested by the customer. The System Specification Section must evaluate this request in terms of feasibility; changes needed to effect it; time, people, and computer time required; and effect on overall schedule. The request for a change will be worded in operational terms, that is, in terms of what the resulting programs will do, not in programming terms. Part of the problem, then, is to determine which programs are affected and what the effect of the change on other functions will be.

3. One of the section managers in the Programming Department has requested that five more programmers be added to his staff within the next month. The Personnel Section has been requested to look into the problem and see what can be done. The following considerations are involved: a budget must be adhered to; people in other sections may be completing tasks and hence becoming available; there is a long lead time for recruiting (if recruiting is to be done, it must be started soon); and, if new people are hired, a greater demand is placed on the Marketing Section to find new business to support a larger group as the current project nears completion. The alternative to finding new business is to increase the financial risk of the organization, which will have raised its committed level of expenditure.

4. As the end of the project nears, the project manager wants to look at his new business potential, decide what he has to do to win new business, what his probabilities are for success, and what he may have to do if no new business is forthcoming.

12.5.5 Solving the Problems

By and large, the problems we have selected for illustration do not have a "solution" in the mathematical sense; there is no "answer" that pure logic tells us must be "right." With or without the aid of a computer, problems such as these are taken on by real people and organizations daily, and solutions are found in the sense that decisions are made and the organization goes on to its next crisis. The decision may never be made explicitly (*no decision* is a decision, as, in a way, is failure to recognize the existence of a problem); and in any case all the facts surrounding the origin of a problem, the process of solving it, and the consequences of the decision are rarely available for later analysis. Thus we do not know as much as we would like to about how decisions are really made.

So what can the computer do? Put to work on the problems we have raised in the preceding section, it is not going to "solve" them in the sense of performing the work involved or rendering infallible decisions. A mechanized management information system, though, containing a good-quality data base and functioning through a skilled user, can help find both options and objections not otherwise recognized, can force the consideration of questions easy to ignore, and can help document information otherwise likely to be forgotten.

The problems selected for illustration are realistic. As such, they imply complexity and subjectivity. It is up to the reader to supply much of the imagination needed to visualize how the attempts at solutions we present would appear in reality, through the medium of an interactive MIS. In reading them it should be remembered that in many cases there is no obvious question to be asked of a system, and constant trial and error is a necessity.

1. Managing the Design Process. The first of our illustrative problems is one, not so much of being able to ask questions of a MIS or of having it evaluate models, as of rapid collection and dissemination of information. Let us look at the project organization during this period. It is small, having started with just a cadre of managers and a few key technical people, and is in the process of adding new persons at a high rate. Little in the way of established specifications or precedent for this organization exists. There is a rough statement of objective, not yet translated into a specific computer program performance specification. Since the people on the project may not know each other well, informal channels of communication are not yet adequately established.

A first pass at a system design might have established the four major program modules shown in Figure 12.2. We start with the simplest

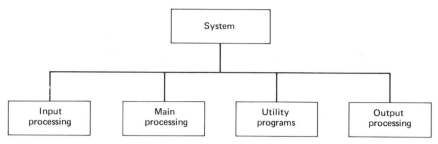

Figure 12.2 Initial concept of program organization.

input-processing-output concept, augmented by a class of expected utility programs. So far, we have nothing more than the start of a classification system, for almost any program fits this model. As more design work is done (Figure 12.3), we begin to identify particular programs or groups of programs, most of which fit under the initial classification. But we can begin to see the trends. Most major program classes rely on utility programs to accomplish their task. Hence *utility* is not so much a separate functional class as a designation of frequently used programs. Even the major classes become interdependent. For example, if our input programs read invalid data, the offending record will be referred to an input error program, which may use an output program to send a message to the originator of the data. Hence we will quickly find that we cannot completely separate one class of program from another. Not that we necessarily want to, but it may initially appear that Input and Output are independent programs and not concerned in each other's planning. We quickly discover the contrary to be true.

Each indicated program will consist of a number of smaller program modules. For each major program, we want to record at minimum a description and a notation of purpose, the list of data files used and produced, the list of subordinate program modules, the people assigned, the responsible person, estimates on completion time, and start and end dates. No one person is going to make all these estimates for any one program, except perhaps at the very lowest level of the program hierarchy, where a single programmer sketches out his own work. After one programmer or designer, say working on input, has designed a data file, another, working on the main processing programs, may find he must request a revision to the file in order to fit his computational needs. We have, then, a number of problems of this type, including the following:

    a. Content of files. This involves (1) joint use of data by more than one program, requiring coordination of data file design, and (2)

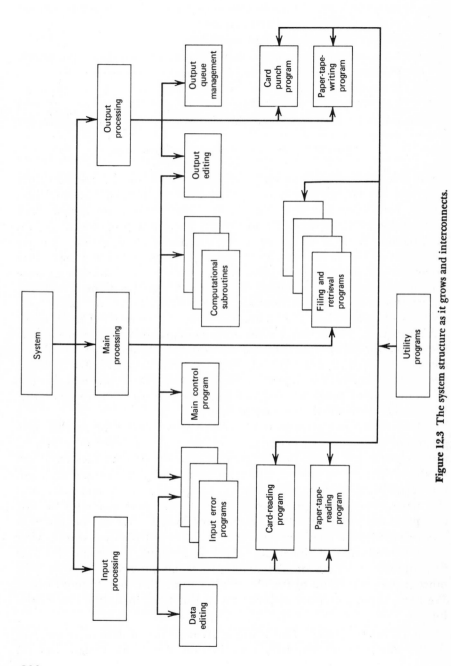

Figure 12.3 The system structure as it grows and interconnects.

agreement on allowable ranges of values of data items and on responsibility for detecting errors.

b. Nature of program interconnections.

c. Competition for people, computer time, and schedule time among different programs.

d. Agreement on performance specifications, particularly passing requirements for performance down the chain of command and passing estimates of the performance that will result from the designs up the chain.

It is not possible to set down either the individual questions to the MIS that would be generated by each person working in the system or the sequence of questions. What will happen is a continuous interchange of information, of proposals and counter proposals, of arguments and compromises. In any real system, there are going to be conflicts or omissions that are overlooked throughout the design period and are discovered only after the system is well into production and the number of possible ways of resolving the problem are severely reduced.

What we require of a MIS for such a situation, then, is frequent updating of files by all users, frequent dissemination of changes to all users, and computer assistance in detecting conflicts. But we also want the MIS to be sufficiently flexible that it does not require information to be entered in a set sequence, or does not need information to be complete in order for it to be able to make preliminary assessments. If, for example, two different people describe the same data item in two different ways, the computer cannot be expected to tell the difference, but it should accept both inputs and assist by referring them to the design group with a request for a resolution, which these people may not be able to make for some time. Similarly, one programmer may describe his output differently from the next programmer to whom it is input. Again the computer cannot reconcile these differences, but it can ask someone to check for consistency.

The computer can offer positive help in the area of manpower and computer planning. As programs are defined and tentatively scheduled, certain amounts of manpower and computer time are implied. The computer can aggregate these and make up cumulative system manpower and computer utilization schedules. More likely than not, too many people and too much computer time will be specified, probably both showing a large build-up at the start of the project, as all designers try to get their own programs implemented immediately. As soon as the magnitude of this peaking problem is apparent, changes can be made, primarily toward shifting some of the work to later times within the development cycle. Also, at this time, more information should be available on what programs are needed first and which ones are dependent on others for testing. The programs actually required first may be less important-seeming ones that are needed to be able to operate the more important programs.

Our MIS for this organization, then, requires each designer or programmer involved in the design process to update his design at least once a week, entering changes into the computer as they occur. The computer stores the information, mostly in its program and data description files, and disseminates current status data as often as daily to all project members. The MIS indicates areas of conflict that it has been able to detect, calls specifically for resolution of all possible multiple-definition problems, and produces a schedule projection (completion, cost, manpower usage, and computer usage) based on the latest estimates available to it.

In a few months (about three months is typical for a large project) this process should have quieted down and resulted in a coordinated system design. It would be naive to assume that all conflicts or errors would have been resolved, but we can be reasonably sure that most of them have. A final schedule, still subject to change but at this point agreed to by all concerned, is prepared and the project budget is laid out. From here on, although changes will still be made, we can expect that they will occur at a far less frequent rate and that the cost of a change will be higher and the system less adaptable to modification. Also, future changes, because of their impact on a production cycle already begun, will have to be documented carefully and approvals made in a prescribed manner.

2. An Individual Design Change. We now place ourselves at another point in the project's development. The design is fairly firm, and production is going on, although not necessarily on schedule. The organization has become stable with no new people expected or needed. In short, if all continues to go as it has, the project will probably be completed reasonably on time and within budget. Now the customer upsets the apple cart: he requests that we consider a change in performance specification. From his point of view the suggestion change is minor, and he sees no need for a schedule modification or for increased cost. However, as a matter of form he has asked that we prepare an estimate of the cost to make the change.

The nature of the change may be something like changing the specifications on input, perhaps raising the arrival rate of new inputs, or increasing or decreasing the allowable range of values. Instead, the customer could request a change in the manner of computing something, perhaps a new tax computation in a payroll program. These are the kinds of changes that computer laymen tend to feel are trivial, whereas to a programmer they can have profound implications to a program system. For example, changing the arrival rate of inputs can require not only more memory, but perhaps also a faster processing cycle, which may not even be possible on the computer selected for the project.

Changing the manner of performing a calculation can be quite simple, so long as all the information needed for the new calculation is the same as for the old one. If new data are required that would not normally be in memory when the computation is performed, however, a major program change may be needed. And if new data are required that are not in the files or are not there in the form needed, the entire system may have to be revamped. Suppose, for example, that a retroactive tax increase is to be imposed, starting on earnings received since last July 1. Then the tax program needs to know not just the cumulative, or year-to-date, earnings of each employee but also the actual dates on which money was earned. This is a figure not necessarily available in a typical payroll file. The example, though, is typical of the problems faced by programmers.

A request to evaluate the cost of a change would first be sent to the System Specification Section, which would serve as the nerve center for the processing of this request. Again without being able to list the precise questions asked, we can foresee the general problems they must resolve. This time, by the way, we are to a greater extent in a question-and-answer situation than in the previous example, for a large number of simultaneous program changes will not be made in this case. Rather, a smaller number of potential changes will be evaluated, with the actual change implemented only when all final decisions have been made.

First, the designers need to know what programs are affected by the proposed change. The answer is not always obvious and may require considerable searching of files. This is particularly true of changes affecting rates and volumes of input or output, for the descriptions of these programs may not include a full set of assumptions on rates and memory availability. Finding out the minimum amount of time a program needs to operate may require detailed searching of the descriptions of all subordinate programs as well as the system monitor, for the logic of the monitor may set some lower bound on elapsed time requirements. For example, it might require x milliseconds for the monitor to be made aware of the arrival of an input message and to call in the appropriate message-processing program. If the arrival rate of input is changed, so that messages can come at smaller intervals than x milliseconds, the particular program system design in use may be completely unable to cope with the data.

Once the programs that *may have* to be changed have been found, the designers need to know *exactly* what has to be changed. This will probably require consultation with the programmers, each of whom will probably be able to think of several more detailed questions than the design team has yet raised. As the individual programmers begin to suggest changes that might be made to their own programs, a cascade of follow-up actions is required. For each one, we need to know how the change impinges on other programs, as far as program interface and joint use of data are concerned. We need to have an estimate of any change in program execution time and to test the effect of this on the overall system. We need to know how much time would be required to make the change and, if the system is far enough into testing, to retest the new versions. We need to know how much manpower and computer time are required and, if these are not available, what changes in the redesign plan can be made.

In answering these questions, we will induce a smaller version of the flurry of changes and counter changes that characterized the original system design. This time, however, we are in a much more controlled environment, all changes being directed at accomplishing a specific end and all being a matter of deviating from a known initial assumption, instead of starting from scratch. Once again, we can see that data related to the redesign must be entered into the MIS as soon as they are available and disseminated immediately to all interested parties. We have one new point here, and that is that all these changes are speculative. Actual design or schedule changes will not be made until the entire change has been planned and fully coordinated. Hence all the estimates are provisional, to take effect only when so ordered by the project staff. However, we want to enter the provisional data in order to find what their effect will be on existing records, and therefore our MIS files must make provision for such entry.

In practice, although major design changes are never easy, they can be accommodated and controlled, especially if an information system such as we are describing is available. Consider, though, the requirements for a system when twenty design changes are being processed simultaneously. Twenty changes is not an unheard-of number to request, but it is almost an impossible number to keep up with. Consider all the combinations and interactions that must be checked, all the multiple versions of estimates and logic descriptions, and all the provisional schedule possibilities. This kind of load can swamp a MIS.

The people concerned must adapt quickly to overload situations, and automatically begin to deal at different levels of abstraction or simply to drop off details or to make fewer checks on the validity of assumptions. We do not necessarily mean that sloppiness is the answer for overloading. It is, however, a frequent result, and a dogged insistence on quality without the provision of relief is no answer. Hence a MIS that is to serve the large-scale project management must be able to adapt itself to overload situations. Programs to accomplish this are among the most difficult kinds to write.

3. Changing Manpower Assignments. With sufficient filed data, a MIS can be of great service in the frequently recurring problem of how to staff each section of the project organization adequately, yet hold the total staff to a minimum and keep overall employment stable. Each individual manager tends to see only his own problem, and from the time that he develops a need or a desire for more people, he is impatient with any delay. Higher management must consider other factors. Hiring new people takes time, is expensive initially, and involves a commitment to keep them on the payroll when the immediate project is over. Moreover, new people must be trained for the project, and a larger staff requires more administrative support, which again raises both dollar costs and the demand for people. Also, there is always the possibility that the manager requesting more people is exaggerating his needs and can actually get along with fewer. On the other hand, if his need is genuine, the project schedule may be in jeopardy.

If one of the programming section managers has asked permission to hire five new people, the managers who make the decisions on whether to approve his request must take the following steps. Obviously, a thorough justification is needed, some firm indication that this manpower requirement is actual and that it cannot be satisfied by overtime, a slight schedule slippage, or some other diversion of resources. Other sections and departments should be canvassed for available workers, or for programs running ahead of schedule that could afford a diversion of people. The Personnel Section should be consulted on the status of its recruiting program and for an assessment of how long it will take to hire the people needed. The Finance Section will have to prepare a cost estimate for hiring these persons and maintaining them on the payroll and will project the increased long-range burden, or risk, of committal to a larger payroll beyond the end of the project.

In short, to make the decision in response to the request for more people, it is necessary first to verify the request and then to find how the people could be made available, either from within or by hiring from outside the project; what the delay in bringing the people in will be; whether, given that some delay is necessary, it will be possible to bring them in on time; whether there is some alternative way to resolve the apparent slippage than by adding people. Finally, the costs and increased business risks of a larger staff must be projected. Much of this could be done by using a personnel model, which keeps track of all project personnel and all prospective new employees as well as the general statistics on recruiting, knows how long it takes for various personnel actions, such as hiring or training, and can estimate the increase in cost. By tying in with a schedule algorithm, the alternative way of solving the problem can also be explored.

Using these tools, managers can test the effectiveness of several possible approaches and can make a final decision based on a thorough examination of all the facts. Use of such techniques will also help management to cope with the complexity that arises when several of these personnel actions are being considered simultaneously and the problems they raise must be solved as a whole, not individually.

4. Predicting the Business Picture. Our final example concerns a problem that is not going to be solved by searching files or by running a simulation model. The problem is how to match the current staff and prospects for increasing the staff with new business opportunities, so that a steady and profitable growth is achieved. Predicting the sales of a programming organization is not the same as predicting retail sales for a nationally sold product. Here we have an organization that will make only a few sales a year. Slight variations from plan can cause large disruptions in budget or in ability to provide needed manpower for a new project.

What management needs, then, is a good market intelligence system, one that has background information on projects forthcoming from customers and that contains reliable information about each customer's previous buying habits, preferences for programming contractors, level of funding, and so on. Any organization can compute a historical probability of winning any proposal for new business that it submits; but since the probability is low to begin with, and since the contract is won or lost in its entirety, estimating income on the basis of weighted probabilities can be hazardous. If company A wins 10 per cent of its bids and it has bid on $1,000,000 worth of business, there is nothing to say that it will necessarily have $100,000 worth of new business. It could well have none, and it could perhaps equally well be swamped by winning two or three of its bids, instead of the one predicted.

What the MIS can do for our organization is assist in laying out all the possibilities, or all combinations of wins and losses in the new business it is currently competing for. This will generate a great many data, but somewhere in the heap is a more realistic picture than the easy-to-obtain aggregate of probabilities. Like all other applications of a MIS, this one depends for its value on valid input data. Far more is gained by having realistic and accurate data on customers and their plans and preferences than by any manipulation of the data to predict market performance.

12.5.6 Problem Summary

We have deviated from our usual practice and shown as an example, not the logic of the programs, but the kinds of questions MIS users need to ask and the kinds of data they require in order to make a MIS useful. From these and previous discussions of information retrieval and design, the reader can infer what the program logic must be. Once again, we stress that, when we apply these techniques to management decision-making, we enter a field that is not deterministic, that is not necessarily governed by a set of mathematical relationships. A MIS must meet the real needs of its users, and this means being responsive to the true complexity of most large organizations and insuring up-to-date information from a wide variety of sources. Perhaps here, more than in any other area we have discussed so far, the dictum *garbage in, garbage out* has meaning. Without meaningful data, a computer cannot help much in decision-making.

On the positive side, we have also indicated, in several contexts, how certain decision-making situations create no particular problem if taken individually, but can be truly overwhelming when a number of simultaneous decisions are called for. The number of possible different outcomes when, say, 20 program change requests are being evaluated may surpass the record-keeping capacity of a manually operated system. This condition easily could swamp the capacity of a MIS as well. The ability to handle overload situations is an important factor in the eventual success of the system. A well-designed MIS can help maintain order in what otherwise would be chaos.

REFERENCES

1. Dearden, John, "Can Management Information Be Automated?" *Harvard Business Review*, **42**, 2 (March-April, 1964), 128–135.
2. *Ibid.*, p. 133.

3. Dodd, George G., ed., *COBOL Extensions to Handle Data Bases,* Research Publication GMR 749, Research Laboratories, General Motors Corp., Warren, Mich., 1968.

4. Hellner, Maurice H., "Evidence and Inference in Foreign Intelligence," *Information System Science and Technology,* Donald E. Walker, ed., Thompson, Washington, D.C., 1967, pp. 295–299.

5. "In a Word, Money," *Time,* **88,** 5 (July 29, 1966), 34.

6. Martin, Francis F., *Computer Modeling and Simulation,* John Wiley, New York, 1968.

7. Melcher, Daniel, "Automation: Rosy Prospects and Cold Facts," *Library Journal,* **93,** 6 (Mar. 15, 1968), 1105–1109.

8. Moder, Joseph J., and Cecil R. Phillips, *Project Management with CPM and PERT,* Reinhold, New York, 1964.

9. Roblin, Daniel A., Jr., "Small Business," *The General Electric Forum,* **X,** 4 (Winter 1967–68), 19.

10. Vazonyi, Andrew, *Scientific Programming in Business and Industry,* John Wiley, New York, 1958.

RECOMMENDED ADDITIONAL READING

1. Ackoff, Russell L., and Patrick Rivett, *A Manager's Guide to Operations Research,* John Wiley, New York, 1963.

2. Dearden, John, "Myth of Real-Time Management Information," *Harvard Business Review,* **44,** 3 (May-June 1966), 123–132.

3. Gass, Saul I., *An Illustrated Guide to Linear Programming,* McGraw-Hill, New York, 1970.

4. Greenberger, Martin, "The Use of Computers in Organizations," *Information,* S. F. Freeman, San Francisco, 1966, pp. 143–156.

5. Stuart-Stubbs, Basil, "Trial by Computer," *Library Journal,* **92,** 22 (Dec. 15, 1967), 4471–4474.

6. "Where IBM Looks for New Growth," *Business Week,* June 15, 1968, pp. 24–27.

Chapter Thirteen

Problems and Perspectives
for Interactive Systems

13.1 INTRODUCTION

To predict accurately the future development of any major segment of the computer industry is nearly impossible. There has been a tendency, throughout the industry's short history, for reality to outstrip our wildest predictions, while some of our more mundane ideas fail to materialize. For example, in the early days of electronic computers, memories were small by present standards, perhaps 1000 words. The attitude was then prevalent that more was not needed because, with stored programs and program-controlled input and output, data or program segments could be temporarily stored in auxiliary memory and brought into main memory only when actually needed.

Today we are no longer quite so ready to accept the delays this approach forces upon us. Each time engineers make more capacity or speed available to programmers, they, in turn, come to depend upon this new level as a minimum. As these expansions have come about, we have undertaken ever more difficult problems; many of today's routine problems would have been virtually impossible to solve on a computer as slow and limited as those of the early 1950s. From the 1000-word memories of less than two decades ago, we have today 1-microsecond-access memories of 250,000 characters in common use, large auxiliary core memories of 1,000,000 characters also in use, and auxiliary storage units of 1 trillion (10^{12}) bits.[5] The net effect of this rapid growth is that computers become cheaper and easier to use at a rapid rate. Hence we can afford to be less efficient in their use and to concentrate instead on getting more programs written faster and on attacking ever more difficult problems.

An almost contradictory growth pattern emerges when we consider certain classes of computer applications, including information retrieval, computer-assisted instruction, and certain types of simulation. In these areas, the computing profession has had a general tendency to promise more, far more, than it has delivered over the years. This is not to say that significant accomplishments have not been made in these areas, but we must face the fact that, particularly with respect to information retrieval, accomplishments have not kept pace either with promises or with developments in other fields. A large part of this lag can be attributed to a failure of the interface between man and machine. Again with information retrieval as the example, one of our principal faults has been to design automatic retrieval systems that are too stilted in use and are unrealistically rigid in structure. Computer-assisted instruction has also suffered from this malady.

In this chapter we shall review the major problems of deficiencies in man-machine communications as carried on today and then consider what the future may hold.

13.2 PROBLEMS TO DATE

To a certain extent, our problems in furthering man-machine communications arise from our impatience, rather than from basic technological weaknesses. We like to feel we can implement any system we can conceive of, and we rush to do so. As we hasten to exploit new ideas, inevitably some progress faster than others. In the struggle for new developments, we often lose the historical perspective in which to view our own progress. It may be that we need a little more time to complete some basic developments before trying to implement them as interactive processes.

The major problems we shall discuss are these: (1) *computer literacy,* or the general extent to which computers are known and comfortable to the public at large, those who, eventually, are their main users; (2) *the linear, or sequential, nature of most modern computers and programming languages,* a condition that forces a disproportionate share of our attention onto problems of how to get to a location in memory rather than of how to describe what we are looking for or what we want to do; (3) the previously mentioned *stiltedness, or artificiality, of the languages* we are often forced to deal with; and, finally, (4) *incompatibility in programs and computers,* which causes much wasteful duplication and, of course, slows down those who would, if they could, build on the work of others.

13.2.1 Computer Literacy

Called by various names, this is the problem of general user familiarity with computers. Most interactive systems are intended to be used by other than professional programmers. However, many of these systems, manufacturers' advertising notwithstanding, require for fully effective use a substantial knowledge of programs, file organization, and even hardware functions. Frequently the designers of these systems do not realize the degree of computer literacy they are requiring of their users.

When the user does not know the program he is dealing with, he cannot see the logic behind the arcane symbols he is forced to use. He cannot think in the language he is given to work with and hence cannot solve his own problems. The natural result is for him to avoid use of the system and to make the claim, very likely valid for him, that it does not "work."

We often talk of using a computer to perform, or to help a man perform, a complex task he has previously accomplished unaided. It makes no sense to think of expecting a skilled practitioner to embrace a computer system that purports to do his job better, but that he cannot understand. Yet this is exactly what we have done in many cases. A truly significant improvement in this situation would be more likely to come from better computer education than from better advertising and public relations by the programmers. As computers become more common, they will be more freely used in new applications. Thus they will be more widely used when they are more effectively used, and they will be more effectively used when they are more widely used. This is not a paradox but rather a matter of parallel development of better technology and increased user acceptance. The same situation was faced, for example, by the television industry when color transmission was introduced. Better programming and consumer acceptance were interdependent. Neither could wholly exist before the other.

13.2.2 Computer Design

In one sense, computer programmers have little to complain of in the way of computer design, for we have not, in general, learned to take full advantage of the designs we have had before new, better ones have arrived on the market. If there is a design limitation, it is that present-day computers are essentially linear, or sequential, machines, whereas the functions we often want to apply them to are multidimensional, or parallel.

For example, most of the applications we have described involve information retrieval, which, from the program's point of view, becomes a problem of finding in a file records having certain stated attributes. The programmer can state these attributes in a single symbolic statement or a concise syntactic expression, and he may visualize the process as a simultaneous one of separating all "hits" from the main file. The computer, however, forces him to go about his search sequentially, recalling and examining records one at a time to see if they conform to the stated criteria. This process can be condensed by the use of indexes; but, when we consider the almost trivial amount of logical work we are asking the computer to do in a file search, the operation still takes an inordinate amount of time. To search for the single record in a file that has the value v in field f can take seconds or even minutes, large time units indeed in modern computers. Therefore, much of the retrieval system designer's attention is necessarily forced onto the mechanics of record acquisition when his real interests lie in the analysis of content.

Time-sharing or multiprogramming can alleviate much of this problem. These, however, are software techniques. They have the effect of turning off the meter that accumulates charges against a program when the CPU is not actually in use by this program, but they do not reduce total elapsed time; in fact, they increase it. The greatest inefficiencies in time-sharing systems themselves involve delays due to file search and data recovery. We intuitively expect the interactive systems of the future to have great problem-solving capability, and indications are that this implies more and more tedious searching of lists, files, and tables. A significant breakthrough in the way these searches are performed should lead to an equally significant breakthrough in what can be accomplished.

Another aspect of the same problem is that most modern computers are still basically mathematical machines. There is a machine instruction to carry out the functions of multiply and divide, which actually are repetitive applications of the more basic operations of adding and subtracting. Normally, however, we do not find individual commands to perform, say, sorting or searching. When an algorithm is interpreted and executed at the hardware level, as is done for multiply and divide, its execution speed is far greater than when interpretation and execution are done by software, that is, by having the algorithm executed by use of a sequence of machine language commands.

Microprogramming [3] is a possible means to this end. In microprogramming complex commands (requiring programs for their interpretation) are interpreted and executed at the machine level, and only one instruction need be decoded by the computer. This speeds up CPU operation considerably, but does not directly affect search time on auxiliary memories or input-output times.

Multiprocessing (Section 4.3.2.) is another approach to this problem. Here two or more CPU's are in use, and all share the same auxiliary memory and I/O facilities. In some systems, a great deal of program logic is built into the I/O control units, so that some degree of searching and screening can be done at this lower command level without tying up the central processor or even one of several processors. Unless the cost of computer hardware is radically reduced (a distinct possibility), however, adding full-power and full-cost CPU's is not the same as a conceptual redesign of the processor that would decentralize expensive processes.

13.2.3 Language

It is difficult for a person to "talk" to a computer while involved in a complex task that makes heavy demands on his attention. Partly, this is a failure or weakness of the programs that interpret messages from console operators, but it is also partly caused by limitations on what these programs can do with information after they have received it. For example, if an information retrieval program expects its user to know his search terms and hence is not programmed to help him find them, there may be no way in its language for him to express any doubts he may have. Suppose the user does not know the names of the files or of the fields within files he wishes to search—for example, that an author's name will be found in a field called *auth*. Then he cannot state his search criteria. Information about the file and field names is probably stored somewhere in the computer and would be as easy to search and retrieve as the subject matter in the files, but most retrieval systems are not programmed to permit searching this bibliographic type of information.

We believe the main problem with interactive systems is inexperience in their design and use. In designing an interactive program, it always seems quite easy to anticipate the possible answers to questions. But in real-life interactive systems, as in real-life man-man communication, it is the penetrating analysis, the ability to understand and tolerate error on the part of another, that makes for smooth, effective conversation. To a large extent, a good conversationalist, man or machine, is an inference drawer, one who asks the question, "What did he (it) really mean?"

In an earlier chapter we gave an example of response analysis for what may appear a straightforward *yes-no* situation. But we immediately found that we must decide whether *Yes, Yes.,* and *YES* are as acceptable as *yes.* We discover that, even when we go through much trouble to word questions so that they call for *yes-no* answers, we must spend considerable time wondering what to do when the answer is neither. What if the answer is unrecognizable? What if the terminal operator persists in entering the same, unrecognizable reply? We would hardly care to talk long with a person who displayed this behavior. He would sound like a broken phonograph record. But another human being conversing with him would immediately recognize that the original question was not being answered, and the dogged persistence would make the observer realize not only that the original question was not going to be answered but that there was something wrong with the responder. Although not every observer is interested enough or is competent to probe for the cause of this offbeat behavior, most are capable of recognizing what is happening. It is possible—and not even particularly difficult—to write interactive programs to do this kind of analysis, but the process can be very time-consuming and short-cut inducing. Hence programmers often fail to face this issue.

We can classify our language deficiency problems as follows:

1. Vocabulary and syntax deficiency; that is, the language is unable to express certain concepts, such as to distinguish between *steel mill* and [*to*] *mill steel,* which demand a level of syntax not present in all information retrieval languages.

2. Imperceptive interpreters; a program that cannot tell *Yes* from *yes* or cannot tell that "Name similar to McFarland" means something like, "NAME = MCFARLAND or MACFARLAND or MACFARLANE . . . ." People, after all, do not think in terms of Boolean expressions. There is really no reason why some standard meaning cannot be assigned to an expression such as "similar to," and the interpreter left to do most of the work of expanding the illustrative word. People who object to writing Boolean expressions might complain less if they were asked to do so only after a short cut had been tried and failed and the user was given the reason why it failed.

3. Lack of forgiveness of errors. When designing a language it is as easy to agree on default assumptions as to ignore them. A default assumption is a decision built into a computer program on what to do, in the absence of a positive statement or in the presence of an ambiguous

one, by a programmer or other system user For example, the FORTRAN programming language assumes that any data item whose name begins with the letter *I* is intended as an integral number, and the data item need not be explicitly declared as such. But this default assumption can be overridden by the programmer if he wishes to make an explicit declaration. This is another attribute of human conversation that can be carried over into machine conversation. We are usually willing to make assumptions about what other people *probably* meant to say.

4. Difficulty in using. It would be ideal if the users of an interactive system could be virtually unaware of the language they are using. Time spent thinking about how to express an idea to a computer may be time away from solving a problem. What is worse, it may actively interfere with problem solving.

By and large these deficiencies are not easy to overcome, and they will not be banished by any single technical discovery or breakthrough. They will be reduced gradually as new ideas are created and made popular. Certainly one great hurdle must be surmounted before a solution is at hand: users of interactive systems must be willing to pay the price for effective communication. Interactive communication can consume a great deal of computer time and of programmer time to prepare the elaborate programs required.

13.2.4 Incompatibility

A characteristic of any new industry is bound to be a lack of standardization among the products of different manufacturers. As an industry that is still in its infancy, in spite of its progress and rate of change in recent years, the computer field has suffered much from this problem. We have, by now, achieved a reasonably standard definition of certain high-order programming languages, such as FORTRAN, COBOL, and ALGOL, which can be used on many different computers. But these languages are not used much in interactive systems, and one reason is the sheer difficulty in implementing such complex languages in an interactive mode. At the level of assembly languages, more nearly the language of the computer, there is hardly any compatibility among different computers, so that a program written, for example, on a PDP-8 will not run on an IBM System/360 computer. For efficiency's sake, most interactive programming systems have been written in assembly languages. Hence they are not transferable to computers of different make, and we find it quite common for not only each manufacturer, but even each major computer user, to develop his own software package. This not only duplicates effort but also creates new areas of confusion by establishing still more procedures, mnemonics, and syntaxes.

At a higher level there are the problems of data file organization, techniques of tracking or "drawing" on the face of a CRT, a bewildering array of methods for initiating a session on an interactive system, methods of handling errors made by the operator, and ways of making changes in existing files or information structures. Not only are the programs that implement an interactive system different, but also a user, once he has learned the techniques of conversing with one, may have to master a completely different mode of operation to use another system. The analogy may be made that this situation is less like the minor difference of driving an automobile on the left side of the road when one is used to the right, but in mechanically the same manner and subject to the same general traffic conventions, and more like the difference between driving one type of vehicle—say an automobile—and then shifting to a completely different type—say a sailboat.

The combined result of all these differences, in hardware, language, and approach to problem solving, is a general inability to build one's system on a foundation established by someone else. Hence, instead of using our most creative people to develop new approaches, we use them to rebuild the same old ideas that others have employed.

The standardization of programming languages and usage procedures need not impose constraints of any significant degree on users or innovators. For example, in Chapter 11 we described one approach to on-line design in which it is appropriate to assume that, when a new structural member is added to a drawing at a point *near* the end point of an existing member, it is added at *exactly* this point—the system closes the small gap between the assumed desired point and the center of the area indicated by the light pen. Now it is not always desirable to do this, and an appeal for standardization does not imply an appeal for a prior decision that the problem can be handled only in this way. It does imply, in the example cited, that a graphic design system should offer this approach as a possibility and that the supporting software should be able to link the points if the user so desires but also to keep them separate. Even more, it implies that a user should be able to tell the program, when he first starts using it, what assumptions he would like the program to make in situations like this one. Standardization, then, does not mean restriction to a limited number of choices but wide recognition of the needs of all users, and the design of systems to accommodate as many alternatives as possible.

13.2.5   Effects

In a sense, all the problems we have just described existed for the computer field as a whole when computers first emerged in the early 1950s as useful commercial products, and they have been gradually overcome for the more traditional areas of application. In those early days there were relatively few programmers, and it is certain that few of the managers who were making business decisions involving the acquisition or use of computers (and sometimes even their design) fully understood them. Although basic processor design has not changed greatly, we have increased the simultaneity of processing and I/O operations and hence decreased the sequential nature of many processes. In the early machines, the entire processor would be idle while, say, some cards were being read in or a record written on tape. Now these operations can be done while the CPU is performing some other useful work, and often many input and output operations can be going on in parallel. Finally, although making use of the work of others still appears distasteful to some, there is a decided increase in this direction, as well as a trend toward the use of higher-order programming languages that foster the interchange of programs and enable programs to operate on different kinds of computers.

Today we face the descendants of these problems in the relatively new world of interactive systems. We can expect that the situation will gradually improve over the years, and when it does we will witness a great spurt in the *practical* application of interactive systems. Until this happens, however, such systems will remain restricted in use and expensive to implement.

13.3   THE FUTURE OF INTERACTIVE SYSTEMS

Clearly, a prediction of the nature of the interactive systems of the future is a subjective thing, and at this stage of the book we shift from a basically tutorial approach to a frankly editorial one. Even with this qualification, we must emphasize that we shall discuss here the *kinds of things* that are likely to be accomplished and the *areas of progress*, not the specific paths to these results or the actual technology that will evolve.

One striking phenomenon we have observed is that many articles and papers on the future of interactive systems have a tendency to describe little more than today's realities. In other words, what is predicted for the future is hardly more than what we have, at least in the form of laboratory models. Although there is, of course, a lag in bringing these systems into productive, operational use, this form of cultural lag is dismaying.

An exception of particular note is one we have previously mentioned (Section 1.2)—that the world has not yet caught up with Vannevar Bush's 1945 description of the interactive information retrieval systems of the future.[1] Although actual technological developments have taken a somewhat different path from the one he envisioned, the capability and ease of use he foresaw have never been approached.

When we examine the world of computer-assisted instruction, we again find the predictors describing largely better, more efficient versions of today's laboratory tools, not totally new ideas. Similarly in design, existing systems perform, in some fashion, most of the functions writers describe in foretelling the world of tomorrow.

13.3.1 Management Systems

It is in the field of management information systems that we find some of the most radical predictions, these often directed at the idea of replacing managers with decision-making computers. Although it is our belief that this will be one of the most dramatic areas of change, we do not anticipate large-scale replacement of people. The main reason for this centers about the continued elusiveness of computer inference drawing. However, as managers become more computer literate, as the man-machine communication languages become more expressive, as computers become faster (hence cheaper to use), and as our repertoire of programs becomes larger, we can expect these developments to cause great changes in the way decision-makers work. For one thing, there will be a great improvement in the extent and quality of data bases, and a large part of this will be attributable to future improvements in interactive information acquisition systems. When the mechanized data bases become truly adequate to serve as the major basis for decision-making, they will be used as such. Today, mechanized data bases do not adequately describe organisms so complex as large business enterprises and cannot, themselves, be used as the sole basis for major business decisions. Overall, as all the factors listed above change, we may expect that, to a far greater extent than is true today, a manager will be expected to take all available information into account, to anticipate all eventualities, to arrive at a decision in a short amount of time, and then to implement his decision flawlessly. It is simply naive to believe that today's decision-makers either work this way or are held as strictly accountable for their actions as if they did.

It is certainly true that as enterprises, business or government, grow larger, decision-making becomes less personalized and less dependent upon personal interaction. This seems to be a development independent of computer evolution. Projecting it into the future, we may expect that decision-making will be less decentralized. As the capability exists to check everything with the head office, that office will insist on being checked with. This is not a particularly happy prospect for the humanist, but it will come about, not through actual replacement of people by computers, but through a gradual evolution of our forms of management and organizational philosophy.

The point made here deserves to be considered also in a larger context. Regardless of the extent to which computers take over what we now think of as human functions, the take-over is likely to come through evolution, not actual replacement. The people of the future who will live with these systems will be much different from us and much better attuned to their symbiotic man-machine world than we could possibly be.

13.3.2 Control of Experiments

Another form of decision-making and control may promise a more exciting future. This is the control of scientific experiments and projects. Let us consider what, in general, are the steps in setting up and conducting an experiment in the physical sciences. First, we must recognize that the purpose of an experiment is to obtain information and that an experiment is judged a success or failure, not according as a hypothesis is proved or disproved, but according to the amount of information or insight gained. Hence a well-designed experiment is not set up just to tell whether or not a hypothesis is correct. It must include a number of contingencies that will provide information, within reason, no matter what the outcome of the test.

The experimental designer, then, must consider how to set up his experiment: what apparatus and subjects to use, and what information he must gather so that he will know not only whether or not the assumed outcome materializes but also, in the event it does not, what else happened. For example, he may wish to measure temperature and decide to use a certain thermometer that is sensitive in the range from zero to 100 degrees. If, in fact, the experiment runs away and this maximum is exceeded, there will be no record of what temperature actually was reached, only the knowledge that it was higher than could be measured.

Of course, we cannot foresee all possible outcomes, and, even if we could, we usually could not afford to guard against them all. Some risks must be taken. One mark of a good scientist (or any good strategist) is understanding these risks and playing the odds so as to conserve resources, yet not be caught unprepared too often. Now, if we place this scientist in a situation where experiments are so highly expensive or otherwise restrictive that they cannot be done a second time, he may find that the traditional technique of designing an experiment, conducting it, and then analyzing the data is not acceptable. He may need feedback during the course of the experiment in order to make decisions on how the remainder of the experiment is to be carried out. He would like, that is, to interact with his experimental subjects and apparatus, and he can make use of a computer to help him interpret the partial information he receives and to examine and select from among alternative paths open to him. Here he finds himself in much the same position as a manager or commander, and a MIS to help him control his experiment is just what he needs.

Is this a realistic situation we have described? Are there experiments so crucial or expensive as to warrant this degree of mechanization? Indeed there are, and there will be more. The space program offers a number of examples, for any manned space flight involves great risk of loss of money, prestige, and even life.

Suppose the experiment involved sending an unmanned probe to another planet to see whether life, in any form, could be found there. It would presumably be possible to build an apparatus that would soft-land, scoop up a sample of soil or whatever material the vehicle landed on, and bring it into a mechanized testing laboratory controlled partially by a computer and partially by scientists on earth who communicate through a computer. It would be most difficult for these people to predict what the first such probe would discover. The expense of the mission would be enormous, and the greatest amount of information possible would have to be obtained to justify the cost. One can conceive, first, of laying out a fairly complex plan of testing, with a large number of decision points, each dependent on previous findings. It is not likely that all desired experiments could be performed on every sample, both because the tests might consume the sample (if a second sample were brought in, it would have to be ascertained whether this was the same as the first one—no mean accomplishment) and because the tests might consume testing and sensing resources—chemical reagents, electric batteries, and so on. Hence planning for each individual test would have to be done on the basis of results from earlier tests.

The problems faced by the human controllers of this experiment are that they are dealing indirectly with what may be highly complex or even completely unknown material, and that they have limited resources, limited time, and great pressure on them to produce results. We are surely going to find computers used in this kind of problem, and these machines must embody a number of the facilities we have described. There must be information retrieval to help in relating any finding to known information. There must be a powerful simulation capability to enable a scientist to describe the known or assumed characteristics of some sample and then have a model try to predict what other characteristics it might have, that is, to extrapolate partial findings. There must be a design system to assist the scientist in designing a future experiment, to include contingency plans. There must be computational facilities to help the controllers to interpret their data. There must be resource allocation models and computational aids available, to help them decide among competing alternatives and to schedule carefully the use of facilities. Finally, there must be a capability to handle speculative information or to help the human scientist draw inferences. Once again, this would be something of the nature of a "what-would-happen-if" system, something like the retrieval, design, and simulation systems we described but intended to work, not with "true" information in the data base, but with hypothetical data put into the system so that the computer could assist in evaluating what would or could happen if this information were true.

A scientist using a system such as this would probably function much like a manager, commander, or senior scientist at a staff meeting. He knows he has certain specialists—those who can provide information, those who add detail to and execute plans, those who know the market, the enemy, etc. At the meeting each specialist uses his particular skill to help evaluate how any proposed course of action will fare. If the manager is an experienced leader, he knows how best to question each person, taking into account both his personality and his particular store of knowledge or skill. The biologist in our illustration would have to function in this same way, using his computer as his multifaceted staff. To do so he must be freed from today's constraints of limited man-machine communication languages and the high cost of using computer time.[11]

We have used a rather esoteric example here, but we can expect this kind of large, expensive experimentation to become more common in the future. When an experiment can be done by a single chemist at a bench, there is little need for these methods, but modern physics, oceanography, and astrophysics place different demands upon the experimentor. Even so, we have not assumed any particularly remarkable development in computer science to make this kind of experimental control possible. It would require primarily a combination of the kind of programs that we have in operation today. The control system of the future needs a versatile information retrieval system fully integrated with decision-making models and simulation models of the physical processes involved, together with a highly articulate language for use by the controller of the experiment. This last point, the articulate language, may be the one truly futuristic requirement in the list.

13.3.3   Artistic Design

Another area of development for interactive systems will be art, using the most general interpretation of this word. We have pointed out how present-day computers help in editing and laying out text. By operating more smoothly and rapidly, perhaps with built-in spelling correctors to forgive typing errors, this kind of system could improve the quality of written composition, partly because it use makes writing easier (less attention to mechanics, more to content) and partly because modification of a manuscript becomes so simple that there is no excuse to avoid it.

As this book is written, a new use of interactive computers is developing—as a medium in the production of graphic art. Almost since computers were built, they have been used to draw designs through cathode ray tubes or mechanical plotters. Many of the results have been trivial—a head of Lincoln or a pin-up girl—but some are serious works of art.

John Whitney has made a film, entitled *Permutations*,[10] by using a computer. Quite elaborate systems of equations are first entered into computer, then parameter values are assigned by a human operator at a console, and next the computer generates the curves specified by these equations and parametric values. The curves can vary from precise geometric patterns to intentionally random effects. The basic patterns can change with time, and two or more patterns can be made to move relative to each other in such a way that the motion itself is part of the total presentation. The images on the CRT are photographed, using color filters, and the result is a striking performance that, set to music, gave this viewer the feeling of watching an abstract ballet. Some frames from *Permutations* are shown in Figure 13.1.

In Whitney's work the selection and entry of the equations and the parameter values to be used in any one run, the filming of the displayed images, and the viewing of the full, moving, colored effect are discrete steps. This is caused by a limitation of the equipment available to him at the time. Whitney likens this manner of composing to the situation of a musical composer at a piano who cannot hear his own composition

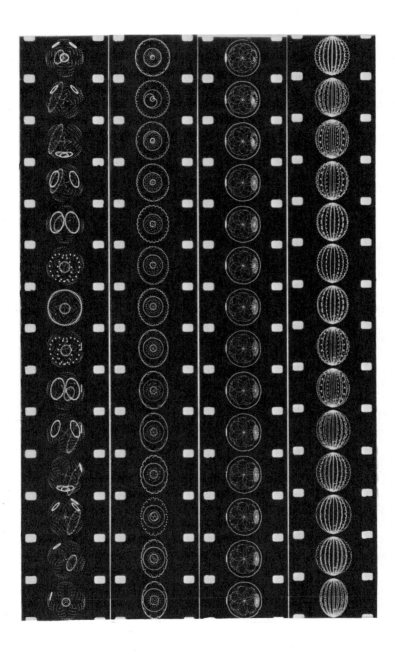

Figure 13.1 Excerpts from the film *Permutations. Photos courtesy IBM Corp.*

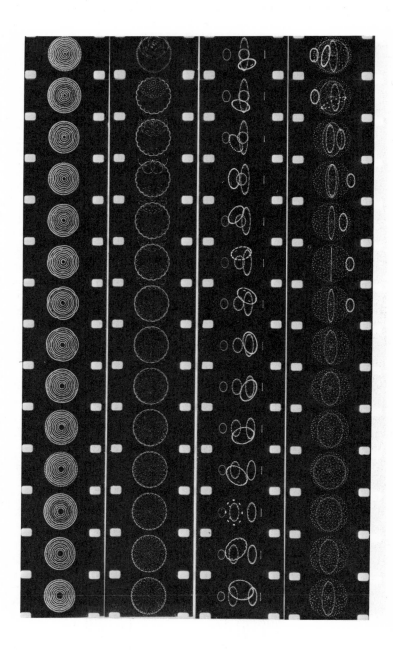

Figure 13.1 Excerpts from the film *Permutations. Photos courtesy IBM Corp.*

410

until sometime after he has finished it. In fact, just this experience is reported of a performance on the Moog Synthesizer, an electronic music-generating device. Walter Carlos, the performer, produced a recording that was [8] ". . . a splicing of sounds that were painstakingly pieced together through trial and error over a three-month period. 'We tried to make music according to Bach,' says Carlos. 'We had a score in front of us. For every phrase, every line, sometimes every chord, we had to decide on and work out color and performance and all that that implies. . . . There's no way of remembering how the sounds were made. That's why I can't wait for the computer.' " * In both cases, graphic and musical composition, communication with the computer is so difficult that what should be an instantaneous feedback process is lengthy and expensive and frustrating. When communication is better, the art form will reflect the difference.

These problems are familiar to the writer who cannot type as fast as he can think. He must then either slow down his rate of composition to the point where he is interfering with the creative process, or he must dictate and then be unable to view his work until after it has been transcribed. This is only one of many situations that will be changed dramatically by the innovation of direct computer recognition of spoken sounds. When we can achieve the state where we are no longer limited by the dexterity of our hands on a keyboard, we will have taken one of the greatest steps forward in man-machine communication.

Another development that promises revolutionary changes in art forms is the hologram.[2] This is a technique for storing and later recovering three-dimensional images on a two-dimensional surface, using lasers. Although we can take a photograph of a three-dimensional scene, store it on a two-dimensional surface, and retrieve it at will, the picture remains flat-looking. The hologram, however, has the property of retaining depth information. It will appear different to viewers looking at it from different angles, just as the original did.

Of course, one may dismiss all these art forms as gimmickry. But the Carlos recording of Bach was given serious consideration by music critics. Whitney, in his film, points out that full development of these media will require extensive experience with them and the development of schools and styles, such as have evolved for other art forms.

13.3.4 Programming

Yet another major change we shall see some day is a great simplification of the programming process. We have already reached the point

---

* Copyright *Newsweek*, Inc., February, 1969.

where an hour of shared computer time costs about what an hour of programmer time costs. The cost of people's time will continue to go up and that of computer time to go down over the years. Hence we can no longer afford to use programmers to assure efficient use of a computer. Rather, we will have to use the computer to assure efficient use of people.

To this end, we have the development of high-order programming languages, which, however, are not enough. Today we find research teams working on programming by drawing flow charts on a graphic input device,[9] programming in natural language,[4] and program generators that produce code according to specifications provided by a programmer in conversation with the generator.[6] The leverage these forms of programming can provide can be great if we think in terms of allowing programmers to spend twice as much time, or even more, on conversational technique as they do now on the mere mechanics of passing messages back and forth in these experimental systems.

13.3.5 Summary

Mechanized management, computer intercession in scientific experiments, computers as art media: what does it all imply for the future of man? Will society be computer-controlled? No one, of course, can know for sure, but our belief is that it will not be. Modern man tends to feel that he is master of the machines that surround him for doing physical work: lifting, carrying, cutting, and the like. This was not always true. The legend of John Henry tells of a man who died pitting his prowess with a sledge hammer against an early model of a steam-powered drill. His pride as a man would not accept the fact that the machine was better than he was. Since then, man has evolved as well as the machine, and we now regard such tools as power drills as essential for our modern society. Indeed, they are liberating tools that free us from the bondage of routine physical work.

The modern-day John Henry, however, also is upset about a machine. He fears that the computer threatens not only his job but also his very role as a thinking human being, dominating nature around him by his superior intellect. But we must consider that, if the kind of thinking men do to attain a superior intellect can so easily be replaced by a machine, perhaps they never really had it. By and large, computer people tend neither to worry about the computer take-over of society nor to aim to accomplish it, for they have a good sense of what can and what cannot be done and a confident knowledge of who controls whom.

It is our belief that, as man evolves, he will make his peace with computers and continue to dominate them as he has dominated physical-work-performing machinery. This form of evolution requires no biological change and will not take millions of years. It requires only a cultural change that can be accomplished through education in one generation.

In the world of the future, then, we feel that the computer will become invisible, as the telephone now is. It will be ubiquitous, so much a part of almost all human activity as to lose the appearance of being unusual and as to make its users, who will understand thoroughly at least its general workings, forget they are using it. In short, computers will gradually cease to be amazing, although the things they will be able to do would astound us today. And this will come about inevitably, just as now we are no longer amazed at steam-powered machinery or interplanetary rockets.

There is a disturbing counter argument to these opinions. It is perhaps significant that two of the three people who reviewed this book in manuscript form took issue with the previous paragraph. One said he has not ceased to marvel at modern machinery in action and that civil engineering—just watching a building go up—amazed him, implying that he will never become inured to the computer and its seeming wonders. The other reviewer put it this way, "We can hope to dominate—but can any man conceive by himself the inner workings of even today's large, man-machine systems? Does this indicate the beginnings of lack of control, and even of concern, over internal operation?" [7]

If we lose concern, we are truly lost. But the choice to be concerned remains with us as long as we want it—no machine can take it from us.

REFERENCES

1. Bush, Vannevar, "As We May Think," *Atlantic Monthly,* **176,** 1 (July 1945), 105–108.
2. El-Sun, H. M. A., "Uses for Holograms," *Science and Technology,* No. 71 (November 1967), pp. 50–59.
3. Grabbe, E. M., S. Ramo, and D. E. Wooldridge, eds., *Handbook of Automation, Computation and Control,* Vol. II, John Wiley, New York, 1959, pp. 2–251 to 2–257.
4. Halpern, Mark, "Foundations of the Case for Natural Language Programming," *Proceedings of the Fall Joint Computer Conference,* 1966, pp. 639–650.
5. Licklider, J. C. R., "Man-Computer Communication," *Annual Review of Information Science and Technology,* Vol. 3, Encyclopaedia Britannica Co., Chicago, 1968, pp. 201–240.
6. Meadow, Charles T., Douglas W. Waugh, and Forrest E. Miller, "CG–1, a Course Generating Program for Computer-Assisted Instruction," *Proceedings of the 23rd National Conference, ACM,* Brandon Systems Press, Princeton, N. J., 1968, pp. 99–110.

7. Pyke, Thomas N., Jr., personal communication.
8. Saal, Hubert, "Electric Bach," *Newsweek*, **LXXIII,** 5 (Feb. 3, 1969), 90.
9. Sutherland, W. R., *On-line Graphical Specification of Computer Procedures,* Technical Report 405, Lincoln Laboratory, Massachusetts Institute of Technology, Lexington, Mass., May 23, 1966 (AD 639 734).
10. Whitney, John, *Permutations* (film), International Business Machines Corp., Armonk, N. Y., 1968.
11. The author is indebted to Mr. Donald Wallis of IBM for much of the material used in this discussion.

RECOMMENDED ADDITIONAL READING

1. Bunker, Don L., "Computer Experiments in Chemistry," *Scientific American,* **211,** 1 (July 1964), 100–108.
2. Greenberger, Martin, ed., *Management and the Computer of the Future,* The MIT Press and John Wiley, Cambridge, Mass., and New York, 1962.
3. *Information,* W. H. Freeman, San Francisco, 1966.
4. Kochen, Manfred, ed., *The Growth of Knowledge,* John Wiley, New York, 1967.
5. Licklider, J. C. R., *Libraries of the Future,* The MIT Press, Cambridge, Mass., 1965.
6. Sackman, H., *Computers, System Science and Evolving Society: The Challenge of Man-Machine Digital Systems,* John Wiley, New York, 1968.

Author Index

415

Subject Index